ENGLISH SYNONYMES

CLASSIFIED AND EXPLAINED;

WITH

PRACTICAL EXERCISES,

DESIGNED FOR

SCHOOLS AND PRIVATE TUITION

BY

G. F. GRAHAM,

AUTHOR OF "ENGLISH, OR THE ART OF COMPOSITION," "HELPS TO ENGLISH GRAMMAR," ETC., ETC

——— Facies non omnibus una.
Nec diversa tamen, qualem decet esse sororum

EDITED,

WITH AN INTRODUCTION AND ILLUSTRATIVE AUTHORITIES,

BY HENRY REED, LL.D.,

PROFESSOR OF ENGLISH LITERATURE IN THE UNIVERSITY OF PENNSYLVANIA

NEW YORK:
D. APPLETON & CO., 443 & 445 BROADWAY.
1867.

INTRODUCTION

TO

THE AMERICAN EDITION.

This treatise is republished and edited with the hope that it will be found useful as a text-book in the study of our own language. As a subject of instruction, the study of the English tongue does not receive that amount of systematic attention which is due to it, whether it be combined or no with the study of the Greek and Latin. In the usual courses of education, it has no larger scope than the study of some rhetorical principles and practice and of grammatical rules, which, for the most part, are not adequate to the composite character and varied idiom of English speech. This is far from being enough to give the needful knowledge of what is the living language, both of our English literature and of the multiform intercourse—oral and written—of our daily lives. The language deserves better care and more sedulous culture; it needs much more to preserve its purity and to guide the progress of its life. The young, instead of having only such familiarity with their native speech as practice without method or theory gives, should be so taught and trained as to acquire a habit of using words—whether with the voice or the pen—fitly and truly, intelligently and conscientiously.

For such training this book, it is believed, will prove serviceable. The '*Practical Exercises*,' attached to the explanations of the words, are conveniently prepared for the routine of instruction. The value of a course of this kind, regularly and carefully completed, will be more than the amount of information gained respecting the words that are explained. It will tend to produce a thoughtful and accurate use of language, and thus may be acquired, almost unconsciously, that which is not only a critical but a moral habit of mind—the habit of giving utterance to truth in simple, clear and precise terms—of telling one's thoughts and feelings in words that express nothing more and nothing less. It is thus that we may learn how to escape the evils of vagueness, obscurity and perplexity—the manifold mischiefs of words used thoughtlessly and at random, or words used in ignorance and confusion.

In preparing this edition, it seemed to me that the value and literary interest of the book might be increased by the introduction of a series of illustrative authorities. It is in the addition of these authorities, contained within brackets under each title, and also of a general index to facilitate reference, that this edition differs from the original edition, which in other respects is exactly reprinted. I have confined my choice of authorities to poetical quotations, chiefly because it is in poetry that language is found in its highest purity and perfection. The selections have been made from three of the English Poets—each a great authority and each belonging to a different period, so that in this way some historical illustration of the language is given at the same time. The quotations from Shakspere (born A. D. 1564, died 1616) may be considered as illustrating the use of the words at the close of the 16th and beginning of the 17th century; those from Milton (born 1608, died 1674) the succeeding half century, or middle of the 17th century; and those from Wordsworth (born 1770) the contemporary use in the 19th century.

In an elementary book like this there was no occasion to introduce earlier illustrations from the immature periods of the language, and why Shakspere and Milton have been chosen as important authorities it cannot be necessary to explain. Why Wordsworth is placed by the side of them may be shown in the words of another, which I prefer using rather than my own:

" Besides the power of Wordsworth's poetry to minister to a sense of the beauty of the world, both material and spiritual, there is a further advantage in it, still more directly connected with education. By no such great poet, besides Shakspere, has the English language been used with equal purity, and yet such flexible command of its resources. Spenser gives us too many obsolete forms, Milton too much unEnglish syntax, to make either of them available for the purpose of training the young of our country in the laws, and leading them to apprehend and revere the principles of their magnificent language. But in Wordsworth is the English tongue seen almost in its perfection; its powers of delicate expression, its flexible idioms, its vast compass, the rich variety of its rhythms, being all displayed in the attractive garb of verse, and yet with a most rigorous conformity to the laws of its own syntax. Those who know how much education must concern itself with man's distinctive organ, speech, will know also how to appreciate such a benefit as this."—*Preface to " Select Pieces from the Poems of William Wordsworth." London :* 1845.

In the quotations I have endeavoured, whenever it was possible, to make choice of passages that might have an interest as words of wisdom or of poetic beauty, and often of both combined, and I should rejoice to think that these fragmentary specimens may allure the student to the willing and happy study of the great masters of English poetry—to feed his moral and intellectual being from their pages.

In transcribing the passages quoted, I have been not seldom painfully sensible of the wrong done by detaching them from the context, especially in observing how the completeness of poetic effect is often impaired by such rude severance. The precise references which accompany the quotations will render it easy to restore them to their connection, as may sometimes be found desirable. It may, however, on the other hand, be found that, so far as the excellence of style is concerned—the fitness and beauty and combination of the words—the fineness of the rhythm and the composition of the sentence, we are made to appreciate these things as well, when we take a passage that is characterized by them and consider it by itself. Look, for example, at the exquisitely simple beauty of the words that follow, and let the music that is made by them be audibly heard or silently felt—the words, each one of them, being no more than our common colloquial words, and yet made expressive of a rich flow of imagery by the admirable choice and apposition.

——— O, hear me breathe my life
Before this ancient sir, who, it should seem,
Hath sometime loved: I take thy hand; this hand
As soft as dove's down, and as white as it;
Or Ethiopian's tooth, or the fanned snow
That's bolted by the northern blasts twice o'er.

Winter's Tale, IV. 3.

Here are words written more than two hundred years ago and yet now as fresh as if first uttered yesterday; and so it is well-nigh always with Shakspere's language, for when a true Poet writes in a matured language, it is in the unchanging and imperishable part of it that his imagination finds its abiding-place.

It is not meant that during the last two centuries the English language has been stationary. No living speech can be unprogressive, for the simple reason that new ideas must be expressed and new thoughts and feelings must have utterance. The text of Shakspere accordingly does not furnish examples for all the words in this volume, and sometimes it gives authority only for a different acceptation. The word '***extravagant***,' for example, is not to be found in Shakspere, in that which is at the present day the most usual sense of the word, which then had not travelled so much away from its origin. When in Hamlet, it is said, that

Whether in sea or fire, in earth or air,
The extravagant and erring spirit hies
To his confine ——

the passage does not exemplify the modern sense of the word, but it throws light upon it by recalling the primitive and etymological meaning.

In this respect the text of Milton may serve an excellent use for instruction in the language. If his diction is sparing in purely English idioms, and his choice and combination of words greatly influenced by his learning and his deep love of antiquity, those very qualities will serve, especially in connection with classical instruction, to call the student's thoughts to the derivative signification of words from Greek and Latin sources, and what may be generally called the Norman as distinguished from the Saxon side of the English tongue. Let the word '*recollecting*,' for instance, be observed in these lines:

> ——— but he, his wonted pride
> Soon recollecting, with high words, that bore
> Semblance of worth, not substance, gently raised
> Their fainting courage, and dispelled their fears.
>
> *Parad. Lost*, i. 528.

or, again, the somewhat curious use of the word '*divert*' in these lines:

> Alas, how simple, to these cates compared
> Was that crude apple that diverted Eve!
>
> *Parad. Regained*, ii. 349.

These cases may suggest how this work can be employed in the etymological study of the language—a process which brings with it more good than mere acquisition. The use of etymology in disciplining the youthful mind to thoughtful habits has been specially commended by Coleridge, in the '*Aids to Reflection*,' and it is his remark that

"In a language like ours, where so many words are derived from other languages, there are few modes of instruction more useful or more amusing than that of accustoming young people to seek for the etymology, or primary meaning of the words they use. There are cases, in which more knowledge of more value may be conveyed by the history of a word, than by the history of a campaign."

The value of the historical consideration of words may be exemplified by one of the titles in the list, in this volume, '*Bravery—Courage*.' The word '*bravery*' has its early and its later use, and it is in the former that it is met with in Shakspere and Milton. The quotation from 'Julius Cæsar:

> ——— and come down
> With fearful bravery, thinking by this face
> To fasten in our thoughts that they have courage.

must not be mistaken for an illustration of what is now the usual sense of the word 'bravery.'

The study of this work may be made to illustrate another important fact in our language—the admirable copiousness that results from the combination of its Saxon and Norman elements. The correspondent words from these two great sources are not mere duplicates—to be used indifferently and at random, but each is often delegated to a distinct duty; each does its own appropriate and peculiar service and shows some shade of meaning, some special variation of the sense. The words '*apt*' and '*fit*,' for example, coming into the language from different sources, might be thought to be closely and strictly synonymous, and yet a delicate distinction of use is made beautifully apparent by the quotations from Shakspere, Milton and Wordsworth.

There is to be observed another and different process by which the language is in some degree impoverished, when one of two corresponding or equivalent words thrusts the other out of use, and when this happens, the Norman is usually the conqueror. We may be said to have given up the good English compound '*to underbear*,' for the Latin-English word '*to support*;' we have well-nigh lost the word, though Shakspere shows its good use from the lips of Constance:

> ——— leave those woes alone, which I alone
> Am bound to underbear, ——

The verb '*to better*' is preserved along with '*to meliorate*,' but the counterpart word '*to worsen*' has been almost given away, perhaps for the sake of the three additional syllables that come in with its synonym '*to deteriorate*.'

Another change in the progress of the language is illustrated under the title '*to learn—to teach*.' The first of these words formerly expressed not only its present sense, but was also synonymous with '*to teach*,' for which use good authority may be cited from early writers and from Shakspere, while modern practice stamps it as somewhat of a vulgarism. The word has dropped one of its meanings, and being limited to the other, there is a gain in point of precision. Not to use Sacred Writ irreverently for this purpose, an historical illustration of this case has occurred to me in two of the English versions of the Bible. In that which is commonly called 'Cranmer's Bible,' and belongs to about the middle of the 16th century, a passage in the 119th Psalm is given in these words:

> "O learn me true understanding and knowledge, for I have believed thy commandments.
> "Before I was troubled, I went wrong; but now have I kept thy word. Thou art good and gracious; O teach me thy statutes."

Here it is seen both words are used, and '*learn*' employed in the sense of '*teach*;' but in the standard version, which belongs to the beginning of the 17th century, much as the style is controlled by adherence to the earlier versions, this passage is changed by the substitution of the word '*teach*' for '*learn*:'

> "Teach me good judgment and knowledge; for I have believed thy commandments.
> "Before I was afflicted I went astray; but now have I kept thy word.
> "Thou art good and doest good; teach me thy statutes."

The use of this volume as a text-book may be extended much beyond the method of instruction prescribed in the 'Practical Exercises,' and in connection with it various considerations of the character and structure of the language will suggest themselves. The synonyms of 'intensity,' or of 'active and passive' words, may induce a more extended examination of words, which, while kindred in meaning, express many different degrees and variations of the meaning. The title "*see—look*" is given and explained, but let it be observed that these are but two of a large family of words connected with the function of sight, which the student might supply and discriminate the several shades of signification. In this way a just sense of the copiousness of the language will be acquired, and the habit by degrees gained, of accurately using and distinctly apprehending words that otherwise would bring only a confused meaning. In studying the nature of that copiousness it will be seen why often there are many names for the same object, or for the same general thought or feeling, as in Arabic, there are, it is said, no less than four hundred names for the lion.* The copiousness of the English tongue may be further illustrated by its etymology, and a word becomes a theme by the study of its origin and history. Let an examination, for example, be made of such words as '*trivial*,' '*pagan*,' '*rustic*,' '*civil*,' '*urbane*,' '*courteous*,' &c., &c.

The teacher, who succeeds in animating the student with an interest in the processes of instruction contained in this volume, need be at no loss to find manifold opportunities for the study of the language to which this text-book may serve as an introduction and a help. Let judicious selections be made, and studied with special reference to the choice and the combination of the words. Single sentences or passages from Shakspere, may show that wonderful mastery of the language which is proved by the impossibility of substituting another for any given word. Take that most familiar passage—Portia's appeal to Shylock, and contemplate not so much the tranquil sublimity of the sentiment as the expression of it, and there will be seen the purity and simplicity and beauty of English speech in its highest perfection :

> The quality of mercy is not strained ;
> It droppeth, as the gentle rain from heaven
> Upon the place beneath : it is twice blessed ;
> It blesseth him that gives, and him that takes ;
> 'Tis mightiest in the mightiest ; it becomes
> The throned monarch better than his crown :
> His scepter shows the force of temporal power ,
> The attribute to awe and majesty,
> Wherein doth sit the dread and fear of kings ,
> But mercy is above this sceptered sway,
> It is enthroned in the hearts of kings,
> It is an attribute to God himself ;

* "Les Arabes ont, dit-on, quatre cents mots pour exprimer le *lion*, tandis que nous n'en avons qu'un, parce que cet animal, étranger à nos climats, ne peut être pour nous qu'un objet de curiosité ; au lieu qu'il est pour l'homme des déserts un ennemi redoutable, un sujet continuel d'aventures et de récits, et que, tenant beaucoup de place dans sa vie, il a dû en prendre davantage dans sa langue. Ainsi, les Arabes, le considérant sous le rapport de sa taille, de sa force, de sa couleur, de son port, de ses appétits, de ses inclinations, etc., l'ont nommé d'autant de noms qu'ils ont observé, ou qu'ils lui ont supposé de qualités physiques ou instinctives. C'est pour la même raison que la langue allemande a un grand nombre de mots pour désigner un cheval."

De Bonald. '*Recherches Philosophiques*,' *tome* 1er.

And earthly power doth then show likest God's
When mercy seasons justice. Therefore, Jew,
Though justice be thy plea, consider this,—
That, in the course of justice, none of us
Should see salvation: we do pray for mercy;
And that same prayer doth teach us all to render
The deeds of mercy. ——

There can of course be no difficulty in choosing passages in the text of Shakspere, illustrative in every way of the language and furnishing subject of verbal study, but I will not forbear pointing out that less familiar though very remarkable passage—the speech of Ulysses, beginning,

'Time hath, my lord, a wallet at his back,'

in the third scene of the third act of Troilus and Cressida. It is not necessary here to show by actual quotation how passages from the text of Milton may also be used, though this should be only when accompanied with a distinct knowledge of the nature of his English. The text of Wordsworth may be used to show what is the English of our own day in admirable purity, and the student of the language will feel it by examining minutely and critically the words in almost any selection from his poems. For example, let the fitness and expressiveness of the words in these stanzas be considered:

Lives there a man whose sole delights
Are trivial pomp and city noise
Hardening a heart that loathes or slights
What every natural heart enjoys?
Who never caught a noon-tide dream
From murmur of a running stream;
Could strip, for aught the prospect yields
To him, their verdure from the fields;
And take the radiance from the clouds
In which the sun his setting shrouds.

A soul so pitiably forlorn,
If such do on this earth abide,
May season apathy with scorn,
May turn indifference to pride;
And still be not unblest—compared
With him who grovels, self-debarred
From all that lies within the scope
Of holy faith and Christian hope;
Or shipwrecked, kindles on the coast
False fires, that others may be lost.

'On the Founding of Rydal Chapel.'

The study of the English language should be cultivated by means of quotations from the prose literature also, with the especial care that no author be resorted to, no matter how brilliant his reputation, unless he be distinguished for the purity of his language and some of the varied excellencies of English style. Instruction may be gained from the gorgeous diction of Jeremy Taylor, or the stately eloquence of Milton's prose; or, on the other hand, from the simple and idiomatic strength of Swift. A style combining in a great measure these opposite qualities may be found in the speeches and writings of Burke, whose manly and statesmanly philosophy found utterance in English that is worthy of his high and practical wisdom. Let such a passage as this be set before the student, to dwell on the language of it with the verbal care that is bestowed on the text of an ancient author:

"Hitherto the name of poor (in the sense in which it is used to excite compassion) has not been used for those who can, but for those who cannot labour—for the sick and infirm; for orphan infancy; for languishing and decrepid age: but when we affect to pity as poor, those who must labour or the world cannot exist, we are trifling with the condition of mankind. It is the common doom of man that he must eat his bread by the sweat of his brow, that is, by the sweat of his body, or the sweat of his mind. If this toil was inflicted as a curse, it is as might be expected from the curses of the Father of all blessings—it is tempered with many alleviations, many comforts. Every attempt to fly from it, and to refuse the very terms of our existence, becomes much more truly a curse, and heavier pains and penalties fall upon those who would elude the tasks which are put upon them by the great Master Workman of the world, who in his dealings with his creatures sympathizes with their weakness, and speaking of a creation wrought by mere will out of nothing, speaks of six days of *labour* and one of *rest.* I do not call a healthy young man, cheerful in his mind, and vigorous in his arms, I cannot call such a man, *poor;* I cannot pity my kind as a kind, merely because they are men. This affected pity only tends to dissatisfy them with their condition, and to teach them to seek resources where no resources are to be found, in something else than their own industry, and frugality, and sobriety."—'*Letters on a Regicide Peace.*' *Let. III.*

Our language, in another of its phases, may be studied in the letters of Cowper, which are justly characterized as the pattern of pure graceful idiomatic English. The merit of the style of Cowper's best biographer—Southey—has also often been acknowledged, and it would be easy to use quotations from his various and voluminous prose works. A passage in one of them—his '*Colloquies*'—is so appropriate to the subject of this introduction, that I am led to insert it here:

"There is another mischief arising out of ephemeral literature, which was noticed by the same great author, (Ben Jonson.) 'Wheresoever manners and fashions are corrupted,' says he, 'language is. It imitates the public riot. The excesses of feasts and apparel are the notes of a sick state; and the wantonness of language of a sick mind.' This was the observation of a man well versed in the history of the ancients and in their literature. The evil prevailed in his time to a considerable degree; but it was not permanent, because it proceeded rather from the affectation of a few individuals than from any general cause. The great poets were free from it; and our prose writers then, and till the end of that century, were preserved, by their sound studies and logical habits of mind, from any of those faults into which men fall who write loosely because they think loosely. The pedantry of one class and the colloquial vulgarity of another had their day; the faults of each were strongly contrasted, and better writers kept the mean between them. More lasting effect was produced by translators, who, in later times, have corrupted our idiom as much as, in early ones, they enriched our vocabulary; and to this injury the Scotch have greatly contributed,—for, composing in a language which is not their mother tongue, they necessarily acquire an artificial and formal style, which, not so much through the merit of a few as owing to the perseverance of others, who for half a century seated themselves on the bench of criticism, has almost superseded the vernacular English of Addison and Swift. Our journals, indeed, have been the great corrupters of our style, and continue to be so; and not for this reason only. Men who write in newspapers and magazines and reviews, write for present effect; in most cases this is as much their natural and proper aim, as it would be in public speaking; but when it is so, they consider, like public speakers, not so much what is accurate or just, either in matter or manner, as what will be acceptable to those whom they address. Writing also under the excitement of emulation and rivalry, they seek, by all the artifices and efforts of an ambitious style, to dazzle their readers; and they are wise in their generation, experience having shown that common minds are taken by glittering faults, both in prose and verse, as larks are with looking-glasses."—SOUTHEY'S '*Colloquies*,' vol. ii. p. 296.

Of another contemporary author, whose writings might be advantageously used as models, it has been well said that 'Arnold's style is worthy of his manly understanding and the noble simplicity of his character.' A few sentences of historical description will show the justice of this praise, while it adds another specimen of the kind of English, which should be employed in the study of the language:

"Before the sweeping pursuit of Hannibal's Numidians, crowds of fugitives were seen flying towards the city, while the smoke of burning houses arose far and wide into the sky. Within the walls the confusion and terror were at their height: he was come at last, this Hannibal, whom they had so long dreaded; he had at length dared what even the slaughter of Cannæ had not emboldened him to venture; some victory greater even than Cannæ must have given him this confidence; the three armies before Capua must be utterly destroyed; last year he had destroyed or dispersed three other armies, and had gained possession of the entire south of Italy; and now he had stormed the lines before Capua, had cut to pieces the whole remaining force of the Roman people, and was come to Rome to finish his work So the wives and mothers of Rome lamented, as they hurried to the temples; and there, prostrate before the gods, and sweeping the sacred pavement with their unbound hair in the agony of their fear, they remained pouring forth their prayers for deliverance. Their sons and husbands hastened to man the walls and the citadel, and to secure the most important points without the city; whilst the senate, as calm as their fathers of old, whom the Gauls massacred when sitting at their own doors, but with the energy of manly resolution, rather than the resignation of despair, met in the forum, and there remained assembled, to direct every magistrate on the instant, how he might best fulfil his duty.

"But God's care watched over the safety of a people, whom he had chosen to work out the purposes of his providence; Rome was not to perish. * * * * *

* * * "Hannibal, at the head of a large body of cavalry, came close up to the Colline gate, rode along leisurely under the walls to see all he could of the city, and is said to have cast his javelin into it as in defiance. From farthest Spain he had come into Italy; he had wasted the whole country of the Romans and their allies with fire and sword for more than six years, had slain more of their citizens than were now alive against him; and at last he was shutting them up within their city, and riding freely under their walls, while none dared meet him in the field. If any thing of disappointment depressed his mind at that instant; if he felt that Rome's strength was not broken, nor the spirit of her people quelled, that his own fortune was wavering, and that his last effort had been made, and made in vain; yet, thinking where he was, and of the shame and loss which his presence was causing to his enemies, he must have wished that his father could have lived to see that day, and must have thanked the gods of his country, that they had enabled him so fully to perform his vow."—ARNOLD'S '*History of Rome*,' chap. 44.

In bringing these somewhat desultory remarks to a close, I must state that I have thought proper to refrain from adding any thing in the way of doubt or difference of opinion to the explanations of the synonyms given in the volume. I have not felt the necessity of interfering with the book in such a way, and will only introduce here a few lines to be taken in connection with the title '*shall* and *will*.' The following is the explanation given by Wallis in his Grammar of the English Language (1699): it is of authority as being the distinction drawn by a mind so logical and so well trained in the processes of exact science as that of the Savilian Professor of Geometry.

"*Shall* et *will* indicant Futurum.

"Quoniam autem extraneis satis est cognitu difficile, quando hoc vel illud dicendum est (non enim promiscue dicimus *shall* et *will*); neque tamen alii quos vidi ullas tradidere regulas quibus dirigantur: has ego tradere necessarium duxi, quas qui observaverit hac in re non aberrabit.

In primis personis *shall* simpliciter prædicentis est; *will* quasi promittentis aut minantis.

"In secundis et tertiis personis, *shall* promittentis est aut minantis; *will* simpliciter prædicentis."—'*Grammatica Linguæ Anglicanæ.*'

I have been tempted to extend this Introduction beyond what I at first intended, by a desire to promote an important but much-neglected subject of study. In pointing out some of the uses of this volume as a text-book, I hoped at the same time to suggest some of the means by which in many and various ways the systematic study of our own language may be made interesting. To prove that I do not speak with undue earnestness respecting the intrinsic value and interest of the study, I add, in conclusion, a few authorities, which, I am sure, cannot fail to make an impression upon those who have the cause of sound education at heart.

"Exceedingly irksome as the mere learning of rules about a language, which we are actually speaking, is, that very irksomeness may be useful if it is made a step to the very delightful exercise (I should think there were very few more delightful) of ascertaining what the laws are which we do actually follow, and must follow, when we speak so as to make ourselves intelligible to others. This is one part of the study of language, but the mind of the pupil will become very cold and formal, though possibly very acute and ingenious, if it is made the only one. The consideration of words, of their connections with each other, of their origin and history, and of the new meanings they contracted as they came in contact with new subjects, is the other and vital part of it. How deep an interest boys at a very early age may take in this pursuit! what clearness, liveliness, honesty, it gives to their minds! At the same time, what a sense of awfulness and mystery in themselves, and in that language which they are every day using! consequently, what a serious meditative habit it cultivates in them, without in the least destroying the gaiety of their spirits, I think we may all have observed. I can conceive scarcely any pursuit a teacher can engage in, which would bring him in so many rewards of increased acquaintance with his pupil's mind, and with his own, or one therefore for which it would be more his duty to train himself diligently and systematically."—'*Lectures on National Education,*' by the Rev. Professor MAURICE, of King's College, London.

"A word which has no precise meaning, can but poorly fulfill its office of being a sign and guide of thought: and if it be connected with matters interesting to the feelings, or of practical moment, it may easily become mischievous. Now in a language like ours, in which the abstract terms are mostly imported from abroad, such terms, when they get into general circulation, are especially liable to be misunderstood and perverted; inasmuch as few can have any distinct conception what their meaning really is, or how they came by it. Having neither taproots, nor lateral roots, they are easily shaken and driven out of line; and one gust may blow them on one side, another on another side. Hence arises a confusion of tongues, even within the pale of the same language; and this breeds a confusion of thoughts. Of all classes of paralogisms the most copious is that in which a word, used in one sense in the premises, slips another sense into the conclusion.

* * * * * *

"They who feel an inward call to teach and enlighten their countrymen, should deem it an important part of their duty to draw out the stores of thought which are already latent in their native language, to purify it from the corruptions which Time brings upon all things, and from which language has no exemption, and to endeavour to give distinctness and precision to whatever in it is confused, or obscure, or dimly seen.

* * * * * *

"A man should love and venerate his native language, as the first of his benefactors, as the awakener and stirrer of all his thoughts, the frame and mould and rule of his spiritual being, as the great bond and medium of intercourse with his fellows, as the mirror in which he sees his own nature, and without which he could not even commune with himself, as the image in which the wisdom of God has chosen to reveal itself to him. He who thus thinks of his native language will never approach it without reverence. Yet his reverence will not withhold, but rather encourage him, to do what he can to purify and improve it."—JULIUS HARE. '*Guesses at Truth.*'

And last, it is COLERIDGE, who says—

"Reflect on your own thoughts, actions, circumstances, and—which will be of especial aid to you in forming a habit of reflection,—accustom your self to reflect on the words you use, hear, or read, their birth, derivation and history. For if words are not things, they are living powers, by which the things of most importance to mankind are actuated, combined, and humanized."—'*Aids to Reflection.*'—*Preface.*

H. R.

Philadelphia, October 23, 1846.

NOTE.

The references for the illustrative authorities under each title are made to the poems, which are respectively quoted, the references to 'Paradise Lost'—'Paradise Regained,' and 'Samson Agonistes' being given with only the initials of the titles of those poems.

PREFACE.

Dr Blair, in his "Lectures upon the English Language," says:—"The great source of a loose style is the injudicious use of synonymous terms." If we examine the style of most of the periodical and light literature of the day, we shall soon be convinced of the truth of this assertion. For one fault in construction or idiom, we shall find at least twenty incorrect applications of words. The want of a critical knowledge of verbal distinctions is obviously the cause of these errors. But though the foundation of this knowledge should undoubtedly be laid at an early stage of the study of language, and before the habit of using words in a loose way has become inveterate, it appears to be generally considered unnecessary for the young student, and is either neglected for other pursuits, or else is wholly excluded from systematic education.

The pernicious result of this neglect is found in the inaccuracy and looseness of style so generally prevalent. The present work has been written with a view to supply what the author believes to be a desideratum in Elementary Education; and though he is far from intending it should be regarded as complete, he hopes it will be found to contain principles sufficiently suggestive to enable those who use it to continue the study to any extent for themselves.

CONTENTS.

PRACTICAL EXERCISES

ON

ENGLISH SYNONYMES.

INTRODUCTION.

It is a common observation, that there are no two objects in nature exactly alike; that however close their apparent resemblance to each other may be, the one will be found, upon examination, to possess some shade, some almost imperceptible tinge of difference by which it may be distinguished from the other. But it is not to the superficial observer that these nice varieties are evident. He who contents himself with a general or casual view of things must remain in ignorance of all those nicely distinctive properties of substances which render them, in certain respects, independent of each other. He can have no knowledge of their peculiar qualities, but must look upon them as belonging to the general mass of natural matter; and though the most indifferent spectator cannot fail to be struck with their more prominent properties, he can have no information respecting their distinctive character or uses. This observation is quite as true of art as of nature. Here, though the artisan exert his utmost skill to make one object exactly like another, we shall find, upon a close inspection, that he never wholly succeeds in his attempt. Some slight variety, either in shape, or form, or color, or weight, will be discovered, sufficient to distinguish the copy from the original. It may, indeed, be more difficult to distinguish between objects purposely constructed alike; still, however, the truth will remain, that a close examination will not fail to detect a peculiarity in substance, construction, dimension, or some other quality, sufficient to mark a difference between the two objects.

Of Nature's intention in making this wonderful variety in her works, it is not necessary here to speak, nor indeed is the present work suited for such a discussion. One reflection, however, which the consideration of this variety will naturally suggest tc our minds, bears more directly upon the subject before us. It is this: that the very habit of indifference to an exact knowledge of distinguishing qualities, even in apparently trivial or insignificant objects, is the main cause of all that vague idea and indefinite conception, which is so common even among those who pass with the world for well-informed and well-instructed men. The extent to which this habit often prevails during our years of education, and the extraordinary influence it has upon us throughout life, are scarcely to be credited. It is this almost inveterate indifference, acquired in early life, which causes us to rest satisfied with general rather than particular knowledge, originates so many indistinct conceptions, produces a positive and violent aversion from thinking, and thus exercises a most pernicious influence upon the intellectual character of the man.

If an infinite variety in the appearance of external things be an admitted fact, it will follow that there must be, in like manner, a great variety in the meaning of those words which are their conventional signs. We must not, however, expect to find the same extent of variety in words as in things, because the system of generalization applied to language does not admit of the same extension. Thus, though the word *table* will represent, generally, a flat substance supported by legs, it will not stand for the many varieties of this piece of furniture which might be presented to the eye. In this respect, single words are imperfect; for, though some have undoubtedly a more specific meaning than others, they cannot express all the varieties of every species of things: all they can do is to supply us with general signs, which must be rendered specific by the addition of those qualifying terms which serve to modify their signification and give them a more definite meaning.

But words, though they do not express individual things, actions, or qualities, are found to approximate so closely in meaning, that it is no easy matter, in many cases, to distinguish them from each other. The leading idea contained in several belonging to the same class of meaning is so prominent, that the mind, in endeavouring to discover their differences, becomes dazzled by the more intensive property of the words, and neglects to examine the attendant shades by which the one may be distinguished from the other. It is not asserting too much to declare, that scarcely any give themselves trouble to search for those nice distinctions of meaning by which words are characterized; nay, we are certain there are few candid persons not ready to admit that they have hitherto contented themselves with *feeling* the difference between the signification of two words of a similar meaning, without having directed the least attention to the cause of that difference, or to any philosophical principle by which a distinction may be established between them.

It is of no weight to argue, that there is no necessity for the study of verbal distinctions, because many writers have composed with accuracy and elegance, who have never bestowed any attention on the philosophy of synonomy. Some are naturally endowed with a more delicate faculty of distinction than others; and such persons, from an almost intuitive sense of the exact meaning and application of words, are seldom likely to use them incorrectly; but it would be utterly absurd to infer from this fact, that some general rules to guide the student in his choice and distinction of words, and in a proper use of them, would not be acceptable to those who are desirous of improving their style in elegance and precision. For, the habit of taking things for granted is not only highly unsatisfactory to an inquiring mind engaged in honestly searching for truth, but it is also replete with danger, and cannot but continually lead us into error. He who always places his dependence on appearances, and never appeals to his own powers of reasoning or investigation, is sure to be constantly involved in difficulties; and though he may possibly be sometimes right he never can explain why he is so, or guard against the recurrence of perplexities.

Accuracy of expression will naturally lead to accuracy of thought, for the practice of carefully examining the shades of difference between words is not only useful in regard to writing, but also exercises a most salutary influence upon the thinking power. Now there are grounds to fear that language is, by many, considered as something existing of itself, and independent, rather than as connected with its proper origin, or as to be referred to a higher principle. In studying language we should never lose sight of the fact, that it is the visible and audible expression of the mind, and that, therefore, all the phenomena of language are to be referred for their source to the intellectual powers. It is, then, only by investigating the modes in which Nature works in the human mind, and by patiently observing her operations, that we can expect to arrive at an accurate knowledge of the philosophy of expression. In these researches, the study of metaphysics is our only way to arrive at any satisfactory result, for from no other source can we acquire any solid information on this subject, nor upon any other principles can we safely proceed in our investigations. Though many scholars have displayed wonderful ingenuity and sagacity in philological research, which cannot fail to command the admiration of all who make this subject their study; no one has yet set forth a system of language referable to the human mind, and applicable to human expression; no one has yet tested the significations of words, their differences, their various classes of differences, and the causes of those differences, in such a manner as to reduce them to a system; or has laid down principles to serve as a basis upon which to ground a general and comprehensive classification of our language.

Though the author of the present work is far from pretending to supply this desideratum, he thinks it may be not wholly useless to mention some opinions he has long entertained on the subject, and to explain some principles to assist in forming a plan by which the unpractised writer may be enabled to avoid the looseness of expression so common with the majority of writers, and to compose in a clear and intelligible style.

It is to be observed, that in every department of science, a classification of its materials is one of the leading principles upon which philosophers have founded their systems. This is a natural and universal principle, drawn from our observation of external objects, and found not in one only, but in every department of natural science. An attempt to acquire solid information upon any other method of instruction will infallibly fill the mind with crude and confused ideas, and impart no sound or lasting knowledge. Hence the maxim "Divide et impera" (divide and conquer) has been successfully applied to every object of human knowledge, and hence it is generally received as the only safe road in which to proceed in every description of study.

Language, among other objects of study, has been subjected to the application of this principle. Grammarians have, accordingly, classified words under the various heads of nouns, verbs, particles, &c., as they observed their signification to possess certain properties. Thus names of things were classed as nouns, names of qualities as adjectives, and names of actions as verbs, &c. But though these classes may be sufficient for grammatical purposes, and though they *are* sufficient to distinguish the more striking differences of words, they are wholly useless when we wish to distinguish more nicely among those of each class, and between the exact shades of meaning in those more closely related to each other; that is, though there may be no difficulty in determining between a verb and a noun, or between an adjective and a conjunction, we have no unerring principle upon which to found a difference between two nouns or two verbs which approximate closely in signification. Thus the difference between *an answer* and *to answer* presents no difficulty as to the grammatical distinction of their two natures ; but if we wish to distinguish between *to answer* and *to reply*, we are immediately at a loss to determine their respective meanings, because we have no fixed principle upon which to proceed in our investigation of their difference.

It so happens that, in respect of synonymy, the English language presents the student with greater difficulties than any other language of Europe. This peculiarity may be accounted for by its structure, and by the circumstances which led to its formation. The difference of its materials, and the great variety of the respective modes of feeling and expression in those nations which contributed to its formation, are sufficient in themselves to explain the cause of this difficulty. In connection with this remark, it may be observed, that there are many words in our language which, on a superficial view, appear to convey precisely the same signification, and present, even to the scholar, no other than an etymological difference. This is the case with many pairs of words, one of which is of Saxon, and the other of Latin origin, such as: *freedom—liberty; happiness—felicity; help—assistance;* and many others. The notion which many entertain of such words is, that as they were respectively drawn from different sources, and as each word stood in its original language for the same idea, they have no difference of meaning in English. But this must be the notion of those who probably do not bestow much attention on the subject; for it requires but little reflection to convince us that such a fact would be an anomaly in the history of language, and strongly opposed to a first principle of nature. And even supposing that two words could have precisely the same meaning in the same language for a short space of time, it is altogether contrary to every law of language that they should continue in that state for any lengthened period. The intensity with which Nature is said to abhor a vacuum can only be equalled by her abhorrence of identity; an exact sameness is nowhere to be found among her works, and she seems to take delight in baffling every attempt to interfere with her dominion and oppose her laws. It cannot, however, be denied, (in applying this law to our own case,) that at the Norman conquest in 1066, many words were introduced by the conquerors into England which were identical in meaning with others in common use among the people of the country before the invasion. In fact, at that time, and during a considerable period after, two distinct languages existed in this island: one used by the lord, and the other used by the tiller of the soil. But this state of things could not continue very long: for, by a natural law, as soon as the two dialects amalgamated, and became one language, one of two terms which had till then identically corresponded, either lost a portion of its original meaning, or suffered some alteration in use; or, if this did not happen, it met with the common fate of all words so situated—it disappeared from the language. In this we see the direct effect of a universal law of nature, viz., the necessity for one of two identical things becoming altered, or else the impossibility of its remaining in existence.

There can be little doubt that the same principles of difference which our senses discover in the external world operate in the very constitution of the human mind; and that properties belonging to the nature of material bodies and external action find corresponding conceptions in the mind, and consequently, corresponding expressions in language. Thus, many words may be observed to differ from each other, as the *species* from the *genus*, as we may perceive between *to do* and *to make;* a very large class of words may be distinguished under the heads of *active* and *passive*, as between *ability* and *capacity;* the principle of *intensity* may be observed to operate in the difference between the words to *see* and to *look;* others have a *positive* and *negative* difference, as between *to shun* and *to avoid*, and many, which do not appear to depend on any uniformly acting principle, may be ranged under the head of *miscellaneous*.

The heads, then, under which the words explained in the body of this work are arranged in their respective sections are:—1. Generic and Specific; 2. Active and Passive; 3. Intensity; 4. Positive and Negative; and 5. Miscellaneous. It is not pretended that this classification is perfect or complete; but, in the absence of any other, it is hoped it may prove useful to the student, not only in supplying him with the information required concerning the words here treated, but in furnishing him with principles applicable to other pairs of words, not here explained, which may present him with any difficulty.

A very large class of synonymes may be ranged under the heads of GENERIC and SPECIFIC; that is, the one word will be found to differ from the other, as the species from the genus: as in such words as *to do* and *to make; to clothe* and *to dress; praise* and *applause, &c.* But as these terms, *generic* and *specific*, may not be familiar to the generality of young students, it may be useful here to explain them. In their classification of natural objects, philosophers have divided them under three grand heads, or, as they are termed in scientific language, kingdoms. These kingdoms are divided into classes and orders. These orders again are divided into genera, and the genera into species. This system of classification, though it may not be applied so extensively to language as in natural philosophy, will in many cases assist in discovering differences not so easily perceived by the application of any other principle. Rejecting the terms *kingdom* and *class*, we may consider the part of speech, as noun or verb, to represent the order; then the genera may be classed under each order as expressing some general or leading principle, and the species under the genus, as describing the latter more particularly. Let it be required to discover the difference between *to do* and *to make*:—Applying the principle above explained, both words will fall under the order verb:—as *to do* expresses general action, it will be the generic; and as *to make* describes a more specific mode of doing, it will be the specific term. By the same principle, *applause* will be a species of the genus *praise*, both belonging to the order noun. Again, *robust* will be a species of the genus *strong*, and belonging to the order adjective. In the exercises under this head, we have to do only with the genus and species, for the order, or part of speech, is equally applicable to both words, and will be of no assistance in our endeavour to determine their respective meanings.

It will be here necessary to explain the signification of the terms ACTIVE and PASSIVE as applied to the philosophy of synonymy, and under which head the words in the second section of this work are arranged. Many words possess an active or passive meaning, wholly independent of the grammatical sense of these two terms. A word that expresses a passive or recipient state may thus often be distinguished from one that contains the same idea in an active state. Between many abstract nouns we shall find this principle to operate. This may be illustrated by the respective meanings of the two words *ability* and *capacity*. The idea of power is here common to both words, but the latter expresses a power of receiving, and has a recipient or passive meaning; whereas the former expresses a power to execute, and consequently has an active signification. Again, the idea of reason enters into the meaning of both the adjectives *reasonable* and *rational;* but the former qualifies a being who exercises reason, and the latter one who possesses reason, and consequently, the difference between them is to be found in the active and passive meaning of each respectively. Lastly, even in the case of verbs into which the idea of action more fully enters, we may frequently observe a difference in meaning dependent upon this principle. This may be exemplified by the two verbs *to keep* and *to retain*. We keep, by the exertion of our own power; we retain, from the want of power or will in others. We keep what we prevent others from taking, we retain what is not taken from us. In the first, we are in an active, in the second, in a passive state. It is undeniable that attention to this phenomenon would, in many cases, solve a doubt which might exist as to the exact difference in the meaning of words.

Another extensively prevalent principle in nature is that of INTENSITY. In the material world, its effects meet us at every turn. Scarcely at any two moments does fire burn with exactly the same degree of heat, nor does the sun shine with the same brilliancy without some intervening circumstance which modifies or increases its degree of brightness. We may then confidently look for the same principle in words which is applied so extensively to objects of sense. It must here again be remembered that this principle of intensity has no reference to *comparison*, as applied to a grammatical class of words, but imports a higher degree, as marked by the difference of meaning between two words in another respect similar. We find it not only in adjectives, but also in nouns and verbs, and indeed, in some cases, in prepositions. The distinction between the two adjectives *bright* and *brilliant* is marked by the intensive degree expressed in the latter word. Brilliant is bright and something more, or it expresses a higher and more intensive degree of bright. A difference of degree will also mark the distinction between the words *breeze* and *gale;* a breeze signifies a gentle wind; a gale, a stronger wind. Again, the difference between *to see* and *to look*, or *to hear* and *to listen*, will depend upon the same principle, the latter expressing a more intensive degree of the former. Whenever the differences between two words may be accounted for on this principle, such words may be termed synonymes of intensity.

A fourth class of differences may be formed under the head of POSITIVE and NEGATIVE. Here also we find the same idea common to both words; but in the one it appears in a positive or independent form, whilst in the other it has a negative meaning. The two verbs *to shun* and *to avoid* will come under this head of differences. To shun means positively to turn from; whereas to avoid is merely *not* to go in the way of, and has a negative sense. The same remarks will apply to the difference of meaning between the two nouns *fault* and *defect.* A fault is something positively wrong; a defect is something negatively wrong. What is faulty has what it should not have; what is defective has *not* what it should have. This class may not be found to contain so many words as those above explained, but the principle will be frequently available in determining the difference of words which cannot be brought under another category.

But although some of the principles above explained will test the difference of a large majority of synonymous terms, there are, undoubtedly, many to which none of them will apply. The difference between two words will, in many cases, be so slight, and will consist in so nice and delicate a variation, that it can be explained only by the individual circumstances of the case. And here it must be confessed that the synonymous words explained in this manner lie open to the objections mentioned in another part of this introduction; for the student will here gain no further information than that given him concerning the words themselves—he will acquire a knowledge of the difference between the two words under consideration; but that knowledge will be strictly limited to the words themselves, and the explanation itself will not suggest any power of distinguishing between other words. Such terms are explained in the fifth section of this work, and are ranged under the head of "MISCELLANEOUS."

In concluding my remarks upon this classification of synonymous words, I must again repeat that I do not set forth this system as a complete or perfect classification of such terms, but that I have adopted it for want of a better, or rather, for want of any existing arrangement. In all the works on synonymy which have fallen under my notice, I have in vain searched for some rule, the application of which would bring any required word under a certain class, and thus enable a student to ascertain its precise meaning, as distinguished from its nearest relative. As far as I am aware, no system of classification has been adopted by any writer on the subject. But though it is true that none of these writers has adopted such a classification as might suggest to the learner uniformly acting principles of difference, there can be no question that they were acquainted with these principles, for they have frequently employed them in their definitions. On the other hand, though the meaning of some words is explained in these works, in many instances, with great ingenuity and acuteness, many others are defined upon very vague, and some upon very arbitrary principles. The student, it is true, may gain the information he requires with respect to certain words; but here his knowledge stops; it is restricted to the words immediately under consideration; nothing is done towards enlarging his views of the philosophy of language, nor is any rule given him by which he may for himself discover the real difference which exists between words apparently identical.

Every one who has had any habit or practice in composing must remember the doubts he has frequently entertained of the proper use of many words suggesting themselves in the course of writing. In all cases of this sort, there is a word, and but one word, which will exactly convey our meaning;

but the difficulty is how to get at it. The writer lays down his pen—begins to think—becomes more and more embarrassed—till, at last, by some lucky association, a word, which he fancies the right one, strikes his mind, and he imagines the difficulty removed. Very far from it; another word, apparently as appropriate as the first, presents itself to his mind, and he now is more perplexed between the two, than he was before puzzled about the one. With many, it now becomes a mere question of euphony, and the more harmonious word is adopted without hesitation. But the conscientious writer, though he may regard harmony as a very desirable attainment, cannot be satisfied with sound for sense, and he looks for some principle upon which he can securely rely, to guide him in his choice. It is true, that he can search for tne difference between the two words in some work of reference, and will probably obtain the required information, as regards the word itself, the precise meaning of which he wishes to fix; but he will perhaps not have written a few lines, before the same difficulty again presents itself, and he thus finds himself continually involved in the most discouraging perplexities. These observations will, of course, not apply to the careless writer. To him it is of little consequence in what form he exhibits his thoughts, or what words he employs in expressing them; however just his views on any subject may be, or whatever merit he may possess, either of novelty or originality of thought, his total indifference to accuracy of expression will not only cause him to fail in his attempts to make his readers understand him, but will produce much positive harm in their minds, by the looseness and inaccuracy of his style.

But to those who would write sensibly and carefully—who are not satisfied with sound for sense, and who are honestly desirous of acquiring a clear and perspicuous style, the following rule may be useful:—Where a difficulty of choice in two or more words occurs, collect together all those which bear upon the meaning desired, and apply to them some of the principles above explained. It will be found, that some may be ranged under the class of generic and specific, others may belong to the active and passive class, a third pair may be distinguished by the principle of intensity, others again may be to each other as positive and negative, and so forth By thus applying some general principle of difference to words, the precise limits to the meaning of each will not be so difficult to ascertain, and the habit of testing their signification in this manner will soon produce a marked effect on the style of those who practise the rule.

There is one science intimately connected with the subject of synonymy, upon which it will be naturally expected that some remarks should here be made. I mean Etymology. A knowledge of the derivation of words is unquestionably of great service in enabling us to determine their meaning, and it may be confidently asserted, that they who are wholly ignorant of those languages from which English is derived can never have that clear conception of the primary signification of words which every good etymologist must possess. On the other hand, it should not be forgotten, that as words are continually undergoing some alteration in meaning, and in course of time, acquiring an incrustation, as it were, of signification, we should not place too firm a reliance on a knowledge of their original meaning, in endeavoring to fix the exact limits of their modern acceptation. A love for antiquity and classical associations, however natural and admirable in itself, may, like all other strong passions, prove in some respects pernicious; and it is much to be feared, that undue admiration for the beauty of ancient languages has, in many instances, caused us to underrate the qualities of our mother tongue. But we should remember, that in order to gain any sound knowledge of a subject, it is necessary not only to make ourselves acquainted with its origin, but also to be able to trace it through all the phases of its existence, a rule particularly applicable to language, the materials of which are so fluctuating and changeable. Now, the principles before explained do not belong to any one language in particular, but are applicable to every language on the globe, both ancient and modern; they are universal—they are founded in the very nature of things—they existed before any language was spoken, and we may presume that they will last as long as the world continues to exist. I would not have it supposed, that in making these remarks, I entertain any disrespect for the languages or literature of antiquity; so far from this being the case, I yield to none in my respect and veneration for the ancients; and I am impressed with a firm conviction, that antiquity is the source from which all the poets and philosophers of modern times have most copiously drawn. I would merely caution the young student against allowing his prejudices in favour of the ancients to interfere with the application of universal principles. Indeed, there can be little doubt that the ancients were as well acquainted with these principles as ourselves, for every day brings to light some new proof of how much further advanced they were even in practical science than we are inclined to give them credit for; and we are not justified in inferring, because they have left us no distinct works upon this subject, that they were not aware of these principles, and did not apply them in the same way as the moderns.

It is not a little surprising that the English, who in some questions have displayed such admirable patience of research and sagacity of investigation, should have produced so few works on the subject of synonymy. During the last century, France reckoned a considerable number of writers on this subject; among others, Girard, Voltaire, D'Alembert, Duclos, Dumarsais, Diderot, Beauzée, Roubaud, Lavaux, &c. The German writers on synonymy are Eberhard and Maass. The Italians and Spanish have also directed some attention to this subject: among the former may be mentioned, Grassi, Romani, and Tommaseo; and among the latter, Huerta and March. The only works on synonymy deserving of notice which we possess in English are, those of Dr. Trusler, Mr. W. Taylor, of Norwich, and Mr. Crabb. These are all books of reference, and not one of them adapted to the wants of younger students, or in any way suited to the purposes of practical education. Dr. Trusler's book, published at London in 1766, was a partial abstract of the Abbé Girard's "Synonymes Français." Most of the articles are little more than translations from this work, and these are interspersed with some original definitions of some contiguous terms peculiar to ourselves. But many of his explanations are very vague; several of the terms which he defines are altered in meaning since his time, and others are growing, or have already become, obsolete. These objections are of themselves sufficient to render his work rather a matter of literary curiosity than a source of instruction. Mr. Taylor's work, which appeared in 1813, displays much learning. He has taken etymology as the basis of his definitions, but in so doing, he appears to have frequently lost sight of the modern acceptation of words, and consequently he has sometimes attempted to force on words a meaning which they do not really possess. Hence many of his definitions and discriminations are purely arbitrary. For these reasons, his work was not so useful as he undoubtedly had the power of making it, and we believe that it never reached a second edition. But the largest work that we possess on the subject of synonymy is that of Mr. Crabb, who, in 1810, published his "English Synonymes arranged in alphabetical order." This is a work of much higher pretensions, and, as a book of reference, is unquestionably of great utility. There is, however, one point connected with its execution which appears to interfere in some measure with its utility. One part of the plan of his work, is to compare four or five, and sometimes as many as six words of the same class of meaning, and explain their differences in one article. In doing this, all the words are so mixed up together, and their explanations so perplexed, that the student, who it may be presumed is searching for the exact meaning of a single word, often finds it utterly impossible to disentangle the one term from the many with which it is mixed up, and thus, in many cases, obtains no satisfactory information. It should be remarked, however, that this practice is not peculiar to Mr. Crabb, but is common to both the others, as well as to all the foreign writers on the subject.*

* Besides the works above mentioned, there was published at Brunswick, in 1841, a work entitled "Synonymisches Handwörterbuch der Englischen Sprache für die Deutschen." The author of this work is Dr. Melford, professor of modern languages in the University of Göttingen. This book, which is merely a translation of some of the principal articles in Crabb, with additional examples, contributes nothing whatever towards an improved knowledge of synonymy.

In the present work, the author has purposely avoided comparing more than two terms in one explanation. This plan, with one or two exceptions, has been uniformly followed throughout the book. It has been adopted for two reasons: 1st, because, in writing, it is almost always between two words that any difficulty of choice exists; and, 2dly, because the writer has been thus better enabled to give the inquirer a distinct conception of their real difference and respective limits, which could not have been so easily done, had he followed the practice of the beforementioned writers. Besides, as the object of this book is not so much to explain, as to lay down principles of explanation, this arrangement was unnecessary. The manner in which the book is intended to be used is as follows:—The explanations under each pair of words having been carefully and attentively read by the pupil, he should be questioned upon them by the teacher, and should be required to determine under which class they may be ranged; then, the exercises under each pair should be written out, the pupil introducing the word in the blank space; and lastly, other sentences of his own composition should be written, in which each of the words is to be employed in its proper signification. This practice will not only insure an accurate knowledge of the difference between the terms, but also, a proper application of the terms themselves; and it will impress that difference, as well as the principle upon which it depends, so strongly on the learner's mind, that he will not be soon likely to forget them.

It would be superfluous to enlarge on the usefulness of such exercises as those here presented to the learner, were it not that this is the first occasion, as far as the author is aware that a practical work on English synonymes has been offered to the public. An admission that something of the sort is a desideratum, does not, however, amount to a conviction that it is necessary, on the same principle that it is much easier to allow that we are in the wrong, than to set about doing right. It may be therefore proper to make some remarks on the effect which a systematic study of synonymy is likely to have, not only on the language and style of the student, but also as regards the general improvement of his mind and his habits of thinking.

Coleridge, in whose writings we may perhaps gather a greater number of valuable hints on education than from any other modern author, says, in the Preface to his "Aids to Reflection," that a leading object of this work was "to direct the reader's attention to the value of the science of words, their use and abuse, and the incalculable advantage of using them appropriately, and with a distinct knowledge of their primary, derivative, and metaphorical senses; and in furtherance of this object, I have neglected no occasion of enforcing the maxim, that to expose a sophism, and to detect the equivocal or double meaning of a word, is, in the great majority of cases, one and the same thing." And, further, addressing the reader, he says: "Reflect on your own thoughts, actions, circumstances, and—which will be of especial aid to you in forming a habit of reflection—accustom yourself *to reflect on the words you use, hear, or read; their birth, derivation, history, &c.* For if words are not things, they are living powers by which the things of most importance to mankind are actuated, combined, and humanized."

When we reflect on the circumstances in which all children are of necessity placed, and the bad example they continually have before them, in respect of language, from servants and others, it is not surprising that they begin at an early age to use words loosely and incorrectly. Though, in this particular, some have much greater advantages than others, all are to some degree affected by this example, and parents cannot well begin too soon to take measures to counteract its effects. If all the English we hear spoken around us during our infancy and childhood were correct, there would be, of course, no necessity for this injunction; but the contrary is so notoriously the fact, that there are very few in whom this pernicious example does not produce an inveterate habit, and whom it does not affect, in some degree, through the whole course of their lives.

There is one principle in education which should never be lost sight of, and which, notwithstanding its importance, does not appear sufficiently obvious to the minds, even of those who devote considerable attention to the subject. It should be remembered, before any study be commenced, that we have two objects in view: one, and this of the greater importance, the effect the study will produce as to the general improvement of the mind; and the other, its practical utility as regards human comforts, or human intercourse. Now, the latter of these objects is that to which most men direct their attention, whilst the former holds but a second place in the opinions of many, and with the majority is considered wholly unimportant. The strength of mind to be acquired by a cultivation of the reasoning faculties is not so perceptible to the generality of mankind as those accomplishments which afford frequent opportunities of exhibition; and hence the exclusive attention paid to lighter accomplishments, and the comparative neglect with which the more valuable branches of education are treated.

The scanty information given to young students in all our schools, on the genius and character of the English language, would, of itself, be sufficient to warrant any writer in endeavouring to promote the knowledge of its nature and philosophy. It is a singular fact, that notwithstanding this unaccountable neglect of what ought to be considered an important branch of every Englishman's education, there are few who are not ready to admit the necessity of their closer acquaintance with their native tongue, and confess that a more accurate knowledge of their own language, acquired in early youth, would have better prepared them for many duties of common life they now feel utterly incompetent to fulfil. It is well known, that the usual course of *instruction* (as it is called) in the English language consists in making a pupil learn by heart the accidence and syntax rules in Murray's Grammar, write out a few dictation exercises, and occasionally compose a theme. But for the more essential acquirements in the language, nothing is done; not a word is mentioned about the philosophy of construction; nothing on facility of expression, forms of idiom, formation of style, accuracy of expression from a proper choice of words, &c. &c. Again, on the subject of versification and poetry. There is not a single book extant which explains the various forms and varieties of English verse in a popular manner, and adapted to early education. It is true, that some scanty remarks on this subject are to be found tacked to the end of one or two of our grammars; but these are mere sketches, and far from sufficient for those who wish to acquaint themselves with the forms and styles of our best poets. On this subject, also, as on many others connected with early education, the most singular ideas prevail. It is thought by many, that an attention to versification is likely to lead young persons into the habit of scribbling verses, and to call them off from the more serious duties of life. It is forgotten that in cultivating an innocent taste, we are purifying the mind from low and grovelling propensities, instilling a love of the true and beautiful, and establishing a most desirable resource in after-life, and one of the best modes of securing an avoidance of vicious or degrading pursuits. The principles on which the present work is based are equally applicable to a poetical and a prose style; that is, a careful choice and accurate use of terms are quite as necessary in the former as in the latter form of composition; and though the versifier must not expect to find here every thing he wants, it may be presumed that an application of the principles here adopted may be of considerable service to him in his studies.

But the importance of the English language, both as a subject of philology and of particular study, is now becoming generally acknowledged. It is high time, then, that something more should be proposed for the younger student than the mere grammatical exercise, or theme. Some mode of study is required which will make him exert his powers of discrimination in the use of words, and bring him into closer acquaintance with the beauties of his language, so that he may thereby acquire a relish for its characteristic power and genius. The attempt in the present work to supply that want is published with a confident hope that, whatever may be its defects, it may assist in giving an impulse to the study and promote the knowledge of that literature, which it should be every educated Englishman's boast to understand and appreciate.

SECTION I.

GENERIC AND SPECIFIC SYNONYMES.

THE principle upon which all the pairs of words in this section are discussed is the same as that adopted by natural philosophers in their classification of external objects. The whole natural world has been divided by them into three heads or kingdoms, viz.—1, the animal; 2, the vegetable; and 3, the mineral kingdom; and each of these is again subdivided into orders, classes, genera, and species. Though, for various reasons, so comprehensive a classification cannot be applied to language, yet in investigating the cause of the difference between words which approximate in meaning, we shall frequently find it to depend upon this principle; that is, the one word will be found to specify precisely what the other expresses more generally. Indeed this occurs so often, that it may be confidently assumed as one mode of testing the difference between words, and thereby acquiring an exact knowledge of the limits of each. We find this difference between such words as *to bury*, and *to inter;* the former being the generic, and the latter the specific word. Whatever is interred is buried, but what is buried is not of necessity interred. To inter is a specific mode of burying; it contains the same idea as that which exists in *to bury*, but with the addition of certain accompanying ideas not found in the generic word.

Adjective—Epithet.

These words differ as the species from the genus. Every adjective is an epithet; but every epithet is not an adjective. *Epithet* is a term of rhetoric.* *Adjective* is a term of gram-

* ["Epithets, in the rhetorical sense, denote, not every adjective, but those only which do not add to the sense, but signify something already implied in the noun itself; as if one says 'the *glorious* sun;' on the other hand, to speak of 'the *meridian* sun' would not be considered as, in this sense, employing an epithet."

WHATELY'S *Rhetoric.*]

mar. The same word may be both an adjective and an epithet. In prose composition, the epithet is frequently put after the noun, as—Henry *the Fowler*, Charles *the Simple*, &c. In the first of these examples, the word "fowler" is, grammatically, a noun; rhetorically, an epithet; in the second, the word "simple" is both an adjective and an epithet. An epithet qualifies distinctively, an adjective qualifies generally. Much of the merit of style depends upon the choice of epithets.

[*Moth.* Once to behold with your sun-beamed eyes,—
—with your sun-beamed eyes.
Boyet. They will not answer to that epithet.
Love's Labour's Lost, v. 2

Remove their swelling epithets, thick laid
As varnish on a harlot's cheek. *P. R.*, iv. 343.]

Exercise.

"All the versification of Claudian is included within the compass of four or five lines; perpetually closing his sense at the end of a verse, and that verse commonly which they call golden, or two substantives and two —— with a verb between them to keep the peace."

"From these principles, it will be easy to illustrate a remark of the Stagyrite on the —— *rosy-fingered*, which Homer has given to Aurora. This, says the critic, is better than if he had said *purple-fingered*, and far better than if he had said *red-fingered*."

"This consideration may further serve to answer for the constant use of the same —— to his gods and heroes; such as the far-darting Phœbus, the blue-eyed Pallas, the swift-footed Achilles, &c."

"A word added to a noun, to signify the addition or separation of some quality, or manner of being, such as good, bad, &c., is an ——."

"I affirm phlegmatically, leaving the —— false, scandalous, and villanous, to the author."

Answer—Reply.

Every reply is an answer, though every answer is not a reply. An *answer* is given to a question; a *reply* is made to an accusation or an objection. The former simply informs, the latter confutes or disproves. When we seek to do more than inform—to bring others to the conviction that the opinions they have expressed are mistaken or unjust, we reply to their arguments. Witnesses who are examined on a trial do not reply to, but answer the questions put to them by the counsel, because, in such a case, information alone is required. The counsel for the defendant, in a trial, does not answer, but replies to the arguments used by the other party, because he seeks to prove that these arguments are false, and do not criminate his client.

[*Macb.* ——————— answer me
To what I ask you. *Macbeth*, iv. 1.

King. Reply not to me with a fool-born jest;
2 Henry IV, v. 5

Cap. Speak not, reply not, do not answer me.
Romeo and Juliet, iii 5.

While thus I called, and strayed I knew not whither,
From where I first drew air, and first beheld
This happy light; when answer none returned—
P. L., viii. 285.

——— and Satan stood
Awhile, as mute, confounded what to say,
What to reply, ——— *P. R.*, iii. 3.

And what are things eternal?—Powers depart,"
The grey-haired wanderer stedfastly replied,
Answering the question which himself had asked,—
The Excursion, v.]

Exercise.

During the night, the sentinel, hearing a rustling noise at some distance from him, demanded in a loud voice, "Who goes there?" and receiving no ———, immediately fired in that direction.

Sir,—In ——— to the statements made in your letter of this morning, I must observe, &c.

As I cannot proceed in this affair, without obtaining information on these points, I shall feel obliged by your ——— my letter at your earliest convenience.

The advocate, in his ——— to the charges brought against the prisoners, fully established their innocence; and they consequently were immediately discharged from custody.

"Perplexed the tempter stood,
Nor had what to ———"

How can we think of appearing at that tribunal, without being able to give a ready ——— to the questions which shall then be put to us?

Bravery—Courage.

Bravery is constitutional; *courage* is acquired. The one is born with us, the other is the result of reflection. There is no merit in being brave, but much in being courageous. Brave men are naturally careless of danger; the courageous man is aware of danger, and yet faces it calmly. Bravery is apt to degenerate into temerity. Courage is always cool and collected. It may be, perhaps, said with justice, that the French are the braver, and the English the more courageous people.

[*Ant.* ——— come down
With fearful bravery, thinking by this face
To fasten in our thoughts that they have courage.
Julius Cæsar, v. 1.

Lady P. Did all the chivalry of England move
To do brave acts. —— *2 Henry IV.*, ii. 3

Mal. ——— The king-becoming graces,
As justice, verity, temperance, stableness,
Bounty, perseverance, mercy, lowliness,
Devotion, patience, courage, fortitude—
Macbeth, iv. 3

his face
Deep scars of thunder had intrenched, and care
Sat on his faded cheek; but under brows
Of dauntless courage ——— *P. L.*, i. 603

——— But, in despite
Of all this outside bravery, within
He neither felt encouragement nor hope.
'*The Excursion*,' ii

The martial courage of a day is vain,
An empty noise of death the battle's roar,
If vital hope be wanting to restore,
Or fortitude be wanting to sustain,
Armies or kingdoms. '*Sonnets to Liberty*.']

Exercise.

King Alfred was conspicuous during the early part of his reign, for the ——— with which he resisted the attacks of his enemies, the Danes.

The first check which Xerxes received in his invasion of Greece was from the ——— of Leonidas and his three hundred Spartans, who disputed with him the pass of Thermopylæ.

Richard I. of England distinguished himself, during his campaigns in the Holy Land, by acts of the most impetuous ———.

It requires quite as much ——— in a minister to guide the state in safety, through all the political storms by which she is beset, as in a general, to insure victory to his country, amidst the difficulties and dangers by which he may be surrounded.

——— is impetuous; ——— is intrepid.

A proper ——— is not confined to objects of personal danger, but is prepared to meet poverty and disgrace.

Bonds—Fetters.

Bonds, from the Anglo-Saxon *bindan*, to bind, means whatever takes away our freedom of action beyond a certain circle. *Fetters*, from the Saxon *fæter*, is strictly what binds the feet; what hinders us from moving or walking. Bonds is the generic term. Fetters are species of bonds.

[*Mar.* What tributaries follow him to Rome
To grace in captive bonds his chariot-wheels.
Julius Cæsar, i. 1.

King. ——— we will fetters put upon this fear
Which now goes too free-footed.
Hamlet, iii. 3.

Eyeless in Gaza, at the mill with slaves
Himself in bonds under Philistian yoke
S. A., 42.

We cannot free the Lady that sits here
In stony fetters, fixed and motionless.
Comus, 819.

Or he, whose bonds dropped off, whose prison-doors
Flew open, by an Angel's voice unbarred.
WORDSWORTH. *Ecclesiastical Sonnets*

Learn by a mortal yearning to ascend—
Seeking a higher object. Love was given,
Encouraged, sanctioned, chiefly for that end;
For this the passion to excess was driven—
That self might be annulled; her bondage prove
The fetters of a dream, opposed to love.
WORDSWORTH '*Laodamia*.']

Exercise.

"Let any one send his contemplation to the extremities of the universe, and see what conceivable hopes, what ——— he can imagine to hold this mass of matter in so close a pressure together."

"Doctrine unto fools is as ——— on the feet, and manacles on the right hand."

The ——— of affection which exists between parent and child can never be broken except by the most unnatural and detestable wickedness.

In this case, I am ——— by circumstances, and, however unwillingly, must remain an inactive spectator of the course of affairs.

"There left me and my man, both bound together,
Till, gnawing with my teeth my ——— asunder,
I gained my freedom."

His legs were so inflamed by the weight of his ——, and the length of time he had worn them, that when they were knocked off his feet, he was too weak to stand, and it was with some difficulty that he was prevented from fainting.

And Paul said: "I would to God, that not only thou, but also all that hear me this day, were both almost, and altogether such as I am, except these ——."

Booty—Prey.

Booty and prey are both objects of plunder: but there is this distinction, that *booty* may be applied to various purposes, whilst *prey* is always for consumption. Soldiers carry off their booty. Birds carry off their prey. Avarice or covetousness incites men to take booty. A ravenous appetite urges animals to search for prey. In a secondary sense, things are said to be a prey to whatever consumes them, either physically or morally. Thus:—a house falls a prey to the devouring flames. The heart is a prey to melancholy. Misfortunes prey on the mind.

[*York.* So triumph thieves upon their conquered booty.
3 *Henry VI.*, i. 4.

Macb. Whiles night's black agents to their prey do rouse.
Macbeth, iii. 2.

Ewes and their bleating lambs over the plain
Their booty. *P. L.*, xi. 650.

As when a vulture on Imaus bred,
Whose snowy ridge the roving Tartar bounds,
Dislodging from a region scarce of prey,
P. L., iii. 433.

And he was free to sport and play,
When falcons were abroad for prey.
WORDSWORTH. '*Song at the Feast of Brougham Castle.*']

Exercise.

The brigands having packed all the —— on mules which they had brought with them, set fire to the premises, and quitted the spot.

There are men of ——, as well as beasts and birds of ——, that live upon and delight in human blood.

The next day, the town was taken by assault; the ferocious assailants vented their rage upon the defenceless inhabitants by massacring them by thousands, and pillaging the churches and treasuries of the place, in which they found an immense ——.

"A garrison supported itself by the —— it took from the neighbourhood of Aylesbury."

Velleius Paterculus states that the sum produced by the ——— which Julius Cæsar brought to Rome was above fifty millions of pounds.

"Who, stung by glory, rave, and bound away,
The world their field, and human-kind their ———."

Conduct—Behaviour.

Behaviour respects our manner of acting on particular occasions, or in individual cases; *Conduct* refers to the general tenor of our actions. Behaviour is connected with the circumstances of the case. Conduct is the result of our habits of thinking, and the standard of morals set up in our own minds. Soldiers behave gallantly in an engagement. A good citizen conducts himself on all occasions wisely and temperately. Our morals or temper influence our conduct. Our humour influences our behaviour. The conduct of Charles I. was marked by mild dignity. Queen Elizabeth's behaviour was undignified when she gave Lord Essex a box on the ear.

[*Bass.* ——— pray thee, take pain
To allay with some cold drops of modesty
Thy skipping spirit; lest through thy wild behaviour
I be misconstrued in the place I go to
And lose my hopes. *Merchant of Venice*, ii. 3.]

Exercise.

The ——— of the firemen was beyond all praise; they exposed themselves at all points to the raging flames, and exerted themselves to the utmost to subdue the fire, which soon yielded to their combined efforts.

At the end of the half-year, the father received a letter from his son's tutor, expressive of his unqualified praise of his pupil's ——— during the six months previous.

A state of happiness is not to be expected by those who are conscious of no moral or religious rule for their ——— in life.

The ——— of the whole school during the master's illness was most exemplary. By common consent, no boisterous or noisy games were allowed, and the pupils all moved about the house as quietly as possible, for fear of disturbing him.

His master parted with him with expressions of much regret, and begged that he would apply to him whenever he should require testimonials of character or ———.

Custom—Habit.

Custom respects things which are done by the majority; *Habit*, those which are done by individuals. We speak ot national customs, and of a man of indolent habits. It is a custom in England to leave town in the summer months. It is a custom to eat hot-cross buns on Good Friday. It is a custom to attend divine service. It is a habit to take snuff, to smoke, &c. Habits will often arise from customs; for instance, the custom of going to church may produce habits of piety. The custom of driving in a carriage may produce habits of indolence. It is of great advantage when the customs of a nation are such as are likely to lead to good habits among the people.

[*Ham.* Assume a virtue, if you have it not.
That monster, custom, who all sense doth eat
Of habit's devil, is angel apt in this;
That to the use of actions fair and good
He likewise gives a frock or livery
That aptly is put on. *Hamlet*, iii. 4.

Cor. What custom wills, in all things should we do't,
The dust on antique time would lie unswept,
And mountainous error be too highly heaped
For truth to overpeer. *Coriolanus*, ii. 3.

Val. How use doth breed a habit in a man!
Two Gentlemen of Verona, v. 4

——— upheld by old repute,
Consent, or custom;——— *P. L.*, i. 640.

Full soon thy soul shall have her earthly freight,
And custom lie upon thee with a weight
Heavy as frost, and deep almost as life.
WORDSWORTH. '*Ode—Intimations of Immortality.*'

The mild necessity of use compels
To acts of love; and habit does the work
Of reason;———
WORDSWORTH. '*The Old Cumberland Beggar.*']

Exercise.

The ——— of early rising is very conducive to health.

The ——— of giving money to servants does not prevail to the same extent as formerly.

Paley has said that "man is a bundle of ———."

In many parts of Germany, it is the ——— to dine as early as twelve o'clock.

The effects of good example and early ——— are equally visible in his conversation.

We have no distinct account of the origin of the Chinese ——— of cramping the feet of their women.

The ——— of representing the grief we have for the loss of the dead by the colour of our garments certainly took its rise from the real sorrow of such as were too much distressed to take the care they ought of their dress.

"The force of education is so great, that we may mould the minds and manners of the young into what shape we please, and give the impressions of such ———s as shall ever afterwards remain."

Comparison—Analogy.

A *comparison* is made between two things that resemble each other in their external appearance. An *analogy* is the resemblance to be found between two things in the effects they produce, or in the relation they bear to other things. We may make a comparison between two trees or two men, because in them may be found an external likeness to each other. The arms of the human body are analogous to the branches of a tree, *i. e.* they stand in the same relation to the body, that the branches do to the tree. The principle of analogy operates very strongly in all the mechanical arts; this has directed the formation of the cupola or dome, which is taken from the human skull; pillars from legs; thatching from hair; tiling from the scales of fish, &c.

[*Flu.* ——— you shall find, in the comparisons between Macedon and Monmouth that the situations, look you, is both alike.

Henry V., iv. 7.

——— the earth
Though, in comparison of heaven, so small
Nor glistering, may of solid good contain
More plenty than the sun that barren shines.

P. L., viii. 92.]

Exercise.

There is something ——— in the exercise of the mind to that of the body.

It is from the principle of ——— that words are used in a secondary sense.

It is absurd to draw a ——— between things which bear no resemblance to each other.

These two persons are so unlike in every respect, that I am surprised any one should ever have attempted to draw a ——— between them.

The ——— between the keel of a vessel and the share of a plough has often been remarked and commonly used.

Plutarch has drawn a ——— between the characters of Julius Cæsar and Alexander the Great.

The bark or outer covering of trees is ——— to the skin of the human body.

"If the body politic have any ——— to the natural, an act of oblivion were necessary in a hot, distempered state."

"If we will rightly esteem what we call good and evil, we shall find it lies much in ———."

Duty—Obligation.

Duty has to do with the conscience, and arises from the natural relations of society. An obligation arises from circumstances, and is a species of duty. No man is exempt from duties. One who guarantees the payment of a sum of money contracts an obligation. He who marries contracts new duties. Duties are between parents and children; husbands and wives; teachers and scholars, &c. When we promise, we contract an obligation. Duty is what is due from one to another. An obligation is what we bind ourselves to do independently of our natural duties.

[*The.* —— in the modesty of fearful duty
I read as much as from the rattling tongue
Of saucy and audacious eloquence.
Midsummer-Night's Dream, v. 1.

King. ——— the survivor bound
In filial obligation, for some term
To do obsequious sorrow. *Hamlet*, i. 2.

——— zeal and duty are not slow
But on occasion's forelock watchful wait.
P. R., iii. 172.

The primal duties shine aloft—like stars;
The charities that soothe, and heal, and bless,
Are scattered at the feet of Man—like flowers.
The Excursion, ix.

——— this imperial Realm,
While she exacts allegiance, shall admit
An obligation, on her part, to teach
Them who are born to serve her and obey.
Id.]

Exercise.

"So quick a sense did the Israelites entertain of the merits of Gideon, and the ——— he had laid upon them, that they tendered him the regal and hereditary government of that people."

It is the ——— of parents to attend equally to the moral and intellectual training of their children.

I feel myself under so many ——— to my uncle, that I could not take so important a step without asking his advice.

"Every one must allow that the subject and matter of domestic ——— are inferior to none in utility and importance."

The offices of a parent may be discharged from a consciousness of their ———; and a sense of this ——— is sometimes necessary to assist the stimulus of parental affection.

If it be the ——— of a parent to educate his children, he has a right to exert such authority, and, in support of that authority, to exercise such discipline as may be necessary for these purposes.

Fear—Terror.

Fear is the generic word. *Terror* is a species of fear. Fear is an inward feeling. Terror is an external and visible agitation. The prospect of evil excites our fear; we feel terror at the evil which is actually before us. We fear an approaching storm; the storm itself excites terror. Fear urges us to action; terror urges us to flight. Fear prompts us to prepare against the coming evil; terror urges us to escape it.

[*Bast.* Possessed with rumours, full of idle dreams,
Not knowing what they fear, but full of fear.
King John, iv. 2.

P. Hen. ——— as the poorest vassal is,
That doth with awe and terror kneel to it.
2 *Henry IV.*, iv. 4

——— and chase
Anguish and doubt, and fear and sorrow, and pain,
From mortal or immortal minds.——
P. L., i. 558.

——— terrour seized the rebel host,
Id., vi. 647.

Whate'er, in docile childhood or in youth,
He had imbibed of fear or darker thought,
Was melted all away. *The Excursion*, i.

——— those that roam at large
Over the burning wilderness, and charge
The wind with terror. while they roar for food.
WORDSWORTH. *Sonnets, &c.*]

Exercise.

The ——— of some persons during a thunder-storm is so great, that it takes away all power of action, and renders them for a time perfectly helpless.

Whatever may occur in the mean time, I have no ——— for the result.

The poor boy felt such ——— at the sight of this hideous mask, that we had some difficulty in calming his agitation, and still more in persuading him that it concealed a human face underneath.

She has been extremely ill; and was for several days in such a precarious state, that ——— were entertained for her life.

The ferocious countenance and gigantic stature of the ancient Germans at first inspired the Roman soldiers with such ———, that Cæsar was obliged to use all his eloquence to persuade his men to oppose them in the field.

Among the many motives which prompt men to obey the laws, ——— of punishment is not the least strong.

The enemy shot through the walls and fortifications of the town, to the great ——— of the inhabitants.

Fancy—Imagination.

Fancy is the power of combining ideas—of bringing them together in such a manner as to produce novel and pleasing scenes for the mind to contemplate. *Imagination* is the power of endowing substances with qualities and faculties, which in reality they do not possess—of making them think, and speak, and act, like beings of another order. The fancy only brings objects together in the mind; it regards but the outward appearances of things. The imagination creates; it gives interest to the simplest and most insignificant things, by investing them with qualities which immediately render them objects of human sympathy.

[*Grif.* ——— such good dreams
Possess your fancy. *Henry VIII.*, iv. 2.

The. —— as imagination bodies forth
The forms of things unknown, the poet's pen
Turns them to shapes, and gives to airy nothing
A local habitation and a name. *Midsummer-Night's Dream*, v. 1

Wrapped in a pleasing fit of melancholy
To meditate my rural minstrelsy,
Till fancy had her fill.—— *Comus*, 548

——— that may lift
Human imagination to such highth
Of godlike power? *P. L.*, vi. 300.

——— Sunbeams, upon distant hills
Gliding apace, with shadows in their train,
Might, with small help from fancy, be transformed
Into fleet Oreads sporting visibly. *The Excursion*, iv.

——— the glorious faculty assigned
To elevate the more than reasoning Mind,
And colour life's dark cloud with orient rays
Imagination is that sacred power,
Imagination lofty and refined — —
WORDSWORTH. *Miscel. Sonnets*]

Exercise.

Shakspeare's "Midsummer Night's Dream," and Pope's "Rape of the Lock," offer numerous instances of the elegant and exuberant ——— of these two poets.

In Homer and Shakspeare, ———, the true test of poetical power, is more abundant than in any other poets the world has ever seen.

——— is creative—lively—glowing; it animates all things which come within the sphere of its magic influence;—makes them think, and feel, and act, and suffer: ——— is whimsical and capricious, it combines strange, and sometimes incongruous elements. Fairies, monsters, gnomes, and spirits, are its offspring.

The following extract from Drayton's "Muse's Elysium" is a charming specimen of a delicate ———:

"Of leaves of roses, white and red,
Shall be the covering of the bed;
The curtains, vallens, tester, all
Shall be the flower imperial;
And for the fringe, it all along
With azure harebells shall be hung
Of lilies shall the pillows be,
With down stuft of the butterfly."

Haste—Hurry.

Haste signifies heat of action. The word *hurry* includes an idea of confusion and want of collected thoughts not to be found in haste. Hurry implies haste, but includes confusion or trepidation. What is done in haste may be done well, but what is done in a hurry can never be done accurately. Haste implies an eager desire to accomplish. Hurry, the same desire, accompanied with the fear of interruption. The derivation of *hurry* from the Anglo-Saxon verb *hergian* (to plunder) will illustrate the proper use of the word. It is the feeling that accompanies those who plunder and take flight

[*Wol.* I have touched the highest point of all my greatness;
And, from that full meridian of my glory,
I haste now to my setting. *Henry VIII.*, iii. 2.

Like youthful steers unyoked, they take their courses
East, west, north, south; or, like a school broke up,
Each hurries toward his home, and sporting-place.
2 Henry IV., IV. 2

——— all this haste
Of midnight march, and hurried meeting here—
P. L., v. 777-8.

A seemly reverence may be paid to power;
But that's a loyal virtue, never sown
In haste, nor springing with a transient shower.
WORDSWORTH. *Sonnets to National Independence*

———, in the motley crowd,
Not one of us has felt the far-famed sight;
How could we feel it? each the other's blight,
Hurried and hurrying, volatile and loud.
Itin. Sonnets, p. 355.]

Exercise.

He ran off in such a ———, that he spilt the ink all over his dress.

If you do not make ———, you will not finish your exercise by one o'clock.

In our ——— to get on board in good time, some of the luggage was left behind, and we were obliged to proceed on our voyage without it.

As I have appointed to meet my brother in Paris, on the 28th of this month, I must ——— on my journey, or I shall arrive there too late to see him, as I know he will be obliged to start the next day for London.

If you wish the work to be finished by next week, it will be necessary to ——— it forward, and consequently it will be badly done; I should strongly recommend you to delay its completion for another week.

Though I am in great ———, I cannot let slip this opportunity of informing you that every thing is going on to our greatest satisfaction.

A List—A Catalogue.

A list contains no more than the names of things or persons to be recorded. *A catalogue* is a systematic list; it has a certain order which we do not find in a list. A catalogue is arranged alphabetically, or according to some determined principle. The reader will now perceive the difference between a list of books and a catalogue of books. A list of books will merely give their titles, put down without any attention to order. A catalogue of books will give not only the titles, editions, and dates of the books it contains, but will divide them under the several heads of History, Poetry, Philosophy, &c., &c.

[*Cæs.* ——— The kings of Mede, and Lycaonia, with a
More larger list of scepters. *Antony and Cleopatra*, iii. 6.

Macb. Ay, in the catalogue ye go for men; *Macbeth*, iii. 1.

Nor am I in the list of them that hope. *S. A.*, 647.

——— that mournful solace now must pass
Into the list of things that cannot be!
WORDSWORTH. '*Vaudracour and Julia*']

Exercise.

"After I had read over the ——— of persons elected into the Tiers Etat, nothing which they afterwards did could appear astonishing."

"In the library of manuscripts belonging to St. Lawrence, of which there is a printed ———, I looked into the Virgil which disputes its antiquity with that of the Vatican."

The Roman Emperor Domitian kept a ——— of those whom he intended to put to death. Three officers of his court, having discovered that their names were among those devoted to destruction, formed a conspiracy against his life.

Take the ——— of music which was sent yesterday, and make a ——— of the pieces you want.

He was the ablest emperor in all the ———.

Some say the loadstone is poison, and therefore in the ——— of poisons we find it in many authors.

The ——— of paintings exhibited this year contains a greater number of pictures than we have ever before seen.

Manners—Address.

An *address* is the mode of directing ourselves to one person. Our *manners* signify the way in which we generally behave. Those who, in speaking to others, hesitate, blush, stammer, and betray a want of self-possession, have a bad address. Those who loll on a sofa, whistle, and pay no attention to those who address them, are ill-mannered. Manners are elegant or vulgar. An address is confident or awkward.

[*Oli.* Fit for the mountains and the barbarous caves,
Where manners ne'er were preached!
Twelfth Night, iv. 1.

——— Civility of manners, arts, and arms,—
P. R., iv. 83.

Or must we be constrained to think that these spectators rude,
Poor in estate, of manners base, men of the multitude,
Have souls which never yet have risen, and therefore prostrate lie?
No, no, this cannot be;—men thirst for power and majesty.
WORDSWORTH. '*The Star-Gazers*']

Exercise.

Many persons pay exclusive attention to intellectual pursuits, and are so enamoured of literature or science, that they neglect those external ——— which every well-bred person possesses, and which form an essential part in the character of a gentleman.

A good ——— is not to be acquired by any fixed rules; we must mix much in polished society, and acquire that confidence in acting and moving which the well-educated unconsciously possess.

It is very possible to be perfectly well ———, and yet to have an awkward ———; good ——— are the necessary result of our habits of thinking as well as acting—they are the colours, so to speak, of our moral and intellectual nature, exhibited externally—the outward effects of our inward turn of thought.

An awkward ——— is perfectly compatible with a very amiable disposition, and is most frequently found in those who, either from peculiarity of physical temperament, or from defect of character, are of shy and reserved habits.

His education has been deplorably neglected; he was so ignorant of the lowest rudiments of knowledge, and so rude in ———, that we found it impossible to remain in his society.

Negligence—Neglect.

Negligence is the habit of leaving undone. *Neglect* is the act of leaving undone. Negligence applies to a state or frame of mind. Neglect is applied to some individual person, or thing, to which we do not pay due attention. The neglect of our duties exposes us to censure. We are negligent in generals, we are neglectful in particulars. Negligent men are neglectful of their duties. Negligence is a quality which should never be suffered to grow up in children. The neglect of moral culture in youth leads to the most baneful effects in after-life.

[*Iago.* As when, by night and negligence, the fire
Is spied in populous cities. *Othello*, i. 1.

Bru. Nor construe any further my neglect
Than that poor Brutus, with himself at war,
Forgets the shows of love to other men.
Julius Cæsar, i. 2.

To tell thee sadly, shepherd, without blame,
Or our neglect, we lost her as we came.
Comus, 510.

——— her house
Bespake a sleepy hand of negligence. *The Excursion*, i.]

Exercise.

"The two classes of men most apt to be —— of this duty (religious retirement) are the men of pleasure and the men of business."

"By a thorough contempt of little excellences, he is perfectly master of them. This temper of mind leaves him under no necessity of studying his air; and he has this peculiar distinction, that his —— is unaffected."

"It is the great excellence of learning that it borrows very little from time or place; but this quality, which constitutes much of its value, is one occasion of ——."

By —— to do what ought to be done, we shall soon acquire habits of ——.

He who treats the counsels of the wise with ——, will be made to repent of his folly by bitter experience.

The boy's —— of his master's strict orders led to this consequence; the stable-door being left open, the horse broke loose, and bursting through the fence, trespassed upon a neighbour's property.

His —— nearly caused his losing the situation.

News—Tidings.

Tidings is a species of *news.* The difference between tidings and news is, that we are always more or less interested in tidings; whereas, we may be indifferent as to news. We *may* be curious to hear news, but we are always anxious for tidings. We receive news of the political events of Europe; but we receive tidings of our friends in their absence. No tidings have been received of the steam-ship *The President,* since she sailed from New York, in March, 1841.

[*Cleo.* Though it be honest, it is never good
To bring bad news: Give to a gracious message
An host of tongues; but let ill tidings tell
Themselves, when they be felt. *Antony and Cleopatra,* ii. 5

Mes. —— Lest evil tidings, with too rude irruption
Hitting thy aged ear, should pierce too deep.
Man. Suspense in news is torture; speak them out.
S. A., 1567.

—— pleading on the shore,
Where once came monk and nun with gentle stir
Blessings to give, news ask or suit prefer.
WORDSWORTH. *Itiner. Sonnets.*

—— and talked
With winged messengers; who daily brought
To his small island in the ethereal deep
Tidings of joy and love. *The Excursion,* iv.]

Exercise.

"But perhaps the hour in which we most deeply felt how entirely we had wound and wrapt our own poetry in himself, was that in which the ——— of his death reached this country."

"Yusef reluctantly took up arms, and sent troops to the relief of the place; when, in the midst of his anxiety, he received ——— that his dreadful foe had suddenly fallen a victim to the plague."

"I wonder that, in the present situation of affairs, you can take pleasure in writing any thing but ———."

"His parents received ——— of his seizure, but beyond that they could learn nothing."

"They have ——— gatherers and intelligencers distributed into their several walks, who bring in their respective quotas, and make them acquainted with the discourse of the whole kingdom."

"Too soon some demon to my father bore
The ——— that his heart with anguish tore."

"In the midst of her reveries and rhapsodies ——— reached Newstead of the untimely death of Lord Byron."

An Occasion—An Opportunity.

Opportunities are particular *occasions*. An occasion presents itself, an opportunity is desired. Opportunities spring out of occasions. When the circumstances of an occasion are favourable to our purpose, the occasion produces the opportunity. We may have frequent occasion to converse with a person, without getting an opportunity of speaking to him on some particular subject. We act as the occasion may require; we embrace or improve an opportunity.

[*Ham.* How all occasions do inform against me
And spur my dull revenge! *Hamlet*, iv. 4.

Rom Farewell! I will omit no opportunity,
That may convey my greetings, love, to thee.
Romeo and Juliet, iii. 5.

——— zeal and duty are not slow
But on occasion's forelock watchful wait.
P. R., iii. 173

And opportunity I here have had
To try thee, sift thee, and confess have found thee
Proof against all temptation. *Id.* iv. 531.

Is placable—because occasions rise
So often that demand such sacrifice.
WORDSWORTH '*Character of the Happy Warrior*

Turning, for them who pass, the common dust
Of servile opportunity to gold;
Filling the soul with sentiments august—
The beautiful, the brave, the holy, and the just!

'Desultory Stanzas,' p 269.]

Exercise.

"Waller preserved and won his life from those who were most resolved to take it, and in an ——— in which he ought to have been ambitious to lose it."

"If a philosopher has lived any time, he must have had ample ——— of exercising his meditations on the vanity of all sublunary conditions."

"'Tis hard to imagine one's self in a scene of greater horror than on such an ———, and yet (shall I own it to you?) though I was not at all willing to be drowned, I could not forbear being entertained at the double distress of a fellow-passenger."

"At the Louvre, I had the ——— of seeing the King, accompanied by the Duke Regent."

Have you ever heard what was the ——— and beginning of this custom?

"A wise man will make more ——— than he finds. Men's behaviour should be like their apparel, not too strait, but free for exercise."

"Neglect no ——— of doing good, nor check thy desire of doing it by a vain fear of what may happen."

A Picture—A Painting.

A picture is a representation of objects. A painting is a representation by means of colour, Colour is essential to a painting, though not to a picture. Every painting is a picture, because it represents something; but every picture is not a painting, because every picture is not painted. Form, drawing, outline, composition, are the essentials of the picture: these, together with the colouring, make up the painting. In a secondary sense, the same distinction is to be observed The poet paints in glowing colours. The historian draws a lively picture.

[*Bora.* ——— sometime, fashioning them like Pharaoh's soldiers in the reechy painting.

Much Ado About Nothing, iii 3

K. Phi. ——— they were besmeared and overstained
With Slaughter's pencil; where revenge did paint
The fearful difference of incensed kings.

King John, III. 1.

Ham. Look here upon this picture, and on this:
The counterfeit presentment of two brothers.

Hamlet, iii. 4.

——— beautiful as when first
The appropriate Picture, fresh from Titian's hand
Graced the Refectory ——— WORDSWORTH, p. 384.]

Exercise.

The historian draws such a lively ——— of the follies and vices of that period, that it is impossible to read his account without taking a deep interest in the events which he relates.

The art of mixing colours, as applied by the old masters in their old ———s, is now lost to the world.

Most children are delighted with ———, and many will pore over them with rapture for hours together.

You cannot easily ——— to yourself any thing more unpleasant than my situation. In a foreign country, far from home and friends, and without money, I should have perished for want, had it not been for some benevolent merchants, who pitied my forlorn condition and supplied my necessities till I should receive remittances from England.

The prize destined for him who should make the greatest improvement in drawing, was a beautiful water-colour ——— by a first-rate artist, mounted and set in an elegant gold frame.

A Pillar—A Column.

A pillar is a supporting pile. A column is a round pillar. A pillar is smaller than a column. Columns may or may not support the roofs or arches of buildings. Pillars are always used in the sense of supporters. Pillars may be square, or even triangular; columns are always round. We say "Nelson's column," the "Duke of York's column," but the Doric or Ionic pillar. We say a column of smoke, because it assumes a round form. Roundness is the distinguishing characteristic of the column.

[*Wol.* ——— from these shoulders
These ruined pillars, out of pity, taken
A load would sink a navy. *Henry VIII.*, iii. 2

Built like a temple, where pilasters round
Were set, and Doric pillars overlaid
With golden architrave—— *P. L.*, i. 714.

As in a fiery column charioting
His godlike presence—— *S. A.*, 27.

Like pillars fixed more firmly, as might seem,
And more secure, by very weight of all
That, for support, rests on them; *The Excursion*, v.

Oft is the medal faithful to its trust
When temples, columns, towers are laid in dust;
And 'tis a common ordinance of fate
That things obscure and small outlive the great.
'*Inscriptions*.']

Exercise.

"Withdraw religion, and you shake all the ——— of morality."

"Some of the old Greek ——— and altars were brought from the ruins of Apollo's temple at Delos."

"The palace built by Picus vast and proud,
Supported on a hundred ——— stood."

"The whole weight of any ——— of the atmosphere, as likewise the specific gravity of its bases, are certainly known by many experiments."

"A simultaneous crash resounded through the city, as down toppled many a roof and ———! the lightning, as if caught by the metal, lingered an instant on the imperial statue—then shivered bronze and ———!"

"Ev'n the best must own
"Patience and resignation are ———
"Of human peace on earth."

"Round broken ——— clasping ivy twined."

"I charge you by the law,
"Whereof you are a well deserving ———,
"Proceed to judgment."

Populace—Mob.

Populace is from the Italian *popolazzo*, and signifies the lowest orders of the people taken collectively. *Mob*, from the Latin *mobilis*, moveable, characterizes the fickleness of the populace. Both the words signify an assemblage of the people. When the lower orders meet peaceably, and disperse quietly, they are the populace. When the populace commit excesses, riot, or act tumultuously, they become the mob. The populace are vulgar, illiterate, and unrefined. A mob is noisy, riotous, and tumultuous.

Exercise.

"The tribunes and people, having subdued all competitors, began the last game of a prevalent ———, to choose themselves a master."

As the ——— began to shew symptoms of a riotous disposition, a body of police was ordered to the spot, to prevent any outbreak.

Instead, however, of displaying any signs of dissatisfaction, the ———

received them with three hearty cheers, and the very best understanding prevailed during the whole day, between the people and the civil authorities.

"By the senseless and insignificant clink of misapplied words, some restless demagogues had inflamed the minds of the sottish ——— to a strange, unaccountable abhorrence of the best of men."

When the new member reached the gates of the town, he was received with deafening cheers by the ———, who, unharnessing the horses from his carriage, dragged him to his hotel in the market-place.

Several women and children, getting into the thickest of the crowd, were much bruised by the ——— before they could extricate themselves.

Posture—Attitude.

An *attitude* is an expression of internal feeling by that disposition of the limbs which is naturally suited to such an expression. A *posture* designates no more than the visible position of the body. We therefore speak of a horizontal posture, an erect posture, or a sleeping posture: and of an attitude of despair, an attitude of melancholy. If a painter wished to represent a figure in an attitude of devotion, he would draw him in a kneeling posture, with joined, outstretched hands, and eyes uplifted to heaven. An attitude always implies expression; a posture, in itself, has none. The attitude is the posture, with expression.

[*Bru.* As if that whatsoever god, who leads him,
Were slily crept into his human powers,
And gave him graceful posture. *Coriolanus*, ii. 1.

Or in this abject posture have ye sworn
To adore the Conquerour? *P. L.*, i. 322.

That posture, and the look of filial love
Thinking of past and gone ——— WORDSWORTH, p 384.]

Exercise.

The bishop was kneeling at the altar in ——— of the deepest devotion, and was so absorbed in meditation, that he did not hear the assassins' steps in the cathedral till they were quite close to him.

In this ——— of affairs, he determined no longer to hold out against the demands of the council.

He was shut up for three days in a dark closet, which was so small, that he was forced to remain the whole time in a most inconvenient ———.

The other nations, which had hitherto stood well-affected towards him, now began to assume a threatening ———, and he soon found himself hemmed in on every side by formidable enemies.

It is certain that no poet has given more graceful and attractive images of beauty than Milton in his various portraits of Eve, each in a new situation and ———.

Praise—Applause.

Praise is the general, and applause the specific term for the expression of our approbation. There is less reflection in applause than in praise. We applaud from impulse. There is reason in our praise. A man is praised for his general conduct, his steadiness, sobriety, &c. He is applauded for some particular action. Applause is spontaneous, and called forth by circumstances. We applaud one who saves a fellow-creature from drowning. We praise a boy for his attention to study, and obedience to his superiors.

[*Ant.* I come to bury Cæsar, not to praise him.
Julius Cæsar, iii. 2.

Arch. O thou fond many! with what loud applause
Didst thou beat heaven with blessing Bolingbroke.
2 *Henry IV.*, i. 3.

Millions of spiritual creatures walk the earth
Unseen, both when we wake, and when we sleep:
All these with ceaseless praise his works behold
Both day and night. *P. L.*, iv. 679

——— as the sound of waters deep,
Hoarse murmur echoed to his words applause
Through the infinite host. *Id.*, v. 873.

On him and on his high endeavour
The light of praise shall shine forever!
WORDSWORTH. '*The White Doe of Rylstone*

For him, who to divinity aspired
Not on the breath of popular applause,
But through dependence on the sacred laws,
'*Dion.*']

Exercise.

It is far better to secure for ourselves the ——— of the wise and judicious than the ——— of the multitude.

This statement was received by the people with shouts of ———, and preparations were immediately made for the proper reception of this distinguished visiter.

The ——— of so eminent a scholar was for him a higher gratification than all the success he had met with.

The resolution met with general ———.

He was much ——— not only for his diligence and regularity, but also for his general good conduct.

"I would ——— thee to the very echo,
That should ——— again."

How many are greedy of public ———, and how little do they taste it when they have it!

The justice and moderation he discovered in the administration of the affairs of the island gained him the ——— and esteem of the inhabitants during the whole time he resided among them as governor.

Robber—Thief.

A *robber* attacks us openly and takes away our property by main force. A *thief* enters our house in the dark, conceals himself, and takes away our property by stealth. The robber plunders; the thief steals. The robber employs violence; the thief, guile for the same purpose. The robber braves the laws; the thief fears detection. An active police may prevent the frequent occurrence of robbery; but thieves are more difficult to catch than robbers: nothing but an improved tone of morality will entirely banish thieving.

[*K. Rich.* —— when the searching eye of heaven is hid
Behind the globe, and lights the lower world,
Then thieves and robbers range abroad unseen.
Rich. II., iii. 2.

Duke. The robbed, that smiles, steals something from the thief.
Othello, i. 3.

K. Hen —— that have before gored the gentle bosom of peace with pillage and robbery
Henry V., iv. 1

Some roving robber calling to his fellows.
Comus, 485.

—— as a thief, bent to unhoard the cash
Of some rich burgher, whose substantial doors
Cross-barred and bolted fast, fear no assault,
In at the window climbs, or o'er the tiles:
So clomb this first grand thief into God's fold.
P. L., iv. 188

He met a traveller, robbed him, shed his blood;
And when the miserable work was done,
He fled, a vagrant since, the murderer's fate to shun.
WORDSWORTH. '*Guilt and Sorrow*

——— a heap of dry leaves,
That he's left, for a bed, to beggars or thieves.
Id. p. 55.]

Exercise.

During the night, when all were asleep, some ——— had entered the house, and stolen plate and jewels to a large amount.

Travellers in the mountains of Italy are frequently stopped by ——, and stripped of all their property.

The country, which is very thinly inhabited, is infested with bands of —— who attack travellers in the open day, and escape, almost without fear of detection, to the mountain fastnesses with which the whole of this region abounds.

"Take heed, have open eye, for —— do foot by night."

What was his surprise, on his return, to find that his desk and trunks had been broken open by —— in his absence, and plundered of every thing valuable they contained!

The whole of the property was taken from the warehouse between twelve and one o'clock, while the workmen were gone to dinner; and though every attempt has been made to discover the ——, we have been as yet unsuccessful.

Safety—Security.

Those who are out of danger are in *safety*: those who are beyond the reach of danger are in *security*. Safety regards the present moment with respect to the past; security regards the future as well as the present. Security implies the absence of all apprehension; safety merely imports the absence of danger. Those who are in a vessel during a storm at sea are not in safety during the storm, nor are they in security from the dangers of the sea till they have reached the shore. Money is placed in fire-proof boxes for security.

[*Hot* —— out of this nettle, danger, we pluck this flower safety.
1 *Hen. IV.*, ii. 3.

Eno. Give up yourself to chance and hazard,
From firm security. *Antony and Cleopatra*, iii. 7

—— with like safety guided down,
Return me to my native element. *P. L.*, vii. 15.

—— in a place
Less warranted than this, or less secure,
I cannot be, that I should fear to change it.
Comus, 327

Half of a vessel, half—no more; the rest
Had vanished, swallowed up with all that there
Had for the common safety striven in vain,
Or thither thronged for refuge.
WORDSWORTH. '*Grace Darling*

—— O human life
That never art secure from dolorous change!
'*Epitaphs.*']

Exercise.

"It cannot be ——— for any man to walk upon a precipice and to be always on the very border of destruction."

"No man can rationally account himself ——— unless he could command all the chances of the world."

"For, as Rome itself is built on an exhausted volcano, so in similar ——— the inhabitants of the south tenanted the green and vine-clad places around a volcano whose fires they believed at rest for ever."

"I am now, my dear sister ———ly arrived at Vienna, and, I thank God, have not at all suffered in my health, nor, what is dearer to me, in that of my child, by all our fatigues."

"Whether any of the reasonings are inconsistent, I ———ly leave to the judgment of the reader."

"As long as he was rich, none pried into his conduct; he pursued the dark tenor of his way undisturbed and ———."

"Who is there that hath the leisure and means to collect all the proofs concerning most of the opinions he has, so as ———ly to conclude that he hath a clear and full view?"

Shape—Form.

The *form* of a thing is what results from the arrangement of the parts of its substance, and includes not only its exterior surface, but also its internal solidity. *Shape* refers to the entire surface of the form; not merely its outline, but its whole superficies. The form includes length, breadth, and thickness. The shape is merely what we can see of the outside. A marble has the form of a sphere, *i. e.* the qualities of rotundity and solidity. It has the shape of a sphere, because it presents a spherical surface to the eye or touch.

[*Lion.* In every lineament, branch, shape and form.
Much Ado About Nothing, v. 1

Mer. In shape no bigger than an agate-stone
On the fore-finger of an alderman. *Romeo and Juliet*, i. 4.

Mac. I see thee yet, in form as palpable
As this, which now I draw. *Macbeth*, ii. 1.

——— he, above the rest,
In shape and gesture proudly eminent,
Stood like a tower; his form had yet not lost
All her original brightness, nor appeared
Less than archangel ruined,—— *P. L.*, i. 590

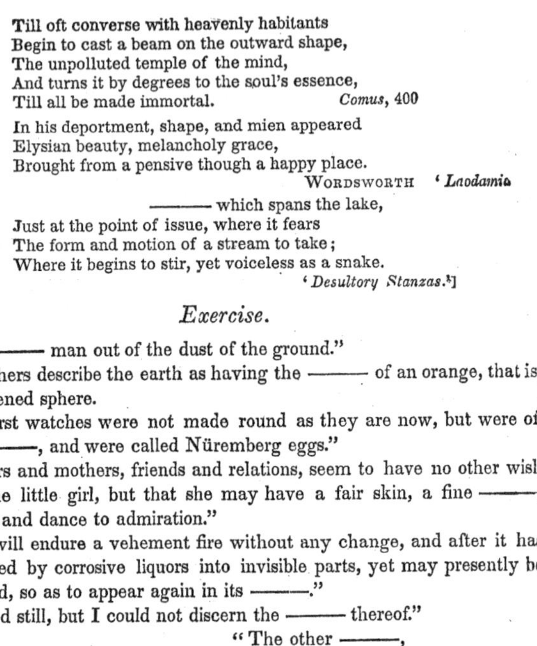

Till oft converse with heavenly habitants
Begin to cast a beam on the outward shape,
The unpolluted temple of the mind,
And turns it by degrees to the soul's essence,
Till all be made immortal. *Comus*, 400

In his deportment, shape, and mien appeared
Elysian beauty, melancholy grace,
Brought from a pensive though a happy place.
WORDSWORTH '*Laodamia*

——— which spans the lake,
Just at the point of issue, where it fears
The form and motion of a stream to take;
Where it begins to stir, yet voiceless as a snake.
'*Desultory Stanzas*.']

Exercise.

"God ——— man out of the dust of the ground."

Philosophers describe the earth as having the ——— of an orange, that is, like a flattened sphere.

"The first watches were not made round as they are now, but were of an oval ———, and were called Nüremberg eggs."

"Fathers and mothers, friends and relations, seem to have no other wish towards the little girl, but that she may have a fair skin, a fine ———, dress well, and dance to admiration."

"Gold will endure a vehement fire without any change, and after it has been divided by corrosive liquors into invisible parts, yet may presently be precipitated, so as to appear again in its ———."

"It stood still, but I could not discern the ——— thereof."

"The other ———,
If ——— it could be called which ——— had none,
Distinguishable in member, joint, or limb."

"The ——— of the locusts were like unto horses prepared for battle."

Talent—Genius.

Genius is a strong bent of the mind to some occupation in which the faculty of imagination is chiefly employed. Genius originates ideas, creates new forms, new expressions. *Talent* is employed in reducing to practice the ideas of others. Talent imitates faithfully, copies correctly, evolves diligently; but originates nothing. Great artists are geniuses. Great historians are men of talent. We speak of a genius for poetry, painting, music, &c.; and of a talent for mathematics, history, diplomacy. In genius, the imagination is exercised, in talent, the memory.

[*Clown.* Well, God give them wisdom that have it; and those that are fools, let them use their talents. *Twelfth Night*, i. 5.

—— that one talent which is death to hide,
Lodged with me useless, though my soul more bent
To serve therewith my Maker, and present
My true account, lest He, returning, chide.
MILTON. *Sonnets.*

——— ye proud
Heart-swoln, while in your pride ye contemplate
Your talents, power, or wisdom, deem him not
A burthen of the earth!
WORDSWORTH. '*The Old Cumberland Beggar*

——— by science led,
His genius mounted to the plains of heaven.
The Excursion, vi.]

Exercise.

His ——— unfitted him for the every-day routine of ordinary life, and he longed for an opportunity to distinguish himself against the enemies of his country.

The unparalleled cruelty and intolerable severity of this general towards his soldiers made him generally detested; but he was a man of such ——— that the state could not dispense with his services, and he was appointed to take the command of the expedition.

In the greatest emergencies the greatest ——— are called forth.

Napoleon Bonaparte was one of the greatest military ——— that ever lived; and he was born at a time in which the most favourable opportunities for the display of his ——— were afforded him.

It is a melancholy reflection, that the most brilliant ——— are oftener employed in vicious pursuits than in furthering the cause of truth and virtue.

The ——— of Homer shines like the morning star on the horizon of antiquity.

Temper—Humour.

Temper is fixed; *humour* is temporary. The former belongs to the permanent character of the individual, and exercises an influence, for good or for evil, over all the actions of his life; the latter expresses a state of mind produced by particular circumstances, and extends over a comparatively short space of time. The best-tempered men are occasionally in an ill-humour, and those of the worst temper have their moments of good-humour. The good-tempered are, of course, much more frequently in a good-humour than those of a contrary disposition. Temper seems to be the principle: humour, its result. Cheerfulness has been defined—"An habitual good-humour."

[*Mort.* He holds your temper in a high respect
And curbs himself even of his natural scope,
When you do cross his humour. 1 *Henry IV.*, iii. 1.

K. Hen. As humourous as winter, and as sudden
As flaws congealed in the spring of day.
His temper, therefore, must be well observed.
2 *Henry IV.*, iv. 4

——— Remember with what mild
And gracious temper he hath heard——
P. L., x. 1046.

——— suggestions which proceed
From anguish of the mind and humours black
That mingle with thy fancy. *S. A.*, 600.

Some silent laws our hearts will make,
Which they shall long obey:
We for the year to come may take
Our temper from to-day. WORDSWORTH, p. 362.

——— his good humour soon
Became a weight in which no pleasure was:
And poverty brought on a petted mood
And a sore temper. *The Excursion*, i

Type of a sunny human breast
Is your transparent cell;
Where Fear is but a transient guest,
No sullen Humours dwell.
'*Gold and Silver Fishes in a Vase.*']

Exercise.

My friend is a man of such excellent ———, that I do not think I ever saw him in an ill ———.

The moment he entered the room, I saw that something had vexed him, for he was in such an ill ———, that he seemed resolved to be pleased with nothing I could say or do.

Since my cousin's return, I find her very much altered; she has no longer the same even ——— for which she was so remarkable, but frequently falls into fits of ——— which make her far from an agreeable companion.

He was a man of very grave and reserved ———, but when in the ———, he could unbend, and be as communicative and agreeable as others.

Temple—Church.

The gods of the ancients were worshipped in *temples*. The God of Christians is worshipped in *churches*. Church signifies the house of the Lord; temple is derived from *templum*, the Latin word for a building consecrated to the worship of a divinity. The word temple, however, is used by modern writers to signify the place where God chooses to dwell; in contradistinction from church, as conveying the idea of the place in which he is worshipped. This may be illustrated in the expressions, "the temple of the Lord;" and "the Christian church." Since, however, God is omnipresent, it is evident that every church must be a temple, though every temple is not a church. The leading idea in temple is *place*, *i. e.* holy place. The prominent idea in church is *worship*, *i. e.* place of worship.

The word church is frequently employed in the sense of "an assembly of the faithful," or to specify a sect of Christians; as, "the church of Christ," "the church of England," the "Catholic church," &c. &c. The word temple is never so used.

[*Cor.* The noble sister of Publicola,
The moon of Rome; chaste as the icicle
That's curded by the frost from purest snow,
And hangs on Dian's temple. *Coriolanus*, v. 3.

Duke. ——— we have seen better days;
And have with holy bell been knolled to church;
As You Like It, ii. 7

The great Emathian conqueror bid spare
The house of Pindarus, when temple and tower
Went to the ground;— MILTON. '*Sonnets.*'

So since into his Church lewd hirelings climb.
P. L., iv. 193.

——— a SPIRIT hung,
Beautiful region! o'er thy towns and farms,
Statues and temples, and memorial tombs;
'*The Excursion*,' iv

——— And this gracious Church,
That wears a look so full of peace and hope
And love, benignant mother of the vale,
How fair amid her brood of cottages!
Id., vi.]

Exercise.

In the earliest times, there appear to have been very few ——— at Rome, and in many spots the worship of a certain divinity had existed from time immemorial, though we hear of no building of a temple to the same divinity till a comparatively late period.

It is said that Ethelbert, on his conversion, gave up his own palace to the missionaries, and the ——— which they built adjoining it occupied the site of the present cathedral of Canterbury.

The character of the early Greek ——— was dark and mysterious, for they had no windows, and they received the light only through the door, which was very large, or from lamps burning in them.

Henry the Second, the most powerful monarch of his time, having ended his contest with the ——, now looked forward to the enjoyment of peace and tranquillity

---

Vestige—Trace.

A *vestige* is properly the mark made by a footstep; a *trace* s a succession of marks. They both refer to indistinct appearances of bygone things or actions. A vestige is an isolated mark. A trace consists of a number of succeeding marks, partly obliterated, but still indistinctly connected. Vestiges are scattered; traces are followed. Vestiges are points by which we may trace. If a plough should be dug up on an uninhabited island, it might be considered as a vestige of its former cultivation. If, in the same island, the remains of hedges, old gates, tools, ruins of farm-houses, &c., were discovered, they might be looked upon as traces of agriculture.

[*Pisa.* He hath been searched among the dead and living,
But no trace of him. *Cymbeline*, v. 5.

Ere Julius landed on her white-cliffed shore,
They sank, delivered o'er
To fatal dissolution; and I ween,
No vestige then was left that such had ever been
WORDSWORTH. '*Artegal and Elidure*

—— Of that day's shame
Or glory, not a vestige seems to endure,
Save in this Rill that took from blood the name
Which yet it bears, sweet Stream! as crystal pure
So may all trace and sign of deeds aloof
From the true guidance of humanity,
Thro' Time and Nature's influence, purify
Their spirit;—— '*Near the Lake of Thrasymene.*']

Exercise.

Many —— of the Roman dominion are still to be found in all the southern, and some of the northern countries of Europe.

In many parts of England, —— of Roman roads, encampments, and fortifications have been discovered, which prove the state of perfection in arts, as well as arms, which the ancient rulers of the world had attained.

The patient, though he had suffered severely from his long illness, was now perfectly recovered; and neither his countenance nor frame bore the slightest ——— of the effects of the disease under which he had so long laboured.

The walls of ancient Jerusalem were destroyed to their very foundations by the soldiers of Titus; so that the prophecy was literally fulfilled, that not a ——— of her former greatness should remain.

Vice—Sin.

Sin is an offence against the commands of God. *Vice* is an offence against morality. Whatever is contrary to the Divine law is a sin; whatever is contrary to the precepts of morality is a vice. Sin has reference to the relation between God and man; vice refers to the relation between man and man. The harm we do ourselves by sin is, that we thereby incur the anger of our Maker. The harm we do ourselves by vice is, that we thereby render ourselves less capable of fulfilling our duties to our fellow-creatures. The same act may be both sinful and vicious; sinful, because it is contrary to the law of God; vicious, because it is injurious to society.

[*Edg.* The gods are just, and of our pleasant vices
Make instruments to scourge us.
King Lear, v. 3

Cleo. ——— Then is it sin,
To rush into the secret house of death,
Ere death dare come to us. *Antony and Cleopatra*, iv. 13

K. Hen. ——— is in your conscience washed
As pure as sin with baptism. *Henry V.*, i. 2.

——— for his thoughts were low;
To vice industrious, but to nobler deeds
Timorous and slothful. *P. L.*, ii. 116.

——— and the rebel king
Doubled that sin in Bethel and in Dan,
Likening their Maker to the grazed ox.
Id., i. 485.

Of Man degraded in his Maker's sight
By the deformities of brutish vice. '*The Excursion*,' vi.

That least of all can aught—that ever owned
The heaven-regarding eye and front sublime
Which man is born to—sink, howe'er depressed,
So low as to be scorned without a sin.
'*The Old Cumberland Beggar*']

Exercise.

"If a man makes his ——— public, though they be such as seem principally to affect himself, (as drunkenness, or the like,) they then become, by the bad example they set, of pernicious effect to society."

"Every single gross act of ——— is much the same thing to the conscience that a great blow or fall is to the head; it stuns and bereaves it of all use of its senses for a time."

"Proud views and vain desires in our worldly employments are as truly ——— and corruptions as hypocrisy in prayer, or vanity in alms."

"Virtue and ——— chiefly imply the relation of our actions to men in this world; ——— and holiness rather imply their relation to God and the other world."

"I cannot blame him for inveighing so sharply against the ——— of the clergy in his age."

"It is a great ——— to swear unto a ———,
But greater ——— to keep a sinful oath"

Way—Road.

According to Horne Tooke, *road* is the way which any one has rode (?) over. *Way* is from the Saxon *wegan*, to move; it is the line along which you move. Way is the general term, and road is the species of way. A pathway—a high road. Instead of keeping the high road to a town, you may frequently go a shorter way across the fields. In like manner, abstractly, the high road to preferment is the way commonly taken; the way to preferment is the one which any individual may choose to adopt.

[*Wol.* Say, Wolsey,—that once trod the ways of glory,
And sounded all the depths and shoals of honour,—
Found thee a way, out of his wreck, to rise in;
A sure and safe one, though thy master missed it.
Henry VIII., iii. 2.

Orl. ——— enforce
A thievish living on the common road.
As You Like It, ii. 3

Bru. You know the very road into his kindness,
And cannot lose your way. *Coriolanus*, v. 1

——— led
To God's eternal house direct the way,
A broad and ample road, whose dust is gold.
P. L., vii, 570-7

She dwelt among the untrodden ways
  Beside the springs of Dove,
A Maid whom there were none to praise
  And very few to love. WORDSWORTH. p. 77
Our walk was far among the ancient trees:
There was no road, nor any woodman's path. p. 110.]

Exercise.

The nearest ——— to reach the village is along the high ———.

" The best and the surest ——— to accomplish your wish will be to engage a master, and read with him three or four hours a day."

" To be indifferent whether we embrace falsehood or truth is the great ——— to error."

" I am amazed, and lose my ———
Among the thorns and dangers of this world."

The real ——— to become rich is to be diligent and industrious.

The high ——— to good fortune is through the prince's favour.

" Attending long in vain, I took the ———
Which through a path but scarcely printed lay."

" An old man who was travelling along the ———, groaning under a huge burden, found himself so weary that he called upon death to deliver him."

The traveller had missed his ———, and lost himself in the mazes of an intricate wood.

Word—Term.

A word is something uttered or written which stands for something perceived. Every conventional combination of letters representing an idea is a word. We cannot stretch the meaning of words beyond certain bounds ; *i. e.* they cannot be made to have more or less than a certain meaning, and in this view they are terms. Nouns, verbs, and adjectives, are limited to a certain meaning, and in this sense they are terms. Prepositions and conjunctions, whose meaning is not likely to become disturbed, are not considered as terms. The object of defining is to lay down the precise meaning of *terms*, and show the exact limits to which they extend. The word term is properly applied in defining. It is only to terms that we can apply a definition.

[*Macd.* I have no words,
My voice is in my sword ; thou bloodier villain
Than terms can give thee out ! *Macbeth*, v. 7

The oracles are dumb,
No voice or hideous hum
Runs through the arched roof in words deceiving.
MILTON. '*Ode on the Nativity*

Though in mysterious terms, judged as then best.
P. L., x. 173.

——— Earth is sick
And Heaven is weary, of the hollow words
Which States and Kingdoms utter when they talk
Of truth and justice. *The Excursion*, v.]

Exercise.

"In painting, the greatest beauties cannot always be expressed for want of ———."

"The use of the ——— minister is brought down to the literal signification of it, a servant; for now, to serve and to minister, servile and ministerial, are ——— equivalent."

Purity of style depends on the choice of———

"Had the Roman language continued in common use, it would have been necessary, from the many ——— of art required in trade and in war, to have made great additions to it."

"Among men who confound their ideas with ———, there must be endless disputes, wrangling, and jargon."

"Those parts of nature into which the chaos was divided, they signified by dark and obscure names, which we have expressed in their plain and proper ———."

It is an affectation of style to introduce many technical ——— into our composition.

To augur—to forebode.

Augur, from the Latin *augurium*, refers to the superstition of the ancient Romans, by which they pretended to predict future events. Forebode, from the Saxon *forebodian*, signifies to tell beforehand.

In distinguishing between the modern use of these words, it is to be observed that there is more of chance in augury, and more of reasoning in foreboding. Moreover, an augury may be for good or for evil, whereas foreboding is scarcely ever used in a good sense. It may be almost said that to augur evil is to forebode. Again, an augury is founded upon outward appearances; a foreboding is founded upon induction.

[*Ham.* Not a whit, we defy augury; there is a special providence in the fall of a sparrow. *Hamlet*, v. 2.

Ther. I would croak like a raven; I would bode, I would bode.
Troilus and Cressida, v. 2

——— what they can do, as signs
Betokening, or ill-boding, I contemn
As false portents, not sent from God, but thee.
P. R., iv. 490.

And O, ye Fountains, Meadows, Hills, and Groves,
Forebode not any severing of our loves!
WORDSWORTH. '*Ode on Intimations, &c*]

Exercise.

He never could take a bright view of any question, but whatever appearance it might present, he had always the unhappy knack of ——— some evil consequence from it.

The sun rose clear and bright; the morning air was pure and deliciously fresh; pearly drops of crystal dew stood glittering on leaves of the brightest green, and all nature seemed to ——— a happy result to the ceremony of this eventful day.

"This looks not well!" exclaimed the doctor, raising his head suddenly from the book which he had been examining with apparently the most intense eagerness for the last five minutes—"This looks not well! these characters ——— no success, either to the undertaking or to any engaged in it. I withdraw my name from among its supporters."

I saw by the smile on his countenance that he had succeeded in his wishes; and he soon after informed me that every thing ——— favourably, and that he had every hope of obtaining the situation.

To bestow—to confer.

To *bestow* signifies to place, or lay out; to *confer*, to bear towards or upon. The idea of giving is common to both these verbs. They differ in this—that the former is said of things given between persons in private life; the latter, of things given from persons in authority to those below them in rank. The king confers the honour of knighthood. Princes confer privileges. One friend bestows favours on another. We bestow charity on the poor. It is also to be observed, that these verbs are scarcely ever used with any other than abstract nouns. Honours, dignities, privileges, &c., are conferred Praise, charity, kindness, pains, &c., are bestowed.

[*Grif.* ——— though he were unsatisfied in getting,
(Which was a sin,) yet in bestowing, madam,
He was most princely. *Henry VIII.*, iv 2

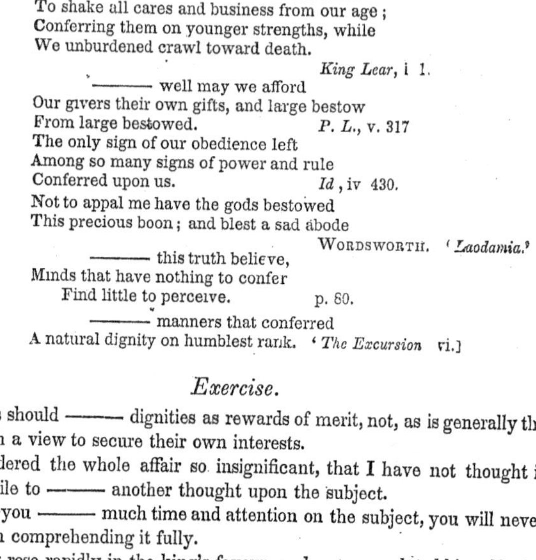

Lear. ——— 'tis our fast intent
To shake all cares and business from our age;
Conferring them on younger strengths, while
We unburdened crawl toward death.
King Lear, i 1.

——— well may we afford
Our givers their own gifts, and large bestow
From large bestowed. *P. L.*, v. 317

The only sign of our obedience left
Among so many signs of power and rule
Conferred upon us. *Id*, iv 430.

Not to appal me have the gods bestowed
This precious boon; and blest a sad abode
WORDSWORTH. '*Laodamia.*'

——— this truth believe,
Minds that have nothing to confer
Find little to perceive. p. 80.

——— manners that conferred
A natural dignity on humblest rank. '*The Excursion* vi.]

Exercise.

Princes should ——— dignities as rewards of merit, not, as is generally the case, with a view to secure their own interests.

I considered the whole affair so insignificant, that I have not thought it worth while to ——— another thought upon the subject.

Unless you ——— much time and attention on the subject, you will never succeed in comprehending it fully.

Wolsey rose rapidly in the king's favour, and accommodated himself with such facility to all Henry's caprices, that the highest honours were ——— upon him, and all the affairs of state were soon intrusted to his management.

Great care was ——— upon his education.

It sometimes happens that even enemies and envious persons ——— the sincerest marks of esteem when they least design it.

"On him ——— the poet's sacred name,
Whose lofty voice declares the heavenly frame."

To bring—to fetch.

To *bring* is to convey to; it is a simple act; to *fetch* is a compound act; it means to go and bring. When two persons are in the same room, and one asks the other to *bring* him something, we must suppose the person addressed to be near the object required. In order to fetch, we must go to some distance for the object. Potatoes are brought to market. Children are fetched from school; *i. e.* when some one *goes* to *bring* them.

[*Cleo.* ——— Go fetch
My best attires; —————
————— Bring our crown and all.
Ant. and Cleop., v. 2

——— Hesperus, whose office is to bring
Twilight upon the earth, *P. L.*, ix. 49

For if such holy song
Enwrap our fancy long,
Time will run back, and fetch the age of gold
'Ode on the Nativity.'

——— a child, more than all other gifts
That earth can offer to declining man,
Brings hope with it, and forward-looking thoughts.
WORDSWORTH. *'Michae.*

——— many a shell
Tossed ashore by restless waves,
Or in the diver's grasp fetched up from caves
Where sea-nymphs might be proud to dwell. p. 385.]

Exercise.

The parliament, however, maintained their power with continued success, and the king was at length ——— to his trial.

On the 20th of next December, just before the Christmas holidays, my father has promised that he will take me with him when he goes to ——— my brothers from school.

If you will call upon me to-morrow at three o'clock, I shall be at home and glad to see you; but do not forget to ——— your books, as without them, you will not be able to take a lesson.

I have desired the servant to ——— your brother home from his uncle's at nine o'clock this evening.

On the evening of the birthday, the prizes were all ——— into the drawing-room, and laid on a large table; the children being then placed on forms arranged across the other end of the room, each, in his turn, was told to ——— his prize from the table and take it to his seat.

This admonition at last produced the desired effect, and ——— him to a proper sense of his guilt.

What appeared to me wonderful was, that none of the ants came home without ———ing something.

I have said before, that those ants which I did so particularly consider, ——— their corn out of a garret

To bury—to inter.

To *bury* is to conceal in the earth; to *inter* is to put into the earth with ceremony. We bury in order to cover up; we inter from a religious motive. Interring is a species of burying. A miser may bury his money in a hole in his garden, or may bury his face in his handkerchief. Those who are buried with religious ceremonies are interred. We can scarcely say correctly that a man is interred in a tomb unless the tomb be below the surface of the earth. Dogs are never interred, though they are frequently buried. To bury is often used in an abstract sense: as to bury animosity, to bury hope, &c. To inter is never used abstractly.

[*Pros.* ——— I'll break my staff—
Bury it certain fathoms in the earth.
Tempest, v. 1.

Kath. ——— although unqueened, yet like
A queen, and daughter to a king, inter me.
Henry VIII., iv. 2

Myself my sepulchre, a moving grave;
Buried, yet not exempt
By privilege of death and burial
From worst of other evils, pains and wrongs.
S. A., 103.

This rich marble doth inter
The honoured wife of Winchester, MILTON '*Epitaph, &c*'

—Call Archimedes from his buried tomb
Upon the grave of vanished Syracuse,
And feelingly the Sage shall make report
How insecure, how baseless in itself,
Is the Philosophy whose sway depends
On mere material instruments; '*The Excursion*,' viii

The corse interred, not one hour he remained
Beneath their roof. —— '*Guilt and Sorrow*.']

Exercise.

The corpse of Henry V. was ——— near the shrine of Edward the Confessor; and the tomb was long visited by the people with sentiments of veneration and regret.

William I. caused the body of Harold to be ——— on the sea-shore, saying: "He guarded the coast when living; let him still guard it now that he is dead."

"The evil that men do lives after them,
The good is oft ——— with their bones."

It was formerly the custom in England to ——— the dead at some distance from any town or city.

The ashes, in an old record of the convent, are said to have been ——— between the very wall and the altar where they were taken up.

They determined henceforward to live on good terms with each other, and to ——— all past animosities in oblivion.

The house suddenly fell in, and six of the workmen were ——— in the ruins.

To clothe—to dress.

To *clothe* is to cover the body ; to *dress* is to cover it in a certain manner. Dressing is a mode of clothing. We clothe to protect our bodies from the inclemency of the weather ; we dress in conformity with the custom of the country. The dress is all the clothes taken together. Savages are clothed in skins. In Europe, men are generally dressed in coats and trousers. The clothing, again, is the material. The dress is the manner in which it is made up.

[*Ham.* That no revenue hast, but thy good spirits
To feed and clothe thee. *Hamlet*, iii. 2.

Hot. Came there a certain lord, neat, trimly dressed
Fresh as a bridegroom ;—— 1 *Henry IV.*, i. 3

—— and his hands
Clothed us, unworthy, pitying while he judged.
P. L., x. 1059

To dress, and troll the tongue, and roll the eye.
Id., xi. 620

—— and in the stormy day
Her tattered clothes were ruffled by the wind
Even at the side of her own fire. '*The Excursion*,' i.

Delivered and Deliverer move
In bridal garments drest '*The Russian Fugitive*.']

Exercise.

Being exposed to the rigour of a severe winter, without sufficient —— to protect him from the inclemency of the season, his health became so materially injured, that he never again recovered his strength, and died in the ensuing autumn.

The North-American Indians are generally —— in buffalo skins, but on grand occasions they decorate their bodies with a profusion of feathers and shells.

The stranger presented a striking, and not unattractive appearance ; he was —— in a Spanish doublet, with slashed sleeves, a dark-brown mantle, carelessly thrown over one shoulder, with a broad-brimmed hat drawn over his brow, and surmounted with a long plume.

"The —— of savage nations is everywhere pretty much the same, being calculated rather to inspire terror than to excite love or respect."

"Some writers say that the girdle worn by the ancient Jewish priests was thirty-two ells long ; according to others, it went twice round the waist. The latter account seems the more probable, because in a warm climate, such a —— would have been highly inconvenient."

To calculate—to reckon.

To *calculate* is the general science by which we arrive at a certain result. To *reckon* refers to the details of calculation in attaining a sum total or amount. Calculation is any operation whatever—not confined to arithmetic or geometry—by which a certain knowledge is arrived at. The astronomer calculates; the statesman calculates. The accountant reckons; the merchant reckons his losses or gains.

[*Cas.* Why old men, fools and children calculate;
Julius Cæsar, i. 3.
Ant. There's beggary in the love that can be reckoned
Ant. and Cleop., i. 1

Hereafter when they come to model Heaven
And calculate the stars. —— *P. L.*, viii. 80

—— whether heaven move or earth
Imports not, if thou reckon right ——
Id., viii. 71

—— to foretell
By calculations sage, the ebb and flow
Of tides, and when the moon will be eclipsed.
'*The Excursion*,' vi.]

Exercise.

Astronomers are able to —— eclipses with astonishing precision.

—— from the foundation of Rome to the birth of Christ, there are seven hundred and fifty-three years.

In chronology, there are two modes of ——; one, from the creation so many years before the birth of Christ, and the other, so many years from the birth of Christ up to the present time.

The epoch of the era of the Hegira is, according to the common ——, Friday, the 16th of July, A. D. 622, the day of the flight of Mahomet from Mecca to Medina.

The Gregorian calendar was adopted in the Low Countries on the 15th [25th] of December, 1582: Francis, duke of Alençon, having on the 10th of that month ordered that the day next following the 14th of December should be —— as the 25th instead of the 15th.

In England, in the seventh, and so late as the thirteenth century, the year was —— from Christmas-day.

The greater the number of elements that enter into a ——, and the greater the discord among those elements, the more difficult must it be to arrive at any thing like a certain result.

—— from last Monday, it will be eight weeks before we see him again

To do—to make.

To *do* is the generic term to express action; to *make*, the specific. Making is a mode of doing. We cannot make without doing, though we may *do* without making. To do is more frequently used with abstract things; to make, with concrete We do right or wrong; we do our duty. Children make a noise; a carpenter makes a table. Again, to do is a simple act; to make is compound, as it implies thought and contrivance, and contains the ideas of formation and production.

N. B. Both these verbs are used idiomatically in a great variety of senses. These idioms do not, however, interfere with the above explanation, which is of their general acceptation

[*Ari.* What shall I do? say what? what shall I do?
Pros. Go make thyself like to a nymph of the sea.
Tempest, i. 2.

Macb. I dare do all that may become a man;
Who dares do more, is none. *Macbeth,* i. 7

Ham. That makes calamity of so long life,
* * * * *
When he himself might his quietus make,
* * * * *
And makes us rather bear those ills we have,
* * * * *
Thus conscience does make cowards of us all.
Hamlet, iii 1.

Virtue could see to do what Virtue would
By her own radiant light, though sun and moon
Were in the flat sea sunk *Comus,* 373.

The mind is its own place, and in itself
Can make a heaven of hell, a hell of heaven.
P. L., i. 255

—— gladsome spirits and benignant looks
That for a face not beautiful did more,
Than beauty for the fairest face can do.
'*The Excursion,*' vi.

——— to its gentle touch how sensitive
Is the light ash! that pendent from the brow
Of yon dim cave, in seeming silence makes
A soft eye-music of slow waving boughs,
Powerful almost as vocal harmony
To stay the wanderer's steps and soothe his thoughts.
WORDSWORTH, p. 142]

Exercise

What are you ——— ? I am ——— a silk purse for my brother
He who ——— every thing in a hurry, can ——— nothing well.

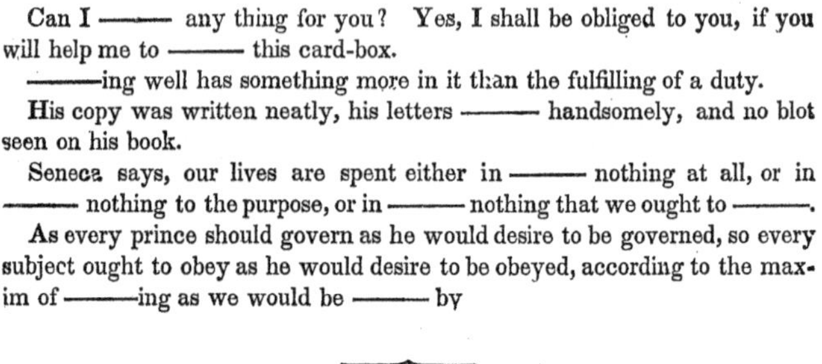

Can I ——— any thing for you? Yes, I shall be obliged to you, if you will help me to ——— this card-box.

———ing well has something more in it than the fulfilling of a duty.

His copy was written neatly, his letters ——— handsomely, and no blot seen on his book.

Seneca says, our lives are spent either in ——— nothing at all, or in ——— nothing to the purpose, or in ——— nothing that we ought to ———.

As every prince should govern as he would desire to be governed, so every subject ought to obey as he would desire to be obeyed, according to the maxim of ———ing as we would be ——— by

To divide—to separate.

To *divide* is to cut into parts; to *separate* is to place those parts at a distance from each other. Objects may be divided, and yet near; to be separated, they must be removed from each other. A hermit is separated from the rest of the world. Society is divided into classes. The highest are separated from the lowest classes. A man may divide his time into hours of study and hours of recreation. Divisions are natural, separations more violent. The year is divided into months, weeks, and days. Two vessels become separated in a storm. There cannot be a separation without a division, though there may be a division without a separation.

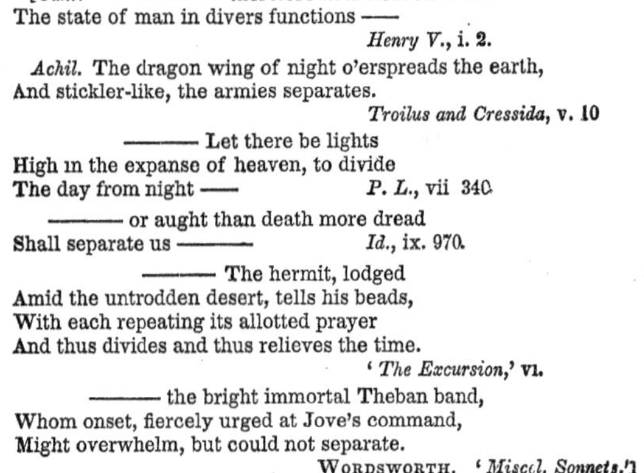

[*Cant.* ——— therefore doth heaven divide
The state of man in divers functions ——
Henry V., i. 2.

Achil. The dragon wing of night o'erspreads the earth,
And stickler-like, the armies separates.
Troilus and Cressida, v. 10

——— Let there be lights
High in the expanse of heaven, to divide
The day from night —— *P. L.*, vii 340

——— or aught than death more dread
Shall separate us ——— *Id.*, ix. 970.

——— The hermit, lodged
Amid the untrodden desert, tells his beads,
With each repeating its allotted prayer
And thus divides and thus relieves the time.
'*The Excursion*,' vi.

——— the bright immortal Theban band,
Whom onset, fiercely urged at Jove's command,
Might overwhelm, but could not separate.
WORDSWORTH. '*Miscel. Sonnets*.']

Exercise.

Alfred the Great ——— his time into three equal parts; allotting the first to prayer and pious exercises, the second to business, and the third to sleep and refreshment.

England is ——— from France by the English Channel.

The river Rhine ——— France from Germany.

Alexander Selkirk, from whose adventures De Foe took his story of "Robinson Crusoe," lived for several years on an uninhabited island in the Pacific Ocean, wholly ——— from human society.

Opinions on the question of the Irish Union were ———, some holding that it should be immediately repealed, and others contending that the repeal would involve a ——— of the two countries.

Ireland is ——— into four provinces. Ulster is ——— from Munster by the provinces of Leinster and Connaught.

If we ——— the life of most men into twenty parts, we shall find at least nineteen of them filled with gaps and chasms, which are neither filled up with pleasure nor business.

To doubt—to question.

We *doubt* within ourselves. The cause of our doubt is our imperfect knowledge. When we *question*, it is with the view that our doubts should be removed. By questioning, we endeavour to remove our ignorance, and thus resolve our doubt. Thus, we doubt the veracity of an historian; *i. e.* the knowledge we possess prevents us from assenting to what he has stated. If we set about resolving our doubts by inquiring into the truth of his writings, we question his veracity. We may doubt without questioning, but we cannot question without doubting.

Isab. —— Alas! I doubt,—
Lucio. Our doubts are traitors,
And make us lose the good we oft might win
By fearing to attempt. *Meas. for Meas.*, i. 5

Kath. ——— It is not to be questioned
That they had gathered a wise council to them.
Henry VIII., ii. 4

Yet doubt not but in valley and in plain
God is, as here. *P. L.*, xi. 349

I question it; for this fair earth I see,
Warmed by the sun, producing every kind,
Id., ix. 720

While stand the people in a ring
Gazing, doubting, questioning,
WORDSWORTH '*White Doe of Rylstone*

——— holy Star,
Holy as princely, who that looks on thee
Touching, as now, in thy humility
The mountain borders of this seat of care,
Can question that thy countenance is bright
Celestial Power, as much with love as light.

'*Itiner. Sonnets.*']

Exercise.

There are many things of which it would be very irrational to ——— but there are also others which we may ——— with great reason.

The Pyrrhonians were a sect of philosophers, who not only ——— of every thing they saw and heard, but even of their own existence.

I have never ——— his veracity, for I have too high an opinion of his regard for every thing honourable and just, to suppose him capable of saying any thing false.

It is a ——— whether, if Hannibal had taken Rome, and destroyed the empire of the Romans, it would have been more advantageous for the human race.

Some truths are intuitive; such as, for example, "the whole is greater than its part;" "two straight lines cannot inclose a space," &c.: it would argue a want of common sense to ——— such truths for a moment; they are self-evident propositions.

He told me that he had never ——— that the prisoner had committed the crime, although he was aware there would be great difficulty in convicting him

To expect—to hope.

We *expect* what we think will probably occur. We *hope* what we strongly desire to happen. We may expect an occurrence which will give us pain, but it is not in human nature to hope for such an occurrence. Thus, I may expect—though I cannot hope—to hear of the death of a dear friend. Expectation regards merely the anticipation of future events without any reference to their being agreeable or otherwise. Hope is always accompanied with pleasure, and is employed upon those events which are likely to be attended with gratification to ourselves.

[*Hel.* Oft expectation fails, and most oft there
Where most it promises; and oft it hits
Where hope is coldest, and despair most sits

All's Well, &c., II 1

Des. These are portents; but yet I hope, I hope,
They do not point at me *Othello*, v. 2

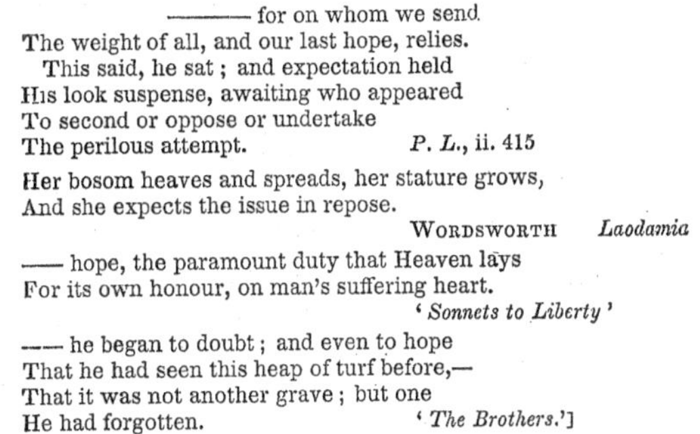

——— for on whom we send
The weight of all, and our last hope, relies.
This said, he sat; and expectation held
His look suspense, awaiting who appeared
To second or oppose or undertake
The perilous attempt. *P. L.*, ii. 415

Her bosom heaves and spreads, her stature grows,
And she expects the issue in repose.
WORDSWORTH *Laodamia*

—— hope, the paramount duty that Heaven lays
For its own honour, on man's suffering heart.
'Sonnets to Liberty'

—— he began to doubt; and even to hope
That he had seen this heap of turf before,—
That it was not another grave; but one
He had forgotten. *'The Brothers.'*]

Exercise.

In the middle of the night, the storm raged with such violence, that none of the passengers ——— the vessel would outlive the gale.

The father had ——— that his son would occupy the same distinguished rank in his profession as himself.

He was doomed, however, to be cruelly disappointed; for he soon after received news that his son was dangerously ill, and that his death was hourly ———.

Every man ——— one day to withdraw from the bustle and tumult of the world, and spend the remainder of his life in quiet ease.

He had ——— that his friends would arrive in the course of the afternoon, and had prepared every thing for their reception.

My cousin sailed for India some months ago: I ——— to hear soon of his safe arrival at Calcutta.

"Regions of sorrow, doleful shades, where peace
And rest can never dwell; ——— never comes
That comes to all."

"All these within the dungeon's depth remain,
Despairing pardon, and ———ing pain."

To finish—to conclude.

To *conclude* is a species of finishing; it means to bring to a close for a time, implying a possibility, if not a probability, that we shall continue the action. To *finish* is to cease from acting, with either no power or no intention of resuming. In reading a book we may conclude when we come to the end of a chapter or paragraph; but we finish when we come to the end of the last page. A sermon which is divided into many sections may be concluded on one Sunday, and finished on the next.

Exercise.

He —— his observations by calling the attention of the meeting to the marked improvement in the condition of the poorer classes in that part of the country.

I have not yet quite —— reading the book you were kind enough to lend me; but I have already begun the —— chapter, and I hope to return you the volume by to-morrow evening.

According to the established rules of the society, the competitors had all —— their pictures, and sent them in for exhibition by the 1st of May.

The prizes were distributed among the successful candidates, after which, the members of the society dined together; and the entertainments of the day were —— by a dance.

Every evening, after his daily labour was ——, he occupied himself in reading; his master kindly supplying him with books from his own library.

This exercise must be —— before five o'clock.

The great work of which Justinian has the credit, although it comprehends the whole system of jurisprudence, was ——, we are told, in three years.

"Destruction hangs on every word we speak,
On every thought, till the ——ing stroke
Determines all, and closes our design."

To give—to grant.

To *give* is the simple term which expresses the act of conveying property from one individual to another. To *grant* implies a previous desire expressed by the receiver of the gift. We give on familiar occasions. We grant on occasions of importance. Permission, requests, favours, prayers, petitions, &c., are granted. Meat, clothes, wine, &c., are given. We grant what we have the power of withholding. To give is not necessarily coupled with such a condition.

[*Gon.* Now would I give a thousand furlongs of sea for an acre of barren ground.
Tempest, i. 1.

Cor. Or if you'd ask, remember this before
The things, I have forsworn to grant, may never
Be held by you denials *Coriolanus*, v. 3.

——— like Alcestis, from the grave,
Whom Jove's great son to her glad husband gave.
MILTON. '*Sonnets.*'

——— therefore as far
From granting he, as I from begging peace.
P. L., iv. 104

When, from the soft couch of her sleeping Lover
Up-starting, Cynthia skimmed the mountain-dew
In keen pursuit—and gave, where'er she flew,
Impetuous motion to the Stars above her.
WORDSWORTH. *Itin. Sonnets*'

Father of all! though wilful Manhood read
His punishment in soul-distress,
Grant to the morn of life its natural blessedness
p. 262.]

Exercise.

Having the most confident anticipation that his petition would be ———, he incurred many unnecessary expenses; great, then, was his mortification on learning, that, instead of presenting his petition to the king, the minister had ——— the document to his secretary without even reading it through.

Three more days were ——— to the prisoner to collect evidence for his approaching trial.

These desperate men, who had led an abandoned life, had long ceased to be recognized as citizens; and a war ensued in consequence of the republic refusing to ——— their demand to be admitted to the rights of citizenship.

Those who cannot ——— reasons for their ordinary actions have scarcely a right to be treated as rational persons.

We are all required to ——— a portion of our substance towards alleviating the sufferings, and providing for the wants of the poor.

If you will but ——— me this favour, I shall hold myself bound to you through life.

Nature ——— us many children and friends to take them away; but takes none away to ——— them us again.

"He heard, and ——— half his prayer;
The rest the winds dispersed."

To gain—to win.

To gain is a general—to win is a specific term.

These words express different modes of acquiring possession, and are to be distinguished by the circumstances which respectively attend them. We *gain* with intention, we *win* by chance. We may reasonably count upon our gains. Our winnings depend on fortune. We do not gain, but win a prize in the lottery. We do not win, but gain a fortune by continued attention to business. A victory may be both gained and won: gained, as concerns the endeavours of the victors; won, as far as it was a question of chance which fortune decided in their favour. Credit, friends, power, influence, &c., are gained. A race, a wager, a prize, &c., are won.

[*Macb.* ——— Better be with the dead
Whom we, to gain our place, have sent to peace.
Macbeth, iii. 2.

Wol. By that sin fell the angels; how can man then,
The image of his Maker, hope to win by't?
Love thyself last: cherish those hearts, that hate thee;
Corruption wins not more than honesty.
Henry VIII., iii. 2.

Help waste a sullen day, what may be won
From the hard season gaining. MILTON. '*Sonnets*'

A leper once he lost, and gained a king.
P. L., i. 471.

——— winning cheap the high repute
Which he through hazard huge must earn.
Id., ii. 472.

To win some look of love, or gain
Encouragement to sport or play.
WORDSWORTH. '*The White Doe, &c.*

For things far off we toil, while many a good
Not sought because too near, is never gained.
'*Itin. Sonnets.*'

——— the Wolf, whose suckling twins
The unlettered Ploughboy pities when he wins
The casual treasure from the furrowed soil.
'*Miscel. Sonnets.*']

Exercise.

He determined to deposit a portion of his weekly ——— in the savings bank, in order that he might have some provision against sickness or old age.

Those who ——— large sums of money by betting, or in lotteries, seldom apply them to useful purposes.

Though I have looked into several books of reference, I can ——— no satisfactory information on this subject.

My cousin, who is inferior in abilities to many of his school-fellows, was much surprised on being informed, after the examination, that he had ——— the prize.

The horse who ——— the race dropped down immediately after reaching the goal, and expired in a few minutes.

How often do we strive to ——— things which possess no real advantages!

Neither Virgil nor Horace would have ——— so great a reputation in the world, had they not been the friends and admirers of each other.

Where the danger ends, the hero ceases; and when he has ——— an empire, the rest of his story is not worth relating

To have—to possess.

What we *have* does not always belong to us, and therefore we cannot dispose of it according to our will. We have entire power over what we *possess*, and it is peculiarly our own. What we have does not remain long ours, but is continually shifting, as money, which circulates in all classes of society. What we possess is permanently our own, as an estate or a house. We are masters of what we possess, but not always of what we have.

To have is the generic term; to possess is a species of having. He who possesses has, but he who has does not always possess.

[*Cal.* ——— Remember
First to possess his books; for without them
He's but a sot, as I am, nor hath not
One spirit to command. *Tempest*, iii. 2

From whom I have that thus I move and live
And feel that I am happier than I know.
P. L., viii. 281

——— now possess
As lords, a spacious world *Id.*, x. 466

I, too, will have my Kings that take
From me the sign of life and death:
Kingdoms shall shift about, like clouds
Obedient to my breath.
WORDSWORTH. '*Rob Roy's Grave.*'

Great God, who feel'st for my distress,
My thoughts are all that I possess,
O keep them innocent! '*Lament of Mary Queen of Scots.*']

Exercise.

I ——— a small parcel at home belonging to you, which shall be sent to your house early to-morrow morning.

He is in all respects an excellent man, and ——— every desirable quality

What has become of the books which were delivered here yesterday? I

——— them up stairs in my library, and you shall ——— them before you go home.

He must be extremely wealthy, for besides funded property to a large amount, there is scarcely a county in England in which he does not ——— an estate.

How many sheets of paper will you require for your exercise? I ——— three, but I think I shall want one more.

When the will was opened, it was found, to the great surprise and astonishment of all his relations, that he had left every thing he ——— to a perfect stranger.

He found, after paying all his debts, that he ——— literally nothing left for himself

---

To help—to assist.

To *help* is the generic term, and expresses a simple act; to *assist* is a specific term, and expresses a mode of helping. A man is helped at his labour; assisted in any intellectual pursuit. Help is more immediately wanted than assistance. Help is wanted in labour, danger, difficulties, &c.; assistance is required in the pursuit of some study, or the performance of some work. When a man is attacked by robbers, he calls for help, not for assistance. He who rescues a man in this situation from danger helps him; but if he should do more—if he should second his endeavours to put the ruffians to flight, or to capture some of them, he assists him. In fine, he who is suffering is helped; he who is doing is assisted

[*Cas.* Cæsar cry'd 'Help me, Cassius, or I sink.'
Julius Cæsar, i. 2

Pom. If the great gods be just, they shall assist
The deeds of justest men. *Ant. and Cleop*, ii. 1

It were a journey like the path to heaven
To help you find them. *Comus*, 303

With God not parted from him, as was feared,
But favouring and assisting to the end.
S. A., 1720.

Not long the Avenger was withstood—
Earth helped him with the cry of blood.
WORDSWORTH. '*Song at Brougham Castle*

Not unassisted by the flattering stars
Thou strew'st temptation o'er the path
When they in pomp depart. P 168.]

Exercise.

It is said that the author was materially ——— in his work by a friend, who carefully revised his manuscript, making many corrections, and supplying several deficiencies.

Had it not been for a friend, who ——— him out of his difficulties, he must have gone to prison.

In the middle of the night, I was awakened by loud cries of "———! ———!" I immediately started up, and hastening to the window, I saw just in front of the house a single traveller attacked by two ruffians.

He was on the point of yielding to the superior strength and skill of his antagonists; when, seizing my sword, I hastened to his ———, and soon turned the scale of victory in his favour.

"Their strength united best may ——— to bear"

"'Tis the first sanction nature gave to man,
Each other to ——— in what they can."

To leave—to quit.

To *quit* is a species of to *leave*. In *leaving* a place, we merely go away from it; in *quitting* a place, we go away from it with the intention either of not returning, or, at any rate, not for some time. It is then evident that we cannot quit without leaving, though we may leave without quitting. In leaving, the idea of what is left is prominent; in quitting, the person who acts is uppermost in the mind. A man *leaves* his house early in the morning for his business; he does not return at his usual hour; and upon inquiry, it is found that he has *quitted* the country.

[*York.* As in a theatre, the eyes of men,
After a well-graced actor leaves the stage,
Are idly bent on him that enters next.
Richard II., v. 2

Pros. ——— the very rats
Instinctively had quit it. *Tempest*, i. 2

——— leave not the faithful side
That gave thee being, still shades thee and protects
P. L., ix. 265

——— which the starved lover sings
To his proud fair, best quitted with disdain.
Id., iv. 770.

When, in the eagerness of boyish hope
I left our cottage-threshold —— WORDSWORTH. *Nutting*'

Unforced by wind or wave
To quit the ship for which he died '*Elegiac Poems.*']

Exercise.

"Such a variety of arguments only distract the understanding; such a superficial way of examining is to ——— truth for appearances, only to serve our vanity."

Dogs have frequently evinced their fidelity, even to the remains of their masters, by not ———ing the spot where they are laid.

"Why ——— we not the fatal Trojan shore,
And measure back the seas we cross'd before?"

I shall ——— my house for a month this autumn, but I shall not be obliged to ——— it before next Christmas.

"Then wilt thou not be loath
To ——— this paradise; but shalt possess
A paradise within thee, happier far."

'He who is prudent ——— all questions on minor matters in religion and politics to men of busy, restless tempers."

"The old man, taking my hand in his, looked earnestly in my face. 'I feel I am not long for this world,' said he, 'but I ——— life without regret, where I have met with nothing but vexation and sorrow, and I look forward with confident hope to another and a better world.'"

"The sacred wrestler, till a blessing giv'n,
——— not his hold, but, halting, conquers heaven."

To punish—to chastise.

Punishment is the general term. *Chastisement* is a species of punishment. Chastisement always proceeds from a superior to an inferior in rank or condition; not so punishment, which is a compensating principle, and applies generally. A man may be punished for his misdeeds by his inferiors, or even by himself. Our own reflections are sometimes our severest punishment. The immediate object of chastisement should be to improve the person chastised. The proper object of punishment should be that the community should benefit Thus, children are chastised, malefactors are punished. Chastisement is intended to amend the individual; punishment to repair the mischief done to society by the crime.

[*Glo.* —— as basest and contemned'st wretches,
For pilferings and most common trespasses
Are punished with. *Lear*, ii. 2.

Cleo. Nor once be chastised with the sober eye
Of dull Octavia —— *Ant. and Cleop.*, v. 2.

——— by which the spirits perverse
With easy intercourse pass to and fro
To tempt or punish mortals. *P. L.*, ii. 1032

Slow be the statutes of the land to share
A laxity that could not but impair
Your power to punish crime.
WORDSWORTH. '*Sonnets on Punishment of Death.*

——— the line of comfort that divides
Calamity, the chastisement of Heaven,
From the injustice of our brother men ——
'*The Excursion*,' ii.]

Exercise.

No species of ——— had the least effect upon him; he seemed not to be affected by it in the same way as others, and set all authority of his superiors at defiance.

The master had severely ——— the scholars several times before for the same fault, and determined not to let this occasion pass without making an example.

He confessed, however, that this was a well-merited ——— for his former follies; and resolved from that moment to compensate by his future good conduct for his past irregularities.

The laws against thieves and burglars were more strictly enforced than ever, and offenders against them were ——— with the utmost rigour.

On several occasions, the father had ——— his son with such severity, that the neighbours had been obliged to interfere.

To put—to place.

Put is to *place* as the genus to the species. To put is a general term; to place, specific Placing is a mode of putting. When we put a thing in a particular situation, we place it. A plant may be put into a flower-pot, and then placed in the green-house. All the parts of a clock may be put together, and the clock then placed in the hall.

[*Hor.* The very place puts toys of desperation,
Without more motive, into every brain.
Hamlet, i. 4.

Macb. Upon my head they placed a fruitless crown,
And put a barren sceptre in my gripe.
Macbeth, iii. 1.

When God into the hands of their deliverer
Puts invincible might ——— *Samson Agon.* 1271.

Was placed in regal lustre. —— *P. L.*, x. 447.

In my own house I put into his hand
A bible ——— WORDSWORTH. '*The Brothers.*'

——— nor any course
Of strange or tragic accident, hath helped
To place those hillocks in that lonely guise
'*The Excursion*,' VII.]

Exercise.

"I had a parcel of crowns in my hand to pay for Shakspeare; and as she had let go the purse entirely, I ——— a single one in, and tying up the riband in a bow-knot, returned it to her."

"Nydia smiled joyously, but did not answer; and Glaucus ———ing the violets he had selected in his breast, turned gaily and carelessly from the crowd."

"Then youths and virgins, twice as many, join
To ——— the dishes, and to serve the wine."

"In saying this, he presented his snuff-box to me with one hand, as he took mine from me in the other; and having kissed it, with a stream of good-nature in his eyes, he ——— it in his bosom, and took his leave."

"Our two first parents, yet the only two
Of mankind, in the happy garden ———."

"He that has any doubt of his tenets, received without examination, ought to ——— himself wholly into this state of ignorance, and throwing wholly by all his former notions, examine them with a perfect indifference"

"'Twas his care
To ——— on good security his gold."

To reprove—to rebuke.

When we rebuke or reprove we express strong disapprobation. A rebuke is given by word of mouth, whilst a reproof may be expressed in a variety of ways. A father who has reason to find fault with his son's conduct may reprove him by letter, or by means of a third person, as well as verbally. There is more of impulse in a rebuke, more of reason in a reproof. Our anger or indignation prompts us to rebuke. The wish to convince another of his fault prompts us to reprove. A rebuke is given on the spur of the moment; a reproof may be conveyed some time after the fault reproved. For this reason, rebukes are not so effectual or so convincing as reproofs.

[*Ant.* My very hairs do mutiny; for the white
Reprove the brown for rashness, and they them
For fear and doting. —— *Ant. and Cleop.*, iii. 9

Macb. My genius is rebuked; as, it is said,
Mark Antony's was by Cæsar. —— *Macbeth*, iii. 1.

Prove disobedient, and, reproved, retort—
P. L., x. 761

——— his grave rebuke
Severe in youthful beauty, added grace
Invincible. —— *Id.*, iv. 844

Life, which the very stars reprove,
As on their silent tasks they move! WORDSWORTH. '*Gipsies.*'

Thou Power supreme! who, arming to rebuke
Offenders, dost put off the gracious look,
And clothe thyself with terrors like the flood
Of Ocean roused into his fiercest mood.
'*Evening Voluntaries.*']

Exercise.

Though his father had ——— him several times in the course of the day, the son persisted in his idleness; and when the examination took place, he was found unable to answer a single question correctly.

Confident of success, he had embarked all his property in a wild speculation, and lost every thing he had in the world. It was now too late for ———, and all his friends could do for him was to assist him, as well as their means would allow, to patch up his broken fortunes.

The popular story of the plan which Canute the Great adopted to ——— his courtiers for their abject flattery in styling him lord and master of the winds and ocean, is well authenticated, and is mentioned by many respectable historians.

"He who endeavours only the happiness of him whom he ———, will always have the satisfaction of either obtaining or deserving kindness."

To ridicule—to deride.

Both these words include the idea of laughter, but the purposes of laughter differ in each. In *ridiculing*, we laugh in order to correct. In *deriding*, we laugh with a view of exposing. Ridicule is good-humoured; it is often employed to work an improvement. Derision is malicious; it is the gratification of a malignant feeling. Mistakes which provoke laughter are ridiculed; the foolish and absurd are derided. We ridicule when we are amused; we deride when we are piqued or offended. It is wrong to ridicule serious things, but it is much worse to turn them to derision.

[*Cor.* Who cover faults, at last shame them derides
King Lear, i. 1

All these our motions vain, sees and derides.
P. L., ii. 191

It ill befits us to disdain
The altar, to deride the fane,
Where simple sufferers bend, in trust,
To win a happier hour. WORDSWORTH. 'Itin Poems

Exercise.

The entreaties of the unfortunate prisoners for water to quench theit burning thirst were neglected or ——— by the guards, and consequently scarcely ten survived the horrors of that dreadful night.

The efforts which he made to regain his equilibrium were so ———, that the whole company burst into a loud laugh.

Many persons have a strong tendency to turn every thing into ———: where this inclination is not checked, it is often productive of very serious consequences.

To ——— any one for a personal deformity is a certain sign of a base mind.

Though it was growing dark, and they were passing through a dangerous part of the country, the guide appeared perfectly insensible to the probability of their being attacked, and ——— the fears of the travellers, marched boldly before them.

He was stung to the quick by the ——— in which his companions held his opinions, and he determined to take the first opportunity of separating himself fiom them.

"Satan beheld their plight,
And to his mates thus in ——— called:
O friends, why come not on those victors proud?"

"Those who aim at ———
Should fix upon some certain rule,
Which fairly hints they are in jest."

To try—to attempt.

To *try* is the generic, to *attempt* is the specific term. We cannot attempt without trying, though we may try without attempting. When we try, we are uncertain as to the result; when we attempt, it is always with intention. We may be indifferent as to the result of a trial, but we never attempt without a desire tc succeed. An *endeavour* is a continued or a repeated attempt. Though a single attempt be fruitless, yet we may at last succeed in our endeavours. An endeavour implies a partial failure in the attempt.

[*Macb.* Yet I will try the last.— *Macbeth*, v. 7.
Rom. —What love can do, that dares love attempt.
Romeo and Juliet, ii. 2.

——— to speak I tried, and forthwith spake.
P. L., viii. 271.

——— Advise, if this be worth
Attempting;— *Id.*, ii 377.

Thy works and alms, and all thy good endeavour.
MILTON. '*Sonnets*'

So vain was his endeavour
That at the root of the old tree
He might have worked forever. WORDSWORTH. '*Simon Lee.*'

——— his palsied hand,
That still attempting to prevent the waste,
Was baffled still. '*The Old Cumberland Beggar.*']

Exercise.

"If we be always prepared to receive an enemy, we shall long live in peace and quietness, without an ——— upon us."

"There is a mixed kind of evidence, relating both to the senses and understanding, depending upon our own observation and repeated ——— of the issues and events of actions or things, called experience."

"At length, as if tired of ——— to escape, the lion crept with a moan into its cage, and once more laid itself down to rest."

"I ——— to seize him, but he glided from my grasp."

"Though Boccaccio and Petrarca followed Dante, they did not employ themselves in cultivating the ground which he had broken up, but chose each for himself an un——— field, and reaped a harvest not less abundant."

"A natural and unconstrained behaviour has something in it so agreeable, that it is no wonder to see people ———ing after it. But, at the same time, it is so very hard to hit when it is not born with us, that people often make themselves ridiculous in ———ing it."

"Whether or not (said Socrates on the day of his execution) God will approve of my actions, I know not; but this I am sure of, that I have at all times made it my ——— to please Him."

To worship—to adore.

Adoration is a species of *worship*. There appears in adoration a strong sense of our own inferiority; for it is always accompanied by an attitude expressive of humility. In worshipping, the prevailing feeling is the superiority of the object worshipped. In worshipping, we pay homage to the power, wisdom, and goodness of the Creator; in adoring, we express our own weakness and dependence on Him. There is no attitude peculiar to worship; it is included in the usual forms

7*

of prayer and thanksgiving. In adoring, we prostrate ourselves

[*Eros.* ——— that noble countenance,
Wherein the worship of the whole world lies.
Ant. and Cleop., iv. 12

Hel. ——— Indian-like,
Religious in mine error, I adore
The sun, that looks upon his worshipper
But knows of him no more. —— *All's Well, &c.*, i. 3

——— wave your tops, ye pines,
With every plant, in sign of worship wave.
P. L., v. 194

Gladly behold though but his utmost skirts
Of glory; and far off his steps adore.
Id., xi. 333

——— the Sun,
Source inexhaustible of life and joy,
And type of man's far-darting reason, therefore
In old time worshipped as the god of verse,
A blazing intellectual deity. —— WORDSWORTH. '*To the Clouds*

The future brightens on our sight;
For on the past has fallen a light
That tempts us to adore. '*Elegiac Stanzas*']

Exercise.

"Let Indians, and the gay, like Indians, fond
Of feathered fopperies, the sun ———;
Darkness has more divinity for me."

"He loved to keep alive the ——— of Egypt, because he thus maintained the shadow and the recollection of her power."

"Menander says that God, the Lord and Father of all things, is alone worthy of our ———, being at once the maker and giver of all blessings."

"The ——— of God is an eminent part of religion, and prayer is a chief part of religious ———; hence religion is described by seeking God."

"Adorned
With gay religions, full of pomp and gold
And devils to ——— for deities."

"By reason man a Godhead can discern,
But how he should be ——— cannot learn."

"In the earliest times there appear to have been very few temples at Rome, and in many spots, the ——— of a certain divinity had been established from time immemorial, while we hear of the building of a temple for the same divinity at a comparatively late period."

"It is possible to suppose, that those who believe in a supreme, excellent Being, may yet give him no external ——— at all."

Ancient—Antique.

Ancient qualifies the manners, institutions, customs, &c., of the nations of antiquity. *Antique* refers to the style of their works of art. Ancient architecture signifies the abstract science as it existed among the ancients. Antique architecture refers to the style of building among the ancients. We speak of an antique coin, an antique cup, or gem; and of ancient laws and customs. Ancient is generic—antique specific; an ancient temple is one built by the ancients; an antique temple is one built in the style of the ancients. Ancient is not modern; antique is not new-fashioned.

[*Pem.* This act is as an ancient tale new told.
Sal. In this, the antique and well-noted face
Of plain old form is much disfigured. *King John,* iv. 2.

Those ancient, whose resistless eloquence
Wielded at will that fierce democratie. *P. R.*, iv. 268

With mask, and antique pageantry. '*L'Allegro*,' 128

Thou dost preserve the stars from wrong;
And the most ancient Heavens through thee are fresh and strong.
WORDSWORTH. '*Ode to Duty*'

——— the rustic Lodge
Antique ——— '*Inscriptions*.']

Exercise.

The room had a very ——— appearance; the furniture was old and worn, the walls hung with tapestry, and the ceiling adorned with relievo.

The remains of an ——— temple have been lately found in the neighbourhood of the modern town, and in the vicinity, many remains of Roman handicraft have been discovered.

"The seals which we have remaining of Julius Cæsar, which we know to be ———, have the star of Venus over them."

The poems of Homer throw great light upon the domestic manners and customs of the ——— Greeks.

"With this view, Lorenzo appropriated his gardens, adjacent to the monastery of St. Marco, to the establishment of a school or academy for the study of the ———."

Several tribes, as ——— tradition asserts, were natives of the Hellenic soil: two, viz. the Pelasgi and the Hellenes, are especially mentioned by Herodotus.

"But seven wise men the ——— world did know;
We scarce know seven who think themselves not so."

"I leave to Edward, Earl of Oxford, my seal of Julius Cæsar; as also another seal, supposed to be a young Hercules, both very choice ———s, and set in gold."

Clear—Distinct.

Objects are *clear* when there is sufficient light to enable us to perceive their general form; they are *distinct*, when we can discern their parts, or separate them from surrounding objects. Suppose, during the twilight of a summer evening, an orange is lying in a dish with some other fruit; there may be light enough for me to see it clearly, that is, to perceive its general form and colour; but when, lights being introduced, I am enabled to form a just idea of its exact shape and colour, and can distinguish it from the other fruit—I see it distinctly.

[*Buck.* ——— proofs as clear as founts in July, when
We see each grain of gravel: *Henry VIII.*, i. 1.

Achil. And make distinct the very breach, whereout
Hector's great spirit flew. *Troil. and Cress.*, iv. 5

——— where the Muses haunt
Clear spring, or shady grove, or sunny hill.
P. L., iii. 28

High, and remote to see from thence distinct
Each thing on earth. *Id.*, ix. 812.

Because the unstained, the clear, the crystalline
Have ever in them something of benign;
Whether in gem, in water, or in sky.
A sleeping infant's brow, or wakeful eye
Of a young maiden, only not divine. WORDSWORTH. '*Itin. Sonnets.*
Nor does the Village Church-clock's iron tone
The time's and season's influence disown;
Nine beats distinctly to each other bound
In drowsy sequence. ——— '*Evening Voluntaries.*']

Exercise.

There are many objects we may see, even in hazy weather ———ly, without being able to see them ———ly. A telescope will often make what is ———, ———.

The night was so bright, and our glasses so good, that we were able to perceive Saturn's ring most ———ly.

One thing is quite ———, that without some knowledge as to the management of the propelling power, the whole machine must have proved useless.

In this country, the English language should form a ——— branch of education, and should be regularly and systematically studied.

The vessel now spread all her sails, and was ———ly seen approaching the harbour.

In about half an hour, the spectators, with which the whole shore was lined, ———ly saw seven men on the raft, one of whom was waving a handkerchief tied to a pole, as a signal of distress.

"Whether we are able to comprehend all the operations of nature, it matters not to inquire; but this is certain, that we can comprehend no more of them than we can ———ly conceive."

I now understand ———ly what you mean.

Entire—Complete.

The word *entire* respects the whole substance of an object considered collectively; it qualifies that which has all its parts: the word *complete* has reference to the appendages of an object, considered apart from the object itself; it qualifies that which wants nothing that properly belongs to it. An *entire* week consists of the seven days of which it is composed, taken together. On Friday, the week wants another day to make it complete. An entire work consists of a certain number of volumes. A complete work contains every thing that can be said on the subject of which it treats. Books of travels which are published without maps cannot be called complete.

[*Oth.* If heaven would make me such another world,
Of one entire and perfect chrysolite. *Othello*, v. 2.

Ham. That thou, dead corse, again, in complete steel,
Revisit'st thus the glimpses of the moon.
Hamlet, i. 4.

Or how the sun shall in mid-heaven stand still
A day entire ——— *P. L.*, xii. 264.

——— so absolute she seems,
And in herself complete ——— *Id.*, viii. 548

——— thereto incline
More readily the more my years require
Help and forgiveness speedy and entire.
WORDSWORTH. *Memorials of Tour in Italy*.']

Exercise.

The embassy did not occupy an ——— house, but were accommodated with temporary lodgings in the viceroy's palace.

Having received this reinforcement, the army was now ———, and it was determined to march immediately against the enemy.

He was so careless of his property, that, every time he went to sea, it was necessary to purchase for him a new and ——— set of mathematical instruments.

The ——— session has been occupied in frivolous discussions on questions of secondary importance.

Many of the houses in that country are built ——— of wood.

When another row of houses is built on the north side, the square will be ——.

My apprehensions were ——ly removed by this intelligence

"And oft, when unobserved,
Steal from the barn a straw, till soft and warm,
Clean and ——, their habitation grows."

Exterior—External.

That which is outside, but yet forms part of a substance, is its *exterior*. What is contiguous to the exterior is *external.* The skin of a nut is its exterior, and the shell its external covering. The exterior of a house is what we see of the house itself from without; such as the brick walls, ornaments, colour, &c. The external parts of a house refer to the garden, stables, offices, &c., by which it is surrounded. Morally speaking, a man's exterior is the visible expression of his mind within, and has reference to his countenance and manners. One who is particular in the arrangement of his dress, house, furniture, pictures, &c., pays much attention to externals.

[*Bart.* Exterior form, outward accoutrement.
King John, i. 1.

K. Rich. And these external manners of lament
Are merely shadows to the unseen grief.
Rich. II., iv. 1

And what is faith, love, virtue, unassay'd
Alone, without exterior help sustained?
P. L., ix. 336

—— all external things
Which the five watchful senses represent.
Id., v. 105.

How exquisitely the individual Mind
(And the progressive powers perhaps no less
Of the whole species) to the external World
Is fitted:—and how exquisitely, too—
Theme this but little heard of among men—
The external World is fitted to the Mind.
WORDSWORTH. *Pref. to the 'Excursion.'*]

Exercise.

The way in which men proceeded in the formation of abstract language was, to take words used originally to designate the states and actions of —— nature, and employ them to express the various faculties and conditions of the mind.

We should never judge any thing by its ———, but in order to ascertain its just value, we should defer our opinion till we become acquainted with its real merits.

Though he is a man of rough ———, you will find, on a closer acquaintance with him, that he has an excellent disposition, and much merit.

A considerable part of the popular religion in all countries is found to have consisted of ——— ceremonies.

The ——— forms of social life are necessary to keep alive feelings of kindness and benevolence among members of the same community.

"Shells, being exposed loose upon the surface of the earth to the injuries of weather, to be trodden upon by horses and other cattle, and to many other ——— accidents, are in course of time broken to pieces."

Extravagant—Profuse.

Etymologically, *extravagant* is *wandering out of* the right way; and *profuse* is *pouring forth* our substance. We are extravagant when we spend more than we can afford. We are profuse when we give away in excess. Profusion is a mode of extravagance. We are extravagant in the cost of what we spend for ourselves; profuse in the quantity we spend upon others. A man displays extravagance in his dress, plate, books, pictures, &c., and he displays profusion in his dinners, entertainments, presents, &c. to his friends. One who is extravagant in his language uses inapplicable, forced expressions. One who is profuse in his thanks says more and repeats oftener than is necessary.

[*Hor.* ——— and at his warning,
Whether in sea or fire, in earth or air,
The extravagant and erring spirit hies
To his confine. *Hamlet*, i. 1.

——— yet for a dance they seemed
Somewhat extravagant and wild. *P. L.*, vi. 616

——— which not nice art
In beds and curious knots, but nature boon,
Poured forth profuse on hill, and dale, and plain,
Id., iv. 243.]

Exercise.

He had acquired so many expensive habits, and was so ——— in his expenditure, that he soon found his fortune wholly inadequate to supply all the wants his artificial mode of living had created.

By ——— liberality and frequent entertainments to the people, the cunning demagogue contrived to raise himself to an unprecedented height of popularity.

Every sensible man will be inclined to doubt the judgment of him who is ——— in his praises of what he is but little acquainted with.

The apartment was decorated with the most exquisite taste and the greatest magnificence; on all sides, a ——— of fruit and flowers met the eye, and the senses were simultaneously ravished with the sweetest perfumes and the softest music.

"New ideas employed my fancy all night, and composed a wild, ——— dream."

"Cicero was most liberally ——— in commending the ancients and his contemporaries."

Frail—Brittle.

Substances which are apt to break are *frail;* those which are apt, in breaking, to split into many irregular particles, are *brittle.* The form or shape of an object may make it frail, though the material of which it is constructed be not brittle. Brittle is a quality essential to the nature of certain materials; frail is applied to those which are put together, or formed in such a way as to be easily broken. A reed, or a hastily-constructed house, is frail; glass, coal, shells, &c., are brittle. What is frail snaps; what is brittle breaks into many parts by collision. Frail is used in a secondary sense, as applied to the moral weakness of human beings. Brittle is scarcely ever so used.

[*P. Hen.* (which some suppose the soul's frail dwelling-house.)
King John, v. 7

K. Rich. A brittle glory shineth in this face:
As brittle as the glory is the face;
For there it is, cracked in a hundred shivers.
Rich. II., iv. 1.

Confined and pestered in this pinfold here,
Strive to keep up a frail and feverish being.
Comus, 8.

Nor founded on the brittle strength of bones.
P. L., i. 427

Too much from this frail earth we claim,
And therefore are betrayed WORDSWORTH. '*Elegiac Stanzas.*']

Exercise.

Though drenched with the rain, and exhausted with excessive fatigue, we were obliged, notwithstanding, to set to work immediately, and construct something to serve as a temporary shelter from the inclemency of the weather.

A ——— hovel, made of deal boards, hastily nailed together and covered with matting and remnants of old sails, was our only dwelling for some months after our arrival.

Nelson, though possessed of perhaps as much personal bravery as any man that ever existed, was of a ——— and weakly constitution; and it is well known that he never went to sea without suffering severely from sickness.

The shell-basket, though it had been packed with the greatest care, was so ——— that it was found broken into a thousand pieces when we arrived at the end of our journey.

Glass of every kind would be much more ——— than it is, if it were not subjected, immediately after it is fashioned, to the process of annealing.

"When with care we have raised an imaginary treasure of happiness, we find at last, that the materials of the structure are ——— and perishing, and the foundation itself is laid in the sand."

"These," said Harley, "are quotations from those humble poets who trust their fame to the ——— tenures of windows and drinking-glasses."

Great—Big.

Bulk that is capable of expansion is big when expanded. *Great* is applied to every species of dimension; so that *big* is a species of great. An animal, a bottle, a balloon, may be called big. The frog that swelled herself out, asked her young if she was bigger than the ox. A great house, is one that has much length, breadth, and height. Again there is a rotundity in big, which does not of necessity belong to great. In a secondary meaning, power, knowledge, strength, &c., are represented as great. Big is not often used in a moral sense. We have, however, a year "big with events," and "big with the fate of Cato," in the sense of *on the point of producing*.

[*Pro.* The solemn temples, the great globe itself.—
Tempest, iv. 1.

1 *Lord.* ——— and the big round tears
Coursed one another down his innocent nose
In piteous chase *As You Like It*, iv. 1

——— the tallest pine,
Hewn on Norwegian hills to be the mast
Of some great ammiral *P. L.*, i. 294.

Behemoth, biggest born of earth, upheaved
His vastness *Id.*, vii. 471.

If this great world of joy and pain
Revolve in one sure track;
If freedom, set, will rise again,
And virtue, flown, come back; WORDSWORTH. p. 381

They sweep distemper from the busy day,
And make the chalice of the big round year
Run o'er with gladness *'The Excursion,'* ix]

Exercise.

This bag will not be ——— enough to hold all we wish to put into it.

The ———er the difficulty, the more should we endeavour to overcome it.

This hat is not ——— enough for him—it hurts his head.

How ——— is the pleasure of doing good, is known only to the benevolent and charitable!

The bottle which he brought with him was ——— enough to hold water for the whole party.

Hamilcar is said to have founded a ——— city, which he destined to be the capital of the Carthaginian Empire in Spain, at a place called the White Promontory; but this was probably superseded by New Carthage, and its situation is now unknown.

His younger brother, whom I had not seen for three years, was now grown a ——— boy, and was old enough to go to school.

"An animal no ———er than a mite cannot appear perfect to the eye, because the sight takes it in at once."

"At one's first entrance into the Pantheon at Rome, how the imagination is filled with something ——— and amazing!"

Heavenly—Celestial.

The Latin word *cœlum* (heaven) leads us to the idea of its natural appearance of hollowness or concavity. *Heaven*, from the Anglo-Saxon *heafan*, (to heave, or raise up,) points to height, moral or physical, as a leading idea. *Celestial* and *heavenly* are adjectives derived, respectively, from these two nouns. Hence, *heavenly* refers rather to what is sublime and exalted, whilst *celestial* is applied to the natural phenomenon of the heavens. Thus we speak of the celestial globe, celestial bodies, &c., and of heavenly music, heavenly joys, &c. The expressions celestial music, celestial joys, &c., are also used, but not in exactly the same sense. Heavenly music raises us above our mortal condition. Celestial music is the music heard in heaven, considered as the abode of the just. In the former, we have the idea of something sublime and superhuman; in the latter, we have the idea of place.

[*Oth.* ——— This sorrow's heavenly;
It strikes, where it doth love. *Othello*, v. 2

Kath. ——— whilst I sit meditating
On that celestial harmony I go to. *Henry VIII.*, iv 2

Celestial voices to the midnight air,
Sole or responsive each to other's note,
Singing their great Creator oft in bands
While they keep watch or nightly rounding walk,
With heavenly touch of instrumental sounds
In full harmonic number joined, their songs
Divide the night, and lift our thoughts to heaven.
P. L., iv. 682–6.

—— guidance have I sought in duteous love
From Wisdom's heavenly Father.
WORDSWORTH. '*On the Punishment of Death*

Reflected beams of that celestial light
To all the Little-Ones on sinful earth
Not unvouchsafed. '*Maternal Grief*.']

Exercise.

Abstracted from all the cares and anxieties of this world, he fixed his mind intently on the ——— joys of a future state, waiting with patient, though longing anxiety for the moment which should dissolve him for ever from all earthly ties.

The artificial contrivance called a ——— globe is a hollow sphere, on the surface of which are represented the stars and constellations, each in its proper situation.

The countenance of St. Cecilia is painted glowing with enthusiasm and rapt in a "fine frenzy," and her ——— features are directed upwards, while she seems to catch the divine inspiration which fills her soul.

"There stay, until the twelve ——— signs
Have brought about their annual reckoning."

"As the love of heaven makes one ———, the love of virtue, virtuous, so does the love of the world make one become worldly."

High—Tall.

High is a generic term; *tall*, a specific term. What is tall is high, but what is high is not always tall. That which attains considerable height by growing is tall. So we speak of the height of a tall man. The reverse of high is low, the reverse of tall is stunted. We may say, a high house, a high church, &c.; and a tall girl, a tall horse, a tall tree, &c. Metaphorically, tall is sometimes used for high, as in the phrase, "*a tall spire.*"

[*Hor.* —— the morn, in russet mantle clad
Walks o'er the dew of yon high eastern hill.
Hamlet, i. 1.

Salar —— a very dangerous flat, and fatal, where the carcases of many a tall ship lie buried. *Merch. of Ven.*, iii 1

Or let my lamp at midnight hour
Be seen in some high lonely tower.
MILTON. *Il Pens.*, 85

——— that proud honour claimed
Azazel as his right, a cherub tall. *P. L.*, i. 534

Yet when above the forest-glooms
The white swans southward passed,
High as the pitch of their swift plumes
Her fancy rode the blast;
WORDSWORTH. '*The Russian Fugitive.*'

And yon tall pine-tree, whose composing sound
Was wasted on the good Man's living ear,
Hath now its own peculiar sanctity;
And, at the touch of every wandering breeze,
Murmurs, not idly o'er his peaceful grave.
The Excursion, vii.]

Exercise.

"Reason elevates our thoughts as ——— as the stars, and leads us through the vast spaces of this mighty fabric; yet it comes far short of the real extent of even corporeal being."

"Two of far nobler shape, erect and ———
Godlike erect, with native honour clad,
In naked majesty, seemed lords of all."

"The ———er parts of the earth, being continually spending, and the lower continually gaining, they must, of necessity, at length come to an equality."

"Prostrate on earth their beauteous body lay,
Like mountain firs, as ——— and straight as they."

"They that stand ———, have many blasts to shake them,
And, if they fall, they dash themselves to pieces."

"They lop, and lop, on this and that hand, cutting away the ——— sound, and substantial timber, that used to shelter them from the winds.'

"——— o'er their heads a mouldering rock is placed
That promises a fall, and shakes at every blast."

"When you are tried in scandal's court,
Stand ——— in honor, wealth, or wit,
All others who inferior sit,

Conceive themselves in conscience bound
To join and drag you to the ground."

Laudable—Praiseworthy.

Laudable is the generic; *praiseworthy* the specific term. Things that are generally entitled to praise are laudable; when circumstances make an action deserve praise, it is praiseworthy. What is laudable is so under all circumstances; what is praiseworthy is so only under certain circumstances. The merit of what is laudable lies in the abstract nature of he thing. The merit of what is praiseworthy depends upon the circumstances of the case. In praiseworthy, there is an implied reference to the agent. More generally, things are qualified as laudable, and actions as praiseworthy. Ambition, confidence, &c., may be laudable. To encourage trade, and discourage immorality, are praiseworthy in a king.

[*L. Macd.* I am in this earthly world: where to do harm
Is often laudable: *Macbeth*, iv. 2.

Bened. So much for praising myself, (who, I myself will bear witness, is praiseworthy.) *Much Ado About Nothing*, v. 2.]

Exercise.

"Nothing is more ——— than an inquiry after truth."

"Ridicule is generally made use of to laugh men out of virtue and good sense, by attacking every thing ——— in human life."

"He had in general a ——— confidence in his own judgment, and never took advice."

"Firmus, who seized upon Egypt, was so far ——— that he encouraged trade."

"Affectation endeavours to cctrect natural defects, and has always the ——— aim of pleasing, though it always misses it."

"But who shall say that the feelings which produced such emotions even in such men were not ——— and good?"

Lucky—Fortunate.

Though both these words are employed to qualify those persons to whom things turn out as they wish, there is this distinction between them. Those are properly called *fortunate* who are continually successful in their undertakings. *Lucky* refers to that which is pure hazard, and wholly unexpected. A fortunate man obtains what he wishes and hopes to gain. A lucky man gets what he may desire, but does not expect to gain. The fortunate merchant grows rich by successful speculations; the lucky man becomes rich by a prize in the lottery, or by an unexpected legacy.

[*Ant.* ——— when mine hours
Were nice and lucky, men did ransom lives
Of me for jests. —— *Ant. and Cleop.*, iii. 11.

Bru. As Cæsar loved me, I weep for him; as he was fortunate, I rejoice at it;
Julius Cæsar, iii. 2.

So may some gentle Muse
With lucky words favour my destined urn;
Milton. '*Lycidas*,' 20

Like those Hesperian gardens, famed of old,
Fortunate fields, and groves, and flowery vales,
Thrice happy isles; *P. L.*, iii. 569

In days of yore how fortunately fared
The Minstrel' wandering from hall to hall
'*The Excursion*,' ii.]

Exercise.

After many fruitless attempts, I was at last so ——— as to find him at home; and having obtained an interview, I explained my views to him, and solicited his interest in my favour.

On his arrival in town, he advertised in the public papers, and, by the ——— chance, the advertisement struck the eye of a gentleman who was in need of some one to superintend his affairs; this led to an interview, and he was so ——— as to obtain the situation.

I met him by the merest chance, an event which has led to all my good ——— throughout life, and which I cannot but consider as the ——— accident that ever befel me.

He has been most ——— in all his transactions; every thing has prospered with him through life, and in all cases of doubtful success, enterprises seemed to want but his sanction to turn the scale in their favour.

It was a ——— circumstance for the Duke that the King died at this conjuncture; for, in consequence of his death, he was liberated from prison, and restored to all his dignities and honors.

"The ——— moment the sly traitor chose,
Then starting from his ambush, up he rose."

"O ——— old man, whose farm remains
For you sufficient, and requites your pains."

Mute—Dumb.

A *dumb* man has not the power to speak. A *mute* man either does not choose, or is not allowed to speak. Whatever takes away the faculty of speech, even for a time, causes a man to be dumb. Men are dumb from some organic defect: circumstances may make us mute. Deafness from birth will make a man dumb. Beasts, birds, and fishes are dumb. Mutes are men who stand on each side of the entrance of a deceased person's house, on the day of his funeral, and who are ordered to preserve strict silence.

[*Cant.*——— when he speaks,
The air, a chartered libertine, is still,
And the mute wonder lurketh in men's ears
To steal his sweet and honeyed sentences.
Henry V., i. 1.

Mess. ——— I have seen
The dumb men throng to see him, and the blind
To hear him speak. —— *Coriolanus*, ii. 1

More safe I sing with mortal voice, unchanged
To hoarse or mute, though fallen on evil days,
On evil days though fallen, and evil tongues.
P. L., vii. 25

His gentle dumb expression turned at length
The eye of Eve to mark his play —— *Id.*, ix. 527.

Mute as the snow upon the hill,
And, as the saint he prays to, still. WORDSWORTH, p 262

Yet, spite of all this eager strife,
This ceaseless play, the genuine life
That serves the stedfast hours,
Is in the grass beneath, that grows
Unheeded, and the mute repose
Of sweetly-breathing flowers. *Id.*, p. 376

——— I forgive him;—but
'Twere better to be dumb than to talk thus:
'*Michael.*']

Exercise.

"We went in an open carriage, drawn by two sleek old black horses for which W. Scott seemed to have an affection, as he had for every ——— animal that belonged to him."

"'Tis listening fear and ——— amazement all."

"Long ——— he stood, and leaning on his staff,
His wonder witnessed with an idiot laugh."

"Some positive terms signify a negative idea: blind implies a privation of sight, ———, a denial of speech."

"All sat ———
Pondering the danger with deep thoughts."
"The whole perplexed ignoble crowd
——— to my questions, in my praises loud,
Echoed the word."

"The truth of it is, half the great talkers in the nation would be struck ——— were this fountain of discourse (party lies) dried up."

In a few minutes, however, several ——— appeared, at the sight of whom, Mustapha, knowing what was his doom, cried with a loud voice, "Lo, my death!" and attempted to fly.

"Sometimes we stand in silence, and with a full heart, gazing upon those hard, cold eyes which never again can melt in tenderness upon us. And our silence is ———,—its eloquence is gone."

New—Novel.

What we get in exchange for the old, is *new.* What has never occurred before, is *novel.* New is opposed to old; novel, to known. New supposes something previous; novel is strange and unexpected. The new year is opposed to the old year. A new edition is one just published. A novel style is one which no one has yet attempted. A novel principle is one hitherto unknown. Novelty—not newness—is the great charm in travelling. A new book may exhibit a subject in a novel manner. Novel is a species of new; it is the new and the unknown combined.

[*Macb.* Approach the chamber, and destroy your sight
With a new Gorgon ——— *Macbeth*, ii. 3.

Duke. ——— novelty is only in request; and it is as dangerous to be aged in any kind of course, as it is virtuous to be constant in any undertaking.
Meas. for Meas., iii. 2.

The winds with wonder whist,
Smoothly the waters kist,
Whispering new joys to the mild ocean.
MILTON. '*Ode on the Nativity*

——— create at last
This novelty on earth ——— *P. L.*, x. 891.

——— flower after flower has blown,
Embellishing the ground that gave them birth
With aspects novel to my sight,
* * * * *
——— where'er my feet might roam,
Whate'er assemblages of new and old,
Strange and familiar, might beguile the way.
WORDSWORTH. '*Memorials of Tour in Italy.*']

Exercise.

This doctor adopts altogether a ——— mode of treatment with his patients.

It is customary in many foreign countries, on the first day of the ——— year, for every one to pay visits of ceremony, and make presents to his friends and acquaintance.

This was a ——— and unheard-of innovation, and so opposed to the feelings of the members, that they unanimously declared they would withdraw their support from the society, if the council should persist in bringing it into practice.

Every thing I find here is so ——— and strange, that scarcely an hour passes without something to engage my attention, and this produces so pleasing an excitement, that I am now strongly prejudiced in favour of the place.

As a reward for his diligence and good conduct at school, his uncle had made him a present of a ——— kite, which he is now engaged in flying in the fields at the back of the house.

"We are naturally delighted with ———."

"When the ——— of success was cooled, he began to feel that the olive crown had its thorns."

> "'Tis on some evening, sunny, grateful, mild,
> When nought but balm is beaming through the woods,
> With yellow lustre bright, that the ——— tribes
> Visit the spacious heavens."

Particular—Peculiar.

Particular qualifies that which belongs to one sort or kind only, exclusively of others. *Peculiar* qualifies that which belongs to the individual. Pineapples have a particular flavour, *i. e.* a flavour not belonging to other kinds of fruit. One individual pineapple may have a peculiar flavour, *i. e.* a flavour to be found in no other pineapple.

> [*Hel.* ——— It were all one
> That I should love a bright particular star
> And think to wed it, he is so above me. *All's Well, &c.*, i. 1.

> *Ros.* The single and peculiar life is bound
> With all the strength and armour of the mind
> To keep itself from 'noyance ——— *Hamlet*, iii. 3.

> Beauty, which, whether waking or asleep
> Shot forth peculiar graces; —— *P. L.*, v 15.

> ——— save only for a hope
> That my particular current soon will reach
> The unfathomable gulf, where all is still. '*The Excursion*,' iii

———we die, my Friend,
Nor we alone, but that which each man loved
And prized in his peculiar nook of earth
Dies with him or is changed; and very soon
Even of the good is no memorial left. '*The Excursion*,' i.

Exercise.

It is so long since this adventure happened to me, that I can do no more than give you a general account of the transaction, for I cannot now recollect every ——— circumstance connected with the affair.

Eccentric men have ——— habits; they do not seem to move in the same sphere with other mortals, but are actuated by different influences from those which affect the bulk of mankind.

I was present during the whole course of lectures; but though I paid the strictest attention to the system and explanations of the lecturer, I could not discover any ——— novelty either in his system or arrangement.

I was once acquainted with a gentleman who had the ——— habit of repeating several times, in a gradually lower tone, the last syllable of every sentence he uttered.

His general conduct was that of an irritable man; and though I do not remember any ——— occasion on which he displayed his violent temper, I know that it was a subject of continual complaint among his friends.

Is there any thing new? No, nothing in ———

" Great father Bacchus, to my song repair,
For clustering grapes are thy ——— care."

" When we trust to the picture that objects draw of themselves on the mind, we deceive ourselves without accurate and ——— observation; it is but ill-drawn at first; the outlines are soon blurred, the colours every day grow fainter"

Prevalent—Prevailing

What generally prevails is *prevalent*. What actually prevails is *prevailing*. There are many pairs of adjectives of this sort in English, the former preserving the Latin, and the latter the Saxon participial ending—such as, Consistent, consisting; different, differing; repentant, repenting, &c. &c. The former of which will be found to qualify as to generals, and the latter as to particulars. Thus, in the above pair of words—Consumption is a prevalent disorder in England: after a bad harvest, distress is a prevailing cause of discontent.

Exercise.

" This was the most received and ——— opinion when I first brought my collection up to London."

"Probabilities, which cross men's appetites and ——— passions, run the same fate; let never so much probability hang on one side of a covetous man's reasoning, and money on the other, it is easy to foresee which will outweigh."

"The evils naturally consequent upon a ——— temptation are intolerable."

"But the great ——— characteristic of the present intellectual spirit is one most encouraging to human hopes; it is benevolence."

"As I consider that the architecture of a nation is one of the most visible types of its ——— character, so, in that department all with us is comfortable, and nothing vast."

It must be admitted, to the honor of our nation, that the vice of drunkenness is far less ——— in England now, than it was some years past.

Commerce and war transplant so many Franks into the East, that at Smyrna and Alexandria it has occasionally been asked whether hats or turbans were the ——— fashion.

Strong—Robust.

Strong is here the generic term; robust the specific. A *strong* man is able to bear a heavy burden. A *robust* man bears continual labour or fatigue with ease. There is in robust the idea of roughness or rudeness, which strong does not contain. A strong man may be active, nimble, and graceful. An excess of muscular development, together with a clumsiness of action, exclude these qualities from the robust man. Ploughmen and labourers are robust: soldiers and sailors are generally strong men.

[*Boling.* Strong as a tower in hope, I cry—amen!
Richard II., i. 3

O impotence of mind, in body strong!
But what is strength without a double share
Of wisdom? *Samson Agon.*, 52.

Alas! when evil men are strong
No life is good, no pleasure long
WORDSWORTH. '*Song at Brougham Castle.*

For one, who, though of drooping mien, had yet
From nature's kindliness received a frame
Robust as ever rural labour bred. '*The Excursion*,' vi.]

Exercise.

Having lived all his life in the country, and being habitually engaged in active occupations, he was in possession of ——— health, and its constant attendant, excellent spirits.

Though naturally of a ——— constitution, his frame was so shattered by the excessive fatigue and hardships he had undergone, that he fell into a bad state of health, from which he never afterwards recovered.

This news threw him into such a state of excitement, that it brought on a fit; and three ——— men could scarcely hold him down, or prevent him doing some injury to the bystanders.

We should never forget that though it is excellent to be ———, it is shameful to abuse our strength.

Sallust describes Catiline as a man of extraordinary powers, both of mind and body; able to bear heat and cold, fatigue and watching to an incredible degree, and displaying every sign of a ——— frame.

Those who are physically ——— are sometimes weak in mind.

"The huntsman, ever gay, ——— and bold,
Defies the noxious vapour."

"The weak, by thinking themselves ———, are induced to proclaim war against that which ruins them; and the ——— by affecting to be weak, are thereby rendered as useless as if they really were so."

Translucent—Transparent.

Whatever admits the light through it in such a way, as to enable us to clearly distinguish objects placed on the other side of it, is *transparent*. What merely admits the light, but does not enable us to distinguish objects through it, is *translucent*. Glass, water, ice, &c., are transparent substances. Ground glass, silver paper, horn, &c., are translucent su stances. What is transparent is also translucent; but wh is translucent is not always transparent.

[*King*. Through the transparent bosom of the deep
Love's Labour Lost, iv. :

——— and God made
The firmament, expanse of liquid, pure,
Transparent, elemental air ——— *P. L.*, vii. 265.

Under the glassy, cool, translucent wave. *Comus*, 861.

——— a brook
Hurled down a mountain-cove from stage to stage,
Yet tempering, for my sight, its bustling rage
In the soft heaven of a translucent pool.
WORDSWORTH. '*Eccles. Sonnets*'

——— while the morning air is yet
Transparent as the soul of innocent youth, p. 373.

I see the dark brown curls, the brow,
The smooth transparent skin,
Refined as with intent to show
The holiness within. '*Jewish Family*']

Exercise.

"A poet of another nation would not have dwelt so long upon the clearness and ———cy of the stream; but in Italy, one seldom sees a river that is extremely bright and limpid, most of them being muddy."

"The quarry has several other ——— stones, which want neither beauty nor esteem."

"Nor shines the silver moon one-half so bright,
Through the ——— bosom of the deep,
As doth thy face through tears of mine give light,
Thou shin'st in every tear that I do weep."

'——— forms, too fine for mortal sight,
Their fluid bodies half dissolved in light."

"Lumps of rock crystal heated redhot, then quenched in fair water, exchanged their ———cy for whiteness, the ignition and extinction having cracked each lump into a multitude of minute bodies."

"Each thought was visible that rolled within,
As through a crystal case the figured hours are seen,
And Heaven did this ——— veil provide,
Because she had no guilty thought to hide."

Weak—Infirm.

Weak is a generic term, and is opposed to strong: *infirm* is a species of weak. Weakness may proceed from various causes, and may exist at any period of life. Infirmity is the weakness of old age. Those who are infirm are weak; but those who are weak are not always infirm. We never hear of infirm children. The term weak, is applied to animate and inanimate things. Infirm, only to human beings. A sick man is too weak to walk; an old man is too infirm to stand.

[*Lear.* ——— here I stand, your slave
A poor, infirm, weak, and despised old man.
King Lear, iii. 2.

Kath. ——— What can be their business
With me, a poor weak woman, fallen from favour,
Henry VIII., iii. 1

Fallen cherub, to be weak is miserable,
Doing or suffering: *P. L.*, i. 157

Thy frailty and infirmer sex forgiven.
Id., x. 956.

Fame is the spur that the clear spirit doth raise,
(That last infirmity of noble mind)
To scorn delights and live laborious days.
'*Lycidas*,' 71

—Come hither in thy hour of strength;
Come, weak as is a breaking wave!
Here stretch thy body at full length;
Or build thy house upon this grave.
WORDSWORTH. '*A Poet's Epitaph*'

——— he shall gain
The clearest apprehension of those truths,
Which unassisted reason's utmost power
Is too infirm to reach. '*The Excursion*,' v.]

Exercise.

The younger brother had suffered a long and painful illness, and was so ——— from exhaustion and depletion, that it was doubtful for some time, whether he would ever recover his strength.

Though of great age, he is one of the most active men know; for, at a time of life when most men are ——— and ailing, he performs all the ordinary duties of life with the energy and vigour of youth.

"There can be little doubt that vice and luxury operate quite as strongly as any hereditary influence or physical debility, in making the mental faculties ——— and inefficient."

Every man must naturally look forward to a time when he will become old and ———, and should lay up in his youth a provision for that period of his life in which he will no longer be able to work.

The workmen had scarcely left the building, when the roof fell in with a loud crash; and on examining the ruins, it was discovered that the walls, being too ——— to support the weight of the roof, had consequently given way.

"At my age, and under my ———, I can have no relief but that which religion furnishes me."

Weighty—Heavy.

Every thing is *weighty*, since weight is the natural tendency which all bodies have to the centre of the earth. Those bodies which have much weight, either in proportion to their bulk, or the strength applied to them, are *heavy*. Heavy qualifies what cannot be easily lifted. A bag of gold is heavier than a bag of feathers of the same size, because gold has more weight than feathers. The nature of the substance causes its weight. The quantity of the substance causes its heaviness. A pound of feathers and a pound of gold have equal weight; but feathers and gold have not equal heaviness. In a moral sense, the same difference is perceptible. A weighty affair is one which is intrinsically important; a heavy charge is one difficult to be got rid of.

[*K. Hen.* There ye shall meet about this weighty business.
Henry VIII., ii. 2.
Cant. The poor mechanick porters crowding in
Their heavy burdens at his narrow gate.
Henry V., i. 2.
That burden heavier than the earth to bear;
Than all the world much heavier — *P. L.*, x. 835
——— that blessed mood,
In which the burthen of the mystery,
In which the heavy and the weary weight
Of all this unintelligible world
Is lightened — WORDSWORTH '*Tintern Abbey*']

Exercise.

" The finest works of invention are of very little ———, when put in the balance with what refines and exalts the rational mind."

" Mersennus tells us, that a little child, with an engine of a hundred double pulleys, might move this earth, though it were much ———er than it is."

" Reverend patriarch," answered the emperor, " do not deem that we think lightly of your ——— scruples, but the question is now, not in what manner we may convert these Latin heretics to the true faith, but how we may avoid being overrun by their myriads, which resemble those of the locusts by which their approach was preceded and intimated."

" The subject is concerning the ———ness of several bodies, or the proportion that is required betwixt any ——— and the power which may move it."

" Thus spoke to my lady the knight full of care,
' Let me have your advice in a ——— affair' "

Whole—Entire.

The parts of any object may be divided, but if they are not separated, that object may be called *whole.* Thus, if an orange be cut into several pieces, all the parts, taken together, will make up the *whole* orange. But if the orange be not cut, then it is *entire.* That is entire which has not been divided. That is whole which has suffered no diminution. (See *To separate* and *To divide*, p. 62.)

[*Ulys* One touch of nature makes the whole world kin —
Troil. and Cress. iii. 3
Oth. —— one entire and perfect chrysolite.
Othello, v. 2
——— that Serbonian bog
Betwixt Damiata and Mount Casius old
Where armies whole have sunk — *P. L.*, ii. 594

In cubic phalanx firm, advanced entire.
Id., vi. 399

Meantime the sovereignty of these fair Isles
Remains entire and indivisible. '*The Excursion*,' ix.

——— equally require
That the whole people should be taught and trained *Id.*]

Exercise.

"An action is ——— which is complete in all its parts; or, as Aristotle describes it, when it has a beginning, a middle, and an end."

"Looking down, he saw
The ——— world filled with violence, and all flesh
Corrupting each their way."
"And all so forming an harmonious ———."

"Thus his ——— conduct was made up of artifice and deceit."

"The ——— conquest of the passions is so difficult a work, that they who despair of it should think of a less difficult task, and only attempt to regulate them."

"And feeling that no human being is ———ly good, or ———ly base, we learn that true knowledge of mankind which induces us to expect little and forgive much."

"A ruined chapel, flanked by a solemn grove, still reared its front ———."

"There was a time, when Ætna's silent fire
Slept unperceived, the mountain yet ———;
When conscious of no danger from below,
She tower'd a cloud-capped pyramid of snow."

His boots are the only thing splendid in his ——— costume.

"How my adventures will conclude, I leave ———ly to Providence; if comically, you shall hear of them."

On—Upon.

In speaking of objects of sense, we say that one thing is *on* another when the former is in contact with the upper surface of the latter. The preposition *upon* is often used synonymously with *on;* though it would be more correct to employ it only when the lower substance of the two is raised considerably from the floor or earth. According to this distinction, we speak of an object lying *on* the floor, but we place something *upon* a shelf. So also, a pigeon perched upon a house may fly down and light on the ground. A boy hangs his hat upon a peg, and throws his ball on the floor.

In a secondary sense, *upon* shews a closer connection than *on*. "Upon the receipt of this letter, he gave orders, &c. (immediately.") "On the death of the king, &c. (*i. e.* in consequence of,) the prince succeeded to all his dominions and titles."

[*Post.* ——— As I slept, methought
Great Jupiter, upon his eagle back,
Appeared to me, with other spritely shows
Of mine own kindred ; when I waked, I found
This label on my bosom. *Cymbeline*, v. 5.

Tita. ——in the spiced Indian air, by night
Full often hath she gossiped by my side ;
And sat with me on Neptune's yellow sands
Marking the embarked traders on the flood.
Midsummer-Night's Dream, ii 2

Paul. ——— A thousand knees
Ten thousand years together, naked, fasting,
Upon a barren mountain, and still winter
In storm perpetual, could not move the gods
To look that way thou wert. *Winter's Tale*, iii. 2

——— As when heaven's fire
Hath scathed the forest oaks or mountain pines,
With singed top their stately growth, though bare
Stands on the blasted heath. *P. L.*, i. 615.

——— for God had thrown
That mountain as his garden mould, high raised
Upon the rapid current — *Id.*, ii. 227.

As the mute swan that floats adown the stream,
Or, on the waters of the unruffled lake,
Anchors her placid beauty. *The Excursion*, vi

And, like the water-lily, lives and thrives,
Whose root is fixed in stable earth, whose head
Floats on the tossing waves. *Id.* v.

Loud is the Vale ;—this inland Depth
In peace is roaring like the Sea ;
Yon star upon the mountain-top
Is listening quietly. '*Elegiac Lines*.']

Exercise.

The door of the cage being left open, the bird flew out, and after making several turns in the air, perched ——— the top of a high tree, where it remained seated all the afternoon.

Immediately ——— the receipt of this news, orders were given to prepare every thing for an invasion.

Nothing was seen ——— all sides but the most abject misery and destitution.

He was so weak, that he could proceed no further; and being suddenly seized with a dizziness, fell ——— the ground before any one could hasten to his relief.

The boy placed his toys ——— the top of a high wall, where none of his companions could reach them.

"As I did stand my watch ——— the hill
I looked towards Birnam, and anon methought
The wood began to move."
"——— me, ——— me, let all thy fury fall."

SECTION II.

ACTIVE AND PASSIVE SYNONYMES.

THE synonymes ranged under this division are distinguished from each other by the active and passive qualities which they respectively contain. It must be understood that the terms *active* and *passive* are not here taken in a grammatical sense. There are many verbs, nouns, and adjectives, which, wholly independently of their grammatical nature, contain in the very ideas they represent either an active or a passive quality. The difference between the two adjectives *contented* and *satisfied* may be referred to this principle. The former qualifies one who has restrained his mind or desires within a certain limit. Here, there is evidently an action from within. On the other hand, the word *satisfied* refers to some one who is in a recipient or passive state. The contented man has acted upon his own mind. The satisfied man has been acted upon by others. In some cases, we even find the active and passive principle existing, under different circumstances, in the same word. Of this, the word *fearful* will furnish a curious example. When it signifies "inspiring fear," it is used in its active—when it means "filled with fear," it is used in its passive sense. A fearful man may mean, either one who makes others afraid, or one who is himself afraid. The difference in many hundred pairs of words may be determined by the application of this principle; the same idea being found in both words; but the one possessing it in an active, and the other in a passive or recipient state.

Ability—Capacity.

Capacity is the power of receiving and retaining knowledge with facility ; *ability* is the power of applying knowledge to practical purposes. Both these faculties are requisite to form a great character ; capacity to conceive, and ability to execute designs. Capacity is shewn in quickness of apprehension. Ability supposes something done ; something by which the mental power is exercised in executing or performing what has been perceived by the capacity.

[*Iago.* And though it be fit that Cassio have his place
(For, sure, he fills it up with great ability.
Othello, iii. 3.

Bru. ——— holding them
In human action and capacity
Of no more soul, nor fitness for the world
Than camels in their war. *Coriolanus*, ii. 1.

If aught in my ability may serve
To lighten what thou suffer'st. *Samson Agon.*, 743.

Capacity not raised to apprehend
Or value what is best. *Id.*, 1028.

The liberal donor of capacities
More than heroic — *The Excursion*, vii.]

Exercise.

Those who are once convinced that they have ———, should instantly act upon that conviction, and do something worthy of themselves.

It is never necessary to explain a difficulty twice to a pupil of good ———.

Few persons exert their ——— to the utmost, or do all the good that lies in their power.

"*Whatever man has done, man may do*," is a saying expressive of the confidence a man should place in his own ———.

The rules and exercises in the book which I lent you are so clearly and accurately explained, that they are intelligible to the lowest ———.

The courage of the soldier and the ——— and prudence of the general are required to extricate an army from a dangerous position.

The object is too big for our ——— when we would comprehend the circumference of a world.

"Though a man has not the ——— to distinguish himself in the most shining parts of a great character, he has certainly the ——— of being just, faithful, modest, and temperate."

"I look upon an ——— statesman out of business like a huge whale, that will endeavour to overturn the ship, unless he has an empty cask to play with."

Aversion—Antipathy.

Aversion is a turning-from; *antipathy* is a feeling-against. An antipathy is not so strong as an aversion. The former is a state of feeling; the latter is a mental act. There is more of reason in aversion, and more of impulse in antipathy. It is something in our own nature which causes our aversion. It is something in the nature of others which produces our antipathy. Antipathy is opposed to sympathy; aversion is opposed to inclination. Many persons feel antipathies to worms, mice, insects, &c. The idle have an aversion from work. We should endeavour to overcome antipathies, and resist aversions.

[*Kent.* No contraries hold more antipathy.
King Lear, ii. 2.

What if with like aversion I reject
Riches and realms? *P. R.*, ii. 457

——— but Discord first,
Daughter of Sin, among the irrational
Death introduced, through fierce antipathy.
P. L., x. 709.]

Exercise.

There is a natural and necessary ——— between good and bad, in the same way as we may imagine the same to exist between any two directly contrary qualities.

They took great pleasure in compounding lawsuits among their neighbours, for which they were the ——— of the gentlemen of the long robe.

There are some persons for whom we entertain an ——— without being able to give any reason for our dislike; we may suppose, as some bodies have naturally a greater affinity for each other, and others a repelling principle within them which prevents their coming together, that the same principle operates on the minds and affections of men.

When a man indulges in solitude to such a degree as to feel a positive ——— from mixing in society, he may depend upon it that his mind is not in a very healthy state.

"To this perhaps might be justly attributed most of the sympathies and ——— observable in men."

"I cannot forbear mentioning a tribe of egotists, for whom I have always had a mortal ———; I mean the authors of memoirs who are never mentioned in any works but their own."

"There is one species of terror which those who are unwilling to suffer the reproach of cowardice have wisely dignified with the name of ——— A man has indeed no dread of harm from an insect or a worm, but his ——— turns him pale whenever they approach him."

Approval—Approbation.

Approbation is the state or feeling of approving. *Approval* is the act of approving. Our approval is expressed positively; our approbation is not necessarily made known. Approbation is taken in a passive sense; approval in an active signification. A virtuous conduct will insure the approbation of all good men. Tradesmen often send articles to their customers on approval. We may be anxious for the approbation of our friends; but we should be still more anxious for the approval of our own conscience.

[*K. Hen.* ——— how many, now in health,
Shall drop their blood in approbation
Of what your reverence shall incite us to.
Henry V., i. 2.

This is true glory and renown; when God,
Looking on earth, with approbation marks
The just man —— *P. R.*, iii. 61

And now, in preference to the mightiest names,
To Thee the exterminating sword is given.
Dread mark of approbation justly gained!
Exalted office, worthily sustained!
WORDSWORTH. '*Thanksgiving Ode.*']

Exercise.

"Precept gains only the cold ——— of reason, and compels an assent which judgment frequently yields with reluctance even when delay is impossible."

"There is a censor of justice and manners, without whose ——— no capital sentences are to be executed."

"The bare ——— of the worth and goodness of a thing is not properly the willing of that thing; yet men do very commonly account it so."

It is certain that at the first you were all of my opinion, and that I did nothing without your ———.

"He who is anxious to obtain universal ——— will learn a good lesson from the fable of the old man and his ass."

The work has been examined by several excellent judges, who have expressed their unqualified ——— of its plan and execution: it will, therefore, be published without delay.

"There is no positive law of men, whether received by formal consent, as in councils, or by secret ———, as in customs, but may be taken away."

"There is as much difference between the ——— of the judgment, and the actual volitions of the will, with regard to the same object, as there is between a man's viewing a desirable thing with his eye and reaching after it with his hand."

Burden—Load.

Whatever we bear is a *burden;* that which is laid upon us is a *load.* A load may be more than we can bear: a burden is troublesome to bear. In the case of the burden, we act, for a burden does not prevent, but impedes action. In the case of the load, we are acted upon, for a load may take away our power of acting. We sink under a load. We are uncomfortable under a burden. Both the load and the burden oppress us, but not in an equal degree. An evil conscience is a burden; a load of guilt overwhelms the wicked.

[*Wol.* ——— from these shoulders,
These ruined pillars, out of pity, taken
A load would sink a navy, too much honour:
O 'tis a burden, Cromwell, 'tis a burden
Too heavy for a man that hopes for heaven.
Henry VIII., iii. 2

——— strive
In offices of love how we may lighten
Each other's burden, in our share of woe.
P. L., x. 961.

For other things mild Heaven a time ordains,
And disapproves that care, though wise in show,
That with superfluous burden loads the day
And, when God sends a cheerful hour, refrains.
MILTON. '*Sonnets.*'

Meekly thou didst resign this earthly load
Of death, called life. —— *Id.*

——— while in your pride ye contemplate
Your talents, power or wisdom, deem him not
A burthen of the earth.
WORDSWORTH. '*The Cumberland Beggar.*

See, where his difficult way that old man wins,
Bent by a load of mulberry leaves! ———
'*Memorials of Tour in Italy.*']

Exercise.

I am sure, you that know my laziness and extreme indifference on this subject will pity me, entangled in all these ceremonies, which are a wonderful ——— to me.

"I understood not that a grateful mind
By owing, owes not, but still pays, at once
Indebted and discharged: what ——— then?"

The poor horse appeared to move forward with extreme difficulty, and after having performed about half the journey, sank to the ground utterly overwhelmed with the weight of the ——— he had to drag.

He had too much spirit, however, to become a ——— to his friends, and immediately determined to qualify himself for some office which would enable him to earn his livelihood and be independent of others' assistance.

"Let India boast her groves, nor envy we
The weeping amber and the balmy tree,
While by our oaks the precious ——— are borne,
And realms commanded which these trees adorn."

The idle cannot be happy; they are a ——— to themselves and others.

"None of the things they are to learn should ever be made a ——— to them, or imposed on them as a task."

Chief—Head.

Chief has an active meaning. *Head* is used in a passive sense. Head is a natural distinction; chief is an acquired distinction. Chief is the principal actor, head is the principal person. The chief of a tribe; the head of a family. A chief magistrate, a commander-in-chief. The head of a profession, the head of the church.

[*Men.* ——— my friends
(Of w om he's chief) *Coriolanus*, v. 2.

Dau. Of what a monarchy you are the head. *Henry V.*, ii. 4.

O prince, O chief of many throned powers,
That led the imbatteled seraphim to war *P. L.*, i. 128.

Forthwith from every squadron and each band
The heads and leaders thither haste. *Id.*, 358.

——— Less vivid wreath entwined
Nemæan victor's brow; less bright was worn,
Meed of some Roman chief—in triumph borne
With captives chained ——— WORDSWORTH, p. 349.]

Exercise

"No ——— like thee, Menestheus, Greece could yield
To marshal armies in the dusty field."

"The ———s of the ——— sects of philosophy, as Thales, Anaxagoras, and Pythagoras, did consent to this tradition."

"A prudent ——— not always must display
His powers in equal ranks and fair array,
But with th' occasion and the place comply,
Conceal his force, nay, sometimes seem to fly."

"Your ——— I him appoint,
And by myself have sworn, to him shall bow
All knees in Heaven, and shall confess him Lord."

As three weeks had now elapsed without the arrival of the expected reinforcement, the ——— met together to consult upon what was best to be done in this emergency.

She was a woman of such uncommon talent and singular prudence, that at the age of nineteen, she was already judged fit to be the ——— of a large establishment.

"Waverley pursued his course silently in the same direction, determined to let the ——— take his own time in recovering the good-humour which he had so unreasonably discarded, and firm in his resolution not to bate him an inch of dignity."

"The queen is acknowledged as the ——— of the church of England."

"As each is more able to distinguish himself as ——— of a party, he will less readily be made a follower or associate."

Consent—Assent.

Assent is given to a wish or an opinion; *consent*, to an act The former word is applied to abstract ideas; the latter, to actions. We say properly—It was with great difficulty that his consent to the marriage was gained. When we say, he nodded assent, it signifies that he expressed that his opinion or wish was in accordance with that of another person. We may consent to what does not please us, but we cannot assent to what we do not believe. We refuse what we do not consent to do; we deny what we do not assent to. Consent is used in an active, assent in a passive sense.

[*Apoth.* My poverty, but not my will consents.
Romeo and Juliet, v. 1.

Sur. ——— without the king's assent, or knowledge,
You wrought to be a legate: *King Henry VIII.*, iii 2

Hear what assaults I had, what snares besides,
What sieges girt me round, ere I consented.
S. A., 846.

——— with full assent
They vote —— *P. L.*, ii. 388

——— these inward chains,
Fixed in his soul, so early and so deep;
Without his own consent or knowledge fixed!
'*The Excursion*,' viii.

——— the thoughts
That in assent or opposition, rose
Within his mind —— *Id.*]

Exercise.

He declared that he would never ——— to such pernicious principles.

We never could gain his ——— to join our party.

He entirely ——— to the truth of the proposition.

Charles I., in his last moments, was filled with remorse for having ——— to the execution of the Earl of Strafford.

"O no! our reason was not vainly lent,
Nor is a slave by its own ———!"

In this situation of affairs, the king found himself obliged to accede to the wishes of the nation which were so unequivocally expressed; he therefore gave his ——— to the bill, and thus secured his power, if not durably, at least for some years longer.

King Edward ——— to spare the town of Calais, on condition that six of its principal citizens should be delivered over to him.

"All the arguments on both sides must be laid in the balance, and, upon the whole, the understanding determine its ———."

Cultivation—Culture.

Cultivation denotes the act of cultivating: culture, the state of being cultivated. *Culture* applies to the soil: *cultivation*, to what grows in it. The culture of the earth; the cultivation of corn. Metaphorically, the same distinction exists. We speak of the culture of the intellect; and of the cultivation of any one of its powers, as the taste, memory, &c. The object of culture is to cause production: thus the culture of the mind is attended to in early years, in order to prepare the soil to bear fruit. The object of cultivation is to improve and perfect: thus, we direct our attention to the cultivation of those arts or sciences in which we wish to excel. Cultivation is sometimes used to represent the state of being cultivated, as well as the act of cultivating.

[——— on the mountain-top
Or in the cultured field —— '*The Excursion*,' iv]

Exercise.

Those excellent seeds implanted at an early age will by ——— be most flourishing in production.

"If vain our toil,
We ought to blame the ———, not the soil."

"The plough was not invented till after the Deluge; the earth requiring little or no ———, but yielding its increase freely, and without labour or toil."

There is no duty more incumbent upon us than the ——— of our tastes · by this we shall never be at a loss for occupation, and consequently less liable than others to fall into temptations.

The state of ——— among this rude people was so imperfect, that it was with difficulty they could afford subsistence to their new guests.

In many of the West-India islands the soil is naturally so rich, and requires so little ———, that it produces many plants and vegetables almost spontaneously

The tea-plant has never been ——— successfully out of China

Deity—Divinity.

Deity signifies the person; *Divinity*, the essence or nature of God. Deity regards God as an agent; divinity is an attribute of God. When we speak of the deities of the Grecian mythology, we mean the persons of their gods. The divinity of Christ signifies the divine nature of Christ. We speak of the wisdom, power, and goodness of the Deity; not of the divinity.

[*Com.* ——— he leads them like a thing
Made by some other deity than nature. *Coriolanus*, iv. 6.
Ham. There's a divinity that shapes our ends
Rough-hew them how we will. *Hamlet*, v. 2.
By prayer the offended Deity to appease *P. L.*, xi. 149.
——— and fancy that they feel
Divinity within them breeding wings. *Id.*, ix. 1010.
——— empowers him to perceive
The voice of Deity, on height and plain,
Whispering those truths in stillness, which the WORD
To the four quarters of the winds, proclaims.
'*The Excursion*,' v
——— the tempestuous sea
Of Ignorance, that ran so rough and high,
And heeded not the voice of clashing swords,
These good men humble by a few bare words,
And calm with fear of God's divinity. '*Ecclesias. Sonnets*.']

Exercise.

The habitual contemplation and study of the works of Nature are well formed to increase our veneration for the ———.

The temples of the Greeks took their names from the ——— to whose honor they were erected; some were dedicated to the worship of one ———, others to that of many

The —— who presided over agriculture were the daughters of Cecrops who are called the earliest priestesses of Pallas.

The word *oracle* was used by the ancients to designate not only the revelations made by the —— to man; but also, the place in which such revelations were made.

The Scriptures were written by the inspiration of the ——.

Among the ancient Romans, the sources of rivers were sacred to some ——, and cultivated with religious ceremonies.

Before proceeding any further, he offered a sacrifice to the —— of the fountain.

Whatever occurred to those who were sacrificing, and in doubt what to say, was supposed to be suggested by some ——.

"Will you suffer a temple, how poorly built soever, but yet a temple of your ——, to be razed?"

"But first she cast about to change her shape, for fear the —— of her countenance might dazzle his mortal sight, and overcharge the rest of his senses."

Example—Instance.

An *example* is a thing or person. An *instance* is something done. The former has an active, the latter a passive sense. An example practically illustrates a rule; the object of an example is to instruct. An instance is a case in which something is represented as done; the object of an instance is to illustrate. Men are examples of virtue or vice; the actions of men are instances of virtue or vice. An example is held up for imitation or avoidance; an instance is related in order to shew us why we should imitate or avoid. An example incites us to act; an instance excites us to reflect.

[*Ham.* —— Examples, gross as earth, exhort me.
Hamlet, iv. 4.

Jaq. Full of wise saws and modern instances
As You Like It, ii. 7

—— the only son of light
In a dark age, against example good. *P. L.*, xi. 809

Let no mean hope your souls enslave;
Be independent, generous, brave;
Your Father such example gave,
And such revere;
But be admonished by his grave,
And think and fear! WORDSWORTH. '*To the Sons of Burns.*'

—— as we stand on holy earth,
And have the dead around us, take from them
Your instances. '*The Excursion*,' v.]

Exercise.

He conducts himself in every respect so properly, that he is an ——— to all the other boys in the school.

I am acquainted with many ———s of his kindness and generosity not only to his relations and friends, but also to all those whom he may know to stand in need of his assistance.

Demosthenes is commonly cited as an ——— of the most determined perseverance the world ever beheld; he surmounted every natural obstacle by his undaunted resolution, and finished by becoming the most renowned orator that ever existed in any age or country.

Innumerable ——— are related of his perseverance; among others, the accounts of his repeating his verses by the seashore, his reciting with pebbles in his mouth, his shutting himself in his room and studying a whole month at a time, &c., &c.

If we wish others to be good, we should set them an ——— by doing well ourselves; for we may be sure that what we do will have a much more lasting effect on others than what we say.

"Are sculpture and poetry thus debased," he cried, "to perpetuate the memory of a man whose best advantage is to be forgotten; whose no one action merits record, but as an ——— to be shunned?"

Facility—Ease.

Ease denotes the state of a person or thing. *Facility* refers to the doing of a thing. It is something real or apparent in the nature of the thing which causes it to be done with ease. Facility is a power belonging to the agent, and regards the peculiar skill of him who performs. A practised hand performs with facility. An easy task may be accomplished with facility. We now see why a man is said to live at his *ease*, and not at his *facility*.

[*Iago.* Why, he drinks you, with facility, your Dane dead drunk.
Othello, ii. 3.

Mira. ——— and I should do it,
With much more ease; for my good will is to it,
And yours against. *Tempest*, iii. 1

——— and winds with ease
Through the pure marble air his oblique way
Amongst innumerable stars. ——— *P. L*, iii. 563]

Exercise.

"——— is the utmost that can be hoped from a sedentary and indolent habit."

"Every one must have remarked the ——— with which the kindness of others is sometimes gained by those to whom he never could have imparted his own."

"True ——— in writing comes from art, not chance,
As those move easiest who have learnt to dance."

"Nothing is more subject to mistake and disappointment, than anticipated judgment concerning the ——— or difficulty of any undertaking"

"They who have studied, have not only learned many excellent things, but also have acquired a great ——— of profiting themselves, by reading good authors."

Every thing appeared ——— to him; and, by dint of continued practice, he acquired a wonderful ——— of execution.

From this time forward, he lived at his ———, as he was thus freed from the necessity of providing for his daily bread.

"The ——— which we acquire of doing things by habit makes them often pass in us without our notice."

"Nobody is under an obligation to know every thing; knowledge and science, in general, is the business only of those who are at ——— and leisure."

Faith—Belief.

Belief exists; *faith* acts. Belief is a passive faith, and faith is an active belief. It has been said that "*faith will remove mountains.*" We could not here substitute the word belief for faith, because belief is merely the passive quality. Faith impels us to action, and is grounded on our belief.

[*Sal.* A voluntary zeal, and unurged faith.
King John, v. 2.

Bra. Belief of it oppresses me already. *Othello*, i. 1.

——— with what faith
He leaves his gods, his friends, and native soil.
P. L., xii. 128

Yet hope would fain subscribe, and tempts belief.
S. A., 1535.

——— acquiescence in the Will supreme
For time and for eternity; by faith,
Faith absolute in God, including hope,
And the defence that lies in boundless love
Of his perfections ——— '*The Excursion*,' iv

One solace yet remains for us who came
Into this world in days when story lacked
Severe research, that in our hearts we know
How, for exciting youth's heroic flame,
Assent is power, belief the soul of fact. '*Memorials of Tour in Italy.*']

10*

Exercise.

"No man can attain ——— by the bare contemplation of heaven and earth; for that they neither are sufficient to give us as much as the least spark of light concerning the very principal mysteries of our ———."

"——— builds a bridge across the gulf of death,
To break the shock blind nature cannot shun,
And lands thought smoothly on the farther shore."

"The Epicureans contented themselves with a denial of Providence, asserting, at the same time, the existence of gods in general, because they would not shock the common ——— of mankind."

"There ——— shall fail, and holy hope shall die,
One lost in certainty, and one in joy."

"Supposing all the great points of atheism were formed into a kind of creed, I would fain ask whether it would not require an infinitely greater measure of ———, than any set of articles which they so violently oppose?"

"I reject all sectarian intolerance—I affect no uncharitable jargon; frankly, I confess, that I have known many, before whose virtues I bow down ashamed of my own errors, though they were not guided and supported by ———."

"Felix heard Paul concerning the ———."

Falsehood—Falsity.

Between falsity and falsehood there is this difference—that *falsity* is passive, and *falsehood* active falseness. Some men practise falsehood; but we cannot say that they practise falsity, since this latter word is the state or quality of being false; not the act of doing falsely. "Probability does not make any alteration, either in the truth or falsity of things." Falsity is always used as the abstract false; falsehood is used in both senses; as the abstract false, and as a false assertion. When the falsity of an assertion is made evident, it is proved to be a falsehood.

[*Cym.* Winnow the truth from falsehood —— *Cymbeline*, v 5.

——— for no falsehood can endure
Touch of celestial temper ——— *P. L.*, iv. 811

By falsities and lies the greatest part
Of mankind they corrupted to forsake
God their creator ——— *Id.*, i. 367.]

Exercise.

"All deception in the course of life is, indeed, nothing else but a lie reduced to practice, and ——— passing from words to things."

The ——— of his pretensions was, however, discovered, and universally admitted, so that he soon lost all his followers, and was obliged to quit the country.

"Many temptations to ——— will occur in the disguise of passions, too specious to fear much resistance."

"Neither are they able to break through those errors, wherein they are so determinately settled, that they pay unto ——— the whole sum of whatsoever love is due unto God's truth."

"Artificer of fraud; he was the first
That practised ——— under saintly show."

It must not be forgotten that these are not arguments, but mere assertions; and we can hardly be expected to believe them till their truth or ——— be tested.

Travellers, from a love of exaggeration, frequently introduce ——— into their narratives.

Force—Strength.

Strength expresses the quality of being strong. *Force* is active: it is strength exerted. An argument has the same strength, whether it be employed or not; but it has no force unless it be applied. Force, in fact, is strength put in action. A man collects his strength, to strike with force. We speak of the strength of a wall or tower, and of the force of water or stream. Strength resists attacks; force puts the invaders to flight.

[*Bast.* Against whose fury and unmatched force
The awless lion could not wage the fight. *King John*, i. 1.

Isab. ——— O, it is excellent
To have a giant's strength; but it is tyrannous
To use it like a giant. *Meas. for Meas.*, ii. 2.

——— like Alcestis, from the grave,
Whom Jove's great son to her glad husband gave,
Rescued from death by force ——— MILTON. '*Sonnets*

——— she has a hidden strength
Which you remember not.
Sec. Bro. What hidden strength
Unless the strength of Heaven, if you mean that.
Comus, 415.

O joyless power that stands by lawless force!
WORDSWORTH. '*Sonnets to Liberty.*'

——— Winds blow and waters roll,
Strength to the brave, and Power, and Deity;
Yet in themselves are nothing ——. *Id.*]

Exercise.

Feats of ——— or agility excite our wonder and surprise, but they seldom raise in us any great degree of admiration.

The lightning struck the oak with such ———, that all the branches on one side of it were stripped off, and a deep mark left in the bark from the top to the bottom of the tree.

The Grecian mythologists represent Atlas as a man of such immense ———, that he could bear the world on his shoulders.

While endeavouring to reach the shore, one of the rowers pulled the oar with such ———, that it suddenly snapped asunder, and the party were consequently delayed an hour.

Nothing can resist the ——— of truth; the most wicked and abandoned acknowledge her power, and are confounded by her steady gaze.

The pier had not sufficient ——— to withstand the ——— of the waves, and in the morning the whole structure was a miserable wreck.

He attacked the enemy's entrenchments with such ———, that they were taken, and the camp abandoned in less than half an hour.

"No definitions, no suppositions of any sect, are of ——— enough to destroy constant experience."

Forgetfulness—Oblivion.

These two words will fall under the class of active and passive. *Forgetfulness* refers to persons; *oblivion*, to things. We cannot speak of things buried in forgetfulness, nor can we allude to the oblivion of men. The former is an act of the mind—the latter, a state of things. Oblivion refers to things forgotten; forgetfulness, to those who forget them Persons are forgetful; things are lost in oblivion.

[*Buck.* ——— the swallowing gulf
Of dark forgetfulness and deep oblivion. *Richard III.*, iii. 7

Cor. ——— That we have been familiar,
Ingrate forgetfulness shall poison, rather
Than pity note how much ——. *Coriolanus*, v. 2.

Duke. A forted residence, 'gainst the tooth of time
And razure of oblivion ———. *Meas. for Meas.* v. 1

——— with one small drop to lose
In sweet forgetfulness all pain and woe. *P L.*, ii. 608.

Nameless in dark oblivion let them dwell. *Id.*, vi. 380.

Our birth is but a sleep and a forgetting:
The soul that rises with us, our life's star,
Hath had elsewhere its setting,
And cometh from afar;
Not in entire forgetfulness,
And not in utter nakedness,
But trailing clouds of glory do we come
From God, who is our home. WORDSWORTH. '*Ode, &c.*']

Exercise.

"I have read in ancient authors invitations to lay aside care and anxiety, and give a loose to that pleasing ——— wherein men put off their characters of business."

"Thou shouldst have heard many things of worthy memory, which shall now die in ———, and thou return unexperienced to thy grave."

"O gentle sleep!
Nature's soft nurse, how have I frighted thee,
That thou no more wilt weigh my eyelids down,
And steep my senses in ———!"

"By the act of ———, all offences against the crown, and all particular trespasses between subject and subject, were pardoned, remitted, and utterly extinguished."

"Have you not love enough to bear with me,
When that rash humour which my mother gave me
Makes me ———?"

"Water-drops have worn the stones of Troy,
And blind ——— swallowed cities up,
And mighty states, characterless, are grated
To dusty nothing."

"The debt immense of endless gratitude,
So burdensome, still paying, still to owe
——— what from him I still received."

Grief—Affliction.

Grief signifies the heaviness of heart which is caused by calamity or misfortune. *Affliction* signifies a prostration of the feelings, and is the strongest term we have to express the sufferings of the heart. Grief is generally loud in expression, and shews itself by violent gestures, such as wringing the hands, beating the breast, &c. Affliction is the sadness of silence. Grief requires to be soothed; affliction, to be comforted. Grief complains, affliction suffers. We raise up the afflicted; we pacify grief; hence grief is an active, and affliction a passive quality,

[*Const.* Grief fills the room up of my absent child,
Lies in his bed, walks up and down with me;
Puts on his pretty looks, repeats his words,
Remembers me of all his gracious parts,
Stuffs out his vacant garments with his form;
Then, have I reason to be fond of grief. *King John*, iii. 4.
Oth. Had it pleased Heaven
To try me with affliction —— *Othello*, iv 2.
——— for grief and spite,
Cast herself headlong from the Ismenian steep.
P. R., iv. 574
Which is my chief affliction, shame, and sorrow.
S. A., 457.
No more shall grief of mine the season wrong:
WORDSWORTH '*Ode Intim Immor*
——— Blest are they
Whose sorrow rather is to suffer wrong
Than to do wrong, albeit themselves have erred.
This tale gives proof that Heaven most gently deals
With such in their affliction. —— *The Excursion*, vii.]

Exercise.

——— caused by the death of her only son had so worked upon the poor widow's feelings, that in a few weeks she was reduced almost to a skeleton

In addition to her other misfortunes, the old woman had now become quite blind; she bore this new ———, however, with the greatest fortitude, and soon resumed her wonted cheerfulness of manner.

On receiving this sad news, he burst out into exclamations of the most passionate ———, declaring that he had now nothing to live for, and that there was no more happiness for him in this world.

I endeavoured to soothe his ———; and, after some time, succeeded in satisfying him of the necessity of submitting to the ———.

In all our ———, the reflection that there is a compensating power, which will make up for every partial evil, must be an unfailing source of consolation.

——— and ——— are the common lot of mankind.

"The mother was so ——— at the loss of a fine boy who was her only son, that she died for ——— of it."

"Where shall we find the man that bears ———,
Great and majestic in his ——— like Cato?"

"Some virtues are only seen in ——— and some in prosperity"

Hatred—Odium.

Hatred is an active feeling. *Odium* is the feeling in a passive state. We do hatred, but we suffer odium. Odium is the feeling as respects those who are hated; hatred is the feeling as concerns those who hate. A tyrant incurs the hatred of all good men, and by his actions brings upon himself the public odium. The odium of an offence will sometimes fall upon the innocent. He persecuted his victim with unrelenting hatred.

> [*Nor.* What his high hatred could effect, wants not
> A minister in his power. *Henry VIII.*, i 1.
>
> Busiris and his Memphian chivalry
> While with perfidious hatred they pursued
> The sojourners of Goshen. *P. L.*, i. 308.
>
> ——— vowing that the stream should bear
> That name through every age, her hatred to declare.
> WORDSWORTH. '*Artegal and Elidure.*']

Exercise.

"——— is the passion of defiance; and there is a kind of hostility included in its very essence; but then, if there could have been ——— in the world when there was scarcely any thing ———, it would have acted within the compass of its proper object."

The king incurred all the ——— which should have fallen on the projectors or inventors of all these unpopular measures.

The slightest and most innocent occasions often produce ———, and propagate quarrels in the world.

Religious wars have always been characterized by the ——— and ruthless cruelty with which they have been carried on.

Notwithstanding all the services he had rendered his country, Miltiades incurred the ——— of his fellow-citizens, and fell a victim to the jealousy of his countrymen.

Henry VII. was personally brave, but he was a lover of peace: but the great blemish of his character was avarice; and on all occasions he evinced an implacable ——— to the house of York.

"Retain no malice nor ——— against any; be ready to do them all the kindness you are able."

"The ——— and offences which some men's rigour and remissness had contracted upon my government, I was resolved to have expiated."

Inclination—Disposition.

A *disposition* is that state of mind which may be easily turned towards some particular object. An *inclination* is a positive tendency towards an object. Disposition regards the whole frame of mind; inclination has reference to single acts.

A disposition for study expresses merely a passive state, which exhibits natural capacity for it; an inclination for study expresses a leaning of the mind, or ability for it. I am disposed to do that to which I have no objection. I am inclined to do what I have a wish for. On solemn occasions, the mind is disposed to be grave and serious. The sight of what is absurd raises in us an inclination to laughter. Dispositions are cherished or overcome; inclinations are yielded to or repressed.

[*Oli.* ——— for 'tis
The royal disposition of that beast
To prey on nothing that doth seem as dead.
As You Like It, iv. 3.

King. ——— Pray can I not,
Though inclination be as sharp as will.
Hamlet, iii. 3.

Go whither fate and inclination strong
Leads thee. *P. L.*, x. 265.

The gracious inclination, the just rule,
Kind wishes, and good actions, and pure thoughts.
The Excursion, ix.

——— constant disposition of his thoughts
To sympathy with man. *Id.*, i.]

Exercise.

Julius Cæsar is said to have been a man of most amiable ———; his first care, after gaining a victory, was to spare the vanquished, and on all occasions he shewed more ——— to mercy than severity.

One of the most essential points in forming a good ——— is to repress every ——— to satire and vanity.

On beholding so ludicrous a scene, it was with the greatest difficulty that I could check my ——— to laughter.

Henry VIII. was never known to sacrifice ——— to the interest or happiness of another.

Towards the latter part of Charles the Second's reign, the indolent ——— of the king threw the direction of affairs very much into the hands of his brother, the Duke of York.

"The love we bear to our friends is generally caused by our finding the same ——— in them which we feel in ourselves."

Intellect—Understanding.

The *understanding* is the faculty by which all who are not idiots perceive evident truths. The *intellect* is the understanding in a state of action, and is engaged in the discovery of abstract and hidden truths. Children have understandings; men have intellect. It requires but a common understanding to perceive the truth of such a proposition as: "The fire burns," or "the fields are green." It requires an operation of the intellect to perceive the truth of the proposition: "Every triangle contains two right angles." Understanding is a passive word; it simply admits or perceives truth. The intellect is active, it does something—works—invents—discovers. Newton's intellect, not his understanding, led to his discovery of gravitation.

[*Queen.* ——— Hath Bolingbroke
Deposed thine intellect? *Rich. II.*, v. 1.

King. An understanding simple and unschooled.
Hamlet, i. 2.

All heart they live, all head, all eye, all ear,
All intellect, all sense — *P. L.*, vi. 351.

——— while we can preserve
Unhurt our minds and understanding sound.
Id., 444.

A few strong instincts and a few plain rules,
Among the herdsmen of the Alps, have wrought
More for mankind at this unhappy day
Than all the pride of intellect and thought!
WORDSWORTH. '*Sonnets to Liberty.*']

Exercise.

Among the various powers of the ———, there is none which has been so attentively examined by philosophers, or concerning which so many facts and observations have been collected, as the faculty of memory.

An inquiry into the philosophy of the mind is one of the noblest and most interesting pursuits in which the human ——— can be engaged.

Some studies require but a common ———, but there are others which demand a very laborious and continued exertion of the ———.

Those who have a clear ——— have no difficulty in perceiving truths which are laid before them; those who are endowed with a strong ——— have the power of discovering truths without the help of others.

"By ——— I mean that faculty by which we are enabled to apprehend the objects of knowledge, general, as well as particular."

"There was a select set, supposed to be distinguished by superiority of ———, who always passed the evening together."

Pretence—Pretext.

Both pretexts and pretences deceive us: the former, as to facts; the latter, as to consequences. A *pretext* conceals the motive, a *pretence* conceals the purpose of an action. When we say, " Justice has been often used as a pretext for murder," we mean that justice has often been put forward falsely as a motive for taking away life; the real motive being concealed. When we say, " The man obtained money under false pretences," we mean that he deceived others in respect of the purpose for which they gave him the money. The pretext covers the thing done; the pretence covers the thing to be done. Hence the distinction is as active and passive.

[*Auf.* To keep your great pretences veiled, till when
They needs must show themselves ——
Coriolanus, i. 3.

Auf. And my pretext to strike at him admits
A good construction —— *Id.*, v. 5.

—— under fair pretence of friendly ends
Comus, 160.

These false pretexts and varnished colours failing. *S. A.*, 901.]

Exercise.

Unable any longer to find a ——— for such barbarities, he threw off all appearance of justice, and from thenceforward shewed himself to the world in his real nature—as an unrelenting tyrant.

He endeavoured to conceal his real intentions by the shallowest ———, but his crafty designs were detected and frustrated by the very men he had hoped to make his victims.

Though conscious of his error in allowing himself to be betrayed into the commission of this rash act, he had not the generosity to confess his fault, but invented continual ——— to excuse his conduct with the people.

The officer received orders from the superintendent to keep a strict watch over his prisoner, and under no ——— whatever, to allow him to quit his place of confinement.

When the conspirators saw that their whole plot was discovered, they each made various ——— to excuse their being concerned in it; some alleging that they were not aware of the real designs of the plot, and others declaring that they entirely mistook the views of the leaders.

Proposal—Proposition.

The distinction is here again as active and passive. A *proposal* is something offered to be done. A *proposition* is something submitted to our consideration. Propositions are acceded to or rejected; proposals are accepted or refused. A proposal, when accepted, is followed by an act on the part of the proposer; a proposition, when acceded to, is followed by an act on the part of those to whom it is submitted. If you propose to your friend that he shall accept you as a partner, you make him a proposition: if you propose to your friend to take him into partnership with yourself, you make him a proposal.

[*Agam.* The ample proposition, that hope makes
In all designs begun on earth below
Fails in the promised largeness. *Troil. and Cress.*, i. 3

If our proposals once again were heard.
P. L., vi. 618.]

Exercise.

He made a ——— to accompany us in our excursion, but as we had already made all our arrangements for the occasion, we were under the necessity of declining his offer.

Some time will be necessary for me to consider the nature of this ———; and even then, before acting upon it, I shall probably be obliged to consult a friend.

Though the ——— is very advantageous in many respects, I have not yet decided upon accepting it, as I foresee that it may involve me in a heavy responsibility.

Yesterday morning, after breakfast, my uncle came in, and offered to take us all out for a walk. We immediately accepted his ——— with joy, and putting on our bonnets and cloaks, accompanied him in a delightful stroll for two hours along the banks of the river Lea.

The terms offered by the general were, that they should lay down their arms, and promise not to appear again in the field against the English They joyfully acceded to this ———.

Rashness—Temerity.

Temerity expresses a certain passive state or quality of a man's mind. *Rashness* is its corresponding active quality. Temerity refers to the disposition; rashness, to the act. We discover temerity in our resolutions, conclusions, &c.; rashness, in the common actions of life. We may possess, but we do not exercise, temerity. Our rashness appears in what we do; our temerity is the principle of our rashness. "A man of temerity," not a man of rashness. "A rash act," not a temerarious act.

[*Ham.* ——— Rashly,
And praised be rashness for it,—Let us know.
Our indiscretion sometimes serves us well
When our deep plots do pall. *Hamlet*, v. 2.
——— for life
To noble and ignoble is more sweet
Untrained in arms, where rashness leads not on.
P. L., xii. 222.]

Exercise.

"All mankind have a sufficient plea for some degree of restlessness, and the fault seems to be little more than too much ——— of conclusion in favour of something not experienced."

"To jump into a river without being able to swim, or to leap over a hedge without being an expert horseman, is ———."

"Still the kindness with which he is treated encourages him to go on, hoping in time that he may acquire a steadier footing; and thus he proceeds, half venturing, half shrinking, surprised at his own good fortune, and wondering at his own ———."

"In so speaking, we offend indeed against truth; yet we offend not properly by falsehood, which is a speaking against our thoughts, but by ———, which is an affirming or denying, before we have sufficiently informed ourselves."

"Her ——— hand in evil hour
Forth reaching to the fruit, she plucked, she ate."

"To distrust fair appearances, and to restrain ——— desires, are instructions which the darkness of our present state should strongly inculcate."

Reason—Cause.

Causes are natural; *reasons* are logical. Causes are for things; reason, for actions. Causes are hidden or evident; reasons are true or false. A fair wind is the cause of a vessel sailing. To discover the reason why the vessel sails, we must apply to the captain. Cause produces effect, reason produces a conclusion. There are many things for which we cannot assign a satisfactory cause; but every one should be able to give a reason for his conclusions.

[*Macb.* Masking this business from the common eye
For sundry weighty reasons. *Macbeth*, iii. 1.

Lear. I have full cause for weeping; but this heart
Shall break into a hundred thousand flaws
Or ere I'll weep. —— *King Lear*, ii. 4.

——— and could make the worse appear
The better reason. —— *P. L.*, ii. 114.

——— say first what cause
Moved our grand parents, in that happy state
Favoured of Heaven so highly, to fall off
From their Creator. *Id.*, i. 28.

There surely must some reason be
Why you would change sweet Liswyn farm
For Kilve by the green sea.
WORDSWORTH. '*Anecdote for Fathers.*'

——— What he draws
From sense, faith, reason, fancy, of the cause,
He will take with him to the silent tomb.
'*Itin. Sonnets.*']

Exercise.

Though I have had many conversations with him on the subject, he has never yet been able to assign a ——— for rejecting his former views, and adopting his new opinions.

The ——— of volcanic eruptions arises from the combination of combustible materials in the bowels of the earth, which, becoming ignited, explode, and find a vent through the outer surface of the globe.

He never thought proper to explain the ——— of his acting in this extraordinary manner; and although the event proved successful, it did not tend to raise him in the opinion of his acquaintance, as they rightly judged this success rather a lucky chance than the result of any mature deliberation.

When the appointed day arrived, and the vessel did not make her appearance, every one was at a loss to account for her prolonged absence; the next day, however, she sailed into port, the ——— of her delay being accounted for by the strong head-winds she had encountered during her passage.

"I mask the business from the common eye,
For sundry weighty ———."

"Good ——— must of course give way to better."

Recovery—Restoration.

Of these two words, *recovery* has an active, and *restoration* a passive meaning. The former implies an act of our own; the latter, an act of another. The recovery of what we have lost regards ourselves; its restoration comes from others. The difference between the recovery of our property and the restoration of our property will then be obvious. His health was recovered (by him.) His health was restored (to him.)

[*War.* Speak lower, princes, for the king recovers.
2 Hen. IV., iv. 4.

Cor. ——— Restoration, hang
Thy medicine on my lips —— *King Lear*, iv. 7

Adam, by this from the cold sudden damp
Recovering —— *P. L.*, xi. 294.

Deucalion and chaste Pyrrha, to restore
The race of mankind drowned, before the shrine
Of Themis stood devout. *Id.*, 12.

——— of glory lost,
May be, through pains and persevering hope
Recovered. —— '*The Excursion*,' v.

——— sensations sweet,
Felt in the blood, and felt along the heart;
And passing even into my purer mind
With tranquil restoration. —— '*Lines—Tintern Abbey*.'

Thy call a prostrate Nation can restore,
When but a single Mind resolves to crouch no more.
'*To Enterprize*.']

Exercise.

"I left you both in France, and in two years after, I went to Italy for the ——— of my health."

"He is now on the eve of visiting foreign parts; a ship of war is commissioned by its royal master to carry the author of 'Waverley' to climates in which he may possibly obtain such a ——— of health as may serve him to spin his thread to an end in his own country."

"Let us study to improve the assistance which this revelation affords to the ——— of our nature, and the ——— of our felicity."

"After the pages which have been already devoted to enumerate the services rendered by Leo X. to all liberal studies, by the establishment of learned seminaries, by the ——— of the works of the ancient writers, and the publication of them by means of the press, by promoting the knowledge of the Greek and Latin languages, and by the munificent encouragement bestowed by him on the professors of every branch of science, of literature, and of art, it would surely be as superfluous to recapitulate his claims, as it would be unjust to deny his pretensions, to an eminent degree of positive merit."

His health was ——— chiefly by the use of goat's milk.

"Any other person may join with him that is injured, and assist him in ———ing from the offender so much as may make satisfaction."

Reformation—Reform.

These words differ as active from passive. *Reformation* is the act of reforming; *reform* is the state of being reformed.

The reformation brings about the reform. The reformation of the church—Parliamentary reform. The former designates the process of reforming the church; the latter, the state of Parliament when in a new form. In strict propriety, it cannot be said that *a reform is going on;* or that *a reformation is effected.*

[*Caer.* Never came reformation in a flood
With such a heady current, scouring faults. *Henry V.*, i 1]

Exercise.

"Examples are pictures, and strike the senses, nay, raise the passions, and call in those (the strongest and most general of all motives) to the aid of ———."

"He was anxious to keep the distemper of France from the least countenance in England, where he was sure some wicked persons had shown a strong disposition to recommend an imitation of the French spirit of ———."

"Satire lashes vice into ———."

"The ——s in representation, and the bills for shortening the duration of Parliaments, he uniformly and steadily opposed for many years together."

"The pagan converts mention this great ——— of those who had been the greatest sinners, with that sudden and surprising change, which the Christian religion made in the lives of the most profligate."

"There are many clamorous for ——— in the political institutions of their country, who forget the ——— requisite in themselves."

"The burden of the ——— lay on Luther's shoulders."

"One cannot attempt a perfect ——— in the languages of the world, without rendering himself ridiculous."

Repentance—Contrition.

Contrition is that state of mind into which we bring ourselves by continued repentance; in which the heart is, as it were, bruised at the remembrance of sin. *Repentance* is a more active term, and simply expresses lively sorrow for past offences. Repentance is felt not only for sin, but also for actions which may influence our worldly affairs or condition. The motives for contrition are always religious. Sorrow for having offended God produces contrition. The reflection that we have done wrong in any way produces repentance. The heart is contrite—our reason repents. When we repent, we act; when we are contrite, we are in a passive state.

[*Mont.* ——— thou wilt mind
Thy followers of repentance; that their souls
May make a peaceful and a sweet retire
From off these fields. —— *Henry V.*, iv. 3

K. Hen. I Richard's body have interred new;
And on it have bestowed more contrite tears
Than from it issued forced drops of blood
Id., iv. 1.

——— the great proclaimer, with a voice
More awful than the sound of trumpet, cried
Repentance. —— *P. R.*, i. 20.

Fruits of more pleasing savour, from the seed
Sown with contrition in his heart —— *P. L.*, xi. 27

——— who cannot judge amiss,
And wafts at will the contrite soul to bliss.
WORDSWORTH. '*Son. on Punishment of Death.*']

Exercise.

During the remaining short period of his life, the prisoner maintained a sullen and obstinate silence; he expressed no ——— for his crime; nor evinced the least desire to see any member of his family.

He now clearly saw the probable consequences of his folly, and bitterly lamented having taken so rash a step; but ——— came too late, and it now only remained for him to prevent, as far as lay in his power, the injury which his rashness might cause to others.

I was told that he was really sincere in his ———, and that he had made a strong resolution to conduct himself for the future like an honest man and a virtuous citizen.

Her sighs and tears bore testimony to the depth of her ———, and every one present was so firmly convinced of her sincerity, that several of those who witnessed her protestations offered to take her into their service.

"———, though it may melt, ought not to sink or overpower the heart of a Christian."

"Who by ——— is not satisfied,
Is not of heaven nor earth"

Smell—Odour.

The word *smell* is used in both an active and passive sense; *odour*, properly, only passively. The smell is active, as affects our organs, and passive as it exists in certain bodies. Odour is also generally used, in a favourable sense, of what has an agreeable or sweet smell. The word *smell* is also used for the faculty of smelling: it is to be regretted that *the smelling* should not be always used for the faculty.

[*Ban.* ——— that the heaven's breath
Smells wooingly here — *Macbeth*, i. 6

Oth. ——— when I have plucked thy rose
I cannot give it vital growth again,
It needs must wither;—I'll smell it on the tree.
Othello, v. 2.

Duke. ——— like the sweet south,
That breathes upon a bank of violets
Stealing and giving odour. ——— *Twelfth Night*, i.

Sabæan odours from the spicy shore
Of Araby the blest; with such delay
Well pleased they slack their course, and many a league
Cheered with the grateful smell old Ocean smiles.
P. L., iv. 162.

More sweet than odours caught by him who sails
Near spicy shores of Araby the blest.
WORDSWORTH. '*Eccles. Sonnets*

A rainbow, a sunbeam,
A subtle smell that Spring unbinds,
Dead pause abrupt of midnight winds,
An echo or a dream. '*Presentiments*.']

Exercise.

"Democritus, when he lay dying, sent for loaves of new bread, which having opened and poured a little wine into them, he kept himself alive with the ——— till a certain feast was past."

"The sweetest ——— in the air is the white double violet, which comes twice a year."

"The Levites burned the holy incense in such quantities as refreshed the whole multitude with its ———, and filled all the region about them with perfume."

"Cheered with the grateful ———, old Ocean smiles."

"Me seemed I smelt a garden of sweet flowers,
That dainty ——— from them threw around."

"By the application of heat, the coffee bean increases to nearly twice its original size, and emits a powerful and agreeable ———."

"There is a great variety of ———, though we have but a few names for them; the ——— of a violet and of musk, both sweet, are as distinct as any two ———."

"To the north of China are found both apples and pears; but the latter are tasteless, and the former mealy and bad, though with a fine colour and ———."

Tyranny—Oppression.

He who exercises arbitrary power is a *tyrant;* he who directs that power against the people is an *oppressor.* In oppression, the idea of suffering is prominent; in tyranny, the active quality is uppermost in the mind. Tyranny is exercised, oppression is borne. In the word tyrant, the ideas of haughtiness and imperious cruelty are comprised. Oppressor is a more limited term, and is confined to one mode of tyranny.

[*Bru.* So let high-sighted tyranny range on
Till each man drop by lottery. —— *Julius Cæsar*, ii. 1

Ham. But I am pigeon-liver'd and lack gall
To make oppression bitter —— *Hamlet*, ii. 2.

——— tyranny must be;
Though to the tyrant thereby no excuse. *P. L.*, xii 95

——— so violence
Proceeded, and oppression, and sword-law *P. L.*, xi. 672.

Forget thy weakness, upon which is built,
O wretched man, the throne of tyranny.
WORDSWORTH. '*Sonnets to Liberty.*'

By Uri's lake, where Tell
Leapt, from his storm-vext boat to land
Heaven's Instrument, for by his hand
That day the Tyrant fell. '*Composed at Cora Linn.*'

Such look the Oppressor might confound,
However proud and strong. '*Elegiac Stanzas.*']

Exercise.

"Boundless intemperance
In nature is a ———; it hath been
Th' untimely emptying of the happy throne,
And fall of many kings."

"Power, when employed to relieve the oppressed, and to punish the ———, becomes a great blessing."

"Tarquin having governed ———ly, and taken from the senate all authority, was become odious to the senate, nobility, and people."

"Her taxes are more injudiciously and more ———ly imposed, more vexatiously collected."

"Domitian had been ———; and in his time many noble houses were overthrown by false accusations."

"If thou seest the ——— of the poor, marvel not at the matter, for He that is higher than the highest regardeth."

"By force of that commission, he in many places most ——— expelled them."

'I from ——— did the poor defend,
The fatherless, and such as had no friend."

"Our grand foe,
Who now triumphs, and in th' excess of joy,
Sole reigning, holds the ——— of heaven."

Unity—Union.

When two or more things are together, so as to make but one, the state in which they then are is their *union;* and the feeling by which they are held together, after being made one, is their *unity*. Union, then, is the state of being one; unity is the state of having but one sentiment or feeling. Hence "unity" has an active, and "union" a passive meaning. Marriage is often termed a union; *i. e.* it is the being together of two persons: all married persons, however, though united, do not live together in unity. Children who are affectionate and kind to each other are said to dwell in unity.

[*Ulys.* The unity and married calm of states
Troi and Cress., i. 3.

Hel. But yet a union in partition
Two lovely berries moulded on one stem.
Midsum. N. Dream, iii. 2.

——— his image multiplied,
In unity defective —— *P. L.*, viii. 425

——— which declare unfeigned
Union of mind —— *Id.*, 604.

That which the heavens displayed, the liquid deep
Repeated; but with unity sublime. '*The Excursion*,' ix

——— how shall man unite
With self-forgetting tenderness of heart
An earth-despising dignity of soul?
Wise in that union, and without it blind! *Id.*, v.]

Exercise.

"Take ——— out of the world, and it dissolves into a chaos"

The want of ——— which exists between England and Ireland has been the chief cause of the clamour for the repeal of the ———, which has so long distracted the latter country.

"Behold how good and how pleasant a thing it is for brethren to dwell together in ———!"

The ——— of the two armies was at length effected, and their operations were effectively directed against the enemy.

"We, of all Christians, ought to promote ——— among ourselves and others."

To avoid dissension, it avails much that there be among them a ———, as well in ceremonies as in doctrine.

"One kingdom, joy, and ——— without end."

"And gladly of our ——— hear thee speak."

Utility—Usefulness.

Of these words, usefulness is the passive, utility the active term. Our *utility* is discovered by what we do; our *usefulness*, by what we are. One person is of utility to another, when he assists him, or does him some service. A man's usefulness consists in the power—not in the act—of making himself useful. Utility is usefulness exerted. For this reason, utility is more frequently said of persons; usefulness, of things. The utility of a thing is discovered by the effects which it produces when brought into action; its usefulness is perceived in its nature or inherent qualities.

[*Bur.* Losing both beauty and utility *Henry V.*, v. 2.]

Exercise.

"The gentleman desired that I would give a relation of a cure of the gout, that it might be made public, as a thing which might prove of common —— to so great numbers as were subject to that disease."

"The grandeur of the commonwealth shews itself chiefly in works that were necessary or convenient. On the contrary, the magnificence of Rome, under the emperors, was rather for ostentation than any real ——."

"Those things which have long gone together are confederate; whereas new things agree not so well; but though they help by their ——, yet they trouble by their inconformity."

It is hoped that every sensible person who reads these exercises will have no difficulty in perceiving their ——, and the author ventures to assert that those who practise them will soon acknowledge their ——.

"I had occasion to refer several times to the work you mentioned in your last letter, but I soon found the book was of no —— whatever, and I have now discontinued referring to it."

Value—Worth.

Value has an active; *worth*, a passive meaning. The quality "worth" is what a thing has in itself. Its "value" is determined by what it *does* for you.

The *worth* of any thing depends upon its real merit; its *value* is determined by the price it would fetch in an open market. Worth is intrinsic; value depends upon circumstances. Worth is an essential, value an accidental property. That which is really of little worth may be of great value in consequence of its scarcity, or the great demand for it. Worth is permanent; value is changeable. The worth of a picture is always the same; its value varies with the taste of purchasers, scarcity of pictures by the same master, &c.

> [*Friar.* —— what we have we prize not to the worth,
> Whiles we enjoy it; but being lacked and lost,
> Why, then we rack the value; then we find
> The virtue, that possession would not show us
> Whiles it was ours. *Much Ado Ab. Noth.*, IV. 1
>
> *Isab.* —— stones, whose rates are either rich or poor,
> As fancy values them. —— *Meas. for Meas.*, ii. 2.
>
> *Oth.* For the sea's worth. —— *Othello*, i. 3.
>
> —— So little knows
> Any, but God alone, to value right
> The good before him —— *P. L.*, iv. 202.
>
> —— the uncontrouled worth
> Of this pure cause would kindle my rapt spirits
> *Comus*, 793.
>
> And something also did my worth obtain;
> For fearless virtue bringeth boundless gain.
> WORDSWORTH. '*Laodamia.*

Exercise.

I know his ——, and appreciate it fully, in proof of which, I have given him the appointment in preference to all the other candidates.

The —— of a book is immediately depreciated by the publication of another and a better one on the same subject.

The —— of the estate is estimated at a much higher sum, in consequence of its being adjacent to some property from which it is said to derive many advantages.

How much is that picture ——? It has been —— at eighty guineas, but I consider it —— much more.

The —— of a man's estate has nothing to do with his moral ——; for every individual should be estimated by what he is, rather than by what he has.

The —— of a thing may differ greatly from its ——; the former depends upon circumstances, whilst the latter is always the same.

Veracity—Truth.

The former word is here active; the latter, passive. *Veracity* regards persons, *truth* regards things. Truth *is*, veracity *does.* We speak of the truth of history, but of the veracity of the historian. We can depend upon the truth of whatever is asserted by a man of known veracity. The thing said is true; the person who says it is veracious.

[*Macb* Two truths are told
As happy prologues to the swelling act
Of the imperial theme. —— *Macbeth*, i. 3.

——— who kept thy truth so pure of old
MILTON. '*Sonnets.*

Truth shows a glorious face,
While on that isthmus which commands
The councils of both worlds she stands.
WORDSWORTH. '*Presentiments.*']

Exercise.

"In real ———, I believe that there is much less difference between the author and his works than is currently supposed."

"Many relations of travellers have been slighted as fabulous, till more frequent voyages have confirmed their ———."

"As we lived near the road, we often had the traveller or stranger visit us, to taste our gooseberry wine, for which we had great reputation; and I profess, with the ——— of an historian, that I never knew one of them find fault with it."

"What can we say? Even that which the man in Terence said to a person whose ——— he suspected."

"There are innumerable ——— with which we are wholly unacquainted."

"I shall think myself obliged for the future to speak always in ——— and sincerity of heart."

"They thought they might do it, not only willingly, because they loved him, and ———ly, because such indeed was the mind of the people; but safely, because she who ruled the king was agreed thereto."

As his ——— has never been called in question, we have no reason to doubt the ——— of his assertion.

To caution—to warn.

We are *cautioned* against acting injudiciously; we are *warned* of what may act injuriously upon ourselves. We warn a man of approaching danger; we caution him against running into it. Heavy clouds warn us of the coming storm. He cautioned his friend not to approach too near the enemy's lines. We are cautioned against speaking rashly; we are warned of the consequences.

[*Macb.* ——— for thy good caution thanks.
Macbeth, iv. 1.

Q. Kath. ——— say I warned ye
Take heed, for heaven's sake, take heed, lest at once
The burden of my sorrows fall upon ye *Henry VIII.*, iii. 1

What meant that caution joined If ye be found
Obedient? *P. L.*, v. 513.

——— or to warn
Us, haply too secure —— *Id.*, xi. 195.

A perfect Woman, nobly planned,
To warn, to comfort, and command. WORDSWORTH, p 143.]

Exercise.

Upon entering into business, he was frequently ——— against having any dealings with Mr. B., whose want of principle made it very dangerous for any one to be connected with him. He, however, disregarded this ———, and was soon induced to embark with this very man in extensive speculations. His friends again strongly urged him to break off all further connection with so unprincipled and daring an adventurer. But the ——— came too late, for he now found himself so deeply involved that nothing could save him from ruin.

When the poor mother left her children, she ——— the eldest not to allow the two youngest to approach the fire.

Though ——— of the consequences, the child paid no attention to her mother's injunctions; and having left her sisters alone in the room for a few minutes, she was horror-struck on her return to find one of them enveloped in flames.

Attention to the forementioned symptoms affords the best ———s and rules of diet, by way of prevention.

"Not e'en Philander had bespoke his shroud,
Nor had he cause; a ——— was denied."

To defend—to protect.

To *defend* is to ward off; to *protect* is to cover over. To defend is an active; to protect, a passive term. We defend those who are attacked; we protect those who are liable to be attacked. In defending, we exert ourselves; in protecting, we merely place ourselves between two parties. Swords and spears are arms of defence; helmets and shields are weapons of protection. A town is defended by its garrison and cannon; a town is protected by its fortifications, and its natural position. Houses protect us from the inclemency of the weather. Brave soldiers defend their country.

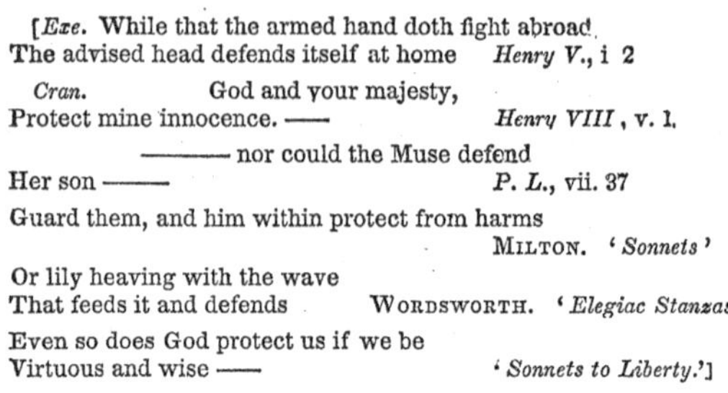

[*Exe.* While that the armed hand doth fight abroad,
The advised head defends itself at home *Henry V.*, i 2

Cran. God and your majesty,
Protect mine innocence. —— *Henry VIII*, v. 1.

——— nor could the Muse defend
Her son ——— *P. L.*, vii. 37

Guard them, and him within protect from harms
MILTON. '*Sonnets*'

Or lily heaving with the wave
That feeds it and defends WORDSWORTH. '*Elegiac Stanzas*

Even so does God protect us if we be
Virtuous and wise —— '*Sonnets to Liberty.*']

Exercise.

The streets were filled with poor, starving wretches, the pictures of misery and poverty, shivering with the cold, and with nothing but a few rags to ——— them from the inclemency of the season.

Just as the magistrate was about to leave the bench, a poor woman entered the court in a state of great agitation, and implored the magistrate to ——— her against the violence of her husband.

As he was on the point of entering the ravine, a huge boar suddenly leaped out upon him; he drew his hanger, and ——— himself as well as he could, till his companions came to his assistance, and soon put the wild beast to flight.

The forty-eighth regiment, being charged with great impetuosity by the enemy's cavalry, ——— themselves for some time with the most determined bravery; but being at length overpowered by the superior weight and number of the enemy, were reluctantly obliged to retreat.

Though well ——— from the weather by a thick great-coat, he caught such a violent cold in travelling outside the stage from Brighton to London, that it brought on a severe attack of fever.

To eat—to feed.

To *eat* is the act of taking in nourishment; to *feed* is the act of deriving nourishment. By eating, we become fed. Infants cannot eat, they are fed. We are fed as much by what we drink, as by what we eat. Men are not said to feed, (in an intransitive sense.) Beasts feed; men are fed. In a metaphorical sense, rust eats into iron. The imagination feeds upon romances.

Exercise.

"The elephant could not have reached the ground without his proboscis; or if it be supposed that he might have ——— upon the fruit, leaves, or branches of trees, how was he to drink?"

At five o'clock in the afternoon, a bell is rung in the Zoological Gardens, Regent's Park, to give notice to the visitors that the keepers are going to ——— the beasts.

The doctor assured his patient that all his indisposition arose from ——— too much; and prescribed no other medicine for him than moderation in his living.

"And when the scribes and Pharisees saw him ——— with publicans and sinners, they said unto his disciples: How is it that he ——— with publicans and sinners?"

Boerhaave ——— a sparrow with bread four days, in which time it ——— more than its own weight.

"Some birds ——— upon the berries of this vegetable."

The child had made itself so ill from ——— a great quantity of unripe fruit, that its life was for some days despaired of.

In winter, when fodder is scarce, cows and sheep ——— upon turnips

---

To employ—to use.

To *use* a thing is to derive enjoyment or service from it; to *employ* is to turn that service into a particular channel. What is employed is made to act; what is used is acted upon. We use words to express our general meaning; we employ certain words on particular occasions. Technical terms are employed in scientific works. Pens, ink, and paper are the materials used in writing. Time and talent are employed in writing, because they are made to produce an intended effect.

[*P. John.* But you misuse the reverence of your place;
Employ the countenance and grace of Heaven
As a false favourite doth his prince's name. 2 *Henry IV.*, iv. 2.

Lear. Had I your tongues and eyes, I'd use them so
That heaven's vault should crack. —— *Lear*, v. 3.

Here Love his golden shafts employs, here lights
His constant lamp —— *P. L.*, iv 763

Some other means I have which may be used
Comus, 821

——— Our life is turned
Out of her course, wherever man is made
An offering, or a sacrifice, a tool
Or implement, a passive thing employed
As a brute mean, without acknowledgment
Of common right or interest in the end;
Used or abused, as selfishness may prompt. '*The Excursion*,' ix.]

Exercise.

He ——— such strange terms, and in such an uncommon signification, that many of his writings are very difficult to understand.

My brother's business has become so extensive, and he consequently requires so much more assistance, that he has found it necessary to ——— forty additional hands in his manufactory.

The quantity of paper ——— annually for the supply of English newspapers is 121,184 reams, some of which paper is of an enormous size; and thousands of persons are ——— in producing these daily and weekly publications.

There is nothing insignificant, nothing which may not be ——— for some good purpose; and though we are not always able to perceive its utility, we are not justified in concluding, on that account, that it is utterly worthless.

We may often ——— our time profitably, even when not engaged in manual labour, or in any powerful exertion of the intellect.

——— diligence and perseverance, and you cannot fail of success.

To find—to meet with.

What we *find*, we go towards, either by chance or intentionally. What we *meet with* presents itself to us unsought for. In looking for a quotation in some poet, we may not be able to find it, but may meet with one which will answer our purpose equally well. In finding, we act; in meeting with. some person or thing acts upon us. We find what we search for; we meet with what we do not expect to see.

[*Duke.* Finds tongues in trees, books in the running brooks,
Sermons in stones, and good in every thing.
As You Like It, ii. 1.

Jaq. ——— meeting with an old religious man,
After some question with him, was converted
Both from his enterprise, and from the world.
Id., v. 4.

Ask for this great deliverer now, and find him
Eyeless in Gaza at the mill with slaves. *S. A.*, 40.

We sail the sea of life—a Calm one finds
And one a Tempest—and the voyage o'er,
Death is the quiet haven of us all. WORDSWORTH '*Epitaphs.*

——— did seem
Like one whom I had met with in a dream.
'*Resolution and Independence*']

Exercise.

"We ——— many things worthy of observation."

"Ask, and it shall be given you; seek, and ye shall ———."

"What a majesty and force does one ——— in these short inscriptions! Are you not amazed to see so much history gathered into so small a compass?"

"She disappeared, and left me dark; I waked
To ——— her, or for ever to deplore
Her loss."

"Hercules' ——— Pleasure and Virtue, was invented by Prodicus, who lived before Socrates."

"It is agreeable to compare the face of a great man with the character, and try if we can ——— in his looks and features, either the haughty, cruel, or merciful temper."

"He was afraid of being insulted with Greek, for which reason he desired a friend to ——— him a clergyman rather of plain sense than much learning."

The other day, looking carelessly through the leaves of that work, I ——— two or three passages which struck me as being so sensibly conceived, and so forcibly expressed, that I determined to peruse the book

I have lost my book, and can ——— it nowhere.

To found—to ground.

To found is used actively—to ground, passively. A charge is founded—a belief is grounded. We should not accuse without a foundation, nor suspect without good grounds for suspicion. We should have a foundation for our actions, and grounds for our thoughts and feelings. The grounds for suspicion may lead us to suspect, and suspicion itself may be the foundation of a charge.

[*Dis.* Hath founded his good fortune on your love.
Othello, iii. 4.

Le Beau Grounded upon no other argument.
As You Like It, i. 2.

Thy hopes are not ill founded—— *Comus*, 1504.

——— oft times nothing profits more
Than self-esteem, grounded on just and right
Well managed —— *P. L.* viii. 572.

——— the spiritual fabric of her Church,
Founded in truth; by blood of Martyrdom
Cemented —— *The Excursion*, VI

——— and sentence gave
So grounded, so applied, that it was heard
With softened spirit, even when it condemned.
Id., ii.]

Exercise.

"I know there are persons who look upon these wonders of art (in ancient history) as fabulous; but I cannot find any ——— for such a suspicion."

"The only sure principles we can lay down for regulating our conduct must be ——— on the Christian religion."

"The solemn usage of praying for the dead can be ——— only on the belief that there exists a middle state of purification and suffering through which souls pass after death, and from which the prayers of the faithful may aid in delivering them."

"A right to the use of the creatures is ——— originally in the right a man has to subsist."

"Wisdom ——— her laws upon an infallible rule of comparison."

"It may serve us to ——— conjectures more approaching to the truth than we have hitherto met with."

"If it be natural, ought we not to conclude that there is some ——— and reason for these fears, and that nature has not planted them in us to no purpose?"

"Power ——— on contract can descend only to him who has a right by that contract."

To furnish—to supply.

I furnish, that you may use; I supply, that you may not want. What is wanting to make a thing complete must be *supplied;* what is required for occasional use is *furnished.* Our wants are supplied; our comforts are furnished. The poor are supplied with blankets and coals during the winter; the rich man's table is furnished with delicacies. What is furnished we keep by us for use; what is supplied we use immediately. Hence a house is furnished with tables and chairs; a larder is supplied with meat and vegetables.

K. Hen. To furnish him with all appertinents
Belonging to his honour —— *Henry V.*, ii. 2.
Cant. A hundred alms-houses, right well supplied.
Id., i. 1

With all things grateful cheered, and so supplied,
That what by me thou hast lost, thou least shalt miss.
S A., 926.

——— to furnish weapons for the bands
Of Umfraville or Percy ere they marched
To Scotland's heaths; or those that crossed the sea
And drew their sounding bows at Azincour.
WORDSWORTH. '*Yew-Trees*

——— bowers that hear no more
The voice of gladness, less and less supply
Of outward sunshine and internal warmth. '*The Excursion*,' v.]

Exercise.

The demand for cotton goods was so great, that the manufacturers could not ——— the dealers fast enough.

The ships were well fitted out, being ——— with all the necessary nautical instruments, and amply ——— with provisions.

The shelves of his library are ——— with a collection of rare books.

London is ——— with vegetables chiefly from the market-gardens in the neighbourhood of Hammersmith and Fulham.

What he wanted in ability was ——— by unremitting assiduity.

Youth is the season for ——— the mind with sound principles.

The encroachments of Philip of Macedon ——— Demosthenes with the subject-matter of some of his most celebrated orations.

Having obtained entrance to the prison, he ——— his friend with the means of escaping.

The unfortunate crew having lost every thing they possessed, were ——— with clothes, and ——— with money to enable them to reach their homes.

To invent—to discover.

That which always existed, but was never known, is *discovered* when it becomes known. When things are combined in such a way as to produce an effect never before known, the author of such a combination *invents*. Thus, the expansive power of steam was discovered, and the steam-engine was invented. America was discovered—not invented, because, though that continent was unknown to the inhabitants of Europe before the year 1493, we may presume that it had existed from the beginning of time. Printing was invented—not discovered, because it was the effect produced by the combination of metal type, ink, paper, &c. Newton discovered the law of gravitation. Galileo invented the telescope.

[*Cas.* I could well wish courtesy would invent
Some other custom of entertainment. *Othello*, ii. 3.

Pan. Some to discover islands far away.
Two Gent. of Verona, i 3

——— his throne itself
Mixt with Tartarean sulphur and strange fire,
His own invented torments — *P. L.* ii. 70.

On bold adventure to discover wide
That dismal world — *Id*, 571.

——— to principles and powers
Discovered or invented —— 'The Excursion,' v

How insecure, how baseless in itself,
Is the Philosophy whose sway depends
On mere material instruments; how weak
Those arts and high inventions, if unpropped
By virtue —— *Id.*, viii.

Not with more transport did Columbus greet
A world, his rich discovery. —— *Id.*, vi.]

Exercise.

There has lately been ——— by M. Menas, in the convent of Santa Laura, on Mount Athos, a manuscript containing one hundred and twenty-one Greek fables of Babrius.

There appear to be reasonable grounds for the belief that what are justly regarded in Europe as two of the most important ——— of modern times, viz.: the art of printing, and the composition of gunpowder, had their first origin in China.

The Chinese had ——— the attractive power of the load-stone from remote antiquity; but its property of communicating polarity to iron is for the first time noticed in a Chinese dictionary, finished A. D. 121.

The date of the ——— of gunpowder is involved in obscurity. It has been said that it was used in China as early as A. D. 85. It has also been stated, that about 1336, Berthold Schwartz, a monk, ——— the mode of manufacturing it.

To keep—to retain.

To *keep* is an active—to *retain* is a passive term. We keep, by our own power; we retain, through want of power or want of exertion in others. What we have power to prevent others taking from us, we keep; what others do not choose, or cannot manage, to take from us, we retain. We keep money in trust for others. We retain our authority over others. Men sometimes retain their faculties to a great age.

[*Hot.* I'll keep them all,
By Heaven, he shall not have a Scot of them.
1 *Henry IV.*, i. 3.

Kent. ——— where is the patience now
That you so oft have boasted to retain?
Lear, iii. 6.

What makes a nation happy, and keeps it so
P. R., iv. 363.

——— still she retains
Her maiden gentleness —— *Comus*, 842.

——— because the good old rule
Sufficeth them, the simple plan,
That they should take who have the power,
And they should keep who can.
WORDSWORTH. 'Rob Roy s Grave

The fragrant air its coolness still retains
'The Excursion,' v.]

Exercise.

In spite of the most strenuous efforts of the opposite party, the new member ——— such influence in the county, that at the next election he was returned to Parliament by an overwhelming majority.

The prince was a man of most extravagant habits; he ——— a numerous stud of horses, a pack of hounds, and an expensive establishment; he gave splendid entertainments, and ——— open house for all his friends.

In Scotland, many people live to a great age; and are not only active and cheerful, but ——— all their faculties to the last.

Those who ——— themselves clear of bad company will be less likely to acquire bad habits, and may ——— their innocence.

The unfortunate prisoner, when led to the place of execution, betrayed no weakness or fear of death, but ———ing his firmness to the last, laid his head upon the block with the most dignified composure.

We have a right to ——— what belongs to us, but no arguments can justify our ——— the property of another.

To lay—to lie.

The confusion in the use of these verbs has arisen from the fact, that the present tense of the first verb is spelt and pronounced exactly in the same way as the past tense of the second; the parts of both verbs are as follows:—

Pres.	*Past.*	*Part.*
Lay	laid	laid
Lie	lay	lain

To *lay* is a transitive verb, and means *to place down;* to *lie* is an intransitive verb, and means *to place one's self down.*

1.	*Lay* down the book	=Place the book down.
	I *laid* down the book	=I placed the book down.
	The book was *laid* down	=The book was placed down.
2	*Lie* down	=Place yourself down.
	I *lay* down	=I placed myself down.
	I had *lain* down	=I had placed myself down.

[*Laer.* Lay her in the earth —— *Hamlet*, v. 1
Lady M. ——— I laid their daggers ready
Macbeth, ii. 2.
Jul. ——— when I am laid into the tomb
Rom. and Jul., iv. 3
Rom. ——— there lies more peril in thy eye
Id., ii. 2.
Len. ——— Where we lay,
Our chimnies were blown down ——
Macbeth, ii. 3
Arth. Many a poor man's son would have lain still
King John, iv. 1.
——— How glad would lay me down,
As in my mother's lap! *P. L.*, x. 777.
Where armies lie encamped —— *Id.*, 276.
——— that horror-striking blade
Drawn in defiance of the gods, hath laid
The noble Syracusan low in dust.
WORDSWORTH. '*Dion.*
Like a fair sister of the sky
Unruffled doth the blue lake lie
The mountains looking on. '*Septem.*, 1819.'
When Philoctetes in the Lemnian isle
Like a Form sculptured on a monument
Lay couched —— '*Miscel. Sonnets.*']

Exercise.

"As a man should always be upon his guard against the vices to which he is most exposed, so we should take a more than ordinary care not to ——— at the mercy of the weather in our moral conduct."

"Europe ——— then under a deep lethargy, and was no otherwise to be rescued but by one that would cry mightily."

"It was a sandy soil, and the way had been full of dust; but an hour or two before, a refreshing, fragrant shower of rain had ——— the dust."

He had not ——— down a quarter of an hour, before the bell rang for dinner.

"Homer is like his Jupiter, has his terrors, shaking Olympus; Virgil, like the same power in his benevolence, counselling with the gods, ———ing plans for empires."

"He intends to ——— in a store of wood and coals for the winter."

"Ants bite off all the buds before they ——— it up, and therefore the corn that has ——— in their nests will produce nothing."

To persevere—to persist.

To *persevere* has to do with the action; to *persist*, with the spirit or will that prompts it. We persevere in doing; we persist in thinking. We persevere in study; we persist in an opinion. By persisting we remain unchanged—that is, we lose nothing of our state. By persevering, we attain our end. Men persist in belief, error, conceit, &c.; they persevere in kindness, virtue, &c.—that is, in kind and virtuous actions. To persist is more frequently used in a bad sense; to persevere, in a favourable acceptation.

[*Edm.* I will persevere in my course of loyalty.
Lear, iii. 5.

Wid. ——— for he persists,
As if his life lay in't. *All's Well, &c.*, iii. 7.

——— who in the worship persevere
Of spirit and truth —— *P. L.*, xii. 532.

I had persisted happy —— *Id.*, x. 874.

—— not content that former worth stand fast
Looks forward, persevering to the last
From well to better, daily self-surpast.
WORDSWORTH. '*The Happy Warrior*'

Persisted openly that death alone
Should abrogate his human privilege
'*Vaudracour and Julia.*']

Exercise.

If you are determined to ——— in your error, you must abide by the consequences; and you will find, perhaps when too late, that you are farther than ever from the accomplishment of your design.

Those who ——— in doing well will, in the end, be rewarded.

Having resolved to finish his task by the end of the second week, he ——— in writing a portion of it every day.

Though repeatedly cross-questioned by the whole bench, the witness ——— in the same story, and his evidence being afterwards corroborated by that of another witness, all the assertions he had made were proved to be true

No argument could induce him to alter his sentiments; he ——— in maintaining the same opinions which he has always entertained on this subject.

There are many who make good resolutions, but few who ——— in them.

To err is human, but to ——— in error is diabolical.

"If we ——— in studying to do our duty towards God and man, we shall meet with the esteem, love, and confidence, of those who are around us."

"A spoiled child ——— in his follies from perversity of humour."

To teach—to learn.

It is to be remarked, that in many European languages, the same word is used for to teach and to learn. In Shakspeare* and Spenser,† the verb to learn frequently occurs in the sense of to teach. This sense is now obsolete. To *learn* is to receive, and to *teach* is to give, instruction. He who is taught, learns, not he who teaches.

[*Cal.* You taught me language ; and my profit on't
Is, I know how to curse : The red plague rid you
For learning me your language. *Tempest*, i. 2.

Ros. Unless you could teach me to forget a banish'd father, you must not learn me how to remember any extraordinary pleasure.
As You Like it, i. 2.

Cor. —— by my body's action, teach my mind
A most inherent baseness. *Coriolanus*, iii. 2.

Scroop. Thy very beadsmen learn to bend their bows
Of double-fatal yew against thy state.
Rich. II., iii. 2.

To teach all nations what of him they learned
P. L., xii. 440

O dearest, dearest boy ! my heart
For better lore would seldom yearn
Could I but teach the hundredth part
Of what from thee I learn.
WORDSWORTH. '*Anecdote for Fathers.*']

Exercise.

"In imitation of sounds, that man should be the teacher is no part of the matter ; for birds will ——— one of another."

"I am too sudden bold ;
To ——— a teacher ill beseemeth me."

"Dissenting ———ers are under no incapacity of accepting civil and military employments."

"Nor can a ———er work so cheaply as a skilful, practised artist."

"If some men ——— wicked things, it must be that others should practise them."

Locke, in his "Thoughts concerning Education," says that pupils should ——— every rule by the practical application of it, and not by tedious illustrated precepts, which cannot make half the impression."

"If there are several children, there is no better way of fixing things in

* "He would *learn*
The lion stoop to him in lowly wise,
A lesson hard."

† "Hast thou not *learn'd* me how
To make perfumes ?"

the memory than when one has ——— something to make him ——— it to the others, which the distinction attending the act will always cause him to be eager to do."

"Let a pupil understand every thing that it is designed to ——— him If he cannot understand a thing this year, it was not designed by his Creator that he should ——— it this year."

To trust—to credit.

Both these words signify to put faith in. We *credit* what has happened; we *trust* what is to happen. We give credit to good news, and we trust it will not prove false. We give a man credit for his good intentions; we trust he will turn out as we have reason to expect. Trust looks forward; credit looks back. When we trust our property to others, we give them credit for their honesty.

[*Ban.* That, trusted home,
Might yet enkindle you unto the crown.
Macbeth, i. 3.

Pro. Who having, unto truth, by telling it
Made such a sinner of his memory
To credit his own lie — *Tempest*, i. 2.

——— in trusting
He will accept thee to defend his cause
S. A., 1178.]

Exercise.

They thought his character was not well enough established to justify his being ——— to execute so important an enterprise; and he was consequently withdrawn from the command.

To the surprise of all present, the youthful lecturer displayed a profound knowledge of his subject, and an extent of reading hardly to be ——— in one so young and inexperienced.

He has deceived me so often, that I can no longer put the least ——— in his promises, nor give any ——— to his statements.

Though it wears some appearance of likelihood, we attach but little ——— to the report; and we ——— that affairs will not turn out so bad as they have been represented.

I have placed the whole affair in his hands, ———ing to his talents and ingenuity to bring it to a happy conclusion.

The account differs so widely from that previously received, and is so irreconcilable with known facts, that it is not worthy of the least ———.

We can put no ——— in a liar, nor give any ——— to his tales.

To waver—to fluctuate.

To *waver* has an active signification. When we waver, we are undecided as to what we shall *do*. The meaning of to *fluctuate* is passive. In fluctuating, we are acted upon. Our state of mind, or passion, is affected when we fluctuate. We waver in action, we fluctuate in passion. He who cannot make up his mind as to whether he shall or shall not act in a certain way—*wavers*. He who is alternately affected by conflicting passions or feelings—*fluctuates*.

[*Duke*. Our fancies are more giddy and unfirm,
More longing, wavering, sooner lost and won
Than women's are. *Tw. Night*, ii. 4

——— propense enough before
To waver, or fall off and join with idols
S. A., 456.

——— as to passion moved
Fluctuates disturbed —— *P. L.*, ix. 668.

——— to guard against the shocks,
The fluctuation and decay of things.
'*The Excursion*,' v.]

Exercise.

"So ingenious is the human heart in deceiving itself, as well as others, that it is probable neither Cromwell himself, nor those making similar pretensions to distinguished piety, could exactly have fixed the point at which their enthusiasm terminated, and their hypocrisy commenced; or rather, it was a point not fixed in itself, but ———ing with the state of health, of good or bad fortune, of high or low spirits, affecting the individual at the period."

"Let a man, without trepidation or ———ing, proceed in discharging his duty."

"As the greatest part of my estate has been hitherto of an unsteady and volatile nature, either tossed upon seas, or ———ing in funds, it is now fixed and settled in substantial acres and tenements."

"The tempter, but with show of zeal and love
To man, and indignation at his wrong,
New parts puts on, and as to passion moved,
——— disturbed."

"Thou almost mak'st me ——— in my faith,
To hold opinion with Pythagoras,
That souls of animals infuse themselves
Into the trunks of men."

Authentic—Genuine.

The term *authentic*, as an active quality, is applied to historical documents, memoirs, news, &c., which are considered good authority, and worthy of belief, as regards the subjects of which they treat. *Genuine* is a passive word. A document is correctly said to be genuine when it *is* what it professes to be, but it is not always, for that reason, authentic. Genuine has to do with the connection between a work and its reputed author. Authentic regards its character, as deserving of consideration as a standard work. Sir Walter Scott's "Life of Napoleon Bonaparte" is not considered *authentic*. Chatterton's "Rowley's Poems" were discovered to be not *genuine*.

[On him who had stole Jove's authentic fire
P. L., iv. 719.

Authentic epitaphs on some of these
Who, from their lowly mansions hither brought
Beneath this turf lie mouldering at our feet
'*The Excursion*,' v

That were indeed a genuine birth
Of poesy; a bursting forth
Of genius from the dust. p. 375.]

Exercise.

The question of the ——— of Ossian's poems has been long set at rest

The most ——— account of this transaction may be found in "Sonnini's Travels in Egypt."

The character of this extraordinary scholar was made up of the most ——— simplicity, accompanied with the quickest sagacity and the deepest penetration.

His memory was so wonderful, that there was scarcely a Greek or Roman author of whose works he could not describe all the ——— manuscripts, and inform you of their exact worth, as throwing any light on the history of their times.

We have reasonable grounds to doubt the ——— of the account concerning the discovery of Richard the First by his favourite minstrel, Blondel.

It was Niebuhr's opinion that several of the books said to have been written by Julius Cæsar are not ———.

"We are surprised to find verses of so modern a cast as the following at such an early period; which in this sagacious age we should judge to be a forgery, was not their ———ness ———ated, and their antiquity confirmed by the venerable types of Caxton."

Actual—Real.

Actual qualifies what is done, and refers to a previous act; *real* refers to what simply exists as an object of thought. The former is active, the latter passive in meaning. When we speak of the actual condition of a country, we signify the condition into which it has been brought by previous acts; when we speak of its real condition, we mean the state in which it exists as an object of contemplation. Actual is opposed to supposititious; real is opposed to imaginary, feigned, or artificial. An actual fact, a real sentiment.

[*Doct.* In this slumbry agitation, besides her walking and other actual performances, &c. *Macbeth*, v. 1.

Cor. ——— or must omit
Real necessities —— *Coriolanus*, iii. 1.

——— whereat I waked and found
Before mine eyes all real —— *P. L.*, viii. 310

——— to the gazer's eye
Deeper than ocean, in the immensity
Of its vague mountains and unreal sky!
WORDSWORTH. '*Evening Voluntaries.*']

Exercise.

"When I place an imaginary name at the head of a character, I examine every letter of it, that it may not bear any resemblance to one that is ———."

"In this slumbry agitation, besides her walking and other ——— performances, what, at any time, have you heard her say?"

"We do but describe an imaginary world, that is but little akin to the ——— one."

"For he that but conceives a crime in thought
Contracts the danger of an ——— fault;
Then what must he expect that still proceeds
To finish sin, and work up thoughts to deeds?"

"The very notion of any duration being past implies that it was once present; for the idea of being once present is ———ly included in the idea of its being past."

"Imaginary distempers are attended with ——— and unfeigned sufferings."

"These orators influence the people, whose anger is ———ly but a short fit of madness."

"All men acknowledge themselves able and sufficient to do many things which ———ly they never do."

Awkward—Clumsy.

An *awkward* man wants grace of action; a *clumsy* man wants grace of shape. Awkward is opposed to adroit; clumsy is opposed to elegant. Awkward has an active; clumsy, a passive meaning. We do not discover awkwardness before something is done; clumsiness is seen in the very appearance of a thing or person. A clumsy man may have an awkward gait. We speak of an awkward manner, and a clumsy appearance. An awkward man is not always clumsy; for many persons of elegant figure and appearance are any thing but adroit in their actions. In the expression "an awkward excuse," we regard the maker of it; the phrase "a clumsy excuse" points to the nature of the excuse when made.

[*Ulys* —— with ridiculous and awkward action
Troil. and Cress., i. 3.]

Exercise.

"I hardly know any thing so difficult to attain, or so necessary to possess, as perfect good breeding; which is equally inconsistent with a stiff formality, an impertinent forwardness, and an ——— bashfulness."

"All the operations of the Greeks in sailing were ——— and unskilful."

"Their own language is worthy their care; and they are judged of by their handsome or ——— way of expressing themselves in it."

This is, after all, but a ——— contrivance, and I fear will not answer the purpose for which it is intended.

"Montaigne had many ——— imitators, who, under the notion of writing with the fire and freedom of this lively old Gascon, have fallen into confused rhapsodies and uninteresting egotisms."

All the work he was set to was so ———ly done, that it was soon found necessary to discharge him from the office.

Apt—Fit.

Apt has an active sense, *fit* represents a passive state. We are naturally apt; we are rendered fit. Those who are quick of apprehension are *apt* scholars. Those who have studied sufficiently are *fit* to undertake certain duties. Children are apt to make mistakes. Well seasoned wood is fit for use.

Apt represents a natural tendency; fit represents an acquired power.

[*Luc.* —— hands apt, drugs fit —— *Hamlet*, iii 2

Ghost. I find thee apt; *Id.*, i. 5.

Ham. To take him in the purging of his soul,
When he is fit and seasoned for his passage?
Id., iii. 3.

But apt the mind or fancy is to rove.
P. L., viii. 188.

—— Atlantean shoulders fit to bear
The weight of mightiest monarchies ——
Id., ii. 306.

—— our hearts more apt to sympathize
With heaven, our souls more fit for future glory.
WORDSWORTH. '*Miscel. Sonnets.*]

Exercise.

"Nor holy rapture wanted they, to praise
Their Maker in ——— strains, pronounced or sung."

"If you have a wise sentence or an ——— phrase, commit it to your memory."

"It is a wrong use of my understanding to make it the rule and measure of another man's; a use which it is neither ——— for, nor capable of."

"Men are ——— to think well of themselves, and of their nation, their courage, and strength."

"Men of valour ——— to go out for war and battle."

"Even those who are near the court are ——— to deduce wrong consequences, by reasoning upon the motives of actions."

"He lends him vain Goliah's sacred sword,
The ———est help just fortune could afford."

The poor man had become so weak and emaciated by his long illness, that he was no longer ——— to work, and was wholly unable to maintain his family.

"——— words can strike; and yet in them we see
Faint images of what we here enjoy."

'One who has not these lights is a stranger to what he reads, and is ——— to put a wrong interpretation upon it."

Contented—Satisfied.

Contented refers to the state into which we have brought our mind by our own determination; it represents the result of our own act. *Satisfied* qualifies that state of mind which is the consequence of some external action. Contentment comes from within; satisfaction proceeds from without. We are the authors of our own contentment; others cause our satisfaction. When we restrain our desires, we are contented, when our desires are gratified, we are satisfied. There is merit in contentment, since it argues considerable power of mind. The poor are often contented; the avaricious are never satisfied.

[*K. Hen.* ——— we are contented
To wear our mortal state —— *Henry VIII.*, ii. 4.

Laer. I am satisfied in nature
Whose motive, in this case, should stir me most
To my revenge —— *Hamlet*, v. 2

Angels, contented with their fame in heaven
P. L., vi. 375.

How fully hast thou satisfied me, pure
Intelligence of heaven, angel serene!
Id., viii. 180.

Age steal to his allotted nook
Contented and serene. WORDSWORTH. '*Memory.*

Weeping and looking, looking on and weeping
Upon the last sweet slumber of her child,
Until at length her soul was satisfied.
'*The Excursion*,' vi.]

Exercise.

"No man should be ——— with himself that he barely does well, but he should perform every thing in the best manner he is able."

"It is necessary to an easy and happy life, to possess our minds in such a manner as to be well ——— with our own reflections."

"To distant lands Vertumnus never roves,
Like you, ——— with his native groves."

The poorest man may be ———; but the most enormous wealth and most successful ambition have seldom produced ———.

"As I have been disappointed myself, it will be very hard if I have not the ——— of seeing other people succeed better."

"I ask you whether a gentleman who has seen a little of the world, and observed how men live elsewhere, can ———ly sit down in a cold, damp habitation, in the midst of a bleak country, inhabited by thieves and beggars?"

"I am ———; my boy has done his duty."

"He expressed himself perfectly ——— with his task."

Efficacious—Effectual.

That which possesses a large share of power to bring about an effect is qualified as *efficacious;* that which has already produced an effect is qualified as *effectual.* A remedy is efficacious, which is known to possess all the properties required to produce a cure; a remedy is effectual, which we know, from experience, to have already effected cures. Severity may be efficacious, even when not practised; it is also found to have been effectual, *i. e.* has produced the desired effect.

[*Pro.* ——— the doom
(Which, unreversed, stands in effectual doom)
Two Gent. of Verona, iii. 1.

——— that spirit, that first rushed in thee
In the camp of Dan
Be efficacious in thee now at need! *S. A.*, 1437.

—— the sun with more effectual beams
Had cheered the face of earth —— *P. R.*, IV. 432.

Examples efficacious to refine
Rude intercourse —— '*The Excursion*,' viii.

The bells of Rylstone seemed to say
While she sate listening in the shade,
With vocal music—'GOD US AYDE;'
And all the hills were glad to bear
Their part in this effectual prayer.
'*White Doe of Rylstone*.']

Exercise.

"He who labors to lessen the dignity of human nature destroys many ——— motives for practising worthy actions."

"Sometimes, the sight of the altar, and decent preparations for devotion, may compose and recover the wandering mind more ———ly than a sermon."

"Nothing so ———ly deadens the taste of the sublime as that which is light and radiant."

On this occasion, the government displayed a severity which was well known to be ——— in such cases. The result justified their views, for these severe measures ———ly prevented a repetition of the like offences.

These disturbances at length rose to such an alarming height, that it was found necessary to adopt some ——— means of quelling them; and accordingly, a large body of soldiers was marched into the immediate neighborhood of the riots, which kept the rebels in awe, and soon re-established order throughout the country.

Kindness united with firmness is a more ——— means of securing obedience than indiscriminate harshness and severity.

Efficient—Effective.

What has power to produce an effect is *effective*. What actually does produce an effect is *efficient*. An effective force is one which, when put in action, is capable of bringing about a certain result; an efficient force is one which is actually engaged in action. We judge of what is effective, from its appearance; we judge of what is efficient, from its acts. An efficient body of police is one by whose daily efforts crime is prevented and property preserved; an effective body of police is one which, judging from its force, numbers and other external circumstances, has the power to produce the same effect.

Exercise.

"I should suspend my congratulations on the new liberties of France, until I was informed how it had been combined with government, with the discipline of the armies, and the collection of an ——— revenue."

"No searcher has yet found the ——— cause of sleep."

"Nor do they speak properly who say that time consumes all things, for time is not ———, nor are bodies destroyed by it."

"The magnetic fluid may be an ——— cause in occasioning the inclination of the earth's axis; yet no variation of this dip has been ever observed."

"There is nothing in words and styles but suitableness that makes them ———."

He has applied himself with such diligence to the business of the office, that he is now become one of the most ——— members of the government.

Creosote is now known as an ——— remedy in many diseases.

Expert—Experienced.

Expert has to do with the hand; *experienced*, with the head. Experienced men are tried in counsel; expert men are tried in action. The expert have continual practice; the experienced have had much practice, and have acquired much knowledge. Young persons may be expert, but they can never be experienced. Experience must be gained by time. The experienced form the design, and intrust it for execution to the expert.

[*Cas.* ——— his pilot
Of very expert and approv'd allowance
Othello, ii. 1.

Auf. As best thou art experienced, since thou know'st
Thy country's strength and weakness ——
Coriolanus, iv. 5

What pilot so expert but needs must wreck,
Imbarked with such a steersman at the helm?
S. A., 1044.

——— he through the armed files
Darts his experienced eye —— *P. L.*, i. 568.

—— whose experienced eye can pierce the array
Of past events —— WORDSWORTH. '*Sonnets to Liberty.*']

Exercise.

"——— men can execute, and judge of particulars, one by one; but the general counsels, and the plots and marshalling of affairs come best from those that are learned."

"To him ——— Nestor thus rejoined,
O friend, what sorrows dost thou bring to mind!"

"The meanest sculptor in th' Æmilian square
Can imitate in brass the nails and hair,
——— in trifles, and a cunning fool,
Able t' express the parts, but not dispose the whole."

"We must perfect, as much as we can, our ideas of the distinct species, or learn them from such as are used to that sort of things, and are ——— in them."

"This army, for the ——— and valour of the soldiers, was thought sufficient to have met the greatest army of the Turks."

"He through the armed files
Darts his ——— eye."

Without the faculty of memory, no advantage could be derived from the most enlarged ———.

"Fearless they combat every hostile wind,
Wheeling in many tracks with course inclined,
——— to moor, where terrors line the road."

Fruitful—Fertile.

Ground which requires but little culture is *fertile.* Trees which bear much fruit are *fruitful.* Aptness for cultivation is the cause of fertility; actual production is the proof of fruit fulness. In a moral sense, the same distinction exists. A fertile invention possesses a readiness of contrivance; a fruitful invention has numerous contrivances ready for use.

A fertile country has the power of producing; a fruitful country does produce. Fertility is not fruitfulness, but fruitfulness implies fertility.

[*Lov.* — as fruitful as the land that feeds us
Henry VIII., i. 3

Cal. —— barren place and fertile *Tempest*, i. 2.
—— where nature multiplies
Her fertile growth, and by disburdening grows
More fruitful —— *P. L.*, v. 319

A gentler life spreads round the holy spires;
Where'er they rise, the sylvan waste retires,
And aëry harvests crown the fertile lea.
WORDSWORTH. '*Eccles. Sonnets.*']

Exercise.

In many of the West India islands, the earth is so —— and requires so little human labour, that the plants and herbs may be almost said to grow spontaneously.

It may be said with truth that vanity is the most —— source of human unhappiness, for there is scarcely a single vice to which it may not lead, unless it be checked in early years.

The southern side of the island is very ——, and requires but little cultivation; in other parts, however, the soil is comparatively barren, and with considerable labour, but very poor crops are produced.

Our orchard has proved more —— this year than for many previous summers. The —— of the trees is partly owing to the natural —— of the soil, and partly to the warm sun and refreshing showers which have been so prevalent during the whole of the season.

In the year 1811, the —— of the vine, both in France and Germany, was remarkable. For many years after, the wines of that year's growth were in great request in both those countries, and to this day they are talked of with pride by the old vine-dressers.

Friendly—Amicable.

Amicable is a passive; *friendly* is an active word. The former is applied to conditions of life, or states of being; the latter qualifies persons. Men are friendly; an intercourse is amicable. We discover persons to be friendly by their actions. The state in which persons live may be amicable. Those who entertain a friendly feeling towards each other live amicably together. A friendly visit, offer, &c.; an amicable arrangement, accommodation, &c.

[*Glo* Now let thy friendly hand
Put strength enough to it. *Lear*, iv. 6.

If he be friendly, he comes well; if not
Defence is a good cause, and Heaven be for us.
Comus, 488.]

Exercise.

"What first presents itself to be recommended is a disposition averse from offence, and desirous of cultivating harmony, and ——— intercourse in society."

"Who slake his thirst; who spread the ——— board,
To give the famished Belisarius food?"

"As I acknowledged this, I felt a suffusion of a finer kind upon my cheek—more warm and ——— to man, than what Burgundy (at least of two livres a bottle, which was such as I had been drinking) could have produced."

"In Holland itself, where it is pretended that the variety of sects live so ———ly together, it is notorious how a turbulent party, joining with the Arminians, did attempt to destroy the republic."

"They gave them thanks, desiring them to be ——— still unto them."

"Nations, grown ——— as the flocks and herds, shall depute their monarchs to meet at a festival of the world for commemorating the jubilee of a fifty years' peace."

"Thou to mankind
Be good and ——— still, and oft return."

Healthy—Wholesome.

That is *healthy* which promotes or increases our bodily strength. That is *wholesome* which does no harm to our physical constitution, but possesses the quality of health. Pure air, exercise, occupations, &c., are healthy; plain food, diet, &c., are wholesome. The internal functions of the body are disorganized by unwholesome food; the physical powers are improved by healthy air and regular exercise. In like manner, abstractly, a wholesome doctrine is a preservative to our morality; a healthy tone of mind tends to the improvement of our faculties. What is healthy acts upon us; what is wholesome, we act upon.

[*Lucio.* Nay, not as one would say healthy;
Meas. for Meas., i. 2.

Gard. The noisome weeds that without profit suck
The soil's fertility from wholesome flowers.
Rich. II., iii. 4.

—— the still night, not now, as ere man fell,
Wholesome and cool and mild —— · *P. L.*, x. 847.

— every moral feeling of his soul
Strengthened and braced, by breathing, in content,
The keen, the wholesome air of poverty
And drinking from the well of homely life
'*The Excursion*,' i.]

Exercise.

The severity of the labour, and the un- ——— state of the atmosphere in which they work, operate most injuriously on the physical constitution of this class of the population.

All sour fruits, strong wines, and ardent spirits, are universally condemned as un- ——— food for children.

The ——— situation of the house, and the order and regularity with which the establishment is conducted, have greatly contributed to raise its reputation.

Plain, ——— food, pure air, and regular exercise, will not only strengthen the bodily powers, but will also preserve the mental faculties in a ——— state.

A close, damp situation, accumulated matter in a state of decomposition, and want of proper ventilation, are the certain elements of disease, and make rapid inroads on the most ——— constitution.

He is a strong, ——— man; he rises early, works hard, lives on ——— fare, and enjoys refreshing sleep.

" Gardening or husbandry, or working in wood, are fit and ——— recreations for a man of study or business."

" So that the doctrine contained be but ——— and edifying, a want of exactness in speaking may be overlooked."

Impracticable—Impossible.

The first of these terms has an active, the second a passive sense. The distinction between them is, that the first regards those designs which cannot be accomplished by human skill or ingenuity; whilst the second is applied to those things which are contrary to the *existing* laws of nature, or to common sense. Thus, nothing is impossible to God, because he is above the laws of nature. It is impossible for a man to be in two places at once. It is impossible that two and two should make more or less than four. The design of cutting a canal across the isthmus of Darien may have been hitherto impracticable, but it is not impossible that it may, one day, be carried into execution. Again, the navigation of some rivers may be impracticable, but it is not impossible that improvements in science may so far overcome natural obstacles, as to render it practicable.

[*Ant.* —— 'tis as impossible
That he's widroun'd, as he that sleeps here, swims
Tempest, ii. 1.

The rest was craggy cliff, that overhung
Still as it rose, impossible to climb *P. L.* iv. 548

—— 'tis a thing impossible to frame,
Conceptions equal to the soul's desires.
'*The Excursion*' iv.]

Exercise.

It is ——— to comprehend the nature of God.

We were obliged to abandon the plan, as it was found to be ———.

When you say that two straight lines can inclose a space, you assert what is ———.

It is folly to consider things ——— because they are ———.

It is ——— that a boy of twelve years should have the experience of a man of forty.

With men, this is ——— ; but with God, all things are possible.

"To preach up the necessity of that which our experience tells us is ——— were to affright mankind with a terrible prospect."

Intolerable—Insufferable.

Intolerable is an active quality—*insufferable* has a passive meaning. The former qualifies that which our mind or body has not power to fight against; the latter, that which our moral or physical constitution will not allow us to endure. The same distinction holds good between the verbs to suffer and to tolerate. Cold, heat, pain, thirst, &c., are insufferable; pride, vanity, rudeness, &c., are intolerable. In suffering, we are acted upon; in tolerating, we act.

[*P. Hen.* —— but one halfpenny-worth of bread to this intolerable deal of sack!
1 *Henry IV.*, ii. 4.

——— Those heavenly shapes
Will dazzle now this earthly, with their blaze
Insufferably bright. —— *P. L.*, x. 1084.]

Exercise.

In the last engagement, he received a sabre-wound in his left shoulder, which put him to such ——— pain, that he fainted, and was carried off the field by some of his comrades

The heat of the climate during three months is ——, and causes so great a mortality, that in some places the towns are almost deserted by the inhabitants, who seek the cooler and more refreshing atmosphere of the mountains.

The overseer behaved with such —— harshness and arrogance, that not a man in the establishment would serve under him; and all the workmen signed a petition to the governor praying for his removal.

She —— so intensely from head-ache, that she frequently lies for whole days on her bed, unable to move or to make the slightest exertion.

It is the most rational philosophy to —— those evils for which no remedy can be found.

Likely—Probable.

Likely is an active word; *probable*, a passive. Men and things are likely; things are probable. Likely refers to the present state of a thing with respect to its future state; probable refers to its future state with respect to what it now is. If we take the two expressions: 1, "A likely story," and 2, "A probable story," the difference between them will be, that a likely story is one which, from internal evidence and present appearance, carries conviction of its truth. A probable story is one which has the chances in its favour, but which we are not so readily inclined to believe as the other. What is likely is always probable; but what is probable is not always likely. Likelihood depends upon appearances; probability, upon the number of chances in its favour. A bright morning is likely to turn out a fine day; but it is probable that it will be foggy, if it be during the month of November. We speak of a likely, never of a probable person.

[*Mor.* —— he walked o'er perils, on an edge,
More likely to [illegible] in, than to get o'er.
2 *Henry IV.*, i. 1.

Cæs. Most probable
That so she died —— *Antony and Cleopatra*, v. 2.

Seek not temptation then, which to avoid
Were better, and most likely if from me
Thou sever not. *P. L.* ix. 365.]

Exercise.

It is very —— that I shall be obliged, in the course of next month, to make a journey to the Highlands.

The ——— effect of my delay in the country will be the neglect of my affairs in town, and perhaps the loss of much business.

It is ——— that my cousin will arrive in England towards the end of next month.

From the present appearance of affairs, I should think such a conclusion veiy ———.

It is ——— that if Napoleon had conquered the English, he would have succeeded in establishing a universal monarchy in Europe.

The weather is now settled, and I think it very ——— that we shall have a fine day for our excursion.

"It seems ——— that he was in hopes of being busy and conspicuous."

"That is accounted ——— which has better arguments producible for it, than can be brought against it."

Lovely—Amiable.

Amiable has a passive sense, and signifies deserving of love. *Lovely* is active in its signification, and means inspiring love. The disposition and character are amiable; the outward appearance is lovely. Beauty of form, shape, colour, &c., are lovely; the kind, gentle, tender, and affectionate are amiable. We speak of an amiable wife or daughter; and of a lovely evening, flower, sunset, &c. Amiable is never applied to things, and lovely never to moral qualities. We can neither say an amiable flower, nor a lovely temper.

[*Friar.* And every lovely organ of her life
Shall come apparelled in more precious habit
Much Ado, &c., iv. 1

Oth. 'T would make her amiable, and subdue my father
Entirely to her love —— *Othello*, iii. 4.

More lovely than Pandora, whom the Gods
Endowed with all their gifts —— *P. L.*, iv. 714

With what all earth or heaven could bestow
To make her amiable —— *Id.*, viii. 484

A lovely Apparition, sent
To be a moment's ornament.
WORDSWORTH, p. 143

Exercise.

Though of an excellent temper, and most ——— disposition, he could be very strict and even severe when the occasion required, and managed all the affairs of the institution with the utmost prudence and discrimination.

On arriving at Remagen, we took post-horses to Ahrweiler, and travelling through the ——— valley of the Ahr, arrived in about two hours at Altenahr, about twenty miles from the Rhine.

The door was opened by a young woman of most ——— appearance, who asked us, in the kindest tone, to walk in and take some refreshment after our long journey.

We had scarcely been seated five minutes, when the door opened, and in walked a ——— little girl, apparently about five years old.

He is just the proper person to mediate between the parties; for his ——— temper, inflexible justice, and the esteem in which they both hold him, make it very likely that he will succeed in reconciling them to each other

"More fresh and ——— than the rest
That in the meadows grew."

"Sweet Auburn, ——— village of the plain."

"Tully has a very beautiful gradation of thoughts to shew how ——— virtue is."

Malicious—Malignant.

Malicious is exerting malice; *malignant* is possessing malice. A malicious feeling is one which does harm to others; a malignant disposition is one which may be easily excited to do injury. Malicious implies an active, malignant a passive or dormant feeling. Things are seldom qualified as malicious, though often as malignant; as a malignant fever, disease, influence, climate, &c.

[*Wol.* ——— We must not stint
Our necessary actions, in the fear
To cope malicious censurers ——— *Henry VIII.*, i. 2.

Wol. His will is most malignant *Id.*, i. 2.

——— what malicious foe
Envying our happiness ——— *P. L.*, ix. 252.

To good malignant, to bad men benign.
Id., xii. 538.

To laughter multiplied in louder peals
By his malicious wit ——— '*The Excursion*,' vi

——— remote
From evil speaking; rancour never sought
Comes to me not; malignant truth nor lie.
'*Personal Talk*.']

Exercise.

The disposition of the minister was so ——— against me, that he left nothing untried to compass my ruin. Unhappily for me, an occasion soon presented itself. I was traduced to the king, thrown into prison, and all my honors and estates conferred on another.

I was now in a deplorable condition; my wife lay ill of a ——— fever, my two sons were too young to do any thing for themselves, and I had not a farthing in the world to procure them the commonest necessaries of life

The unhealthy state of many climates is caused by the ——— vapours which rise from extensive tracts of land covered with stagnant water. Fever, ague, and rheumatism are thus engendered to a fearful extent.

It required all his vigilance and caution to keep clear of the intrigues of his ——— foe, who thwarted all his plans, and in many cases successfully interfered with his designs for the public improvement.

Go not near him; his influence is most ———, and it will affect not yourself only, but also your friends.

" Greatness, the earnest of ——— fate
For future woe, was never meant a good."

" Still horror reigns, a dreary twilight round
Of struggling night and day ——— mixed."

Mercantile—Commercial.

Mercantile is used in an active sense ; it qualifies those who buy and sell commodities. *Commercial* is passive in its acceptation ; it has reference to the state of things or persons. Mercantile people are such as are actually engaged in business ; commercial people are those who understand the theory and practice of commerce. The English are a commercial people ; the majority of the inhabitants of London are mercantile men.

Exercise.

" Of the ——— talents of Bonaparte, I can be supposed to know but little ; but bred in camps, it cannot be supposed that his ——— knowledge can be very great."

" Such is the happiness, the hope of which seduced me from the duties and pleasures of a ——— life."

" We usually find that a certain apathy to amusement, perfectly distinct from mere gravity of disposition, is the characteristic of ——— nations."

" Though this was one of the first ——— transactions of my life, yet I had no doubt of acquitting myself with reputation."

" The ——— world is very frequently put into confusion by the bankruptcy of merchants."

" It was the morning of Diomed's banquet, and Diomed himself, though he greatly affected the gentleman and the scholar, retained enough of his ——— experience, to know that a master's eye makes a ready servant."

"Let him travel, and fulfil the duties of the military or ——— life; let prosperous or adverse fortune call him to the most distant parts of the globe, still let him carry on his knowledge, and the improvement of his soul."

"One circumstance prevented ——— intercourse with nations from ceasing altogether."

Owing—Due.

That is *owing* which is to be referred to as an origin or source; that is *due* which ought to be paid as a debt. Justice is due to all men. It was owing to this difficulty that the plan did not succeed. In the first of these examples, justice is qualified as *due—i. e.* to be paid as a natural right. In the second, the difficulty is mentioned as the origin or cause of the plan not succeeding.

In such sentences as "The money is owing," "It was due to the ignorance of the scholars," &c., both words are, undoubtedly, misapplied.

[*Count.* there is more owing her than is paid.
All's Well, &c., i. 3.

Ege. Turned her obedience, which is due to me,
To stubborn harshness. —— *Mid. N. Dream*, i. 1.

——— a slave inrolled
Due by the law to capital punishment
S. A., 1225

Save those who to my sorrows lend
Tears due unto their own.
WORDSWORTH. '*Lament of Mary Queen of Scots.*']

Exercise.

"There is ——— from the judge to the advocate some commendation, where causes are well handled and fairly pleaded. There is likewise ——— to the public a civil reprehension of advocates, where there appears cunning, gross neglect, or slight information."

"This was ——— to an indifference to the pleasures of life, and an aversion to the pomps of it."

"There is a respect ——— to mankind which should incline even the wisest of men to follow innocent customs."

"The custom of particular impeachments was not limited any more than that of struggles between nobles and commons; the ruin of Greece was ——— to the former, as that of Rome was to the latter."

"Mirth and cheerfulness are but the ——— reward of an innocent life."

"If we estimate things, what in them is ——— to nature, and what to labour, we shall find in most of them ninety-nine hundredths to be on the account of labour."

Whatever is ——— to you shall certainly be paid.

Peaceable—Peaceful.

Peaceful qualifies what remains at peace, or is in a state of peace; *peaceable* refers to an inclination to peace. Peaceful is having the quality of peace; peaceable is having the desire of peace. A peaceful valley; a peaceable disposition. A cottage is not peaceful which is disturbed by the brawls of its inmates; a man is not peaceable who is continually quarrelling with his acquaintances. Peaceful describes a passive; peaceable, an active quality.

[*Dogb.* the most peaceable way for you, if you do take a thief is to let him show himself what he is, and steal out of your company.

Much Ado, &c., iii. 3

K. John. Unless thou let his silver water keep
A peaceful progress to the ocean. *King John*, ii. 2.

——— enslave
Peaceable nations ——— *P. R.*, iii. 76.

And may at last my weary age
Find out the peaceful hermitag.

MILTON. *Il Pens*, 168.

——— trophies high
Of more than martial courage in the breast
Of peaceful civic virtue ———

WORDSWORTH. '*Sonnets to Liberty.*']

Exercise.

"I know that my ——— disposition already gives me a very ill figure here!"

"Still as the ——— walks of ancient night,
Silent as are the lamps that burn in tombs."

"The balance of power was provided for, else Peisistratus could never have governed so ———ly, without changing any of Solon's laws."

"Succeeding monarchs heard the subjects' cries,
Nor saw displeased the ——— cottage rise."

"But how faint, how cold is the sensation which a ——— mind can receive from solitary study!"

"The reformation in England was introduced in a ——— manner, by the supreme power in Parliament."

"As one disarmed, his anger all he lost,
And thus with ——— words upraised her soon."

The young king thus finding himself in ——— possession of the throne, directed his attention to the cultivation of those arts which embellish life and refine human nature.

"In this retired and ——— spot he spent the remaining days of his life"

Poetic—Poetical.

Poetic is the active, and *poetical* the passive term. *Poetic* qualifies what produces poetry, or is an agent in producing it: thus we have poetic rage, poetic frenzy, &c. *Poetical* qualifies that which already exists as an object of our thought or contemplation: thus we have poetical language a poetical license, &c.

[*Touch.* Truly, I would the gods had made thee poetical.
As You Like It, iii. 3

Yea, what were mighty Nature's self?
Her features, could they win us
Unhelped by the poetic voice
That hourly speaks within us?
WORDSWORTH. '*Yarrow Revisited.*']

Exercise.

——— language is distinguished from prose, by figure, metre, and harmony.

Those who are said to be of a ——— temperament are generally much more nervous and easily excited than others.

Milton is celebrated not only for his ——— compositions; he was a beautiful prose writer, and one of the best classical scholars of his age.

Though young and inexperienced in writing, he has shewn in these works considerable harmony and smoothness of versification, nor are they wanting in ——— power in many passages.

A ——— reader discovers, without any effort, a thousand beauties which not only are hidden from others, but which no power of explanation can succeed in making them comprehend.

"Truth of every kind belongs to the poet, provided it can bud into any kind of beauty, or is capable of being illustrated and impressed by the ——— faculty."

Pindar is characterized by his ——— energy. Horace says that he rushes along roaring and foaming like a mighty river, carrying every thing with it in its course.

Reasonable—Rational.

One who exercises reason is *reasonable;* one who possesses reason is *rational.* The former is the active; the latter, the passive quality. Man is a rational animal—that is, he is endowed with the reasoning faculty. Reasonable men are those who make use of their reason. The brutes are irrational. Though all men are rational, many are very far from being reasonable.

[*Anne.* It is a quarrel just and reasonable
To be revenged on him, that killed my husband.
Richard III., i. 3

——— affecting to subdue
Rational liberty —— *P. L.*, xii. 82

——— nor Man,
The rational creature, left, to feel the weight
Of his own reason, without sense or thought
Of higher reason and a purer will
To benefit and bliss, through mightier power.
'*The Excursion*,' iv.]

Exercise.

"Human nature is the same in all ——— creatures."

"As that which has a fitness to promote the welfare of man, considered as a sensitive being, is styled natural good; so, that which has a fitness to promote the welfare of man as a ———, voluntary, and free agent, is styled moral good, and the contrary to it, moral evil."

"The Parliament was dissolved, and gentlemen furnished with such forces as were held sufficient to hold in bridle either the malice or rage of ——— people."

"The evidence which is afforded for a future state is sufficient for a ——— ground of conduct."

"It is our happiness to have a ——— nature, that is endued with wisdom and reason."

It is greatly to be lamented that ——— beings are not more ———.

Chaucer makes Arcite violent in his love, and unjust in the pursuit of it yet when he came to die, he made him think more ———ly.

"When the conclusion is deduced from the unerring dictates of our faculties, we say the inference is ———."

"To act in direct opposition to our convictions is ———."

Sociable—Social.

Those who are formed for society are *social;* those who are in active intercourse with their fellow-creatures are *socia-*

ble. Man is a social animal; but all men are not sociable. Social refers to the natural quality of men to congregate together, and live in society. Sociable refers to the particular inclination of some to be in continual intercourse with their friends and acquaintances.

When these words qualify things, (not persons,) the same distinction of active and passive holds good between them. *Social* is that which relates to society. Social morality means that species of morality which affects men living in society. *Sociable* is that which promotes intercourse; hence the word has been used substantively to designate a sort of chair or carriage, which is convenient for familiar conversation.

[*Imo.* ——— Society is no comfort
To one not sociable. —— *Cymbeline*, IV. 2.

Raphael, the sociable spirit, that deigned
To travel with Tobias, and secured
His marriage with the seventimes-wedded maid.
P. L., v. 221

Best with thyself accompanied, seek'st not
Social communication —— *Id.*, viii. 429

Five graves, and only five, that rise together
Unsociably sequestered, and encroaching
On the smooth play-ground of the village-school.
'*The Excursion*,' vii.

——— Turn to private life
And social neighbourhood; look we to ourselves:
A light of duty shines on every day
For all —— *Id.*, v]

Exercise.

A great portion of our happiness in this world arises from the power of that ——— intercourse by which we are enabled to communicate our thoughts and feelings to others, and receive theirs in exchange.

Even those who are most ———ly inclined do not like to be always in the midst of their friends, or in actual intercourse with their fellow-creatures; for all sensible men must require some time for study and meditation.

Man appears to have been made a ——— being in order that he might help his fellow-man, and assist him to provide against those dangers which his unaided power has not strength to resist.

He acquired in early life such un——— habits, that he never could overcome his dislike to society, where he always both looked and felt ill at ease.

We met there several very clever and amiable men, and spent a most ——— and delightful evening with them.

Salutary—Salubrious.

Both these words signify improving the health. *Salutary*, however, is not so immediate in its effects as *salubrious*. This latter word is used in a passive sense; it signifies having the property of improving health. The air in the south of France is equally salubrious, whether we reside there or not. The word salutary has a more active meaning; what it qualifies affects us, as it were, of its own accord. For this reason, salubrious is more frequently used in a proper sense, whilst salutary is generally used metaphorically. Thus we have salubrious air, climate, water, &c.; and a salutary doctrine, influence, practice, &c.

[——— as a power
Is salutary, or an influence sweet
Are each and all enabled to perceive
That power, that influence, by impartial law
'*The Excursion*,' IX.]

Exercise.

"If that fountain (the heart) be once poisoned, you can never expect that ——— streams will flow from it."

"Be that as it may, a ——— reformation was wrought—the muses were brought back from the rattle and the go-cart to lift their voices as of old; and the isle of Britain, east and west, north and south, broke out into one voluntary song."

His mode of life was now entirely changed; no longer pent up within the narrow streets of a crowded city, or the hot rooms of London gaiety, he rose betimes, enjoyed the ——— mountain air the whole day, ate temperately, and retired to rest at an early hour.

"A sense of the Divine presence exerts this ——— influence of promoting temperance, and restraining the disorders incident to a prosperous state."

Instruction or admonition is ——— when it serves the purpose of strengthening good principles, and awakening a sense of guilt or impropriety.

"I boast no song in magic wonders rife,
But yet, O Nature! is there nought to prize
Familiar in thy bosom-scenes of life?
And dwells in daylight truth's ——— skies,
No form with which the soul may sympathize?"

Sufficient—Enough.

Enough has a passive meaning ; it respects self-enjoyment : *sufficient* is an active quality, and respects the necessaries of life. A man has enough who has no longer a desire ; a man has sufficient who has no longer a want. Some men never have enough, though they have much more than sufficient. The measure of enough is the satisfying of our desires ; the measure of sufficient depends on what is to be done with it. We may have enough for ourselves, but not sufficient to provide for the wants of others. A man may have lived long enough, as far as he himself is concerned, without having had sufficient time to do all the good he could have wished.

[*Cant.* —— a wall sufficient to defend
Our inland from the pilfering borderers.
Henry V., i. 2.

K. Hen. If we are marked to die, we are enough
To do our country loss —— *Id.*, iv. 3.

Sufficient introduction to inform
Thee, of thyself so apt, in regal arts *P. R.*, iii. 247

——— each day's lot
Enough to bear —— *P. L.*, xi. 766.

Deeming the evil of the day
Sufficient for the wise.
WORDSWORTH. '*Our Lady of the Snow.*'

Yea, veriest reptiles have sufficed to prove
To fettered wretchedness, that no Bastile
Is deep enough to exclude the light of love
Though man for brother man has ceased to feel.
'*Miscel. Sonnets.*']

Exercise.

During the whole of the long winter, this poor family were in the greatest want ; they had often scarcely ——— food to preserve life, and suffered extremely from the intense cold of the season.

Many who have ——— for themselves never think of whether others are ———ly provided for.

The dealer told me that twenty-nine yards of that silk were quite ——— to make two dresses.

I have seen ——— to convince me that the affairs of the house are very badly managed

As soon as you have heard ——— music, we will adjourn to the other apartment.

Without ——— money, I shall not have the means of proceeding on my journey, and shall be obliged to remain at Brussels, until I procure a fresh supply.

I can easily procure ——— for my own wants; but to provide ——— for the maintenance of a large family is not so easy a matter.

Sure—Certain.

The word *sure* is used actively; the word *certain*, passively. The former is more frequently joined with a verb; the latter, with a participle. What is to be done may be sure; but what is already done is certain. The idiom of our language will not allow us to say "He is certain to do something;" but we may say, "He is sure to do it." We are sure of what we are convinced will happen; we are certain of what we are satisfied is true. We are not sure, but certain, of our existence; we cannot be certain, but may be sure, of what is to happen. Certain has to do with our reason; sure has to do with our feelings.

[*Edg.* Not sure, though hoping, of this good success.
Lear, v. 3.

Cit. Therefore, 'tis certain, he was not ambitious.
Jul. Cæsar, iii. 2.

——— what shall befall
Him or his children; evil he may be sure
Which neither his foreknowing can prevent.
P. L., xi. 772.

——— that honour
Certain to have won by mortal duel from thee
S. A., 1102.]

Exercise.

"If you find nothing new in the matter, I am ——— much less will you in the style."

"Those things are ——— among men, which cannot be denied without obstinacy and folly."

"———ly, it will be owned, that a wise man, who takes upon him to be vigilant for the public weal, should touch proper things at proper times, and not prescribe for a surfeit, when the distemper is a consumption."

"———er to prosper than prosperity
Could have assured us."

"It is very ——— that a man of sound reason cannot forbear closing with religion upon an impartial examination of it."

"Be silent always when you doubt your sense,
And speak, though ———, with seeming diffidence."

"What precise collection of simple ideas modesty or frugality stands for in another's use, is not ———ly known."

"The youngest in the morning are not ———,
That till the night their life they can secure."

"When these everlasting doors are thrown open, we may be ——— that the pleasures and beauties of this place will infinitely transcend our present hopes and expectations."

Thankful—Grateful.

Gratitude is rather the feeling, and *thankfulness* the expression of the feeling. We may look grateful, but we speak our thanks. Thankfulness is uttered; gratitude is sometimes too deep for utterance. Gratitude is on the alert to make a return for kindness; thankfulness publishes a kindness. Gratitude is silent, though lasting; thankfulness is temporary, and is the expression of our gratitude.

[*Buck.* Sir
I am thankful to you —— *Henry VIII.*, i. 1.

King. I cannot give thee less, to be called grateful
All's Well, ii. 1.

And understood not that a grateful mind
By owing owes not, but still pays, at once
Indebted and discharged —— *P. L.*, iv. 55.

—— were humbly thankful for the good
Which the warm sun solicited, and earth
Bestowed —— '*The Excursion*, iv

—— He, whose soul
Ponders this true equality, may walk
The fields [illegible] earth with gratitude and hope
Id., ix.]

Exercise.

"The young girl made me a more humble courtesy than a low one; 'twas one of those quiet, ——— sinkings, where the spirit bows itself down; the body does no more than tell it."

"After we had saluted each other with proper ceremony, we all bent in ——— to that Being who gave us another day."

"He scarcely would give me thanks for what I had done, for fear that ——— might have an introduction of reward."

"The release of pain is the excess of transport. With what ——— we feel the first return of health—the first budding forth of the new spring that has dawned within us!"

"In favor, to use men with much difference is good; for it makes the person preferred more ———, and the rest more officious."

"A ——— mind
By owing, owes not, but still pays, at once
Indebted and discharged."

"He retired, overpowered with his own ———, and his benefactor's respectful compassion."

Vacant—Empty.

That which has nothing in it is *empty*. That which requires something in it is *vacant*. Empty is a natural, vacant, a circumstantial quality. A space is purposely left vacant which is intended to be filled up; a space is empty which is merely not filled up. If we rise from our chair, the seat is empty; if we do not intend to return to it, the seat is vacant. A seat in Parliament becomes vacant by the death of a member. A vacant hour wants filling up; an empty title has nothing solid in it.

[*Const.* Stuffs out his vacant garments with his form
King John, iii. 4.

Ant. When my good stars, that were my former guides
Have empty left their orbs —— *Ant. and Cleop.*, v. 11

——— silent as the moon
When she deserts the night,
Hid in her vacant interlunar cave *S. A.*, 89.

Or in the emptier waste, resembling air
Weighs his spread wings —— *P. L.*, ii. 1045.

——— and clear and bright
And vacant doth the region which they thronged
Appear: —— WORDSWORTH. '*To the Clouds.*'

Lo! in such neighbourhood, from morn to eve
The habitation's empty! —— '*The Excursion*,' viii.]

Exercise.

"Why should the air so impetuously rush into the cavity of the receiver, if there were before no ——— room to receive it?"

"I did never know so full a voice issue from so ——— a heart; but the saying is true, the ——— vessel makes the greatest sound."

"Others, when they admitted that the throne was ———, thought the succession should immediately go to the next heir."

"When you speak, he listens with a ——— eye; when you walk, he watches you with a curled lip; if he dines with you, he sends away your best hock with a wry face."

"Cold is the hearth within their bowers,
And should we thither roam;
Its echoes and its ——— tread
Would sound like voices from the dead"

"The watch-dog's voice that bayed the whispering wind,
And the loud laugh that spoke the ——— mind."

"If you have two vessels to fill, and you ——— one to fill the other, you gain nothing by that; there still remains one vessel ———."

"The pit was ———; there was no water in it."

"The memory relieves the mind in her ——— moments, and prevents any chasms of thought, by ideas of what is past."

Warlike—Martial.

Martial qualifies the external appearance, and is used passively; *warlike* qualifies the spirit, and is active in its meaning. A martial appearance has reference to the "pomp and circumstance" of war; a warlike appearance, to the expression and attitude of warriors. A man who breathes a spirit of hostility has a warlike appearance; a man in armour, or in military uniform, has a martial appearance.

[*Cym.* ——— which to shake off,
Becomes a warlike people ——— *Cymbeline*, iii. 1.

Ros. We'll have a swashing and a martial outside.
As You Like It, i. 3

——— At his approach
The great archangel from his warlike toil
Surceased ——— *P. L.*, vi. 257

Sonorous metals blowing martial sounds. *Id.*, i. 540.

——— urgent to equip
Thy warlike person with the staff and scrip
WORDSWORTH. '*Eccles. Sonnets.*

——— fixing hope and aim
On the humanities of peaceful fame,
Enter betimes with more than martial fire
The generous course, aspire and still aspire.
'*Liberty*.']

Exercise.

"But different far the change has been
Since Marmion, from the crown
Of Blackford, saw that ——— scene
Upon the bent so brown."

"Gifts worthy of soldiers; the ——— steed, the bloody and ever-victorious lance, were the rewards which the champions claimed from the liberality of their chief."

"But when our country's cause provokes to arms,
How ——— music every bosom warms."

"Last from the Volscians fair Camilla came,
And led her ——— troops, a warrior dame."

"Let his neck answer for it, if there is any ——— law in the world"

"When a ——— state grows soft and effeminate, they may be sure of a war."

"They proceeded in a kind of ——— justice with enemies, offering them their law before they drew their sword."

"She, using so strange and yet so well-succeeding a temper, made her people by peace ———."

"The ——— genius of Napoleon at length wearied even the ——— ardour of his soldiers."

"Old Siward, with ten thousand ——— men,
All ready at a point, was setting forth."

"See
His thousands, in what ——— equipage
They issue forth!"

Unavoidable—Inevitable.

These two words, though approximating very closely in signification, do not convey exactly the same meaning. The distinction between them depends on the active or passive sense of the words which they qualify. *Inevitable* respects some fixed law of nature over which no human power can prevail; whereas *unavoidable* qualifies some measure or step which we cannot help taking. That is unavoidable which circumstances will not allow us to escape from *doing;* that is inevitable which our condition, as human beings, will not allow us to escape from *suffering.* Death, fate, and ruin, are represented as inevitable; a bankruptcy or a marriage may be unavoidable.

[*Cor.* 'Tis fond to wail inevitable strokes
As 'tis to laugh at them. —— *Coriolanus,* iv. 2.

——— since fate inevitable
Subdues us, and omnipotent decree *P. L.*, ii. 197.

Why with such earnest pains dost thou provoke
The years to bring the inevitable yoke,
Thus blindly with thy blessedness at strife!
WORDSWORTH. '*Ode on Intimations,*' *&c.*]

Exercise.

His affairs were so deeply involved, that an exposure was become ———.

The ——— consequences of extravagance are ruin and misery.

In consequence of the non-arrival of the packet, we were ——— delayed at the custom-house.

Had not the storm abated, we should have been ——— shipwrecked.

Oppression on one side, and ambition on the other, are the ——— occasions of war.

The evils to which every man is daily exposed are ———.

This step was ———, as without it, our ruin was ———.

" If our sense of hearing were exalted, we should have no quiet or sleep in the most silent night, and we must ———ly be struck deaf, or dead, with a clap of thunder."

" The day thou eat'st thereof, my sole command
Transgrest, ———ly thou shalt die."

Single acts of transgression will, through weakness and surprise, be ——— to the best guarded.

SECTION III.

SYNONYMES OF INTENSITY.

In examining the explanations in this section, it will be found that they are all based upon one leading principle, viz. *intensity*—that is, the difference between the one and the other word will be, that the second expresses a more intensive degree of the first. Here again, the student must be cautioned against confounding this principle with grammatical comparison. In grammar, the comparative is a more intensive form of the same word, (the adjective,) and is confined to one class of words; but here, the second word is wholly unlike the first in form, though it expresses a more intensive degree in signification. We may refer to this principle the difference between the two verbs *to hear* and *to listen*. *To hear* is a simple act, *to listen* is an intensive act. We cannot help hearing, but we listen with intention. The same may be said of *to see* and *to look*. It costs us no effort of the sense, to *see*—it is but " opening the eye, and the scene enters ;" but in *looking*, there is an effort, a desire, an act, in fine, of the mind as well as of the eye, which is not found in the former word. This principle operates to a great extent in language, and a very great number of differences are to be explained by its application. Whenever we find a difference of this sort between two terms, they may be ranged under the head of " *Synonymes of Intensity*."

Act—Action.

An *act* is the simple exertion of physical or mental power. An *action* is a continued exertion of the faculties. An action takes up more time than an act. Many acts make up an action. We set about doing a kind action, viz. to reconcile two friends. Many acts are requisite to effect this purpose : *e.g.*, the act of speaking to both parties ; the act of walking, perhaps, from one to the other, &c. There is this difference between an act of folly and a foolish action : an act of folly is one in which folly is represented as the impulse ; a foolish action is one which is qualified or specified as such when done. The degree of our merit depends upon our actions, not upon our acts. Acts are single ; actions habitual.

[*Lod.* This heavy act with heavy heart relate *Othello*, v. 2.

L. Macd. ——— When our actions do not,
Our fears do make us traitors. —— *Macbeth*, iv. 2.

This day will be remarkable in my life
By some great act —— *S. A.*, 1388.

High actions and high passions best describing *P. R.*, iv. 266.

Resting upon his arms each warrior stood,
Checked in the very act and deed of blood.
WORDSWORTH. '*Sonnets to Liberty*.'

——— our state
Enjoins, while firm resolves await
On wishes just and wise,
That strenuous action follow both,
And life be one perpetual growth
Of heaven-ward enterprise. '*The Wishing-Gate Destroyed*.']

Exercise.

He had raised his hand, and was in the ——— of striking the prince, when a foot-soldier, perceiving his purpose, rushed in between the combatants, and received the blow upon his arm.

For this brave ——— he was handsomely rewarded by his commander, and immediately promoted to the rank of a sergeant.

Many persons judge wrongly of their neighbours, from not sufficiently considering the motives of their ———.

He was in the ——— of shaking hands with a neighbour, when he was suddenly seized with a fit, and fell back senseless into an arm-chair.

Our ——— are generally caused by instinct or impulse ; ——— are more frequently the result of thought or deliberation.

"Many of those ——— which are apt to procure fame are not in their nature conducive to ultimate happiness."

"I desire that the same rule may be extended to the whole fraternity of the heathen gods; it being my design to condemn every poem to the flames, in which Jupiter thunders or exercises any ——— of authority which does not belong to him."

Anguish—Agony.

A struggling against pain is the idea common to both these words. *Agony* denotes the bodily feeling, whilst *anguish* regards the state of mind. The throbbing of a wound produces agony; a mother feels anguish at the idea of being separated from her child. The word agony is used in a secondary sense to express the climax of any state of feeling, as found in the expressions, "an agony of doubt, an agony of suspense," &c. —*i. e.* the highest possible state of painful doubt or suspense. The agonies of death; the anguish of despair.

[*Phy.* —— many simples operative, whose power
Will close the eye of anguish. *King Lear*, IV. 4.

1 *Gent.* ——— he was stirred
With such an agony, he sweat extremely *Henry VIII.*, ii. 2

The anguish of my soul, that suffers not
Mine eye to harbour sleep, or thoughts to rest. *S. A.*, 458.

—— ghastly spasm, or racking torture, qualms
Of heart-sick agony —— *P. L.*, xi. 482.

——— through weight
Of anguish unrelieved, and lack of power
An agonizing sorrow to transmute '*The Excursion*,' iv.]

Exercise.

"The sun had now gone down—another day had passed without bringing us relief—several of the party had begun to suffer dreadfully from intense thirst, and two were in the ——— of death."

The ——— of the father when he heard of the fate of his wretched child is to be imagined rather than described; he fainted immediately on receiving the news, and it was a long time before he recovered his senses.

They had persecutors, whose invention was as great as their cruelty. Wit and malice conspire to find out such deaths, and those of such incredible ———, that only the manner of dying was the punishment, death itself the deliverance.

The thoughts not only of what he himself was about to suffer, but also of the forlorn condition of his wife and family in the event of his death, filled his mind with ——— and despair.

He suffered such ——— from the wound in his leg, that he could proceed no further on his journey.

"There is a word in the vocabulary more bitter, more direful in its import, than all the rest. Reader, if poverty, if disgrace, if bodily pain be your unhappy fate, kneel and bless Heaven for its beneficent influence, so that you are not tortured with the ——— of remorse."

Artisan—Artist.

The word *artisan* signifies one who exercises a mechanical art: the word *artist* is properly applied only to those who practise the fine arts. Carpenters, masons, and shoemakers, are artisans; poets, musicians, and sculptors, are artists. The artisan works by rule, and uses his hands; the artist's occupation requires the exercise of a refined intellect and lively imagination. We shall thus easily distinguish the sign-painter from the historical painter. In an intellectual scale, the artisan ranks above the labourer, but below the artist. Ingenuity and contrivance are the qualities of a good artisan; creative power and refined taste are requisite for a great artist.

[*Agam.* The wise and fool, the artist and unread
Troil. and Cress., i. 3.

——— like the moon, whose orb
Through optic glass the Tuscan artist views
At evening, from the top of Fesolè. *P L.*, i. 288.

——— shoals of artisans
From ill-requited labour turned adrift '*The Excursion*,' i

Might some aspiring artist dare
To seize whate'er, through misty air
A ghost by glimpses may present
Of imitable lineament. *Id.*, p. 233.]

Exercise.

"This poor woman's husband, who was an ingenious ———, had come up to London in hopes of finding employment; but having failed in his attempt, had set off to return to Scotland, and was on his way back when I fell in with him."

Dannecker, the sculptor, one of the most celebrated modern ——— of Germany, was born at Stuttgard, October the 15th, 1758. Two of his works, viz. "Mourning Friendship," and the "Ariadne reclining on a Leopard," are distinguished for beauty and expression.

The close and densely-populated parts of London are inhabited chiefly by labourers, journeymen, and ———, whose health is undoubtedly as much impaired by the situations in which they are obliged to reside, as by the circumstances which force them to work so hard for their daily bread.

Haydn, Mozart, and Beethoven, were the greatest musical ——— the world ever produced.

"If ever this country saw an age of ———s, it is the present; her painters, sculptors, and engravers, are now the only schools properly so called."

"The merchant, tradesman, and ———, will have their profit upon all the multiplied wants, comforts, and indulgences of civilized life"

Compunction—Remorse.

These words express degrees of repentance. *Remorse* is an intensive compunction. *Compunction* signifies a pricking of the conscience. *Remorse* denotes a gnashing or biting. The former is expressive of the sorrow caused by minor offences; the latter conveys an idea of the excessive pain the soul feels at the sense of its crimes, and is analogous to the feeling of bodily pain expressed by grinding or gnashing the teeth. Compunction is felt for sin; remorse for enormous crimes. A miser may feel compunction for his injustice; a murderer is agitated by remorse.

[*Lady M.* Stop up the access and passage to remorse;
That no compunctious visitings of nature
Shake my fell purpose —— *Macbeth*, i. 5

So farewell, hope; and with hope, farewell, fear;
Farewell, remorse: —— *P. L.*, iv. 109.

To feed remorse, to welcome every sting
Of penitential anguish, yea, with tears.
WORDSWORTH. '*The Borderers*.']

Exercise.

All his peace of mind was now destroyed by the ——— he felt for the crimes of his early life; the images of his victims haunted him in his dreams, and in his waking hours he looked upon every stranger as an assassin.

"Stop up th' access and passage to ———
That no ——— visitings of conscience
Shake my fell purpose."

This outcast of society pursued his wicked machinations without cessation; he felt no ——— for the injustice he was practising on the desolate widow and helpless orphan; all fell alike into his meshes, and as long as his coffers were filled, it signified nothing to him that it was at the expense of the sighs and tears of thousands.

He began at length to feel some ——— for the harshness with which he had treated his brother, and wrote him an affectionate letter, in which he begged his forgiveness, and entreated that they should renew their former harmony.

"All men, even the most depraved, are subject, more or less, to ——s of conscience."

"The heart
Pierced with a sharp —— for guilt, disclaims
The costly poverty of hecatombs,
And offers the best sacrifice, itself."

Diligence—Industry.

Diligence signifies the attention we pay to any particular object, because we prefer it to others. *Industry* is the quality of laying up for ourselves a store, either of knowledge or worldly goods. Diligence produces industry: it is applied to one object; industry, to many. To collect accurate information, evidence, &c., from various sources, we must be industrious. To become well-informed upon one subject, we must be diligent. The quality of diligence is not applied to animals. The bee and ant, however, are said to be industrious, because their instinct prompts them to lay up a store.

[*Lord.* There wants no diligence in seeking him,
Cymbeline, iv. 3.

Bel. The sweat of industry would dry, and die,
But for the end it works to. —— *Id.*, iii. 6.

—— redoubled love and care
With musing diligence —— *S. A.*, 924.

—— where thou heard'st the billows beat
On a wild coast, rough monitors to feed
Perpetual industry. Sublime Recluse!
The recreant soul, that dares to shun the debt
Imposed on human kind, must first forget
Thy diligence, thy unrelaxing use
Of a long life —— WORDSWORTH. '*Eccles Sonnets.*]

Exercise.

He was so ——, that before he was twelve years old, he was much better informed on all subjects than most boys of his age.

My cousin studied with such ——, that he soon made himself master of the language.

He immediately applied himself with great —— to every department of knowledge which was connected, however remotely, with the duties of his office.

Without ———, it is impossible to make a satisfactory progress in any branch of learning.

——— is a striking characteristic of all classes of the population in China.

Distress and difficulty are known to operate in private life as the spurs of ———.

If you inquire not attentively and ———ly, you will never be able to discern a number of mechanical motions.

"It has been observed by writers on morality, that, in order to quicken human ———, Providence has so contrived that our daily food is not to be procured without much pains and labour."

Discernment—Penetration.

By *discernment* we obtain a knowledge of the real worth of persons or things. By *penetration* we discover the existence of what is concealed. Discernment is the quality of a clear, sensible understanding; penetration, of an acute intellect. We exercise discernment in forming a just estimate of character; we exercise penetration in discovering the plots of the designing.

Exercise.

He struggled long and hard against the difficulties of fortune, and had it not been for the ——— of a casual acquaintance, who saw his merit, and introduced him to public patronage, he would probably have languished, and died in obscurity.

There were now as many as four deeply-laid plots against his life, and without his amazing ———, which discovered and frustrated all these designs, he must have soon fallen a victim to one or the other of them.

It is the property of a ——— mind to discover hidden truths, and expose perversions. A ——— judgment is perhaps more practically useful than ———, as it is more frequently required in the common affairs of life.

"He is as slow to decide as he is quick to apprehend, calmly and deliberately weighing every opposite reason that is offered, and tracing it with a most judicious ———."

Of these two qualities, ——— argues a higher power of intellect than ———. The latter is indispensable to every station in life, but the former is more necessary for those who are placed in high offices, and to whom the destinies of men are intrusted.

"Cool age advances venerably wise,
Turns on all hands its deep, ——— eyes."

Intention—Purpose.

An *intention* is a leaning towards an action. A *purpose* is that which is laid down or proposed to be done Intentions are more remote; purposes, more immediate. What we purpose to do, we set about at once; what we intend to do, circumstances may oblige us to delay. Purposes are generally executed, intentions may be postponed. An intention is weaker than a purpose.

[*Bast.* This sway of motion, this commodity
Makes it take head from all indifferency,
From all direction, purpose, course, intent. *King John*, ii. 2

——— whence Gaza mourns
And all that band them to resist
His uncontroulable intent. *S. A.*, 1754

——— were not his purpose
To use him farther yet in some great service. *Id.*, 1498.

——— to consummate this just intent,
Did place upon his brother's head the crown
Relinquished by his own. WORDSWORTH. '*Artegal and Elidure*

——— there tried his spirit's strength
And grasp of purpose, long ere sailed his ship
To lay a new world open —— '*Tour in Italy*.']

Exercise.

He determined to set out immediately for Paris; and with this ———, proceeded without delay to the office to procure his passport, and made all the necessary preparations for his journey.

As soon as you have settled upon what course you will pursue, you will let me know your ———, as my movements will depend in a great measure upon your determination.

If you pay no attention to the subject you are reading, you will read, as many do, to no ———.

My ——— at present is to spend next winter at Naples, and to return to England in the following spring.

After spending this evening with some friends, I ——— starting to-morrow for Lausanne, where I hope to arrive on the 13th.

His character was not remarkable for firmness, and though every one gave him credit for the best ———, no class of people ever received much benefit from his measures.

The ——— of my inquiry is to discover the real character of this man, that I may ascertain whether he is a fit candidate for the office.

"I wish others the same ———, and greater success."

"The common material with which the ancients made their ships was the ornus or wild-ash; the fir was likewise used for this ———."

Moment—Instant.

An instant is the smallest conceivable point of time. A moment may be said to be one degree longer than an instant. An instant is, etymologically, the point of time which *stands over* an act, or which exists simultaneously with it. A moment is a moving (however small) of time. We can conceive of a beginning and an end to a moment. The parts of an instant are inconceivable. Strictly speaking, both terms are hyperbolical, though they are both commonly used to denote a very small space of time. Properly, however, the instant is the point, and moment the duration of time.

[*Macb.* Who can be wise, amazed, temperate and furious,
Loyal and neutral in a moment? —— *Macbeth*, ii. 3

Pand. Before the curing of a strong disease,
Even in the instant of repair and health,
The fit is strongest. —— *King John*, iii. 4.

All in a moment through the gloom were seen
Ten thousand banners rise into the air
With orient colours waving —— *P. L.*, i. 544.

—— sleep, which instantly fell on me —— *Id.*, viii. 458.

Not for a moment could I now behold
A smiling sea, and be what I have been:
WORDSWORTH. '*Elegiac Stanzas.*']

Exercise.

The touch-paper being applied to the train, the spark communicated in an ——— to the powder, and a few seconds after, the whole rock fell crashing to the ground.

The ——— the horseman saw the mischief he had done, he was off his horse, and assisting the poor woman to rise, he led her into a cottage by the road-side, where he saw that she was properly attended to before he proceeded on his journey.

The Arab, foaming with rage, grappled with his opponent, and in an ——— plunging his dagger into his heart, struck him to the ground.

I watched the vessel from the summit of the cliff depart from that shore to which she was never again to return. Her shadow now grew more and more dim upon the waters; for a few ——— I lost sight of her altogether—then I saw her again, as I thought, more distinctly than before, till at length she disappeared entirely from my view.

If you will wait here a ———, I will come to you.

"Some circumstances of misery are so powerfully ridiculous, that neither kindness nor duty can withstand them; they force the friend, the dependant, or the child, to give way to ——— emotions of merriment."

"I can easily overlook any present ——— sorrow, when I reflect that it is in my power to be happy a thousand years hence."

Need—Necessity.

Need is exigent and pressing, *necessity* is stern and unyielding. Necessity demands; need requires. Those who are in necessity are in the lowest degree of poverty, and have no means of supplying their commonest wants; those who are in need are in a temporary difficulty, from which a moderate help will relieve them. Necessity forces us to act for ourselves; in our need, we require the assistance of our friends. We may manage to do without what is needful, but what is necessary cannot be dispensed with.

[*Lear.* O, reason not the need; our basest beggars
Are in the poorest things superfluous;
Allow not nature more than nature needs,
Man's life is cheap as beasts'; *King Lear*, ii. 4

——— necessity
Commands me name myself. *Coriolanus*, iv. 5.

Nature hath need of what she asks; yet God
Can satisfy that need some other way. *P. R.*, ii. 253.

So spake the fiend, and with necessity,
The tyrant's plea, excused his devilish deeds *P. L.*, iv. 393.

Long patience hath such mild composure given,
That patience now doth seem a thing of which
He hath no need. —— WORDSWORTH. '*Poems on Old Age.*'

Who, doomed to go in company with Pain,
And Fear, and Bloodshed, miserable train!
Turns his necessity to glorious gain.
'*Character of the Happy Warrior.*']

Exercise.

If the old saying—"A friend in ——— is a friend indeed"—be true, how much more valuable must be a friend in ———!

I find that I shall be able to manage the business perfectly well by myself, and shall stand in no ——— of assistance from any one.

The maxim "——— has no law" is one of the most ancient in existence, and is quoted or alluded to by almost all the writers of antiquity.

We should be always ready to assist our fellow-creatures in time of their ———.

It is our duty, as far as lies in our power, to relieve the ——— of those who are in distress.

We found the poor people in a state of the most horrible destitution: they had been obliged to part with every piece of furniture they possessed to purchase food, and to complete their misery, in the midst of their ———, several of them were attacked with a malignant fever!

"One of the many advantages of friendship is, that we can say to our friend the things that stand in ——— of pardon."

"The cause of all the distractions in his court or army proceeded from the extreme poverty and ——— his majesty was in."

Obstruction—Obstacle.

Both these words are expressive of what interferes with our progress. The difference between them is, that an *obstruction* hinders our proceeding as fast as we wish; whereas an *obstacle* effectually prevents our advancing. An obstacle is something standing before us; an obstruction is something thrown in our way. We stumble at an obstruction; we are stopped by an obstacle. Hence, an obstacle is a more serious matter than an obstruction. A heavy, wet road, is an obstruction to the wheels of a carriage. A gate placed across a road is an obstacle to the progress of a carriage. Metaphorically, the same distinction exists. Obstructions are removed; obstacles are surmounted.

[*Arch.* ——— the obstructions, which begin to stop
Our very veins of life —— *2 Hen. IV.*, iv. 1.

Glo. ——— if all obstacles were cut away,
And that my path were even to the crown. *Richard III.*, iii. 7.

——— no cloud, or, to obstruct his sight,
Star interposed —— *P. L.*, v. 257.

For sight no obstacle found here, nor shade *Id.*, iii. 615.]

Exercise.

The river being now clear of all ———, the two sailing vessels started at eleven o'clock, and were expected to return from the Nore the same night.

The Duke of Gloucester, who allowed nothing to stand in the way of his designs, procured the death of the young princes. his nephews, as well as of all those whose influence or example presented any ——— to his ambition.

Self-conceit is one of the greatest ——— to our improvement.

The opposition, during this session, was more violent than ever, and every conceivable ——— was thrown in the way of the government.

The pertinacity with which the Saxons clung to their own customs and language seemed to increase with the cruel policy of their haughty conqueror, and was for a long time an effectual ——— to his desires.

"One ——— must have stood not a little in the way of that preferment after which Young seems to have panted. Though he took orders, he never entirely shook off politics."

"In his winter quarters, the king expected to meet with all the ——— and difficulties his enraged enemies could lay in his way."

Pertinacity—Obstinacy.

Pertinacity is but an intensive degree of tenacity, which expresses the quality of holding-to. *Obstinacy* is holding to a purpose when violently opposed. People cling to what they consider their natural rights with pertinacity; but if an attempt be made to deprive them of those rights, they defend them with obstinacy. The word obstinacy contains the idea of opposition. We speak of an obstinate dispute, defence, &c. We are pertinacious in maintaining opinions; we are obstinate in maintaining prejudices.

[*Cam.* The queen is obstinate,
Stubborn to justice —— *Henry VIII.*, ii. 4.
Anger and obstinacy, and hate and guile. *P. L.*, x. 114.]

Exercise.

"One of the dissenters appeared to Dr. Sanderson to be so bold, so troublesome, and illogical in the dispute, as forced him to say, that he had never met a man of more ——— confidence, and less abilities."

He was extremely tenacious of his own opinions, and defended them on all occasions with the most determined ———, though his arguments never carried conviction to the minds of any who heard them.

——— is never convinced of its own integrity; it resists reason, and opposes common sense; ——— has to do with our feelings, prejudices, national character, &c.: in the latter, there is an amiable weakness; in the former, a self-sufficient pride.

This controversy was distinguished by the violence with which it was conducted on both sides; for nothing could exceed the ——— which the two parties exhibited in maintaining their opinions, unless it was the malignity with which they denounced those of their opponents.

"Most writers use their words loosely and uncertainly, and do not make plain and clear deductions of words from one another, which it were not difficult to do, did they not find it convenient to shelter their ignorance or ——— under the obscurity of their terms."

"In this reply was included a very gross mistake, and if maintained with ———, a capital error."

Persuasion—Conviction.

In order to persuade, we address the feelings and the imagination. In order to convince, we address the reasoning faculty. The tinsel and glitter of rhetoric persuade ; the arguments of the reasoner convince. After persuasion, a doubt may remain in the mind ; but we have a positive certainty of what we are convinced of. A conviction implies firm belief We may have misgivings concerning the truth of what we are persuaded to believe. Persuasion is liable to change. Conviction is firm and lasting.

[*Fal.* ——— may'st thou have the spirit of persuasion, and he the ears of profiting —— 1 *Henry IV*, i 2

By winning words to conquer willing hearts
And make persuasion do the work of fear — *P. R.*, i. 223.

——— subtle shifts conviction to evade. — *Id.*, iv. 308.]

Exercise.

"When men have settled in themselves a ——— that there is nothing honorable which is not accompanied with innocence ; nothing mean but what has guilt in it ; riches, pleasures, and honors will easily lose their charms, if they stand between us and our integrity."

"Let the mind be possessed with the ——— of immortal happiness annexed to the act, and there will be no want of candidates to struggle for the glorious prerogative."

"I should be glad if I could ——— him to write such another critique on any thing of mine ; for when he condemns any of my poems, he makes the world have a better opinion of them."

"That which I have been all this while endeavouring to ——— men of, and to ——— them to, is no other than what God himself doth particularly recommend to us as proper for human consideration."

"Philoclea's beauty not only ———, but so ——— as all hearts must yield ; Pamela's beauty used violence, and such as no heart could resist."

"History is all the light we have in many cases, and we receive from it a great part of the useful truths we have, with a ——— evidence."

"How incongruous would it be for a mathematician to ——— with eloquence, to use all imaginable insinuations and entreaties that he might prevail with his hearers to believe that *three and three make six !*"

Pleasure—Happiness.

Pleasure is a temporary gratification. *Happiness* is a continued state of enjoyment. We are happy in the exercise of our faculties, we are pleased with whatever is agreeable to our perceptions. Pleasure is derived through the senses. We feel pleasure from what we eat or drink, see or hear. Happiness is an inward feeling, and is derived from consciousness. The beauty of a landscape, the sound of music, the fragrance of flowers, give us pleasure; the consciousness of our power to enjoy these pleasures makes us happy.

[*Ant.* ——— the purest pleasure
By revolution lowering, does become
The opposite of itself —— *Ant. and Cleop.*, i. 2.

Rom. ——— let rich music's tongue
Unfold the imagined happiness —— *Romeo and Juliet*, ii 6

——— all taste of pleasure must forego *P. L.*, xi. 541

——— the face
Of God, whom to behold was then my highth
Of happiness. —— *Id.*, x. 725.

While here I stand, not only with the sense
Of present pleasure, but with pleasing thoughts
That in this moment there is life and food
For future years. —— WORDSWORTH. '*Tintern Abbey Lines*

A temper known to those, who, after long
And weary expectation, have been blest
With sudden happiness beyond all hope. '*Nutting*.']

Exercise.

Having inspected the whole establishment, and partaken of some refreshment which had been prepared for him, he departed, expressing great —— at every thing he had seen.

Wealth, though it assists our ———, cannot procure us ———.

A consciousness of our integrity is a never-failing source of ———.

——— does not consist in the ——— of sense, in whatever profusion or variety they be enjoyed.

When we are in perfect health and spirits, we feel in ourselves a ——— independent of any particular outward gratification whatever, and of which we can give no account.

There is hardly any delusion by which men are greater sufferers in their ———, than by expecting too much from what is called ———.

In strictness, any condition may be denominated ———, in which the amount of ——— exceeds that of pain; and the degree of ——— depends upon the quantity of this excess.

"That every day has its pains and sorrows, is universally experienced; but if we look impartially about us, we shall find that every day has likewise its ——— and its joys."

"The various and contrary choices that men make in the world argue that the same thing is not good to every man alike; this variety of pursuit shows that every one does not place ——— in the same thing."

Plenty—Abundance.

Plenty denotes fulness. *Abundance* signifies an overflowing. Abundance is more than we want; plenty is quite as much as we require. In abundance there is superfluity; in plenty there is satisfaction. From an abundance we can lay by; from plenty we have a full sufficiency. By the best writers, plenty is more frequently used in a primary sense; abundance, in a secondary signification. Plenty of corn, meat, wine, &c.; an abundance of blessings, wealth, riches, &c.

[*Cran.* ——— Peace, plenty, love, truth, terror
That were the servants to this chosen infant,
Shall then be his, and like a vine grow to him. *Henry VIII.*, v. 4

Aust. —— this abundance of superfluous breath.
King John, ii 1.

——— the earth
Though, in comparison of heaven, so small,
Nor glistering, may of solid good contain
More plenty than the sun that barren shines. *P. L.*, viii. 94.

—— do not charge most innocent Nature,
As if she would her children should be riotous
With her abundance —— *Comus*, 764.]

Exercise.

"Those people of quality who cannot easily bear the expense of Vienna choose to reside here, (at Prague,) where they have assemblies, music, and other diversions, those of a court excepted, at very moderate rates, all things being here in great ———, especially the best wild-fowl I ever tasted."

"Ye shall eat in ———, and be satisfied, and praise the Lord."

Last year, the harvest was so ———, that it was estimated we had enough corn to last the whole nation for more than three years.

"The resty knaves are overrun with ease,
As ——— ever is the nurse of faction."

"And God said, let the waters generate,
Reptile with spawn ———, living soul."

"Berne is ———ly furnished with waters, there being a great multitude of fountains."

The banquet was furnished with every delicacy which could be procured; there was ——— of meats and sauces of all kinds, and no want of any thing which the most refined taste could desire.

The charity children were regaled with roast beef and plum-pudding on the occasion. They all had ——— to eat and drink, and went home in the evening highly delighted with the festivities of the day.

Riot—Tumult.

A *riot* arises out of a quarrel in which many are concerned. A *tumult* is a general riot. There are more persons engaged in a tumult than in a riot. There may be many riots at the same time, but there can be but one tumult (in the same place). Riots may lead to a tumult. A riot takes place in a street or court; the whole city is engaged in a tumult. A riot affects the local peace; a tumult destroys the peace and order of the whole community.

[*Cant.* His hours filled up with riots, banquets, sports,
Henry V., i. 1.
K. John. ——— and civil tumult reigns *King John*, iv. 2

——— in luxurious cities, where the noise
Of riot ascends above their loftiest towers *P. L.*, i. 499.

——— a broken foe,
With tumult less and with less hostile din *Id.*, ii. 1040.

The unfettered clouds and region of the heavens
Tumult and peace, the darkness and the light ——
WORDSWORTH. '*The Simplon Pass*'

——— the Gods approve
The depth, and not the tumult of the soul.
'*Laodamia.*']

Exercise.

——— having broken out in several parts of the town, it was judged necessary to send for the assistance of the military.

A body of horse soldiers were immediately ordered from the adjoining barracks, but when they arrived, they found the whole city in a ———.

On many occasions, when bread has been dear, or trade and manufactures depressed, ——— have taken place in various parts of England.

In the midst of this ———, Tiberius Gracchus, having fallen over a dead body that lay in his way, was killed, on attempting to rise, by a violent blow on the head.

Notwithstanding all the exertions of the magistrates, who acted with singular moderation upon this occasion, it was found impossible to quell the ——— which had now extended itself all over the country, and threatened the state itself with destruction.

The people, who considered themselves grievously injured by this decree, met in large bodies, and on one or two occasions behaved in such an unruly manner, that it was found necessary to read the ——— Act.

"The ———ous assembling of twelve persons or more, and not dispersing upon proclamation, was first made high treason by statute."

"In this piece of poetry, what can be nobler than the idea he gives us of the Supreme Being thus raising a ——— among the elements, and recovering them out of their confusion; thus troubling and becalming nature?"

Servant—Slave.

The servant serves according to compact. The slave serves upon compulsion. The servant undertakes to do that for which he shall be remunerated. The slave is no party to his own service; his master has unlimited power over him. The servant may cancel his agreement, and seek another master. The slave is deprived of all liberty. Slaves are oppressed; in this country, servants are generally well treated; if not, they are at liberty to change their master.

[*Macb.* ——— our duties
Are to your throne and state, children and servants,
Which do but what they should, by doing every thing
Safe toward your love and honour. *Macbeth*, i. 4.

Lear. ——— here I stand, your slave,
A poor, infirm, weak, and despised old man.
King Lear, iii. 2.

His servants he, with new acquist
Of true experience, from this great event,
With peace and consolation hath dismissed
And calm of mind, all passion spent *S. A.*, 1754.

Eyeless in Gaza at the mill with slaves.
Id., 41.

——— an ancient State
Strong by her charters, free because inbound,
Servant of Providence, not slave of Fate ——
WORDSWORTH. '*Sonnets to Liberty and Order.*']

Exercise.

"The condition of ——— was formerly different from what it is now, they being generally ———, and such as were bought and sold for money."

"This subjection, due from all men to all men, is something more than the compliment of course, when our betters tell us they are our humble ———, but understand us to be their ———."

"I had rather be a country ——— maid,
Than a great queen with this condition."

"When once men are immersed in sensual things, and are become ——— to their passions, then are they most disposed to doubt the existence of God."

Jeanne d'Arc was a ——— maid at an hotel in the small hamlet of Domremy, in Champagne.

The British government have exerted themselves strenuously to put down the inhuman traffic in ———.

Every station in life has its proper duties; master and ———, teacher and scholar, father and son, &c. &c.

An immense sum of money was some years ago paid by the British government to the West India planters, by way of indemnification for the emancipation of their ———.

"For master or for ——— here to call,
Was all alike when only two were all."

"——— to our passions we become, and then,
It grows impossible to govern men."

Slander—Calumny.

These words both denote the taking away of our neighbour's character. Slander differs from calumny in this, that in *slandering*, we spread abroad an evil report which has reached our ears; but in *calumniating*, we ourselves both forge and propagate a false character. Hence the calumniator is more despicable than the slanderer; for the latter, with the intention of injuring, is heedless of the truth of the report he spreads; whereas the former both fabricates it and spreads it abroad. The falsehood originates with the calumniator, and is disseminated by the slanderer.

[*King.* ——— so, haply, slander,—
Whose whisper o'er the world's diameter
As level as the cannon to his blank
Transports his poisoned shot. —— *Hamlet*, iv. 1.

Duke. ——— back-wounding calumny
The whitest virtue strikes —— *Winter's Tale*, iii. 2.]

Exercise.

Heedless alike of his own reputation, or of the peace of mind of others, he took every opportunity to spread the ———, and before he could reflect upon the consequences, the injury he had occasioned was irreparable.

The accused man suddenly rose; the strongest indignation burned in his countenance; he solemnly protested his ignorance of the whole transaction, and consequent innocence of the charge, concluding by declaring it to be his firm conviction that the whole accusation was a vile and abominable ———, invented for the mere purpose of blasting his character.

Be slow to believe evil of others; so shalt thou shut thine ear to ——— and live charitably with all men

"Give me leave to speak as earnestly in truly commending it, as you have done in untruly and unkindly defacing and ——— it."

"The way to silence ———, says Bias, is to be always exercised in such things as are praiseworthy."

> "———, that worst of poisons; ever finds
> An easy entrance to ignoble minds."

Temperance—Abstinence.

Abstinence is the power of refraining; temperance is the power of enjoying with moderation. We abstain from what is injurious to our health; we are temperate in our use of what is good for us. Abstinence demands self-denial; temperance requires wisdom. We abstain from high-seasoned dishes, spirituous liquors, &c.; we are temperate in food, language, expression, manners, &c. Abstinence is opposed to the use of a thing; temperance, to its abuse. It is a question whether there is not more merit in exercising temperance than in the practice of abstinence, since it argues a greater strength of mind to use a gift moderately, than to refrain from it altogether. We may abstain through fear or necessity; to be temperate, we must have a well-regulated mind.

> [*Mal.* ——— The king-becoming graces,
> As justice, verity, temperance, stableness
>
> *Macbeth*, iv. 3.

> *Duke.* A man of stricture, and firm abstinence.
>
> *Meas. for Meas.*, i. 4.

> — Knowledge is as food, and needs no less
> Her temperance over appetite, to know
> In measure what the mind may well contain.
>
> *P. L.*, vii 127.

> That sacred fruit, sacred to abstinence
>
> *P. L.*, ix. 924.

> In this one man is shown a temperance—proof
> Against all trials; industry severe
> And constant as the motion of the sun.
>
> *The Excursion*, vii.

> —— demand of him, if there be here
> In this cold abstinence from evil deeds
> And these inevitable charities
> Wherewith to satisfy the human soul?
>
> *The Old Cumberland Beggar.*

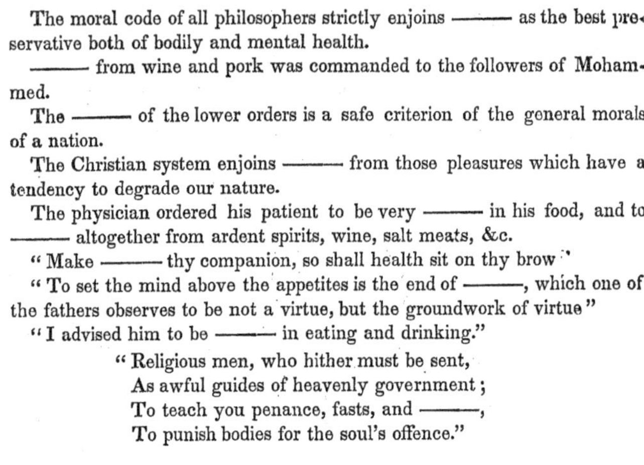

Exercise.

The moral code of all philosophers strictly enjoins ——— as the best preservative both of bodily and mental health.

——— from wine and pork was commanded to the followers of Mohammed.

The ——— of the lower orders is a safe criterion of the general morals of a nation.

The Christian system enjoins ——— from those pleasures which have a tendency to degrade our nature.

The physician ordered his patient to be very ——— in his food, and to ——— altogether from ardent spirits, wine, salt meats, &c.

"Make ——— thy companion, so shall health sit on thy brow."

"To set the mind above the appetites is the end of ———, which one of the fathers observes to be not a virtue, but the groundwork of virtue"

"I advised him to be ——— in eating and drinking."

"Religious men, who hither must be sent,
As awful guides of heavenly government;
To teach you penance, fasts, and ———,
To punish bodies for the soul's offence."

Vicinity—Neighbourhood.

These words differ in degree. Vicinity does not express so close a connection as neighbourhood. A neighbourhood is a more immediate vicinity. The streets immediately adjoining a square are in the neighbourhood of that square. The streets a little farther removed are in the vicinity of that square. Hampstead and Highgate are in the vicinity, not in the neighbourhood, of London. Where houses are not built together in masses, there can be no neighbourhood. In the country, gentlemen's seats are often in the vicinity of a town or village. In London, every square, street, and alley, has its neighbourhood. The word neighbourhood is also used for the inhabitants, taken collectively, who live near, as well as the place near.

[*Fr. King.* Plant neighbourhood and christian-like accord
In their sweet bosoms, that never war advance
His bleeding sword 'twixt England and fair France
Henry V., v. 2

My daily walks and ancient neighbourhood
Comus, 314.

Happy as others of her kind,
That, far from human neighbourhood,
Range unrestricted as the wind
Through park or chase or savage wood.
WORDSWORTH. '*The Russian Fugitive.*']

Exercise.

"We had an elegant house, situated in a fine country and a good ———."

"The Dutch, by the ——— of their settlements to the coast of the Caraccas, gradually engrossed the greatest part of the cocoa trade."

"Though the soul be not actually debauched, yet it is something to be in the ——— of destruction."

"The reader has had a sketch of the interior of the Alhambra, and may be desirous of a general idea of its ———."

"A man in the ———, mortally sick of the small-pox, desired the doctor to come to him."

"I could not bear
To leave thee in the ——— of death."

When the house was discovered to be on fire, every one in the ——— hastened to give assistance; and the whole village was crowded in a few minutes with vehicles of every sort, containing tubs, pails, buckets, &c., filled with water.

Wood—Forest.

A *forest* is a large and uncultivated tract of ground covered with trees. A *wood* is a smaller assemblage of trees. A forest is the resort of wild beasts. A wood is the haunt of smaller animals. Lions, bears, wild boars, &c., live in forests; hares, rabbits, squirrels, &c., in woods. Wood is derived from the Saxon *wod;* forest, from the low Latin *foresta.* The forest is characterized by its uncertain extent and wildness of growth; the wood, by thickness of growth.

[*Duke.* ——— Are not these woods
More free from peril than the envious court?
As You Like It, ii. 1

Macb. Who can impress the forest; bid the tree
Unfix his earth-bound root? *Macbeth*, iv. 1.

In wood or wilderness, forest or den *P. L.*, iv. 342.

——— by blessed song
Forbidding every bleak unkindly fog
To touch the prosperous growth of this tall wood.
Comus, 270

——— or faery elves,
Whose midnight revels, by a forest side,
Or fountain, some belated peasant sees.
P. L., i. 782.

But oft the woods renewed their green,
Ere the tired head of Scotland's Queen
Reposed upon the block!
WORDSWORTH. '*Lament of Mary Queen of Scots*

Yet, when above the forest-glooms
The white swans southward passed,
High as the pitch of their swift plumes
Her fancy rode the blast. '*The Russian Fugitive.*']

Exercise.

"By many tribulations we enter into the kingdom of heaven, because, in a ——— of many wolves, sheep cannot choose but feed in continual danger of life."

I counted yesterday afternoon more than sixty hares in the field below the lake, and, on clapping my hands, they all scampered into the adjoining ———, and disappeared in a moment.

A lion, being fatigued with hunting, lay down to repose under one of the wide-spreading trees of the ———.

The lively fancy of the ancient Greeks peopled all creation with imaginary beings; every fountain had its goddess, every ——— its nymph, and every cave its divinity.

William the Conqueror laid waste a tract of thirty square leagues in Hampshire, burning villages, cottages, and churches, and expelling the inhabitants, to form the New ———, as it is still called.

"The ——— born people fall before her flat,
And worship her as goddess of the ———."

There is a small ——— in the vicinity of the town, whither the inhabitants repair to enjoy themselves on holidays.

To alter—to change.

To change is to substitute one thing for another; to alter is to make some difference in one thing or person. Those persons are changed whose features we cannot recognise after a lapse of time; those persons are altered whom we have difficulty in recognising. To change a dress is to take one off and put another on; to alter a dress is to make it in some respect different. We change our opinions when we give up old and adopt new ones; we alter our opinions when they become no longer in every respect the same as formerly. Changes are intensive alterations. Alterations regard the part; changes, the whole.

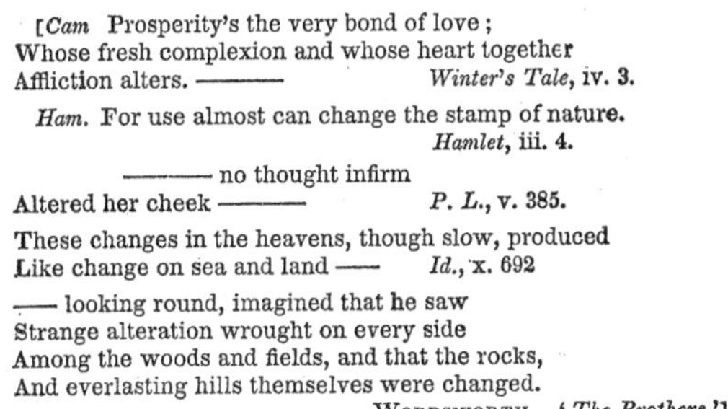

[*Cam* Prosperity's the very bond of love;
Whose fresh complexion and whose heart together
Affliction alters. ——— *Winter's Tale*, iv. 3.

Ham. For use almost can change the stamp of nature.
Hamlet, iii. 4.

——— no thought infirm
Altered her cheek ——— *P. L.*, v. 385.

These changes in the heavens, though slow, produced
Like change on sea and land —— *Id.*, x. 692

—— looking round, imagined that he saw
Strange alteration wrought on every side
Among the woods and fields, and that the rocks,
And everlasting hills themselves were changed.
WORDSWORTH. '*The Brothers*.']

Exercise.

It was now fourteen years since I had left my native village, and I had in that time visited almost every part of the globe. It was then not without reason that I could hardly believe I was again in the place of my birth. Time had worked so many ———, and the appearance of those I knew intimately when I went away was so ———, that I felt quite like a stranger.

This sudden accession of fortune did not appear to affect him in any way; he made no ——— in his style of living, received his friends in the same cordial but frugal manner as formerly, and did not increase his expenses in any particular.

I found upon inquiry that the house had ——— owners since I had last visited the spot. I was a little depressed by this intelligence, but soon recovering my spirits, I knocked at the door, and finding that the family were absent, begged to be permitted to see the house and grounds.

Every thing stood as it was in the old time, and there was nothing ——— either in the grounds or house.

"How strangely are the opinions of men ——— by a ——— in their condition!"

"They who beyond sea go will sadly find
They ——— their climate only, not their mind."

To be—to exist.

The verb *to be* is used to connect what is declared of a subject with the subject itself.

The verb *to exist* is never used with the qualities of things, it simply points to the existence of the things themselves. Thus: Man *is* an animal; children *are* inexperienced; the soul *exists;* the soul *is* immortal. Friendship *exists;* friendship *is* a solace in adversity.

[*Cas.* That by your virtuous means, I may again
Exist, and be a member of his love *Othello*, iii. 4.

How charming is divine philosophy!
Not harsh and crabbed, as dull fools suppose,
But musical as is Apollo's lute *Comus*, 476.

The heavens whose aspect makes our minds as still
As they themselves appear to be,
Innumerable voices fill
With everlasting harmony
WORDSWORTH. '*On the Power of Sound*

Whate'er exists hath properties that spread
Beyond itself, communicating good
A simple blessing, or with evil mixed
'*The Excursion*,' ix.]

Exercise.

"It is as easy to conceive that an Almighty Power might produce a thing out of nothing, and make that to ——— which did not ——— before; as to conceive the world to have had no beginning, but to have ——— from eternity."

"To say a man has a clear idea of quantity without knowing how great it ———, ——— to say he has the clear idea of the number of the sands, who knows not how many they ———."

"When the soul is freed from all corporeal alliance, then it truly ———."

"Herein ——— the exact difference between the young and the old. The young ——— not happy but when enjoying pleasure; the old ——— happy when free from pain."

"Man ——— man, and will ——— man under all circumstances and changes of life; he ——— under every known climate and variety of heat or cold in the atmosphere."

It is difficult to conceive how these poor men could have ——— so long in such dreadful extremities.

"Henry, called of Winchester, the place of his birth, ——— but ten years of age when his father died."

The Pyrrhonians were a sect of Greek philosophers who doubted the ——— of every thing.

To confuse—to confound.

Things become confounded in consequence of being confused. To confuse does not express so high a degree of disorder as to confound. One who is *confused* still retains his senses to a certain degree; he is only thrown into disorder. He who is *confounded* is in the highest state of stupefaction, and no longer knows what he is doing. A criminal is confounded at the discovery of his guilt; liars are confused when suspected. Impudence confounds; severity confuses. The confusion of tongues at Babel confounded the multitude.

[*Cho.* — the shrill whistle, which doth order give
To sounds confused —— *Henry V.*, iii. (*chorus.*)

Macb. ——— though the yesty waves
Confound and swallow navigation up
Macbeth, iv. 1.

And what the people but a herd confused
P. R., iii. 49.

— ruin upon ruin, rout on rout
Confusion worse confounded —— *P L.*, ii. 996

——— as he gazed, there grew
Such a confusion in his memory
That he began to doubt; and even to hope
That he had seen this heap of turf before,—
That it was not another grave ——
WORDSWORTH. '*The Brothers*

——— rock on rock
Descends:—beneath this godlike Warrior, see!
Hills, torrents, woods, embodied to bemock
The Tyrant, and confound his cruelty.
'*Sonnets to National Independence*

Exercise.

"We may have a clear and distinct idea of the existence of many things, though our ideas of their intimate essences are very ——— and obscure."

"Ignorance is the darkener of man's life, the disturber of his reason, and the common ———er of truth."

A ——— report of an accident on one of the French railways has just reached town.

"They who strip not ideas from the marks men use for them, but ——— them with words, must have endless disputes."

He was so ——— at the sudden appearance of his master, that he was unable to utter a word.

"The generality of writers are apt to ——— words with one another, and to employ them with promiscuous carelessness, merely for the sake of filling up a period, or of diversifying the language."

"He has so much to do, and his head is become so ———, that it is not surprising his affairs are falling into disorder."

"I to the tempest make the poles resound,
And the conflicting elements ———."

"A ——— report passed through my ears;
But full of hurry, like a morning dream,
It vanished in the business of the day."

To deprive—to bereave.

To *bereave* is a stronger term than to *deprive:* there is an idea of violence expressed in the former which the latter does not contain. Deprive merely points to what we once had, but have no longer. We are deprived of comforts, of pleasures; we are bereft of what we feel necessary to our existence, or of what there is no possibility of our regaining. Bereaving not only takes away from us, but also violently affects our inclination. Death bereaves us of our children; an accident bereaves us of a limb. What we are deprived of may be restored to us; what we are bereft of never returns.

[*Hor.* ——— some other horrible form
Which might deprive your sovereignty of reason
And draw you into madness —— *Hamlet*, i 4

——— bereaves the state
Of that integrity which should become it.
Coriolanus, iii. 1

——— no wrong
But justice, and some fatal curse annexed,
Deprives them of their outward liberty
P. L., xii. 100

——— bereave me not,
Whereon I live, thy gentle looks, thy aid,
Thy counsel, in this uttermost distress.
Id., x. 918.]

Exercise.

"To ——— us of metals, is to make us mere savages; it is to ——— us of all arts and sciences, of history and letters, nay, of revealed religion too, that inestimable favour of Heaven."

In prison, and ———, by the cruelty of the tyrant, of the consolations of friendship, he endured many bitter reflections.

"That when thou com'st to kneel at Henry's feet,
Thou mayst ——— him of his wits with wonder."

His mother determined, from that day forth, to ——— her son of all pleasure and indulgence, till he should show by his conduct that he was really sorry for what he had done.

Mr. * * was ——— of his excellent wife and two lovely children by the same illness.

I shall be sorry to be ——— of your society; but as I know it is for your advantage, I shall endeavour to bear the loss with fortitude.

To disperse—to dispel.

The latter of these two verbs expresses an intensive degree of the former. To disperse is to scatter abroad; to dispel is to drive away. What is *dispersed* no longer exists in the same form as before; what is *dispelled* no longer exists in any form. An enemy is dispersed; darkness is dispelled. To dispel is used in both a primary and secondary sense; to disperse, only in a primary.

[*Ari.* ——— the rest of the fleet,
Which I dispersed, they all are met again
Tempest, i. 2.

——— if the night
Have gathered aught of evil or concealed,
Disperse it, as now light dispels the dark.
P. L., v. 208.

Hell to the lyre bowed low; the upper arch
Rejoiced that clamourous spell and magic verse
Her wan disasters could disperse.
WORDSWORTH. '*On the Power of Sound.*']

Exercise.

"When the spirit brings light into our minds, it ——— darkness: we see it as we do that of the sun at noon, and need not the twilight of reason to show it."

"And I scattered them among the heathen, and they were ——— through the countries."

"Hail universal Lord! be bounteous still,
To give us only good; and if the night
Have gathered aught of evil, or concealed,
——— it, as now light ——— the dark."

"As when a western whirlwind, charged with storms,
——— the gathering clouds that nature forms,
The foe ———, their bravest warriors killed,
Fierce as a whirlwind now I swept the field."

On the death of the late duke, his extensive library was sold by public auction, and the books were thus ——— over all parts of the country.

Notwithstanding the most strenuous exertions which individuals may make to ——— the ignorance and raise the moral tone of the lower orders, little good will be effected without the cordial co-operation of the government.

To enlarge—to increase.

The verb *to enlarge*, taken either in a moral or physical sense, is applied to extent of surface; to *increase* is used with reference to bulk, number, or quantity. A field is enlarged when, by the removal of its boundary, it is made to contain a greater extent of ground. In like manner, a man's mind is enlarged when, by reading, reflection, or conversation, he has acquired the power of seeing *more of the extent* of whatever may be the object of his attention. A balloon, during the process of inflation, becomes increased in size, and enlarged in extent: increased, so far as it occupies more space; and enlarged, as it presents more surface to the eye of the spectator. Riches, wisdom, appetite, &c. are increased; views, prospects, premises, &c. are enlarged.

[*Puc.* Glory is like a circle in the water
Which never ceaseth to enlarge itself
Till, by broad spreading, it disperse to nought.
1 *Henry VI.*, i. 2.

Eliz. —— hie thee from this slaughter-house,
Lest thou increase the number of the dead.
Rich. III., iv 1

——— love refines
The thoughts, and heart enlarges ——
P. L., viii. 590

——— O voice, once heard
Delightfully, Increase and multiply;
Id., x. 730

——— Rather in the law
Of increase and the mandate from above
Rejoice!—and ye have special cause for joy.
'*The Excursion.*']

Exercise.

The revenue of the country has greatly ——— during the last five years.

Frederic the Great, of Prussia, considerably ——— his territories by the addition of Silesia.

From the time of Hugh Capet, the royal domain (as distinguished from the domains of the great feudal lords) was progressively ——— by the conquest, forfeiture, or inheritance of the greater fiefs.

The French noblesse was exceedingly numerous; for not only all the children of a noble belonged to the class of their father, but that class was continually ——— by the creation of new nobles.

The ——— estimation in which he was held was manifested in his successive appointments to various offices.

"Then as her strength with years ——, began
To pierce aloft in air the soaring swan.'

"Where there is something both lasting and scarce, and so valuable to be hoarded up, there men will not be apt to —— their possessions of land."

To estimate—to esteem.

We *esteem* a man for his moral qualities; we *estimate* him according as we judge of his worth. To esteem is always used in a good sense; to estimate, in either a good or bad, indifferently. We set a high value upon those we esteem. It is possible that we estimate too highly those whom we esteem. There are degrees of estimation. Esteem is in itself a high degree of appreciation. What is good is esteemed. That which is imperfectly known, or which is a mixture of good and bad, is estimated. "He esteemed his friend," means that he highly valued his character. "He estimated his worth," means that he calculated it according to his own standard. Men are esteemed; men and things are estimated.

[*Lady M.* —— Would'st thou have that,
Which thou esteem'st the ornament of life,
And live a coward in thine own esteem.
Macbeth, i. 7

For I esteem those names of men so poor,
Who could do mighty things, and could contemn
Riches, though offered from the hand of Kings.
P. R., ii. 447

How nourished here through such long time
He knows, who gave that love sublime;
And gave that strength of feeling, great
Above all human estimate! WORDSWORTH '*Infidelity.*

—— will not hold in light esteem
A suffering woman's word. '*The Russian Fugitive.*']

Exercise.

His kindness and gentleness of manner, and his strict integrity in all his dealings, have gained him the —— and love of all his fellow-countrymen.

The only way to arrive at a just —— of the difference between a public and a private life is to try both.

There is no prize more worthy of aspiring after than the —— of the good and the wise.

It is impossible to form a just —— of any individual character, without having divested ourselves of all those passions or prejudices which may tend to pervert our judgment.

All articles are not to be ——— merely by the intrinsic value of the material; the form, workmanship, and labour bestowed upon it must also enter into the calculation.

"The extent of the trade of the Greeks, how highly soever it may have been ——— in ancient times, was in proportion to the low condition of their marine."

"I am not uneasy, that many whom I never had any ——— for are likely to enjoy this world after me"

To excite—to incite.

When we *excite*, we raise into existence feelings which were dormant. When we *incite*, we urge the excited feelings to action. When we are in a state of excitement, we are easily incited. First the excitement, then the incitement. Novelty excites us; arguments incite us. By excitement, we feel strongly; by incitement, we are urged to action. Excitement will, undoubtedly, greatly assist incitement; for a man, whose passions are excited, may be much more easily incited to do wrong than he who is calm.

[*Bel.* ——— Beaten for loyalty
Excited me to treason. —— *Cymbeline*, v. 5.

Pro. Incite them to quick motion. ——
Tempest, IV. 1

——— glory, the reward
That sole excites to high attempts ——
P R., iii. 26

——— and other stars
By his attractive virtue and their own
Incited, dance about him various rounds.
P. L., viii. 125.]

Exercise.

"The Lacedæmonians were more ——— to desire of honor with the excellent verses of the poet Tyrtæus, than with all the exhortations of their captains."

"Nature and common reason, in all difficulties where prudence or courage is required, do rather ——— us to fly for assistance to a single person, than to a multitude."

Antony, by his speech over the body of Cæsar, and the reading of his will, so ——— the feelings of the people against his murderers, that the latter were obliged to withdraw from the popular wrath.

He was strongly ——— to study, not only by the hope of honors and rewards, but also with the view of procuring a maintenance for his aged father and mother.

When the news arrived of the disclosures that had taken place in the city, of the complete suppression of the plot, and of the execution of the leading conspirators, many who had joined their standard, from the love of ———, and the hope of plunder, gradually slunk away.

Antiochus, when he ——— Prusias to join in war, set before him the greatness of the Romans, comparing it to a fire that took and spread from kingdom to kingdom

To exert—to exercise.

In order to exercise, we must exert repeatedly: the former is but an intensive form of the latter. To *exert* is simply to put forth; to *exercise* is to put forth often, and involves reiterated exertion. We may exert authority in a single instance, but to exercise authority implies continuance of time, and repetition of action. We exert the voice to make those at a distance hear us; we exercise the voice to attain a good intonation and flexibility in singing.

[*Sici.* No longer exercise
Upon a valiant race, thy harsh
And potent injuries. *Cymbeline*, v. 4

——— thence on the earth
Dominion exercise ——— *P. L.*, x. 400.

The faith partaking of those holy times
Life, I repeat, is energy of love
Divine or human; exercised in pain,
In strife, and tribulation ——— '*The Excursion*,' v.]

Exercise.

"This faculty of the mind, when it is ——— immediately about things, is called judgment."

"When the service of Britain requires your courage and conduct, you may ——— them both."

"Men ought to beware that they use not ——— and a spare diet both; but if much ———, a plentiful diet; if sparing diet, little ———."

"When the will has ——— an act of command upon any faculty of the soul, or member of the body, it has done all that the whole man, as a moral agent, can do for the actual ——— or employment of such a faculty or member."

"The Roman tongue was the study of their youth; it was their own language they were instructed and ——— in."

"How has Milton represented the whole Godhead ———ing itself towards man in its full benevolence!"

"God made no faculty but he also provided it with a proper object upon which it might ——— itself."

"The utmost power of my ———ed soul
Preserves a being only for your service."

"The constitution of their bodies was naturally so feeble, and so unaccustomed to the laborious ——— of industry, that they were satisfied with a proportion of food amazingly small."

"He was strong of body, and so much the stronger, as he, by a well-disciplined ———, taught it both to do and to suffer."

To forgive—to pardon.

Small offences are forgiven; serious offences are pardoned. The former word is used on familiar occasions; the latter, in cases of importance. Forgiveness is exercised between those of the same condition in life. Pardon is granted from those in authority to their inferiors. We forgive each other after a quarrel; a king pardons rebels or conspirators. The expression in the Lord's Prayer, "*Forgive* us our trespasses," is in accordance with the term used at the beginning of the same prayer: "Our *Father*, which art," &c. Kindness prompts us to forgive; mercy inclines us to pardon. Hatred prevents us from forgiving; the laws prevent us from pardoning.

[*Men.* The veins unfilled, our blood is cold, and then
We pout upon the morning, are unapt
To give or to forgive —— *Coriolanus*, v. 1.

Five hundred poor I have in yearly pay,
Who twice a day their withered hands hold up
Toward heaven, to pardon blood ——
Henry V., iv. 1

Let weakness then with weakness come to parle,
So near related, or the same of kind
Thine forgive mine —— *S. A.*, 787.

——— confessed
Humbly their faults, and pardon begged ——
P. L., x. 1101.

——— a fault so natural
(Even with the young, the hopeful, or the gay)
For prompt forgiveness will not sue in vain.
'*Tour in Scotland.*']

Exercise.

Simnel having confessed his imposture, and publicly begged ———, was degraded to a mean office in the king's household, in which employment he soon afterwards died.

The wretched wife, on hearing that her husband was condemned, immediately undertook a journey on foot to the capital, where, throwing herself at the king's feet, she implored ——— for her husband.

The little girl shewed such unequivocal signs of sorrow for her fault, that her mother was induced to ——— her; telling her, however, that she would not find her so lenient again under similar circumstances.

The unfortunate brother, now an outcast and a wanderer on the face of the earth, was so fearful of his father's just anger at his conduct, that he despaired of ever obtaining ———, and determined never again to return home.

Though numerous applications were made for the prisoner's ———, they were all ineffectual, the government having determined to make an example of the next that should be guilty of a like offence.

"What better can we do than prostrate fall
Before him reverent, and there confess
Humbly our faults, and ——— beg; with tears
Watering the ground?"

"A being who has nothing to ——— in himself, may reward every man according to his works."

He whose very best actions must be seen with a grain of allowance, cannot be too mild, moderate, and ———ing.

To grow—to become.

To *become* is to be one thing from having been another; it always has reference to a previous state: to *grow* is to be approaching towards another state. A man is become old when he is of a certain age; a man grows old when he is verging towards that age. To grow is to become by degrees. To grow is continuous; to become is stationary. A dying man grows weaker every hour: a patient who has suffered much pain is become very weak.

[*Ant.* But when we in our viciousness grow hard
(O misery on't!) the wise gods seel our eyes.
Ant. and Cleop., iii. 11.

Sooth. ——— thy angel
Becomes a Fear, as being overpowered ——
Id., ii. 3.

——— the stars grow high;
But night sits monarch ept in the mid-sky.
Comus, 956

——— who, for thee ordained
A help, became thy snare ——— *P. L.*, xi. 165

My heart leaps up when I behold
A rainbow in the sky—:
So was it when my life began;
So is it now I am a man;
So be it when I shall grow old,
Or let me die!
WORDSWORTH. '*On the Period of Childhood*'

——— when a damp
Fell round the path of Milton, in his hand
The Thing became a trumpet; whence he blew
Soul-animating strains—alas too few!
WORDSWORTH. '*Miscel. Sonnets*'

Within the soul a faculty abides,
That with interpositions, which would hide
And darken, so can deal that they become
Contingencies of pomp; and serve to exalt
Her native brightness. ——— '*The Excursion,*' iv.]

Exercise.

We should not only never forget, but we should be deeply impressed with the reflection, that as we ——— older, it is our duty to ——— more virtuous.

The Lord breathed into his nostrils the breath of life, and man ——— a living soul.

Our old coachman is almost recovered from his late attack, and is now ——— stronger every day.

All eyes were now intently fixed on the horizon: a faint light glimmered in the east, which gradually unfolded to our sight the whole expanse of the ocean; it soon ——— brighter; the stars, one by one, ——— extinct; and at length the glorious god of day, rousing himself from his golden couch, stepped majestically forth from the waters, and stood confessed before our wondering and delighted eyes.

During his youth, there never was a more liberal or more hospitable man; but towards the latter part of his life, he ——— penurious and reserved, and at last wholly withdrew from society.

"About this time, Savage's nurse, who had always treated him as her own son, died; and it was natural for him to take care of those effects, which, by her death, were, as he imagined, ——— his own."

"Authors, like coins, ——— dear as they ——— old."

To hate—to detest.

Hate, from the Anglo-Saxon *hæte*, describes the active feeling of dislike, together with that agitation of the spirits which accompanies every strong passion; *detest*, from the Latin *de-*

testor, is a more intensive degree of hate; it calls on others to bear witness to its hatred. Hate is "deep, not loud;" detestation is communicative, and always expressed. What we begin by hating, we may end by detesting. Those who endeavour to injure others are hated; those who secure their own power on the ruin of others are detested. Malice is hateful; hypocrisy is detestable.

[*Char.* In time we hate that which we often fear.
Ant. and Cleop., i. 3.

Ant. Since Cleopatra died,
I have lived in such dishonour that the gods
Detest my baseness. —— *Id.*, iv. 12.

——— and add thy name,
O Sun, to tell thee how I hate thy beams. *P. L.*, iv. 3"

——— nor ever saw till now
Sight more detestable than him and thee. *Id.*, ii. 745.]

Exercise.

Duplicity and cunning deserve to be ———; they may escape detection for a time, but are sure, in the end, to be brought to light.

We are commanded not to ——— any man; there are, however, many qualities which we are justified not only in ———, but even in ———.

Some young persons are so fond of expressing themselves hyperbolically, that they never condescend to use common terms; whatever they entertain any dislike or disinclination to they declare that they ———. Not long since, I heard a young lady protest that she ——— steel forks!

Though we ought to ——— no one, it is not possible that we should love all equally.

"Who dares think one thing, and another tell,
My heart ——— him as the gates of hell."

The character of Catiline is admirably drawn by Sallust, who describes him as possessed of the greatest talents, and yet plunged in the deepest excesses and committing the most ——— crimes.

"Your majesty hath no just cause to ——— me"

"Brutus ——— the oppression and the oppressor."

"A bard was selected to witness the fray,
And tell future ages the feats of the day;
A bard who ——— all sadness and spleen,
And wished that Parnassus a vineyard had been."

To hear—to listen.

The same difference exists between to hear and to listen that may be found between to see and to look; *i. e.* they are synonymes of degree. Listening is an intensive degree of hearing. We hear involuntarily; we listen with intention. Those who have sound ears cannot help hearing. We may hear persons talking without listening to what they say. If you listen to a conversation, you may hear many improving remarks.

[*Macb.* Listening their fear, I could not say, amen,
* * * * * *
Methought, I heard a voice cry, *Sleep no more!*
Macbeth, ii. 2

——— the heavenly tune, which none can hear
Of human mould, with gross unpurged ear
MILTON. *Arcades*, 72

Listen for dear honour's sake,
Goddess of the silver lake;
Listen and save! *Comus*, 864.

I listened, motionless and still;
And, as I mounted up the hill,
The music in my heart I bore,
Long after it was heard no more.
WORDSWORTH. '*The Solitary Reaper*

——— I have seen
A curious child, who dwelt upon a tract
Of inland ground, applying to his ear
The convolutions of a smooth-lipped shell;
To which, in silence hushed, his very soul
Listened intensely; and his countenance soon
Brightened with joy; for from within were heard
Murmurings, whereby the monitor expressed
Mysterious union with its native sea.
Even such a shell the universe itself
Is to the ear of Faith —— '*The Excursion*,' iv.]

Exercise.

On entering the harbour, we ——— a loud explosion, which seemed, from its intensity, to have taken place at no great distance from us. We ——— attentively, thinking it might be repeated, but we ——— nothing more.

There is an old proverb: "——— never ——— any good of themselves." This saying does not apply to all ———, but only to those who are curious to ——— what it is not proper that they should know.

When the prisoners were led across the drawbridge into the castle, and ——— the heavy portcullis fall behind them as they entered the yard, their hearts sank within them, and each felt that he should never leave that prison alive.

Though they ——— with all possible attention, they were so far from the preacher, that they could not ——— a syllable of the sermon.

All discipline was now at an end, and such din and confusion ensued, that even those who were desirous to preserve order, and obey their officers, could not ——— the word of command.

One who is really deaf cannot ——— ; one who is deaf to your entreaties will not ——— to them.

"I looked, I ———; dreadful sounds I ———,
And the dire forms of hostile gods appear."

"When we have occasion to ———, and give a more particular attention to some sound, the tympanum is drawn to a more than ordinary tension."

To lament—to deplore.

These two words represent different circumstances of grief: we *lament* with exclamation ; we *deplore* with tears. Lamentations are accompanied with sobs and cries. In deploring our grief is expressed by weeping. Violent grief produces lamentation ; deep grief causes us to deplore. What is lamentable excites a strong expression ; what is deplorable excites a strong feeling. We lament loudly ; we deplore deeply. The cries of a bird hovering round the nest from which her young have been stolen are lamentable. A mother deplores the death of her son.

[*Vol.* Leave this faint-puling, and lament as I do,
In anger, Juno-like. —— *Coriolanus*, iv. 2.

Vio. ——— never more
Will I my master's tears to you deplore. *Twelfth Night*, iii. 1.

Thus Adam to himself lamented loud,
Through the still night; —— *P. L.*, x. 845.

——— I waked
To find her, or forever to deplore
Her loss —— *Id.*, viii. 479.

——— Babylon,
Learned and wise, hath perished utterly,
Nor leaves her speech one word to aid the sigh
That would lament her. —— WORDSWORTH. '*Eccles. Sonnets.*'

Full oft our human foresight I deplore;
Trembling, through my unworthiness, with fear
That friends, by death disjoined, may meet no more!
'*Poems on the Affections.*']

Exercise.

"The wounds they washed, the pious *tears* they shed,
And laid along their oars, ——— the dead."

"But let not chief the nightingale ———
Her ruined care, too delicately framed
To brook the harsh confinement of the cage."

"This was the ——— condition to which the king was reduced."

He who ——, grieves aloud; he who ——, grieves silently

We —— an honorable, we —— a disgraceful misfortune.

"Hence we may have some idea of the —— state of learning in that kingdom."

"We, long ere our approaching, heard within
Noise, other than the sound of dance or song!
Torments, and *loud* ——, and furious rage."

"In this interval of anguish and expectation, she came to take her last farewell of her husband and deliverer, —— her wretched fate that had saved her from perishing in the waters to be the spectator of still greater calamities."

"The victors to their vessels bear the prize,
And hear behind loud groans and —— cries."

To overcome—to conquer.

By overcoming, we prove our superiority or mastery. By conquering, we acquire possession. An enemy is conquered; an antagonist is overcome. Those who are taken prisoners are conquered; those who prove unequal to the contest are overcome. Alexander the Great conquered the Persians, after having overcome Darius in three great battles. William the First conquered the English. In his march across the Alps, Hannibal overcame every difficulty.

[*Ant.* That day he overcame the Nervii. *Julius Cæsar*, iii. 2.

Cæs. —— for what I have conquered
I grant him part; but then, in his Armenia,
And other of his conquered kingdoms, I
Demand the like. —— *Ant. and Cleop.*, iii. 6

—— courage never to submit or yield,
And what is else not to be overcome. *P. L.*, i. 109.

The conquered also and enslaved by war
Shall, with their freedom lost, all virtue lose. *Id.*, xi. 797.

Such dismal service, that the loudest voice
Of the swoln cataracts (which now are heard
Soft murmuring) was too weak to overcome,
Though aided by wild winds, the groans and shrieks
Of human victims —— '*The Excursion*,' ix.

He conquering, as in joyful Heaven is sung,
He conquering through God, and God by him.
'*Sonnets to National Independence*.']

Exercise.

"There are sometimes little misfortunes and accidents that happen to poor people, which, of themselves they could never be able to ——."

"They had ——— them, and brought them under tribute."

"When a country is completely ———, all the people are reduced to the condition of subjects."

"That he no less
At length may find, who ———
By force, hath ——— but half his foe."

Alexander is said to have wept at the idea that there were no more worlds to ———.

"The patient mind by yielding ———."

"When these happy tidings were communicated to her, the poor woman's feelings were quite ———, and she burst into a flood of tears."

"If it were possible for a man to ——— all his passions, and ——— all his prejudices, we should look upon such a person as being the nearest conceivable approach to a perfect character."

"Not to be ——— was to do more
Than all the conquests former kings did gain."

"Welcome, great Stagirite, and teach me now
All I was born to know,
Thy scholar's victories thou dost outdo:
He ——— th' earth, the whole world you."

To perceive—to discern.

To *discern* expresses that act by which the eye is enabled to separate one object from among several, and to consider it apart from the rest. To *perceive* signifies that act, performed by the eye, by which an object at some distance is brought to make an impression on the mind. Perceiving has reference to objects of the same sort; discerning, to one among many of a different sort from itself. I perceive trees or houses at a distance; I discern a steeple among houses, or a river in a landscape. The same distinction holds good in the abstract sense of the two words. We perceive the truth of a proposition which, perhaps, did not at first strike us obviously. A sagacious mind can discern truth though it be mixed up with falsehood or hypocrisy.

[*Des* I do perceive here a divided duty *Othello*, i 3.

Mon. What from the cape can you discern at sea?
Id., ii. 1

And they, so perfect in their misery,
Not once perceive their foul disfigurement *Comus*, 74.

And in his garland, as he stood
Ye might discern a cypress bud.

MILTON. *Epitaph on March: Winchester*

——— of all the mighty world
Of eye and ear,—both what they half create
And what perceive —— WORDSWORTH. '*Tintern Abbey.*'

——— the discerning intellect of Man,
When wedded to this goodly universe
In love and holy passion, shall find these
A simple produce of the common day.

'*Preface to the Excursion.*']

Exercise.

Long before our vessel had reached the shore, I could ——— the tall elms which skirt our home-field.

Walking along the road, I ———, coming towards me, a crowd of children dressed in their holiday suits, each carrying an oak-branch in his hand.

I soon ——— that the chief's intentions towards me were hostile; and slipping out unobserved, I withdrew hastily from the conference.

The style of the writers of that age is so obscure and affected, and at the same time so diffusive, that it is no easy matter, amidst so many defects, to ——— any meaning in their writings.

"One who is actuated by party spirit is almost under an incapacity of ——— either real blemishes or beauties."

"And lastly, turning inwardly her eyes,
——— how all her own ideas rise."

"Great part of the country was abandoned to the plunder of the soldiers, who not troubling themselves to ——— between a subject and a rebel, whilst their liberty lasted, made indifferently profit of both."

To raise—to lift.

To *raise* is to place upright. To *lift* is to take from the ground. That which is lifted is no longer in contact with its under support. What is raised stands erect, but still touches the ground. If we lift a child who has fallen, we take him in our arms; if we raise a child who has fallen, we make him stand on his legs. In a secondary sense, the same difference exists. Devotion lifts the soul to heaven. "This gentleman came to be raised to great titles."

[*Mon.* I will raise her statue in pure gold. *Romeo and Juliet*, v. 3.

Rom. ——— an unaccustomed spirit
Lifts me above the ground with cheerful thoughts.

Id., v. 1.

——— him the gentle angel by the hand
Soon raised —— *P. L.*, xi. 421

——— their songs
Divide the night, and lift our thoughts to heaven.
Id., iv. 688.

Lords of the visionary eye whose lid,
Once raised, remains aghast, and will not fall!
WORDSWORTH. '*Dion.*'

——— the bulk
Of ancient minster lifted above the cloud
Of the dense air, which town or city breeds
To intercept the sun's glad beams —— '*The Excursion*,' vi.]

Exercise.

Antæus was a mighty giant and wrestler in Libya, whose strength was invincible as long as he remained in contact with his mother earth. Hercules discovered the source of his strength, ——— him up from the earth, and crushed him in the air.

When ——— from the ground, he was so weak that he could not stand upright, and was obliged to be supported home by two men.

"Now rosy morn ascends the courts of Jove,
——— up her light, and opens day above."

As the little girl was too short to see what was going on in the gardens, her father ——— her up in his arms.

The ladder was so heavy, that it required four men to ——— it against the building.

"I would have our conceptions ——— by dignity of thought and sublimity of expression, rather than by a train of robes or a plume of feathers."

By his great natural powers, aided by industry and perseverance, he was so esteemed and respected that he was at last ——— to the highest dignities of the state.

"Hark! was there not
A murmur as of distant voices, and
The tramp of feet in martial unison?
What phantoms even of sound our wishes ———!"

"The mind, by being engaged in a task beyond its strength, like the body strained by ———ing a weight too heavy, has often its force broken."

To receive—to accept.

To *accept* is a voluntary—to *receive* an involuntary act. We cannot help receiving, but we are not obliged to accept what is sent to us. That is received which simply comes to hand; that is accepted which we express our willingness to take for ourselves. Thus, we receive a letter when it comes to hand;

we receive news when it reaches us; we accept a present which is offered us; we accept an invitation to dine with a friend, &c.

[*Ulys.* ——— like a gate of steel
Fronting the sun, receives and renders back
His figure and his heat. —— *Troil. and Cress.*, i. 3

Ner. ——— you should refuse to perform your father's will, if you should refuse to accept him. *Merchant of Venice*, i. 2

——— who, if we knew
What we receive, would either not accept
Life offered, or soon beg to lay it down. *P. L.*, xi. 505

——— But he had felt the power
Of Nature, and already was prepared,
By his intense conceptions, to receive
Deeply the lesson deep of love which he,
Whom Nature, by whatever means, has taught
To feel intensely, cannot but receive. '*The Excursion*,' i.

Nor for their bodies would accept release;
But blessing God and praising him, bequeathed
With their last breath, from out the smouldering flame,
The faith which they by diligence had earned
Or through illuminating grace, received
For their dear countrymen, and all mankind.
Id., vi.]

Exercise.

No further intelligence of his proceedings had been ——— up to the middle of last month.

He was of so independent a character, that though deeply involved in pecuniary difficulties, he did not think proper to ——— the offer of a friend to assist him.

The last accounts we ——— of our friends in India are most satisfactory.

The minister, rising, said that he ——— with pride and satisfaction the token of their friendship which they had that day offered him.

The whole party succeeded in reaching Tinian in about three weeks, where they were ——— with the greatest hospitality, and were treated with all the kindness and attention their deplorable condition required.

The conditions offered by Cæsar, and ——— by Cassivelaunus, were, that he should send to the continent double the number of hostages at first demanded, and acknowledge subjection to the Romans.

"The sweetest cordial we ——— at last,
Is conscience for our virtuous actions past."

"Unransomed here ——— the spotless fair,
——— the hecatomb the Greeks prepare"

To remark—to observe.

To *remark* is to note down casually; to *observe* is to note down intentionally. A slight degree of attention will call forth a remark. An observation is the result of inquiry. We often cannot help remarking; but in observing, we direct our attention specially to some object. A remark will very frequently lead to an observation. A phenomenon in the heavens may be remarked by a casual spectator, but will be observed by an astronomer. A remark is momentary; an observation occupies more time.

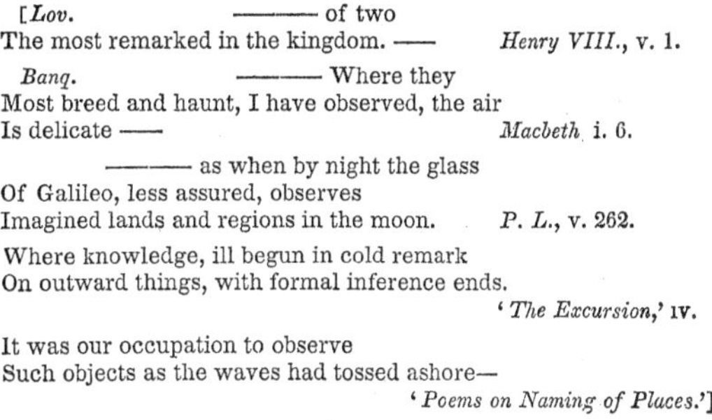

[*Lov.* ——— of two
The most remarked in the kingdom. —— *Henry VIII.*, v. 1.

Banq. ——— Where they
Most breed and haunt, I have observed, the air
Is delicate —— *Macbeth* i. 6.

——— as when by night the glass
Of Galileo, less assured, observes
Imagined lands and regions in the moon. *P. L.*, v. 262.

Where knowledge, ill begun in cold remark
On outward things, with formal inference ends.
'*The Excursion*,' IV.

It was our occupation to observe
Such objects as the waves had tossed ashore—
'*Poems on Naming of Places*.']

Exercise.

"It was also ——— of Cromwell, that though born of a good family, both by father and mother, and although he had the usual opportunities of education and breeding connected with such an advantage, he never could acquire the courtesies usually exercised among the higher classes in their intercourse with each other."

"It should, however, be ———, that Cromwell made religion harmonize with his ambition."

"It is easy to ——— what has been ———, that the names of simple ideas are least liable to mistake."

"I have often had occasion to ——— the fortitude with which women sustain the most overwhelming reverses of fortune."

"Othello is the vigorous and vivacious offspring of ——— impregnated by genius."

"The course of time is so visibly marked, that it is ——— even by birds."

"The rules of our practice are taken from the conduct of such persons as fall within our ———."

"We may ——— children discourse and reason correctly on many subjects at a comparatively early age."

To remember—to recollect.

We *remember* what has happened without any great effort; we *recollect* after some exertion of the memory. When the idea of some past occurrence presents itself spontaneously to the mind, that occurrence is remembered; but when, after several attempts, an idea becomes clear and distinct, it is then recollected. It will therefore be more proper to say—"I *do* not remember"—and, "I *cannot* recollect."

[*North.* ——— his tongue
Sounds ever after as a sullen bell
Remembered knolling a departing friend. 2 *Henry IV.*, i. 1.

Duke. ——— it did relieve my passion much;
More than light airs and recollected terms. *Twelfth Night*, ii. 4.

——— Remember with what mild
And gracious temper he both heard and judged,
P. L., x. 1046

——— he, his wonted pride
Soon recollecting —— *Id.*, i. 528.

——— the scene that lay
Before our eyes, awakened in my mind
Vivid remembrance of those long-past hours.
'*The Excursion*,' vii.

——— crossing the career
Of recollections vivid as the dreams
Of midnight —— '*Desultory Stanzas*.']

Exercise.

"I have been trying to ———," said he, "all the circumstances of that eventful day; but I ——— nothing more than what I have already related to you."

I ——— perfectly what occurred up to a certain point of time; but I cannot ——— what took place afterwards.

There died lately at Hampstead, a gentleman named Thompson, who was endowed with such an extraordinary power of memory, that he ———, and could accurately describe all the most minute objects in any street or road he had once passed through; and that after a considerable lapse of time.

Those who have ready memories learn easily, but do not ———; those whose memories are retentive have but little difficulty in ——— what they have once learnt.

No one can ——— what occurred to him during the first six or seven months of his life.

Do you ——— what I said to you this morning?

"We are said to ——— any thing, when the idea of it arises in the mind with a consciousness that we have had this idea before."

"——— every day the things seen, heard, or read, which make any addition to your understanding."

To reveal—to divulge.

To *reveal* is to make known what is concealed, by withdrawing what covered it. To *divulge* is to spread abroad the knowledge of what is revealed. A man reveals his secret to his friend; that friend divulges the secret by making it generally known. What is once revealed is likely to become soon divulged. What is revealed is imparted to one or to a few; what is divulged is made known to many. We reveal to ease our conscience or our feelings; we divulge what ought to remain concealed.

[*Ham.* You will reveal it. *Hamlet*, i. 5.

King. ——— like the owner of a foul disease,
To keep it from divulging, let it feed
Even on the pith of life —— *Id.*, iv. 1.

The secrets of another world, perhaps
Not lawful to reveal —— *P. L.*, v. 570.

——— when God
Looking on the earth, with approbation marks
The just man, and divulges him through heaven
To all his angels ——— *P. R.*, iii. 62.

——— the ruddy crest of Mars
Amid his fellows beauteously revealed
At happy distance from earth's groaning field
WORDSWORTH. '*Sonnets to National Independence*'

——— a tragic history
Of facts divulged —— '*The White Doe of Rylstone.*

Exercise.

These facts, though they occurred so many years ago, were never ——— to any but two persons, who have most religiously kept the secret ever since.

"The cabinets of the sick, and the closets of the dead, have been ransacked to publish private letters, and ——— to all mankind the most secret sentiments of friendship."

Time, which ——— all other things and brings them to light, is itself the most difficult of all things to be understood.

The mystery attached to the "Man in the Iron Mask" has never been cleared up, and though innumerable conjectures have been made of who he was, his name has never been ——— to the world.

Conscious of the disgrace it would bring upon his family if it should be known that he was implicated in this dreadful transaction, he steadily and constantly refused to ——— his name.

Though no less than forty persons were privy to the escape of Charles II., and concerned in aiding his flight, not one of them ——— his secret.

"In confession, the ———ing is not for worldly use, but for the ease of a man's heart."

> "These answers in the silent night received,
> The king himself ———, the land believed."

To satisfy—to satiate.

Those who have enough are *satisfied;* those who have more than enough are *satiated.* They who do not require more are satisfied; they who feel that they have had too much are satiated. What nature requires is to be satisfied; gluttons satiate themselves. To satisfy brings pleasure; to satiate causes disgust. Injudicious mothers frequently allow their children to satiate themselves. Satisfaction is necessary to preserve a healthy appetite; satiety destroys health.

> [*Jach.* That satiate yet unsatisfied desire,
> That tub both filled and running ——— *Cymbeline*, i. 7.
>
> *Seb.* ——— let us satisfy our eyes
> With the memorials, and the things of fame
> That do renown this city. *Twelfth Night*, iii. 3.
>
> How fully hast thou satisfied me, pure
> Intelligence of heaven, angel serene! *P L.*, viii. 180.
>
> ——— but if much converse perhaps
> Thee satiate, to short absence I could yield. *Id.*, ix. 248.
>
> ——— nor hide his theory
> That satisfies the simple and the meek,
> Blest in their pious ignorance, though weak
> To cope with Sages undevoutly free.
> WORDSWORTH. '*Tour* 1833
>
> ——— while the imperial City's din
> Beats frequent on thy satiate ear. '*The River Duddon.*']

Exercise.

"Whatever novelty presents, children are presently eager to taste, and are as soon ——— with it."

She told me that both herself and her children suffered extremely from hunger, for that the miserable pittance her husband gained was not sufficient to procure them wherewith to ——— the natural cravings of the appetite.

There is no action, the usefulness of which has made it a duty, which a man may not bear the continual pursuit of, without loathing or ———.

I am far from being ——— with the account he gives of the transaction, and believe that he knows much more about the affair than he chooses to disclose.

"He leaves a shallow plash to plunge him in the deep,
And with ——— seeks to quench his thirst."

A hungry man will be always ——— with plain food.

——— with pleasures, and disgusted at the ingratitude of those he had thought his friends, he suddenly resolved to retire to a monastery, there to compensate, by a life of penance and mortification, for the excesses of his past years.

To see—to look.

To *see* is the simple act of using the organ of sight; to *look* is to direct that organ to some particular object. Those who have their eyes open cannot help seeing; but to look implies an act of the will. I see the light, or any objects which are casually in the way of my eyes; I look at something with a view to examine its nature or qualities. If you look at the sun, you may see the spots on its surface. The two words have the same difference of meaning when used in a secondary sense: On looking at the question, he saw the difficulties with which it was surrounded.

[*Por.* That light, we see, is burning in my hall,
How far that little candle throws his beams!
So shines a good deed in a naughty world. *Merchant of Venice*, v. 1

Lor. ——— Look, how the floor of heaven
Is thick inlaid with patines of bright gold;
There's not the smallest orb, which thou behold'st,
But in his motion like an angel sings
Still quiring to the young-ey'd cherubins: *Id*

As I bent down to look, just opposite
A shape within the watery gleam appeared
Bending to look on me: I started back,
It started back; but pleased I soon returned,
Pleased it returned as soon with answering looks
Of sympathy and love; there I had fixed
Mine eyes till now, and fixed with vain desire,
Had not a voice thus warned me: What thou seest,
What there thou seest, fair creature, is thyself.
P. L., iv. 460.

——— a pensive instantaneous gleam
Startles the pensive traveller while he treads
His lonesome path, with unobserving eye
Bent earthwards; he looks up—the clouds are split
Asunder,—and above his head he sees
The clear Moon, and the glory of the heavens.
WORDSWORTH. '*A Night Piece*.
O terror! what hath she perceived?—O joy!
What doth she look on?—whom doth she behold?
Her Hero slain upon the beach of Troy?
'*Laodamia*.']

Exercise.

When his father ——— me, he ——— that I was much agitated.

There is a great deal to be ———, but little worth ———.

On ——— the weathercock, I ——— that the wind had changed.

On ascending the hill, we ——— a man standing in a melancholy attitude, ——— wistfully on the ground. Raising his eyes, he ——— us for some moments with an expression of eager hope; at length, ——— that we did not intend to give him any thing, he walked silently away.

——— this system comprehensively, we may easily ——— that it will never work well.

We ——— the whole affair as a fraudulent design, and ——— from the beginning that it would never succeed.

——— Martin's "Deluge"—it is the most simple of his works—it is perhaps also the most awful.

"They climb the next ascent, and ———ing down,
Now at a nearer distance view the town."

One ——— around sufficed him; his face brightened, he uttered a cry of joy.

Should—Ought.

Both these words imply an obligation; but ought binds more strongly than should. What we *should* do is a social obligation; but what we *ought* to do implies a moral obligation on our part. We ought to love our parents; we ought to respect our superiors. We should be neat and clean in our persons, and kind to our inferiors: we ought always to speak the truth. We should avoid giving offence; we ought to obey the laws.

[*Macb.* She should have died hereafter;
Macbeth, v. 5.
Elb. — that good christians ought to have.
Meas. for Meas., ii. 1
For still they knew, and ought to have still remembered
The high injunction not to taste that fruit.
P. L., x. 12.

But how can he expect that others should
Build for him, sow for him, and at his call
Love him, who for himself will take no heed at all?
WORDSWORTH. '*Resolution and Independence*'

——— Grant that Spring is there
In spite of many a rough untoward blast,
Hopeful and promising with buds and flowers;
Yet where is glowing Summer's long rich day,
That *ought* to follow faithfully expressed?
'*The Excursion*,' v.]

Exercise.

You ——— never to forget the kindness he has shewn you, and how much you are indebted to him for many of the advantages you now enjoy.

In writing, you ——— take care that the letters be perfectly formed, and well joined together.

We ——— to consider it our duty to bear with the moral failings of others, when we remember that we are all weak creatures, and are easily led into temptation.

In accomplishing any design, or completing any work of importance, we ——— proceed systematically and regularly.

He whose honor is intrusted with a secret ——— never to divulge it: no circumstances ——— make him consider it excusable to communicate it to a single individual.

Exercises ——— be written carefully and neatly, and ——— never be shewn to the teacher till they are corrected, as far as possible, by the pupil.

Judges ——— to remember that their office is to interpret law, and not to make or give law.

To slake—to quench.

To *slake* (from the Saxon verb *slacian*, to slacken) is to quench partially. To *quench* is from the Saxon *cwencan*, and means to put out entirely. He who slakes his thirst takes sufficient liquid to prevent great inconvenience. He who quenches his thirst takes enough to fully satisfy his desire of drink. The same difference is preserved between the words when used in a moral sense. To slake desire is to lessen it; to quench hatred is to extinguish it.

[*Clif.* It could not slake mine ire, nor ease my heart
3 *Henry VI.*, i 3.

Oth. If I quench thee, thou flaming minister,
I can again thy former light restore. *Othello*, v. 2.

To slake his wrath whom sin hath made our foe
MILTON. *Ode*, &c

Yet years, and to ripe years judgment mature,
Quench not the thirst of glory, but augment.
P. R., iii. 38

——— The traveller slaked
His thirst from rill or gushing fount, and thanked
The Naiad. —— '*The Excursion*,' iv

The trumpet (we, intoxicate with pride
Arm at its blast for deadly wars)
To archangelic lips applied
The grave shall open, quench the stars.
'*On the Power of Sound.*']

Exercise.

Soon after the fire had broken out, there fell a heavy shower of rain, which effectually ——— it, and prevented any damage, beyond the loss of the furniture in one or two rooms.

"Amidst the running stream he ——— his thirst."

"A little fire is quickly trodden out,
Which, being suffered, rivers cannot ———."

It is a custom in many parts of Ireland to ——— the fires by covering them over with wet coals at night time; by this means, they burn through the whole night at a small cost, and do not require the trouble of lighting afresh in the morning.

The hatred which was thus unhappily occasioned between these two men was never afterwards wholly ———, and they lived and died implacable enemies.

We all suffered intensely from the excessive heat and drought; for water was so scarce as to be sold at four or five shillings the pailful, and we were often whole days without being able to procure a drop of water to ——— our thirst.

"You have already ——— sedition's brand."

"When your work is forged, do not ——— it in water to cool it, but throw it down on the floor or hearth to cool of itself."

To surprise—to astonish.

Both these words imply a disturbing of the senses. To *surprise* is to take one off his guard; to *astonish* is to confound the senses. We are longer in recovering from astonishment than from surprise. We are surprised at what is unexpected; we are astonished at what is beyond our comprehension. Surprise is more temporary; astonishment more lasting. We are *taken* by surprise; we are *struck* with astonishment. What we are prepared for does not surprise us; what we can conceive clearly does not astonish us.

[*Pro* So glad of this as they, I cannot be
Who are surprised with all —— *Tempest*, iii 1

Casca. When the most mighty gods, by tokens, send
Such dreadful heralds to astonish us. *Julius Cæsar*, i. 3

——— surprised with deep dismay
At these sad tidings —— *P. R.*, i. 108.

——— they, astonished, all resistance lost
All courage —— *P. L.*, vi. 838.

Surprised by joy—impatient as the Wind
I turned to share the transport ——
WORDSWORTH. '*Miscel. Sonnets.*'

Had this effulgence disappeared
With flying haste, I might have sent
Among the speechless clouds, a look
Of blank astonishment. '*Evening Voluntaries.*']

Exercise.

"So little do we accustom ourselves to consider the effect of time, that things necessary and certain often ——— us like unexpected contingencies."

"I have often been ———, considering that the mutual intercourse between the two countries (France and England) has lately been very great, to find how little you seem to know of us."

"But the chief merit of this great man (Michael Angelo) is not to be sought for in the remains of his pencil, nor even in his sculptures; but in the general improvement of the public taste which followed his ———ing productions."

"The greatest actions of a celebrated person, however ——— and extraordinary, are no more than what are expected from him."

"——— at the voice, he stood amazed,
And all around with inward horror gazed."

"You see, I am just to my word in writing to you from Paris, where I was very much ——— to meet my sister. I need not add, very much pleased."

"We crossed a large tract of land ———ly fruitful."

"Cromwell was not the meteor which ——— and astounds by the brilliancy and rapidity of its course."

"It is the part of men to fear and tremble,
When the most mighty gods, by tokens, send
Such dreadful heralds to ——— us."

To understand—to comprehend.

To *understand* is to have the free use of our reasoning aculty; to be able to see the relation between cause and effect, or the fitness of things for each other. To *comprehend* requires a stronger exertion of intellect. We understand what is stated in plain terms; we comprehend what at first appeared obscure. I may understand the words of a sentence without being able to comprehend its meaning. The understanding is employed upon practical questions; the comprehension, upon theoretical systems, or speculative truths. A simple fact is understood. To arrive at a conclusion by a process of reasoning, we must comprehend.

[*Macb.* ——— You seem to understand me,
By each at once her choppy finger laying
Upon her skinny lips. —— *Macbeth*, i. 3.

The. Such shaping fantasies, that apprehend
More than cool reason ever comprehends.
Midsum. N. Dream, v. 1

—— a hideous gabble rises loud,
Among the builders; each to other calls
Not understood —— *P. L.*, xii. 58.

What words or tongue of seraph can suffice,
Or heart of man suffice to comprehend.
Id., vii. 114.

That poor men's children, they, and they alone,
By their condition taught, can understand
The wisdom of the prayer that daily asks
For daily bread. —— '*The Excursion*,' iv.

Who comprehends his trust, and to the same
Keeps faithful with a singleness of aim.
'*Character of the Happy Warrior.*']

Exercise.

When a man speaks in a language with which we are unacquainted, we cannot ——— what he says: when a man speaks in a language we ———, but expresses himself loosely and inaccurately, we cannot ——— his meaning.

Natural signs are a language universally ———.

It is impossible to ——— the nature of God.

There are many things which the mind of man is unable to ———.

Though he ——— several languages, and is very accomplished, he has not yet been able to procure any occupation.

The language of a lecturer who does not fully ——— his subject must, of necessity, be unintelligible to his hearers.

Men often commit great injustice in condemning what they have not capacity to ———.

"What they cannot immediately conceive, they consider as too high to be reached, or too extensive to be ———."

"Swift pays no court to the passions, he excites neither surprise nor admiration ; he always —— himself, and his readers always —— him."

" Our finite knowledge cannot ——
The principles of an unbounded sway."

Adjacent—Contiguous.

Places that are *adjacent* lie near to each other; places that are *contiguous* lie close to each other. Two fields which have a common boundary are contiguous. Places that are adjacent to each other may yet have something intervening. Places that are contiguous must touch each other. Hampstead and Highgate are adjacent to London. The houses in Portland-place are contiguous to each other.

[*Eno.* A strange invisible perfume hits the sense
Of the adjacent wharfs. —— *Ant. and Cleop.*, ii. 2.

At once the Four spread out their starry wings
With dreadful shade contiguous —— *P. L.*, vi. 828.

How feelingly religion may be learned
In smoky cabins, from a mother's tongue—
Heard while the dwelling vibrates to the din
Of the contiguous torrent —— '*The Excursion*,' iv.]

Exercise.

" They have been beating up for volunteers at York, and the towns —— but nobody will list."

" We arrived at the utmost boundaries of a wood which lay —— to a plain."

" And now the odours, fanned by a gentle wind creeping from the —— sea, scattered themselves over that chamber, whose walls vied with the richest colours of the most glowing flowers."

" Where, then, ah ! where shall poverty reside,
To 'scape the pressure of —— pride ?"

" This is more particularly the case with the counties —— to London, over which the Genius of gardening exercises his power so often and so wantonly, that they are usually new-created once in twenty or thirty years, and no traces left of their former condition."

" The loud misrule
Of Chaos far removed ; lest fierce extremes
—— might distemper the whole frame."

On the morning of the 27th of March, 1844, not only the town itself, but all the —— villages, felt a violent shock of an earthquake.

" Flame does not mingle with flame, as air does with air, but only remains ——."

Contemptible—Despicable.

These are synonymes of degree. *Despicable* is a more intensive degree of *contemptible*. What is worthless or weak is contemptible; what is actively bad or immoral is despicable. In contemning, we pay no more attention to the thing contemned than is sufficient to perceive its worthlessness. In despising, the mind is more strongly and permanently fixed on the object despised. Circumstances may make despicable that which is in itself only contemptible. An army may be contemptible from its want of numerical force. A traitor to his country is a despicable character. Vanity is contemptible; malice is despicable.

[*Pedro.* —— the man, as you know all, hath a contemptible spirit ——
Much Ado, &c., ii. 3

Vaunting my strength in honour to their Dagon!
Besides, how vile, contemptible, ridiculous!
S. A., 1361.

——— sunk before the spear
Of despicable foes. —— *P. L.*, i. 437

—— Canute (truth more worthy to be known)
From that time forth did from his brows disown
The ostentatious symbol of a crown;
Esteeming earthly royalty
Contemptible and vain. WORDSWORTH. '*Canute and Alfred.*']

Exercise.

He attempted to conceal his designs by shallow and ——— artifices.

Menon contemned simplicity and truth as weaknesses, and so ——— was his character, that he never hesitated to accomplish his ends by perjury and deceit.

Men of ——— understanding mostly pride themselves on qualities that are worthless in the eyes of the wise.

His character was a compound of the most ——— qualities of our nature; his most prominent vices were fraud, duplicity, and the most inordinate avarice, and he had not one redeeming virtue in his whole composition.

Nothing can be more ——— than the attempts of the vain to gain that praise which they are conscious that they do not deserve.

It frequently happens to the weak-minded, that what they regard as ——— proves in the end of more real worth than many things of which they entertain a high opinion.

"To put on an artful part to obtain no other but an unjust praise from the undiscerning is of all endeavours the most ———"

Covetous—Avaricious.

The *avaricious* man is inordinately desirous of gain, by whatever means he may acquire it. The *covetous* man is desirous of appropriating the wealth of others. The avaricious are eager to get, in order to heap up; they cannot bear to part with their wealth. The covetous are eager to obtain money, but not so desirous to retain it. It is very possible for a covetous man to be a spendthrift. The avaricious never spend freely.

[*K. Hen.* —— I am not covetous for gold
Nor care I, who doth feed upon my cost;
It yearns me not, if men my garments wear;
Such outward things dwell not in my desire:
But, if it be a sin to covet honour
I am the most offending soul alive
Henry V., IV. 3.

Mal. Luxurious, avaricious, false, deceitful
Macbeth, iv. 3.

Had it been only coveting to eye
That sacred fruit, sacred to abstinence
P. L., ix. 923

—— In vain doth Valour bleed,
While Avarice and Rapine share the land.
MILTON. '*Sonnets.*

Corrupt affections, covetous desires
Are all renounced —— '*The Excursion*,' v.

Two passions, both degenerate, for they both
Began in honour, gradually obtained
Rule over her, and vexed her daily life.
An unremitting, avaricious thrift
And a strange thraldom of maternal love
Id., vi.]

Exercise.

He was so ———, and in such a hurry to become rich, that he frequently over-reached himself, and entered into speculations which proved heavy losses.

Catiline is said to have been ——— of the wealth of others, at the same time that he was lavish of his own.

About this period, two vices of an opposite nature, luxury and ———, prevailed in Rome.

"No wise man was ever ——— of money."

——— is subversive of truth, probity, and all other good qualities; and introduces in their stead, pride, cruelty, and irreligion.

The ——— are in constant fear, either of losing what they already possess, or of not being able to gain more.

The consideration that happiness does not consist in the possession of what we desire should prevent our becoming ——— of the goods of others.

"He that is envious or angry at a virtue that is not his own, is not —— of the virtue, but of its reward and reputation, and then his intentions are polluted."

"Nothing lies on his hands with such uneasiness as time. Wretched and thoughtless creatures! In the only place where —— were a virtue, we turn prodigals."

"At last Swift's —— grew too powerful for his kindness; he would refuse his friends a bottle of wine."

Different—Various.

It has been said that no two things in nature are exactly alike. The words to be here distinguished express degrees of their unlikeness. *Various* marks the dissimilarity of the species. *Different* shows the unlikeness existing in generals. Things are infinitely various; that is, it is impossible to enumerate all the points in which they vary. We cannot, however, say that things are infinitely different, because this word more exactly defines the point of unlikeness. The flowers on a rose-bush will be various in size and shape, and will be different from the flowers of the pink or dahlia. Different people think differently. A subject affects the minds of men variously, when they all entertain the same opinion of it in the main, but not in detail: it affects them differently, when some entertain an opinion of it totally opposed to that of others.

[*Fri.* Many for many virtues excellent,
None but for some, and yet all different
Rom. and Juliet, ii. 3

But if there be in glory aught of good
It may by means far different be attained,
Without ambition, war or violence *P. R.*, iii. 89

Then herbs of every leaf, that sudden flowered
Opening their various colours —— *P. L.*, vii. 318.

—— We struggle with our fate,
While health, power, glory, from their height decline,
Depressed; and then extinguished: and our state
In this, how different, lost Star, from thine,
That no to-morrow shall our beams restore.
WORDSWORTH. '*Miscel. Sonnets.*

The tears of man in various measure gush
From various sources; —— '*Eccles. Sonnets.*']

Exercise.

The two men were as ——— from each other as it was possible. The one, open, frank, liberal, and kind to his friends and companions; the other, close, mean, avaricious, and unfeeling.

"There are upwards of a hundred ——— species of fern, but they are seldom cultivated in gardens."

"Happiness consists in things which produce a pleasure, and in the absence of those which cause any pain: now these, to ——— men, are ——— things."

"Then they were known to men by ——— names,
And ——— idols through the heathen world."

The northern languages of modern Europe may be divided under three ——— heads, viz., Celtic, Teutonic, and Sclavonic.

"It is astonishing to consider the ——— degrees of care that descend from the parent to the young, so far as is absolutely necessary for the leaving a posterity."

As land is improved by sowing it with ——— seeds, so is the mind by exercising it with ——— studies.

Evident—Obvious.

What is clearly proved is *evident;* what proves itself is *obvious.* The latter is a stronger term than the former. It requires some, though not a great effort of the mind, to perceive what is evident; what is obvious requires no stretch of the mind to understand—it presents itself to our view—nay, thrusts itself upon our notice. Intuitive truths are obvious; deduced truths become evident. It is evident that two straight lines cannot inclose a space; it is obvious that the whole is greater than its part.

[*Emil.* —— your goodness is so evident
That your free undertaking cannot miss
A thriving issue —— *Winter's Tale,* ii. 2.

—— in our faces evident the signs *P. L.,* ix. 1077.

—— the conscience of her worth,
That would be woo'd, and not unsought be won,
Not obvious, not obtrusive, but retired
The more desirable —— *Id.,* viii. 504

That obvious emblem giving to the eye
Of meek devotion which erewhile it gave,
That symbol of the day-spring from on high,
Triumphant o'er the darkness of the grave.
WORDSWORTH. *Rydal Chape.*]

Exercise.

"It is —— to remark that we follow nothing heartily unless carried to it by inclination."

"It is —— that fame, considered merely as the immortality of a name, is not less likely to be the reward of bad actions than of good."

"These sentiments, whether they be impressed on the soul, or arise as —— reflections of our reason, I call natural, because they have been found in all ages."

"It is —— in the general frame of nature, that things most manifest unto sense have proved obscure unto the understanding."

"All the great lines of our duty are clear and ——, the obligation acknowledged, and the wisdom of complying with it freely confessed."

"They are incapable of making conquests upon their neighbours, which is —— to all who know their constitution."

"They are such lights as are only —— to every man of sense, who loves poetry and understands it."

"The printing private letters is the worst sort of betraying conversation as it has ——ly the most extensive ill consequences."

Forsaken—Forlorn.

Forlorn is the intensive of *forsaken.* When we are forsaken, we are partially deprived of society; the forlorn are deprived of all society and help. Forsaken also refers to the act of those who abandon; forlorn qualifies the state of the abandoned. The forsaken are no longer visited by former friends; the forlorn are cared for by no one. Things, places, &c., as well as persons, are forsaken; only persons are forlorn.

[*France.* Most choice, forsaken; and most loved, despised.
King Lear, i. 1.

Prin. To some forlorn and naked hermitage,
Remote from all the pleasures of the world.
Love's Labour Lost, v. 2

—— the rathe primrose that forsaken dies
MILTON. '*Lycidas*'

The nodding horrour of whose shady brows
Threats the forlorn and wandering passenger
Comus.

The world forsaken, all its busy cares
And stirring interests shunned with desperate flight,
All trust abandoned in the healing might
Of virtuous action —— WORDSWORTH. '*Tour in Italy*

Yet how forlorn, should ye depart
Ye superstitions of the *heart*,
How poor were human life! '*Presentiments*.']

Exercise.

Conscience made them recollect that they who had once been deaf to the supplications of a brother were now left friendless and ——.

"But fearful for themselves, my countrymen
Left me —— in the Cyclops' den."

"For here —— and lost I tread,
With fainting steps and slow,
Where wilds immeasurably spread
Seem lengthening as I go."

London is at this period of the year quite ——. In the west end of the town, the private houses are almost all shut up, and no gay equipages strike the eye of the passenger.

Last summer you frequently came to see us, but now you have quite —— us.

The apartments and gardens remain in the nicest order, and though the villa is ——, it is not neglected.

"Disastrous day! what ruin hast thou bred,
What anguish to the living and the dead!
How hast thou left the widow all ——."

"Their purple majesty,
And all those outward shows which we call greatness,
Languish and droop, seem empty and ——,
And draw the wond'ring gazers' eyes no more."

General—Universal.

General bears the same proportion to *universal* as the part to the whole. The former qualifies the majority; the latter, every individual. A general rule has exceptions; a universal rule has none. General is opposed to particular: universal to individual. The chief object of a good government should be to secure the general welfare of the community. Universal prosperity never yet existed in any country.

[*Macb.* As broad and general as the casing air.
Macbeth, iii 4.

Chor. A largess universal, like the Sun
His liberal eye doth give to every one.
Henry V., IV. (*Chorus.*,

—— forthwith from all winds
The living, and forthwith the cited dead
Of all past ages, to the general doom
Shall hasten —— *P. L.*, iii. 328.

—— while universal Pan
Knit with the Graces and the Hours in dance
Led on the eternal spring —— *Id.*, iv. 266.

Creatures that in communities exist,
Less, as might seem, for general guardianship
Or through dependence upon mutual aid,
Than by participation of delight
And a strict love of fellowship, combined.
'The Excursion' iv.

—— the mild assemblage of the starry heavens;
And the great sun, earth's universal lord! *Id.*]

Exercise.

"To conclude from particulars to ——— is a false way of arguing."

"What, cried I, is my young landlord, then, the nephew of a man whose virtues, generosity, and singularities are so ———ly known?"

"Nor failed they to express how much they praised,
That for the ——— safety he despised
His own."

"I have considered Milton's 'Paradise Lost' in the fable, the characters, the sentiments, and the language; and have shewn that he excels, in ——— under each of these heads."

"Divine laws and precepts, simply and formally moral, are ——— in respect of persons, and in regard of their perpetual obligation."

"This excellent epistle, though in the front of it it bears a particular inscription, yet in its drift is ———, as designing to convince all mankind of the necessity of seeking for happiness in the Gospel."

"The ———ty of the English have such a favorable opinion of treason, nothing can cure them."

"The wisest were distracted with doubts, while the ———ty wandered without any ruler"

Idle—Indolent.

The expression "an idle child" does not mean one who is altogether inactive, but one who occupies his time in frivolities. An indolent child is one who has a strong aversion from action of any sort. The idle do not what they ought to do; the indolent would do nothing. The idle boy does not learn his lesson; the indolent boy lies in bed late, and lounges about all day. Idleness is opposed to diligence; indolence, to activity. The idle want steadiness of purpose; the indolent want power of exertion.

[——— The murmuring surge,
That on the unnumbered idle pebbles chafes,
Cannot be heard so high. *King Lear*, iv. 6.

——— other creatures all day long
Rove idle, unemployed, and less need rest.
P. L., iv. 617.

The happy idleness of that sweet morn
With all its lovely images, was changed
To serious musing and to self-reproach.
WORDSWORTH. '*On Naming of Places.*'

—— who might mistake for sober sense
And wise reserve the plea of indolence.
'*Poems on National Independence.*']

Exercise.

"Nothing is so opposite to the true enjoyment of life as the relaxed and feeble state of an ——— mind."

"——— and vice, then, are the chief parents of crime and distress. But how, in so industrious a country, arises the indifference to toil? The answer is obvious—wherever ——— is better remunerated than labour, ——— becomes contagious, and labour hateful."

In the ——— luxuries of a court, what more natural than satiety among the great, and a proud discontent among their emulators?

"Supposing among a multitude embarked in the same vessel, there are several that, in a tempest, will rather perish than work; would it not be madness in the rest to stand ———, and rather choose to sink than do more than comes to their share?"

"Children generally hate to be ———; all the care, then, is that their busy humour should be constantly employed in something of use to them."

The Frankish kings, buried in luxurious ———, resigned the administration of their affairs into the hands of officers, who, after a time, assumed the regal authority, and founded a new dynasty.

Miserable—Wretched.

A *miserable* man is one who is to be pitied or despised on account of his feelings or state of mind; a *wretched* man is one to be pitied by reason of his condition. We are miserable in consequence of our own reflections. It is what we suffer from external circumstances that makes us wretched. A condemned felon is both miserable and wretched; miserable, from his state of mind, and wretched, from the circumstances in which he is placed. The miserable and the wretched are both deserving of pity; the wretched, more so than the miserable, as wretchedness is the extreme of misery.

[*K. Hen.* —— Get you therefore hence,
Poor miserable wretches, to your death.
Henry V., ii. 2.

Lear. As full of grief as age; wretched in both!
King Lear, ii. 4

O miserable mankind, to what fall
Degraded, to what wretched state reserved!
P. L., xi. 500

A dismal prospect yields the wild shore strewn
With wrecks, and trod by feet of young and old
Wandering about in miserable search
Of friends or kindred, whom the angry sea
Restores not to their prayer! ‘*The Excursion*,’ v

O, never let the Wretched, if a choice
Be left him, trust the freight of his distress
To a long voyage on the silent deep! *Id.*, iii.]

Exercise.

Robinson Crusoe, when wrecked on his uninhabited island, was ——— at the thoughts of his being cut off from all human intercourse, and separated from the whole world; and the idea of his ——— and forlorn condition frequently drew from him expressions of the bitterest grief.

Though I have seen poverty in many forms, I never beheld, in any part of the world, such ——— beings as the poor cottagers in the south of Ireland.

"Thus to relieve the ——— was his pride,
And e'en his failings leaned to virtue's side."

He felt ——— at reflecting upon the misfortunes he had unconsciously brought upon an amiable family.

"Man, considered in himself, is a very helpless and a very ——— being."

It was discovered the next morning that the ——— man had committed suicide.

'Tis murmur, discontent, distrust,
That makes you ———.

"Reason tells me that it is more misery to be covetous than to be poor, as our language, by a peculiar significance of dialect, calls the covetous man the ——— man."

Modern—Recent.

The word *recent* refers to what has happened within a comparatively short space of time past—that which has been some time, but not a long time, in existence; the word *modern* refers not only to what has been, but what still does, and will probably remain, in existence for some time. Recent is contradistinguished from what is long past; modern is opposed to ancient. Recent is always used abstractly; modern, in both senses. Recent facts are fresh in our memory; modern fashions belong to the present day.

[Many are the sayings of the wise,
In ancient and in modern books enrolled,
Extolling patience as the truest fortitude.
S. A., 653.

—— subjected to the arts
Of modern ingenuity, and made
The senseless member of a vast machine
'The Excursion,' ix

—— when golden beams,
Reflected through the mists of age, from hours
Of innocent delight, remote or recent,
Shoot but a little way—'tis all they can,—
Into the doubtful future. —— *'Tour in Italy.'*]

Exercise.

——— experiments have proved beyond a doubt, that it is not only possible, but very easy, to freeze water in a red hot crucible.

"Some of the ancient, and likewise of the ——— writers, that have laboured in natural magic, have noted a sympathy between the sun and certain herbs."

On his arrival at court, he found that, in consequence of ——— changes in the administration of the king's household, it would be necessary for him to wait at least a week or ten days before he could obtain an audience of his majesty.

"A ——— Italian is distinguished by sensibility, quickness, and art, while he employs on trifles the capacity of an ancient Roman; and exhibits now, in the scene of amusement, and in search of a frivolous applause, that fire and those passions with which Gracchus burned in the forum, and shook the assemblies of a severe people."

Some ——— regulations of the minister have made him very unpopular in this part of the country.

Scarce—Rare

That of which there is at no time much to be procured, or which is seldom to be met with, is *rare*. That of which there is occasionally but a small quantity is *scarce*. Certain plants are rare in England; that is, they are seldom found in this country. A bad harvest will make corn scarce. Scarce implies a previous plenty, which is not the case with rare. Rare qualifies what is a subject of curiosity, or novelty; scarce qualifies what is an article of necessity. Things *are* rare, and may *become* scarce. Rare is used metaphorically, scarce is never so used.

[*Gaunt.* Where words are scarce, they are seldom spent in vain
Rich. II., ii 1

K. Hen. If thy rare qualities, sweet gentleness,
Thy meekness saint-like, wife-like government
Henry VIII., ii. 4

Or what, though rare, of later age
Ennobled hath the buskined stage.
MILTON. '*Il Penseroso*'

——— rare, at least,
The mutual aptitude of seed and soil
That yields such kindly product. —— '*The Excursion*,' v.

Exercise.

"A perfect union of wit and judgment is one of the ———est things in the world."

"When any particular piece of money grew very ———, it was often recoined by a succeeding emperor."

"Already it is difficult to determine whether his (Michael Angelo's) reputation be enhanced or diminished by the sombre representations of his pencil, in the Pauline and Sistine chapels, or by the few specimens of his cabinet pictures, now ———ly to be met with, and exhibiting only a shadow of their original excellence."

"A Swede will no more sell you his hemp for less silver, because you tell him silver is ———er now in England, than a tradesman of London will sell his commodity cheaper to the Isle of Man, because money is ——— there."

"Far from being fond of any flower for its ———ity, if I meet with any in a field which pleases me, I give it a place in my garden."

"Corn does not rise or fall by the differences of more or less plenty of money, but by the plenty and ———ity that God sends."

Silent—Taciturn.

Taciturnity is an intensive silence. A *silent* man is one who does not speak; a *taciturn* man is one who scarcely ever speaks. We may be silent without being taciturn. Silent respects the act; taciturn the habit. Circumstances may make us silent; our disposition inclines us to be taciturn. The English have a reputation for taciturnity. There are many occasions on which it is proper to be silent; the taciturn lose many opportunities of information from their disinclination to ask questions. Silent is opposed to speaking; taciturn, to loquacious. The taciturn are frequently gloomy and sullen.

[*Cor.* What shall Cordelia do? Love and be silent.
King Lear, i. 1

Æne. —— the secrets of nature
Have not more gift in taciturnity. *Troil. and Cress.* iv. 2

——— silent, and in face
Confounded, long they sat, as stricken mute.
P. L., ix. 1063

The city now doth, like a garment, wear
The beauty of the morning; silent, bare.
Ships, towers, domes, theatres and temples lie
Open unto the fields, and to the sky.
WORDSWORTH. '*Miscel. Sonnets*]

Exercise.

Some men are so fond of hearing their own voices, that they are not ———, even when they have no one to talk to.

He was by fits either very loquacious, or very ———.

It is prudent to be ——— where we find that speaking would be dangerous.

" And just before the confines of the wood,
The gliding Lethe leads her ——— flood."

He did not appear to be in good spirits that evening, and I observed that he was unusually ———.

Our country is not famed for great talkers; Englishmen are in general ——— and reserved.

I have travelled for twenty-four hours in a stage-coach with three companions (?) who did not make a single remark, either to me or to each other, but preserved a strict ——— during the whole journey.

Women are generally much less ——— than men; this may be accounted for in two ways: they are naturally more communicative; and, secondly, they have not the same causes for ——— which operate upon the other sex.

Wonderful—Marvellous.

A *wonder* is natural; a *marvel* is incredible. What is wonderful takes our senses, what is marvellous takes our reason, by surprise. The wonderful is opposed to the ordinary; the marvellous is opposed to the probable. Jugglers' tricks are wonderful; travellers' stories are marvellous. The adventures of Baron Münchausen are full of the marvellous; nature is full of wonders.

[*Exe.* 'Tis wonderful!
K. Hen. Come, go we in procession to the village:
And be it death proclaimed through our host,

To boast of this, or take that praise from God,
Which is his only. *Henry V.*, iv. 8

Gon. Marvellous sweet music! *Tempest*, iii. 3.

——— more wonderful
Than that, which by creation first brought forth
Light out of darkness! *P. L.*, xii. 471.

—— 'Wonderful' hath been
The love established between man and man,
Passing the love of women' ——
WORDSWORTH. '*On the Death of Charles Lamb*.'

I thought of Chatterton, the marvellous Boy,
The sleepless Soul that perished in his pride.
'*Resolution and Independence*.'

Exercise.

"If a man, out of vanity, or from a desire of being in the fashion, or in order to pass for ———ly wise, shall say that Berkley's doctrine is true while at the same time his belief is precisely the same with mine, I leave him to enjoy the fruits of his hypocrisy."

"The ——— fable includes whatever is supernatural, and especially the machines of the gods."

"I could not sufficiently ——— at the intrepidity of these diminutive mortals, who durst venture to mount and walk upon my body."

"The common people of Spain have an Oriental passion for story-telling, and are fond of the ———."

"How poor, how rich, how abject, how august,
How complicate, how ——— is man!
How passing ——— he who made him such!"

"——— causeth astonishment, or an immoveable posture of the body for in ——— the spirits fly not as in fear, but only settle."

Sir John Mandeville, in the narrative of his travels, dedicated to Edward III., inserted parts of such chronicles as were then in existence, and introduced romantic and ——— tales of knight errantry, miraculous legends, monsters, giants, &c.

Below—Beneath.

Below and beneath both refer to what is under us; but *beneath* is farther down than *below*. Small fish sport below the surface of the waters. The larger fish repose beneath the flood. What is beneath is below us; but what is below is not always beneath. Those who are below us in rank are not beneath us; on the contrary, they deserve our respect if they conduct themselves virtuously. The vicious and the profligate are beneath our consideration.

[*Jul.* Methinks I see thee, now thou art below,
As one dead in the bottom of a tomb. *Rom. and Jul.*, iii. 5
Oth. O, I were damned beneath all depth of hell,
But that I did proceed upon just grounds.
Othello, v. 2.
There let the pealing organ blow
To the full-voiced quire below MILTON. '*Il Penseroso.*'
Sunk though he be beneath the watery floor
'*Lycidas.*'
A lofty precipice in front
A silent tarn below! WORDSWORTH. '*Fidelity.*
Then, from thy breast what thought
Beneath so beautiful a sun
So sad a sigh has brought? '*The Two April Mornings.*']

Exercise.

The noble Venetians think themselves at least equal to the electors of the empire, and but one degree ——— kings.

He will do nothing that is ——— his high station, nor omit doing any thing which becomes it.

Standing on the summit of a high rock, when I looked down into the cavern ——— me, I was seized with such a giddiness, that I was obliged to sit down for fear of falling.

His brother, though several years older, was ——— him in the school, and was often reproved by the master for his idleness.

All the numbers ——— ten are called digits.

Those who work in mines are forced to toil the whole day long far ——— the surface of the earth, and to be deprived of the light of the sun and fresh air for a great portion of their lives.

The house consists of three stories, and a suite of kitchens and offices ——— the ground-floor. It stands in the midst of a well-stocked garden, and is not more than a mile from the high-road.

"This said, he led them up the mountain's brow,
And showed them all the shining fields ———."
"Trembling, I view the dread abyss ——— "

Between—Among.

Among is derived from *on many;* between, from *by twain.* The former is used in speaking of a larger number; the latter, never when more than two are concerned. The etymologies of these two prepositions will suggest their proper use. A man is therefore between his friends when he has one on each side of him; and he is among his friends when he is surrounded by several.

[*Ham.* As love between them like the palm might flourish
As peace should still her wheaten garland wear,
And stand a comma 'tween their amities. *Hamlet*, v. 2.

Ben. —— he hath hid himself among those trees.
Rom. and Jul., ii 1

——— gods adored
Among the nations round ; and durst abide
Jehovah thundering out of Sion, throned
Between the cherubim —— *P. L.*, i. 384.

Among the faithless, faithful only he ;
Among innumerable false, unmoved,
Unshaken, unseduced, unterrified. *Id.*, v. 897

—— Sentinels, between two armies
With nothing better, in the chill night air
Than their own thoughts to comfort them '*The Excursion*,' vi

The towering headlands, crowned with mist,
Their feet among the billows, know
That Ocean is a mighty harmonist, '*On the Power of Sound.*']

Exercise.

There exists not the slightest shadow of resemblance ——— the hieroglyphics of Egypt and the Chinese characters.

——— those who are not exposed to the climate, the complexion is fully as fair as that of the Spaniards and Portuguese.

The prize-money was equally divided ——— the ship's crew.

The constant intercourse which subsisted for many centuries ——— this country and France contributed largely to the introduction of French terms into our language.

These two failures, to the aggregate amount of about two millions of dollars, produced, as might be expected, a considerable sensation and loud clamours ——— the foreign merchants at Canton.

The object of all writers on synonymous terms is to explain the distinction ——— words which approximate in signification.

The king endeavoured to promote kindlier and gentler feelings ——— all classes of his subjects, by encouraging and patronizing such sports and pastimes as were consonant with the spirit and habits of the age.

"There were ——— the old Roman statues, several of Venus in different postures and habits; as there are many particular figures of her made after the same design."

"Friendship requires that it be ——— two at east; and there can be no friendship where there are not two friends."

By—With.

The distinction to be made between these prepositions is to be found in the degree of connection which they express.

The etymological meaning of the former is, *close-to;* and that of the latter, *join.* *With* expresses contact; *by*, occasional proximity, or a remoter connection. In speaking of external things, we say—He came *with* his friend; and, he stood *by* me. In an abstract sense, the same difference holds good. The task was accomplished *with* great difficulty. *By* constant diligence, he at length acquired a perfect knowledge of the subject.

The manner or instrument of an action is generally preceded by *with; by* is used before the cause, or direct agent, when a person. The man struck the table with his hand. The table was struck by the man.

[*K. Rich.* My care is—loss of care by old care done;
Your care is—gain of care, by new care won.
* * * * *
With mine own tears I wash away my balm,
With mine own hands I give away my crown,
With mine own tongue deny my sacred state,
With mine own breath release all duteous oaths;
Rich. II., iv. 1

Him thus intent Ithuriel with his spear
Touched lightly —— *P. L.*, iv. 810.

——— from the arched roof
Pendent by subtle magic, many a row
Of starry lamps and blazing cressets, fed
With naphtha and asphaltus, yielded light
As from a sky. —— *Id.*, i. 726.

Nor shall she fail to see
Even in the motions of the storm
Grace that shall mould the Maiden's form
By silent sympathy. WORDSWORTH.

The GIFT to King Amphion,
That walled a city with its melody
Was for belief no dream —— '*On the Power of Sound.*']

Exercise.

The war was at that time carried on between the French and the Italians ——— the utmost inhumanity.

More misery is produced among us ——— the irregularities of our tempers, than ——— real misfortunes.

Lord Anson signalized himself ——— his voyage round the world We are told that he was encouraged in his fondness for naval history and bold adventures ——— his father.

Being sent ——— a squadron of five ships to annoy the Spaniards in the Southern Ocean, he sailed from Portsmouth September 18th, 1740.

Caxton first introduced into England the art of printing ——— moveable types.

"The grammar of a language is sometimes to be carefully studied ——— a grown man"

'——— thy powerful blast,
Heat apace and cool as fast"

Frequently—Often.

That is done *often*, which is repeated after short intervals. That is done *frequently*, which is repeated after longer, but not always after the same intervals of time. Thus, "Our uncle often dines with us;" but, "we frequently have friends to dine with us." "I often walk in the park, and frequently meet some of my acquaintance there." The difference between the two words is to be found not only in the length of time which elapses between the acts they qualify, but also in the variety of persons who perform those acts.

[*Tita.* ——— in the spiced Indian air, by night,
Full often hath she gossiped by my side.
Midsummer Night's Dream, ii 2.

——— How often from the steep
Of echoing hill or thicket have we heard
Celestial voices ——— *P. L.*, iv. 680.

I've heard of hearts unkind, kind deeds
With coldness still returning;
Alas, the gratitude of men
Hath oftener left me mourning. WORDSWORTH. '*Simon Lee.*']

Exercise.

What is done ——— and carelessly, is liable to be ——— done wrong.

He ——— paid us visits, but did not come so ——— as his brother.

The wealth of individuals is ——— dissipated by an extravagant patronage of the fine arts.

Men act wrong scarcely less ——— from the defect of courage, than of knowledge and of prudence.

Though he ——— goes into society, I have not ——— met him at the houses of our common friends.

"How ——— shall my brother sin against me, and I forgive him?"

It ——— happens that young persons of an inquiring turn of mind are discouraged from the pursuit of some studies by failing to perceive their ultimate object.

"I could not without much grief observe how ——— ladies and gentlemen are at a loss for questions and answers."

"Who does not more admire Cicero as an author than as consul of Rome, and does not ———er talk of the celebrated writers of our own country in former ages, than of any among their contemporaries?"

Immediately—Instantly.

An act is performed *instantly* when no time is allowed to elapse before we set about it; it is performed *immediately* when no occupation is allowed to intervene between the present act and the one proposed. To do a thing instantly, we leave our occupation. To do a thing immediately, we may finish what we have in hand before commencing what is required of us. What is done instantly is done sooner than what is done immediately. One who is writing a letter may promise to go somewhere immediately, and yet not go till he have finished his letter; but he must begin nothing else before he goes. One who is writing and promises to go instantly, must leave off writing, and go at once.

[*K. Rich.* Now put it, heaven, in his physician's mind
To help him to his grave immediately. *Rich. II.*, i. 4.

Art. Delay not, Cæsar; read it instantly *Jul. Cæsar*, iii. 1

Reason in man obscured, or not obeyed,
Immediately inordinate desires
And upstart passions catch the government
From reason. —— *P. L.*, xii. 89.

——— sought repair
Of sleep, which instantly fell on me —— *Id.*, viii. 458.

——— I will not say
What thoughts immediately were ours ——
WORDSWORTH. '*On the Naming of Places.*']

Exercise.

"Admiration is a short-lived passion, that ——— decays upon growing familiar with the object."

"The poor man has caught cold on the river; for our order reached him when he was just returned from certain visits in London, and he held it a matter of loyalty and conscience ——— to set forth again."

This good news arrived yesterday, and was ——— spread all over the town, so that this morning there was not a soul in the place unacquainted with all the circumstances.

Seeing his friend struggling hard in the water, and in imminent danger of his life, he ——— stripped off his coat, and jumped into the river to his assistance.

"Moses mentions the ——— cause of the Deluge, the rains and the waters; and St. Peter mentions the more remote and fundamental cause, viz the constitution of the heavens."

"The ——— stroke of death denounced to-day
Removed far off."

Middle—Midst.

Middle is from the Anglo-Saxon *mid*, and *dael*, a part or portion. *Midst* is the superlative or intensive form of middle and is a contraction of *middlemost;* thus: middlemost—middest—midst.

The middle is that part of a substance which is at an equal distance from both its ends. Midst is that point in a substance which is at an equal distance from all parts of its circumference. The middle of the street is half-way between the houses on one side, and those on the other. The middle of June is half-way between the beginning and the end of the month. The midst of the forest is that point which is at an equal distance from all parts of its circumference. In an abstract sense, midst is more frequently used. Thus, we have: In the midst of danger—of difficulties, &c.

[*Per.* ——— these are flowers
Of middle summer; and, I think, they are given
To men of middle age ——— *Winter's Tale*, v. 3.

1 *Sen.* ——— our good city
Cleave in the midst and perish. *Coriolanus*, iii. 2.

——— on the snowy top
Of cold Olympus ruled the middle air
Their highest heaven ——— *P. L.*, i. 516.

——— from whence a voice
From midst a golden cloud, thus mild was heard.
Id., vi. 28.

That secret spirit of humanity
Which, 'mid the calm oblivious tendencies,
Of Nature, 'mid her plants, and weeds, and flowers,
And silent overgrowings, still survived. '*The Excursion*, i.]

Exercise.

The man had laid a wager that he would swim across the river at its widest part in less than ten minutes; he had accomplished half his task with ease, in less than half the allotted time; but just when he had reached the ——— of the stream, he was carried away by the force of the current, and drowned.

Extended on the burning sand in the ——— of the desert, and suffering the greatest pain from fever brought on by excessive fatigue and want of proper nourishment, I should have perished, had it not been for the extreme kindness and attention of my Arab guides.

In the ——— of these imminent and appalling dangers, he did not betray a sign of fear, but gave his orders with the same calmness and composure as usual.

"A ——— station of life is within reach of those conveniences which the lower orders of mankind must necessarily want, and yet without embarrassment of greatness."

He was thankful in the ——— of his afflictions.

While—Whilst.

While is from the Saxon *hwile*, and signifies *time*. *Whilst* is a superlative form, or a more intensive degree of while, and is used for *during the whole time*. "I shall write *while* you work," means that during the time that you are working, I shall occupy myself (perhaps occasionally) in writing. "I shall write *whilst* you work," means that during the whole time that you are occupied in working, I shall not cease from writing.

Whilst is also used to mark a contrast or strong distinction between two things or actions. "Make your mirth *whilst* I bear my misery."

[*Hor.* While one with moderate haste might tell a hundred.
Hamlet, i. 2.

Ant. ——— the queen,—
Whose heart, I thought, I had, for she had mine;
Which, whilst it was mine, had annexed unto 't
A million more, now lost. *Ant. and Cleop.*, iv. 12

For evil news rides post, while good news baits
S. A., 1538.

Whilst from off the waters fleet
Thus I set my printless feet
O'er the cowslip's velvet head
That bends not as I tread. *Comus*, 896.

——— when with eye upraised
To heaven he knelt before the crucifix,
While o'er the lake the cataract of Lodore
Pealed to his orisons —— WORDSWORTH. '*Inscriptions.*]

Exercise.

The two ruffians rushed out upon the traveller unawares; and having knocked him down, the one held his hands ——— the other rifled his pockets of his watch and money.

How did these two men behave in the same circumstances? The one seized with a malicious joy the opportunity thus offered him of gratifying his revenge; ——— the other, with a noble generosity, pardoned his enemies for those offences against him which he could have then so easily punished.

——— we were all engaged in conversation, we heard some beautiful music under our windows, which was continued at intervals during the remainder of the evening.

"Can he imagine that God sends forth an irresistible strength against some sins; ——— in others he allows men a power of repelling his grace?"

——— Cæsar was at Rome, an insurrection broke out among his troops, who were too impatient to wait for the triumph, and the advantages they hoped to derive from it.

SECTION IV.

POSITIVE AND NEGATIVE SYNONYMES.

ANOTHER principle by which we may frequently discover a difference between two approximating meanings, is where one term is positive, and the other negative; that is, where the first expresses some idea independently, and the second, the negation of another idea. The two verbs, *to shun* and *to avoid*, show a difference of this sort; to shun is positively to turn away from, to avoid is merely *not* to approach, or go in the way of. Between many approximating words, we shall have no difficulty in distinguishing, by the application of this test. The difference between *unable* and *not able*, *inability* and *disability*, and many others, becomes thus immediately clear. The two words have the same idea in common, but the one has a negative quality not found in the other, and thus a distinction can be made. The pairs of words treated in this section differ from each other in consequence of this principle.

Despair—Hopelessness.

Despair is positive; *hopelessness* is negative. He who despairs, once hoped, but has now lost his hope The hopeless man may never have hoped; desperate is deprived of hope; hopeless is wanting hope. Affairs are said to be hopeless when their state is such as not to raise any hope of their being successful. An enterprise is said to be desperate when all hope is lost which we once entertained of its success. To be desperate, we must have previously hoped.

[*Hel.* Oft expectation fails, and most oft there
Where most it promises; and oft it hits,
Where hope is coldest and despair most sits. *All's Well, &c.*, ii. 1.

K. Rich. The hopeless word of—never to return,
Breathe I against thee, upon pain of life. *Richard II.*, i. 3

Me miserable! which way shall I fly
Infinite wrath, and infinite despair! *P. L*, iv. 74.

Nor am I in the list of them that hope:
Hopeless are all my evils, all remediless. *S. A.*, 648

And oft his cogitations sink as low
As, through the abysses of a joyless heart,
The heaviest plummet of despair can go. WORDSWORTH. '*Dion.*

For years to me are sad and dull;
My very moments are too full
Of hopelessness and fear. '*Lament of Mary, Queen of Scots.*']

Exercise.

"In a part of Asia, the sick, when their case comes to be thought ———, are carried out and laid on the earth, before they are dead, and left there."

Are they indifferent, being used as signs of immoderate and ——— lamentation for the dead?

I am a man of ——— fortunes, that is, a man whose friends are dead; for I never aimed at any other fortune than in friends.

"The Æneans wish in vain their wanted chief,
——— of flight, more ——— of relief."

"——— is the thought of the unattainableness of any good, which works differently in men's minds, sometimes producing uneasiness or pain, sometimes rest and indolence."

"——— of ransom, and condemned to lie
In durance, doomed a lingering death to die."

"We are troubled on every side, yet not distressed; we are perplexed, but not in ———"

"Before the ships a ——— stand they made,
And fired the troops, and called the gods to aid."

"[He] watches with greedy hope to find
His wish and best advantage, us asunder;
——— to circumvent us joined, where each
To other speedy aid might lend at need."

Disability—Inability.

Inability is a natural want of power to act; *disability* is a want of qualification. One who confesses his inability to account for some phenomenon, gives us to understand that nature has not endowed him with power to explain its cause. One who is disqualified, by reason of his nonage, from entering into a contract, labours under a legal disability.

[*Val.* Leave off discourse of disability.
Two Gent. of Verona, ii. 4.]

Exercise.

There are many questions which have baffled the most sagacious penetration of the human intellect, and which the deepest philosophy is to this day obliged to confess its ——— to fathom.

In the tenth and eleventh centuries, the Jews were persecuted in England with unrelenting cruelty, and even at this moment they labour under many legal ——— in that country.

He accepted, though much against his will, the office vacant by the death of the professor, as he could plead neither ignorance nor ——— as an excuse for refusing it.

The party on the other side grounded their hopes of success on the alleged ——— of the plaintiff, and on the presumption that as he was a minor, he could not be a party to the contract in question.

One who confesses his ——— declares that he is *not able* to perform some action, or explain some question. He who labours under ——— is *unable* to enter into certain contracts or agreements.

"It is not from ——— to discover what they ought to do, that men err in practice."

Want of age is a legal ——— to contract a marriage.

This disadvantage which the Dissenters at present lie under, of a ——— to receive church preferments, will be easily remedied by the repeal of the test.

Disbelief—Unbelief.

Unbelief is a want of belief; *disbelief* is an unwillingness or refusal to believe. I express my unbelief of what I am willing to believe, but am not convinced is true. I express my disbelief of what I have reason to think is false. Unbelief is open to conviction; disbelief is already convinced of the falseness of what it does not believe. Many men have expressed their unbelief in Christianity. I disbelieve the statement of a perjured man. Unbelief is properly applied to opinions, truths, &c. ; disbelief, to facts.

[——— but unbelief is blind.
Comus, 519.]

Exercise.

The magistrate having heard the prisoner's story, expressed his unqualified ——— of every word he had uttered, and turning to the clerk of the office, directed him immediately to make out his committal.

Notwithstanding all the pretensions to the art of magic which this impostor so unblushingly asserted, few, even in those superstitious times, were so far deceived by his artifices as not to suspect him of fraud, and many even openly expressed their ——— of the art he professed.

It is well known that a firm faith in the power of magic is to this day common in all parts of the East; and a dangerous experiment would it be for any European traveller who, in the pride of his philosophy, should venture there publicly to express his ——— in its agency.

One of the most pernicious effects of a close acquaintance with the world is, that it renders us so familiar with the worst parts of human nature, as almost to lead to our ——— in many good qualities which really exist among men.

Freedom—Liberty.

Freedom represents a positive—liberty, a negative quality. The former denotes a natural state; the latter, an exemption from bonds or slavery. Those who have never been slaves enjoy freedom; Those who are exempt from slavery enjoy liberty. Freedom supposes a right; liberty supposes a previous restraint. Freedom is the birthright of every Englishman. A prisoner who is set at liberty regains his freedom We are at liberty to speak on any subject we choose, but circumstances may prevent our speaking with freedom.

[*Bru.* And, waving our red weapons o'er our heads,
Let's all cry, Peace! Freedom! and Liberty! *Julius Cæsar*, iii. 1.

Pro. Shortly shall all my labours end, and thou
Shalt have the air at freedom — *Tempest*, iv. 1.

Jaq. ——— I must have liberty
Withal, as large a charter as the wind
To blow on whom I please — *As You Like It*, ii. 7

The conquered also, and enslaved in war
Shall, with their freedom lost, all virtue lose. *P. L.*, xi. 798.

Since thy original lapse, true liberty
Is lost, which always with right reason dwells

Id, xii 82

That bawl for freedom in their senseless mood,
And still revolt when truth would set them free.
License they mean when they cry Liberty;
For who loves that must first be wise and good.

MILTON '*Sonnet*

How does the Meadow-flower its bloom unfold?
Because the lovely little flower is free
Down to its root, and, in that freedom, bold.
And so the grandeur of the Forest-tree
Comes not by casting in a formal mould,
But from its own divine vitality.

WORDSWORTH. '*Miscel Sonnets*

——— No sea
Swells like the bosom of a man set free;
A wilderness is rich with liberty.
Roll on ye spouting whales, who die or keep
Your independence in the fathomless Deep! '*Liberty*.']

Exercise.

After ten years' confinement, the prisoner's friends contrived to raise the sum necessary for his ransom, and he was at length set at ———.

The question was discussed with great ———, and most of the members of the society took part in the debate.

The ancient Greeks cherished the deepest and most heartfelt love for their country; they fought and bled for their ———, and preferred a thousand deaths to slavery or oppression.

He was one of the most amiable characters of his time, and his disposition was marked by the ——— and frankness with which he communicated his opinions and sentiments to his friends.

Some men appear to have had singular ideas of ———; they seem to have thought that it meant a privilege to do whatever their evil passions might dictate, and to have looked upon it as a state in which the most atrocious crimes might be committed with impunity.

After having suffered three years' imprisonment for this libel, he was set at ———, and he determined thenceforth to express himself with less ——— on the character and conduct of others.

"The ——— of the press is a blessing when we are inclined to write against others, and a calamity when we find ourselves overborne by the multitude of our assailants."

A Lie—An Untruth.

A *lie* is positively—an *untruth* is negatively false. The former is intentional, the latter involuntary. He who says what he knows to be untrue, with an intention to deceive, tells a lie. He who says what is untrue, but who is not aware of its falseness, utters an untruth. The word *untruth* is not unfrequently used as a softened expression for a lie, but this is not a correct use of the word. These two words might also be distinguished by their active and passive meanings—for a lie is the active, and an untruth the passive false.

[*Pro.* ——— like one
Who having, unto truth, by telling of it
Made such a sinner of his memory
To credit his own lie —— *Tempest*, I. 2.

Kath. ——— In the presence
He would say untruths ; and be ever double
Both in his words and meaning —— *Henry VIII.*, IV. 2

His countenance, as the morning-star, that guides
The starry flock, allured them ; and with lies
Drew after him the third part of heaven's host
P. L., v. 709.]

Exercise.

"Above all things, tell no ———, no, not even in trifles."

"The nature of a ——— consists in this, that it is a false signification knowingly and voluntarily used."

"There is little hope for common justice in this dispute, from a man who lays the foundations of his reasonings in so notorious an ———."

"When I hear my neighbour speak that which is not true, and I say to him: 'This is not true,' or 'This is false,' I only convey to him the naked idea of his error ; this is the primary idea: but if I say, 'It is a ———,' the word ——— carries also a secondary idea ; for it implies both the falsehood of the speech, and my reproach and censure of the speaker."

"I can hardly consider this observation as an ———, much less can I condemn the person who made it as a ———."

"Thy better soul abhors a ——— part,
Wise is thy voice, and noble is thy heart."

"In matter of speculation or practice, no ——— can possibly avail the patron and defender long."

"That a vessel filled with ashes will receive the like quantity of water that it would have done if it had been empty is utterly ———, for the water will not go in by a fifth part."

"Truth is the object of our understanding, as good is of our will ; and the understanding can no more be delighted with a ———, than the will can choose an apparent evil."

To permit—to allow

To *allow* consents tacitly; to *permit* consents formally. The former has a negative meaning; it is merely not to forbid; the latter is positive; it signifies to grant leave. We are allowed to do what no one interferes with us for doing; we are permitted to do what we obtain leave to do. An action for which it is not necessary to ask permission is allowed; to permit implies the granting of a request. School-boys are allowed a certain space for their sports or exercise; but if they wish to go beyond the limits of that space, they must ask leave in order to be permitted to do so.

[*P. Hen.* Yet herein will I imitate the sun;
Who doth permit the base contagious clouds
To smother up his beauty from the world. 1 *Henry IV.*, i. 2.

Nor. ——— Anger is like
A full-hot horse; who being allowed his way
Self-mettle tires him. —— *Henry VIII.*, i. 1.

Lear. ——— O heavens,
If you do love old men, if your sweet sway
Allow obedience, if yourselves are old,
Make it your cause. —— *King Lear*, iv. 4

——— Therefore, since he permits
Within himself unworthy powers to reign
Over free reason, God, in judgment just,
Subjects him from without to violent lords. *P. L.*, xii. 90

——— who, while they feel
Vigour divine within them, can allow
Omnipotence to none —— *Id.*, vi. 158.

——— But Heaven's high will
Permits a second and a darker shade
Of Pagan night. —— WORDSWORTH. '*Ecclesias. Sonnets.*

——— Faint the beam
Of human life when first allowed to gleam
On mortal notice. ——— '*Tour of* 1833.'

——— the chancel only showed
Some vain distinctions, marks of earthly state
By immemorial privilege allowed;
Though with the Encincture's special sanctity
But ill according. —— '*The Excursion*,' v.]

Exercise

The boys had finished their studies, and were going to take a walk, but the youngest was not ——— to accompany the others, as he had not been so diligent as usual that morning.

This was a great disappointment to him, and at his earnest request, and faithful promise to do better another time, the master ——— him to join his school-fellows.

It is shameful that we should ——— ourselves to remain in ignorance of what it is our bounden duty to know.

The sailors, having asked leave of the captain, were ——— to go ashore, on condition that they should return to the vessel before nine o'clock the same evening.

As some friends were expected that night whom they very much wished to see, they were ——— to sit up later than usual, and did not retire to bed till nearly ten o'clock.

Soldiers cannot absent themselves from their duty without being specially ———.

"I have obtained his ——— to make these conversations public."

"Plutarch says, very finely, that a man should not ——— himself to hate even his enemies."

"Any of my readers who have studied the biography of men of letters will ——— my assertion is borne out by facts."

To assuage—to mitigate.

To assuage and to mitigate both denote a diminishing of pain. To mitigate is a negative, to assuage is a positive term. He who mitigates, relaxes in harshness; he who assuages, actively lessens the pain of others. We mitigate by being less severe; we assuage by being positively kind. Time mitigates, friends assuage our afflictions. A penalty to be inflicted—rigour to be employed—a sentence to be passed—may be mitigated; grief, fears, affliction, &c., may be assuaged.

[*Men.* The good Gods assuage thy wrath. ——
Coriolanus, v. 2.

Por. To mitigate the justice of thy plea
Merch. of Ven., iv. 1

Nor wanting power to mitigate and 'suage
With solemn touches troubled thoughts ——
P. L., i. 556.

Dire inflammation, which no cooling herb
Or med'cinal herb can assuage
Nor breath of vernal air from snowy Alp.
S. A., 627.

Till she, in jealous fury unassuaged
Had slain his paramour with ruthless sword
WORDSWORTH. '*Artegal and Elidure.*'

——— Man—whose soul
Christ died for—cannot forfeit his high claim
To live and move exempt from all controul
Which fellow-feeling doth not mitigate.
'Ecclesias. Sonnets.'

For the tired slave, Song lifts the languid oar
And bids it aptly fall, with chime
That beautifies the fairest shore
And mitigates the harshest clime. *'On the Power of Sound.'*]

Exercise.

"If I can in any way ——— private inflammations, or allay public ferments, I shall apply myself to it with the utmost endeavours."

"All we can do now is to devise how that which must be endured may be ———, and its inconveniences countervailed as near as may be, that when the best things are not possible, the best may be made of those that are."

"This was necessary for the securing the people from the fears capable of being ——— by no other means."

"The king would not have one penny abated of that granted to him by Parliament, because it might encourage other countries to pray the like release or ———ion."

The prisoner having been found guilty upon this evidence, acknowledged the justice of the verdict, but prayed that the circumstances of the case would induce the judge to ——— his sentence.

The remedies which were applied immediately ——— the pain of the wound, so that by the next day he could use the limb, and in a short time was able to walk about without assistance.

"We could greatly wish that the rigour of their opinion were ———."

"Yet is his hate, his rancour ne'er the less,
Since nought ——— malice when 'tis told."

To shun—to avoid.

To avoid has a negative, to shun, a positive meaning. To *avoid* is merely not to approach; to *shun* is to turn from. We avoid what may do us harm; we shun what we dislike, or what we think is likely to do us harm. We avoid bad habits—that is, we take care not to acquire them; we should shun vice—that is, we should turn away from it. Prudence induces us to avoid; fear or dislike prompts us to shun. A transitive verb can never be used after to shun. We avoid doing; we shun what is already done.

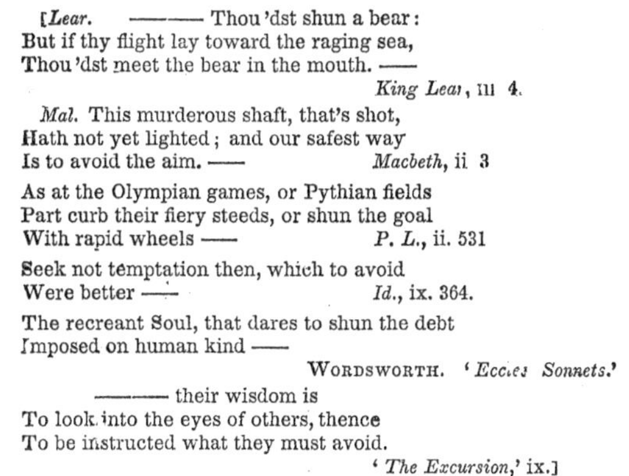

[*Lear.* ——— Thou 'dst shun a bear:
But if thy flight lay toward the raging sea,
Thou 'dst meet the bear in the mouth. ——
King Lear, iii 4.

Mal. This murderous shaft, that's shot,
Hath not yet lighted; and our safest way
Is to avoid the aim. —— *Macbeth*, ii 3

As at the Olympian games, or Pythian fields
Part curb their fiery steeds, or shun the goal
With rapid wheels —— *P. L.*, ii. 531

Seek not temptation then, which to avoid
Were better —— *Id.*, ix. 364.

The recreant Soul, that dares to shun the debt
Imposed on human kind ——
WORDSWORTH. '*Eccles Sonnets*.'

——— their wisdom is
To look into the eyes of others, thence
To be instructed what they must avoid.
'*The Excursion*,' ix.]

Exercise.

"Having thoroughly considered the nature of this passion, I have made it my duty to study how to ——— the envy that may accrue to me from these my speculations."

"Of many things, some few I shall explain,
Teach thee to ——— the dangers of the main,
And how at length the promised shore to gain."

"Let no man make himself a confidant of the foibles of a beloved companion, lest he find himself ——— by the friend of his heart."

"Prudence will enable us to ——— many of the evils to which we are daily exposed."

Here he fell into vicious habits, and associated with such low companions that his society was soon ——— by every respectable person.

I thought I perceived him at some distance from me, but, as if he dreaded an interview, on my approaching him, he ——— me, and mixed among the crowd.

It is wise and prudent to do what is commanded, and ——— what is forbidden, by those whose authority we acknowledge.

To prevent—to hinder.

We are *hindered* from proceeding by something which draws us back. We are *prevented* from advancing by something which comes in our way. A visiter who occupies much of our time hinders us from pursuing our usual occupations. A shower of rain will prevent us from taking a walk.

He who is hindered does not wholly cease from action; but he who is prevented cannot advance a step. The inspection of passports frequently hinders travellers on the continent from proceeding as quickly as they wish. He who would attempt to travel on the continent without a passport, would be prevented by the custom-house officers.

[*Car.* —— wise men ne'er wail their present woes
But presently prevent the ways to wail.
Richard II., iii. 2.

K. Hen. This dangerous treason, lurking in our way
To hinder our beginnings —— *Henry V.* ii. 2.

Perhaps forestalling night prevented them.
Comus, 285.

——— what hinders then
To reach, and feed at once both body and mind?
P. L., ix. 778.

See how her Ivy clasps the sacred Ruin
Fall to prevent, or beautify decay.
WORDSWORTH '*Miscel. Sonnets*

But O restrain compassion, if its course,
As oft befals, prevent or turn aside
Judgments and aims and acts whose higher source
Is sympathy with the unforewarned, who died
Blameless—with them that shuddered o'er his grave,
And all who from the law firm safety crave.
'*On Punishment of Death*'

——— and airy hopes
Dancing around her, hinder and disturb
Those meditations of the soul that feed
The retrospective virtues. —— '*The Excursion*,' vii.]

Exercise.

I should have begun my letter yesterday, but I was ——— by my brothers, who insisted on my accompanying them in their afternoon walk.

I sat down this morning with the full determination to write to you, but I have been ——— by so many circumstances, that I am afraid I shall never finish this letter.

They now attempted to force their way through the entrance, but were ——— by those within, who made a desperate sally from the gate, and successfully repulsed the assailants.

I was ——— from calling on you yesterday by several visiters who came in when I was on the point of setting off.

The delicate state of his health has ——— his education considerably, and ——— his making that advancement which, in ordinary cases, would be expected.

Had not the workmen been ———, they would have finished the building last week.

It is much easier to keep ourselves void of resentment than to restrain it from excess when it has gained admission. To use the illustration of an excellent author, we can ——— the beginnings of some things whose progress afterwards we cannot ———

Barbarous—Inhuman.

Barbarous and inhuman are both higher degrees of *cruel;* but barbarity expresses a positive love of cruelty, whilst inhumanity denotes the cruelty resulting from a want of the natural feelings of kindness and tenderness which are common to human beings. A barbarous man takes pleasure in inflicting pain; an inhuman man is heedless of the pain he gives others. Barbarity delights in cruelty. Many of the Roman emperors committed the most atrocious barbarities. Inhumanity has no feeling for the miseries of others. The slave-trade is an inhuman traffic.

[*Lear.* ——— The barbarous Scythian
Or he that makes his generation messes
King Lear, i. 1.

Duke. A stony adversary, an inhuman wretch
Uncapable of pity, void and empty
From any dram of mercy *Merch. of Ven.*, iv. 1.

A multitude, like which the populous north
Poured never from her frozen loins, to pass
Rhene or the Danau, when her barbarous sons
Came like a deluge on the south, and spread
Beneath Gibraltar to the Libyan sands.
P. L., i. 353.

—— all the miseries of life
Life in captivity
Among inhuman foes. *S. A.*, 109.

——— By Augustin led,
They come—and onward travel without dread,
Chanting in barbarous ears a tuneful prayer—
Sung for themselves, and those whom they would free!
WORDSWORTH. '*Eccles. Sonnets.*']

Exercise.

"By their ——— usage, he died in a few days, to the grief of all that knew him."

"A just war may be prosecuted in a very unjust manner; by perfidious breaches of our word, by ——— cruelties, and by assassinations."

"Each social feeling fell,
And joyless ——— pervades
And petrifies the heart."

"The unfortunate young prince was ———ly assassinated in his mother's arms."

"Among the ———s he exercised during his progress, none was more horrible than the massacre of the Alexandrians; he led the people out of their city, surrounded them with his soldiers, and ordered them all to be cut down."

"The more these praises were enlarged, the more ——— was the punishment, and the sufferer more innocent."

"Relentless love the cruel mother led
The blood of her unhappy babes to shed;
Love lent the sword, the mother struck the blow,
——— she, but more ——— thou."

"Whether it was that her son had instigated it, or that she had herself given some offence, or from the mere wantonness of ———ty, Henry now gave orders for the execution of the Countess of Salisbury."

Defective—Faulty.

That is *defective* which is wanting in some respect. That is *faulty* which has what it ought *not* to have. What is defective requires something to be supplied; what is faulty requires something to be corrected. A book which wants a leaf is defective; a book containing a leaf which belongs to another book is faulty. The same distinction is to be made between the nouns *defect* and *fault*. The former implies the absence of something right; the latter, the presence of something wrong.

[*Bur.* And as our vineyards, fallows, meads and hedges,
Defective in their natures, grow to wildness;
Even so our houses, and ourselves, and children,
Have lost, or do not learn, for want of time,
The sciences that should become our country.
Henry V., v. 2.

Crom. ——— men so noble,
However faulty, yet should find respect
For what they have been: 'tis a cruelty
To load a falling man. *Henry VIII.*, v. 2.

Like of his like, his image multiplied
In unity defective — *P. L.*, viii. 425.

The image of God in man, created once
So goodly and erect, though faulty since
Id., xi. 509.]

Exercise.

The system was found to be ——— in many points: the arrangement was so confused, that it not unfrequently puzzled rather than enlightened the inquirer; and, on several questions connected with the subject, it gave no information whatever.

It was not until several games had been played, that the cards were found to be ——; a discovery made by two of the players throwing down the same card simultaneously; it was consequently agreed that all the money won during the preceding part of the evening should be restored to its original owners.

The book was very badly printed, and so ——, that there was scarcely a page in which several emendations were not required.

In order to render the work useful, it was found necessary to correct its ——, and supply its ——.

It is perhaps better that a work should be —— than ——, for —— will often happen in the haste of composition; whereas —— may generally be traced either to the author's ignorance or imperfect knowledge.

"The low race of men take a secret pleasure in finding an eminent character levelled to their condition by a report of its ——, and keep themselves in countenance, though they are excelled in a thousand virtues, if they believe that they have in common with a great person any one ——"

Excessive—Immoderate.

He who exceeds, goes beyond—he who is immoderate, does not keep within bounds. Consequently the distinction between excessive and immoderate is as positive and negative. They who do not restrain their appetites within the bounds prescribed by nature, eat immoderately; they who load the stomach to satiety, eat to excess. An immoderate indulgence in the pleasures of the table produces uneasiness; excessive indulgence in the same pleasures puts us in danger of a surfeit, or apoplexy. Immoderate is opposed to temperate; excessive to defective. Excessive is frequently used in a favorable sense; immoderate, always in a bad sense.

[*Laf.* Moderate lamentation is the right of the dead, excessive grief the enemy to the living. *All's Well, &c.*, i. 1.

Claud. As surfeit is the father of much fast,
So every scope by the immoderate use
Turns to restraint. —— *Meas. for Meas.*, i. 3.

But pain is perfect misery, the worst
Of evils, and excessive, overturns
All patience *P. L.*, vi. 463.]

Exercise.

Who knows not the languor that attends every ——— indulgence in pleasure?

"One of the first objects of wish to every one is to maintain a proper place and rank in society: this, among the vain and ambitious, is always the favourite aim. With them it arises to ——— expectations founded on their supposed talents and imagined merits."

"A man must be ———ly stupid as well as uncharitable, who believes there is no virtue but on his own side."

"One means very effectual for the preservation of health is a quiet and cheerful mind, not afflicted by passions, or distracted with ——— cares."

"If panicum be laid below and about the bottom of a root, it will cause the root to grow to an ——— bigness."

——— eating takes away sound sleep; ——— eating disorders the digestive functions.

"Moderation is a virtue of no small importance to those who find ——— in every thing to be an evil."

"It is wisely ordered in our present state that joy and fear, hope and grief, should act alternately as checks and balances upon each other, in order to prevent an ——— in any of them."

"His death was caused by an ——— use of opiates."

SECTION V.

MISCELLANEOUS SYNONYMES.

There are many cases in which it is extremely difficult to discover any principle by which the differences of words can be accounted for. Though, as we have already shewn, it is very possible to form, to a certain extent, a classification of differences, by referring them, in different cases, to a distinct principle; there are many pairs of words whose difference does not appear to depend on any uniformly directing principle, but seems the result of a mere caprice of language. These cases baffle all attempts at classifying, and we must, therefore, be content to consider them under the head of "Miscellaneous." Here it will be found that a different cause operates in each single pair, so that we shall here learn nothing more than the explanation of the difference in each individual case, and this explanation will suggest no certain rule in other cases of difficulty. But when we consider the subtile nature of the human mind, and the almost infinite variety of shades and forms which language assumes, we shall not be surprised at this difficulty. Some tinge of colouring, some almost imperceptible shade, will be found to exist in one, which does not belong to the other, and this so capricious, and so infinitely various, that it is impossible to classify such words, or collect those among them in which any one principle is found to act uniformly. The following synonymes are of this nature, for the study of which the learner is referred to the explanations under each pair.

Accent—Emphasis.

An *accent* is a stress or leaning of the voice on certain syllables in every word, by which those syllables are more vigorously pronounced than others. An *emphasis* is a stress of the voice on certain words, by which those words are prominently distinguished in a sentence. Accent respects the pronunciation of a word; emphasis respects the meaning of the sentence. To pronounce the word *náture* with the strain on the second syllable (thus, *natúre*) would be a fault of accent. To give the same force to every word in a sentence, is to read without emphasis.

[*Len.* —— prophecying, with accents terrible,
Of dire combustion, and confused events,
Macbeth, ii. 3.

Ham. What is he, whose grief
Bears such an emphasis? *Hamlet*, v. 1.

And with persuasive accent thus began.
P. L., ii. 118.

—— the sacred Book
In dusty sequestration wrapt too long
Assumes the accents of our native tongue.
WORDSWORTH. '*Eccles. Sonnets.*']

Exercise.

In the time of the Commonwealth, the —— of many words in the English language was unfixed. In the "Paradise Lost" of Milton, several words are found with an —— different from that with which they are now pronounced.

In every sentence, there are certain words which require a greater stress of the voice in reading than others. This stress is called in grammar ——— He who reads without ———, reads monotonously.

Foreigners are very liable to make faults of ——— in pronouncing our language.

Laying a strong ——— on these last words, and giving me another inquiring look of significance, the stranger quitted the room, leaving me in a state of confusion and conjecture, which may be more easily imagined than described.

It is very difficult, if not impossible, to pronounce a dissyllable without placing a stronger ——— on one than on the other of the two syllables.

"Those English syllables which I call long ones receive a peculiar stress of voice from their acute or circumflex ———, as in quíckly, dôwry."

"——— not so much regards the tune, as a certain grandeur, whereby some word or sentence is rendered more remarkable than the rest by a more vigorous pronunciation, and a longer stay upon it."

An address—A direction.

The difference between an address and a direction is, that an *address* comprises the name of the person directed to, as well as the place at which he or she resides. A *direction* signifies no more than the specification of a certain place. The form of an address might be, Mr. John Smith, 19, George-street, Cornwall-square. If I am told to address a letter to the above Mr. Smith, I write down this form; but if some one ask me Mr. Smith's direction, I answer by specifying the place in which he lives, viz. 19, George-street, Cornwall-square. An address comprises a name and direction; a direction excludes the name. We do not address places, though we direct to both places and persons.

Exercise.

I have only to put the ——— to this letter, and I will then accompany you.

I should have written to you before, but I had mislaid your ———, and did not find it till this morning.

Can you give me Mr. Robinson's ———?

The name was written on the outer cover of the parcel, but it had no ———.

This trunk being properly ———, it cannot fail to reach the person for whom it is intended.

Those who travel with much luggage should take the greatest care that all their packages are correctly and legibly ———.

Put the ——— on this letter for me

Arms—Weapons.

In strict propriety of language, *arms* are instruments of offence, and *weapons* instruments of defence. According to this distinction, swords, spears, cross-bows, &c., are arms; whilst helmets, cuirasses, and shields are weapons. This distinction, however, does not always hold good, for the expression "murderous weapons," as well as "coat of arms," is common in modern phraseology. These are in direct opposition to the above explanation. The best distinction, then, to be made between these words is, that arms are instruments made expressly for fighting; and weapons are instruments casually used for fighting. According to this distinction, pokers, staves, or knives, will be equally weapons, but not equally arms with swords, pistols, and guns. The word weapons is used in the singular; arms, never, in this sense.

[*Glo.* Weapons! arms! What's the matter here?
King Lear, ii. 2

K. Rich. —— grating shock of wrathful iron arms
Rich. II., i. 3.

Bru. —— waving our red weapons o'er our heads
Let's all cry, Peace! Freedom! and Liberty!
Julius Cæsar, iii. 1

——— for life
To noble and ignoble is more sweet
Untrained in arms, where rashness leads not on.
P. L., xii. 222

Far other arms and weapons must
Be those, that quell the might of hellish charms.
Comus, 612.

This is the happy Warrior; this is He
That every Man in arms should wish to be.
WORDSWORTH. '*Character of the Happy Warrior.*'

While we go forth, a self-devoted crowd,
With weapons grasped in fearless hands, to assert
Our virtue, and to vindicate mankind.
'*Sonnets to Liberty.*']

Exercise.

The bayonet is a formidable ———; it was so called from having been first made at Bayonne.

Fire ——— are an invention of the middle ages.

The garrison, after sustaining a ten months' siege, in which they endured all the horrors of disease and famine, capitulated on condition of being allowed to march out with their ———, and go wherever they pleased.

The ——— with which the deed was perpetrated was found, after a long search, in a field at some distance from the house.

The ——— used by the savages of the Pacific are chiefly stakes burnt at one end, and sharpened with fish-bones.

He defended himself against the fury of the populace with whatever ——— chance threw in his way.

"Here the pavement is upturned—here the torch is planted—here the ——— is prepared; everywhere you may see the women mingling with the men, now sharing their labours, now binding up their wounds."

"The native Greeks had that mark of a civilized people, that they never bore ——— during the time of peace, unless the wearer chanced to be numbered among those whose military profession and employment required them to be always in ———"

Beast—Brute.

A wild animal is a *brute;* a tamed animal is a *beast.* According to this distinction, lions, tigers, leopards, &c., are brutes; whilst horses, oxen, sheep, &c., are beasts. The prominent idea in the word brute is the presence of ferocity and unrestrained passion; the leading idea in the word beast is absence of reason. Taylor remarks: "We say beasts of burden; never brutes of burden." A tamed brute becomes a beast. The brutes of the forest; the beasts of the field. Applied as terms of reproach, a man is called a brute when he abuses his strength; he is called a beast when he abuses his reason by sensual indulgence.

[*Ant.* O judgment thou art fled to brutish beasts,
And men have lost their reason. ——
Jul. Cæs., iii. 2

Ham. —— a beast that wants discourse of reason
Would have mourned longer —— *Hamlet*, i. 2.

The visage quite transforms of him that drinks
And the inglorious likeness of a beast
Fixes instead, unmoulding reason's mintage
Comus, 528

With lickerish baits, fit to ensnare a brute
Id., 700.

——— beast and bird, the lamb
The shepherd's dog, the linnet and the thrush
Vied with this waterfall ——
WORDSWORTH. '*On Naming of Places*'

See the first mighty Hunter leave the brute—
To chase mankind, with men in armies packed
For his field pastime high and absolute
'*Poems to Liberty*.']

Exercise.

"There is no opposing ——— force to the stratagems of human reason."

"The royal ———, with his usual generosity, immediately set the little trembling captive at liberty."

"Medea's charms were there, Circean feasts.
With bowls that turn enamoured youths to ——— "

"As nature has framed the several species of beings as it were in a chain, so man seems to be placed as the middle link between angels and ———."

"Returning home last night, I was met by my old mastiff, Carlo, who came bounding towards me, and barking with joy at seeing me again. Suddenly, I observed that he ceased barking, and limped in walking. I called him to me, and upon examination discovered that the poor ——— had cut one of his fore-paws very severely."

"The ——— philosopher who ne'er has proved
The joy of loving or of being loved."

"Even ——— animals make use of this artificial way of making divers motions, to have several significations, to call, warn, chide, cherish, threaten."

A consequence—A result.

A *consequence* is that which, of necessity, follows an action, or a course of life; a *result* is produced by combination. Ruin is the consequence of extravagance; four is the result of the addition of two and two. The primary meaning of the word *consequence* may be illustrated by the swell which always follows in the wake of a steam-vessel; it is that which cannot but follow. In the same way, a *result* is the rebounding of a ball, or any thing elastic, which is struck against a wall. In this case, the *result* will not always be the same; it will depend on the elasticity of the ball, the hardness of the wall, and the force of the throw. Many circumstances then, enter into the calculation of a result which is not the case with a consequence. There may be many steps in a calculation before we arrive at a result: consequences are invariable and more immediate; they arise out of the very nature of things.

[*Bass.* —— here choose I; Joy be the consequence!
Merch. of Ven., iii 2

Remember what I warn thee, shun to taste
And shun the bitter consequence ——
P. L., viii. 328

Then of their session ended they bid cry
With trumpets' regal sound the great result
Id., 515.

—— Festive songs
Break from the maddened nations at the sight
Of sudden overthrow; and cold neglect
Is the sure consequence of slow decay.
'*The Excursion*,' vii.]

Exercise.

A premature decay of all the vital functions is the natural —— of a vicious life.

According to the account received yesterday, fortune then appeared inclined to favor the opposite party; but whatever may be the ——, it will be generally known to-morrow.

His health suffered severely in —— of excessive study during his youth, and, at a period of life when most men enjoy the greatest physical and mental vigour, he had lost all his energy and elasticity of mind.

When you have well discussed the matter, and come to some conclusion as to your intention, you will let me know the ——.

" Shun the bitter ——, for know.
The day thou eatest thereof, thou shalt die."

" The state of the world is continually changing, and none can tell the —— of the next vicissitude."

" Jealousy often draws after it a fatal train of ——."

A contest—A conflict.

A *contest* is a strife which arises between two or more persons for some common object, a *conflict* is the violent meeting of two parties incensed against each other. A contest may be, and often has been, decided by a conflict. In the history of the wars of the "Roses," the contending parties were the Houses of York and Lancaster, and in the course of the contest for the crown, a series of conflicts took place. Contests do not of necessity imply violence, but conflicts are always desperate and sanguinary. A man perishes in a conflict, and is defeated in a contest.

[*Edm.* I will persevere in my course of loyalty though the conflict be sore between that and my blood. *King Lear*, iii. 5.

Thus they in mutual accusation spent
The fruitless hours, but neither self-condemning
And of their vain contest appeared no end.
P. L., ix. 1189.

——— dire was the noise
Of conflict, —— *Id.*, vi. 212.

When he had crushed a plentiful estate
By ruinous contest, to obtain a seat
In Britain's senate. —— '*The Excursion*,' vi.

——— that Soul,
Which with the motion of a virtuous act
Flashes a look of terror upon guilt,
Is, after conflict, quiet as the ocean,
By a miraculous finger stilled at once,
'*The Borderers*.']

Exercise.

"Soon after, the death of the king furnished a general subject for poetical ———."

"Bare, unhoused trunks,
To the ———ing elements exposed."

"A definition is the only way whereby the meaning of words can be known, without leaving room for ——— about it."

"Happy is the man who, in the ——— of desire between God and the world, can oppose not only argument to argument, but pleasure to pleasure."

"Leave all noisy ———, all immodest clamours, and brawling language."

"Lashed into foam, the fierce ———ing brine
Seems o'er a thousand raging waves to burn."

"If he attempt this great change, with what labour and ——— must he accomplish it?"

The third candidate, finding there was no chance of success, withdrew from the ———.

"No assurance touching victories can make present ——— so sweet and easy, but nature will shrink from them."

Discretion—Prudence.

Prudence is the quality which enables us to foresee probabilities, and to act accordingly. Discretion has to do with tangible realities—with things that are before us. The prudent man prepares for what is coming; the discreet man judges of present affairs. We are determined by our prudence to follow one course to the exclusion of all others; we are determined by our discretion to do one of two things. It is prudent to provide against bad weather; it is discreet not to allude to an offensive subject.

[*Ham.* Be not too tame neither, but let your own discretion be your tutor
Hamlet, iii. 2.

Kath. A prince most prudent, of an excellent
And unmatched wit and judgment. ——
Henry VIII., ii. 4.

——— that what she wills to do or say
Seems wisest, virtuousest, discreetest, best.
P. L., viii. 550.

—— what the lofty grave tragedians taught
In chorus or iambick, teachers best
Of moral prudence —— *P. R.*, iv. 263.]

Exercise.

Nature has been likened to a ——— mother, who not only supplies her children's present wants, but provides against their future necessities.

It is a strong proof of in——— to speak of family affairs before all persons indiscriminately.

Horace calls the ant a ——— animal, who, not regardless of the future, employs herself in the summer in laying up a store of food against the severity of the winter season.

No ——— person will ever allude to subjects which he knows to be disagreeable to those with whom he converses.

——— is more required in the management of present affairs, ——— in that of future: by the former, we determine promptly what to do or what not to do in the exigency of the moment; by the latter, we predetermine what shall be most expedient for the future. Both qualities are not only desirable, but actually indispensable in the regulation of the common affairs of human life.

"Let your own
——— be your tutor. Suit the action
To the word."

"The ignorance in which we are left concerning good and evil is not such as to supersede ——— in conduct."

Endurance—Duration.

These words are not strictly synonymous; but as they are frequently mistaken for one another, it may be useful to shew in what they differ. Endurance is the power of bearing up against insults or misfortunes; duration signifies merely a continuance of time. The idea of time enters into the meaning of both words, for endurance is the power of bearing with for a length of time. Without duration, we should have no opportunity of enduring.

[*Bene.* —— she misused me past the endurance of a block. ——
Much Ado, &c., ii. 1

——— work ease out of pain
Through labour and endurance. —— *P. L.*, ii. 263.

Her mind she strictly tutored to find peace
And pleasure in endurance. —— '*The Excursion*,' vi.]

Exercise.

"It has been my lot to ——— frequent visitations of ill-health, although my muscular frame is strong, and I am capable of bearing great privation and almost any exertion of mere bodily fatigue."

"Aristotle, by greatness of action, does not only mean it should be great in its nature, but also in its ———, that it should have a due length in it."

"Their fortitude was most admirable in their patience and ——— of all evils, of pain and of death."

"——— is a circumstance so essential to happiness, that if we conceived it possible for the joys of heaven itself to pass from us in an instant, we should find ourselves not much concerned for the attainment of them."

"How miserable his state who is condemned to ——— at once the pangs of guilt and the vexations of calamity!"

"I think another probable conjecture (respecting the soul's immortality) may be raised from our appetite to ——— itself."

"I would fain know whether that man takes a rational course to preserve himself, who refuses the ——— of these higher troubles, to secure himself from a condition infinitely more miserable?"

An era—An epoch

The words era and epoch are both employed to mark specified times of events. An *era* expresses the duration of time for which events are computed chronologically; an *epoch* is a point of time, distinguished by some remarkable circumstance, from which events are reckoned. The era of Rome lasted from 753 B. C. to the birth of Christ; the Christian era, from the birth of Christ to the present time. The nativity of Christ is the epoch from which modern European chronology is computed. The Hegira, or flight of Mahomet, A. D. 622, is the epoch from which the Arabians date.

Exercise.

Seneca, the Roman philosopher, was born at the beginning of the Christian ——.

The foundation of their city was the —— from which the Romans dated the events of their history.

The Christian —— commenced in the seven hundred and fifty-third year of the building of Rome.

The —— of the Julian ——, which precedes the common or Christian —— by forty-five years, is the reformation of the Roman calendar by Julius Cæsar.

In the tenth century, many sovereigns dated their instruments from the different —— of their reign.

"The commencement of the reign of William the Conqueror is usually dated from the day of the battle of Hastings, viz. Saturday, the 14th of October, 1066; but, according to Vilaine, it was dated from two ——; the one, the death of Edward the Confessor, which occurred on the 5th of January, 1066; and the other, William's coronation, which took place at Westminster, on Christmas-day in that year."

"Their several —— or beginnings, as from the Creation of the world, from the Flood, from the first Olympiad, from the building of Rome, or from any remarkable passage or accident, give us a pleasant prospect into the histories of antiquity, and of former ages."

A fault—a mistake.

A *fault* is an error of judgment; a *mistake* is an error of perception. When we determine wrongly, we commit a fault; when we perceive wrongly, we make a mistake. A mistake is less grave than a fault. Children are apt to make mistakes; men often commit faults. A child that would copy a *p* for a *q* would make a mistake; *i. e.* he would take one for the other. To allow children to do as they please is a great fault. The writer was once asked whether the Greeks were called Hellénes because they were descended from Helen, the wife of Menelaus: that was a mistake, the questioner mistook Helen for Hellen.

[*King.* ——— But 'tis not so above:
There is no shuffling, there the action lies
In his true nature; and we ourselves compelled
Even to the teeth and forehead of our faults
To give in evidence. —— *Hamlet*, iii. 3

Ariel. Remember, I have done thee worthy service;
Told thee no lies, made no mistakings ——
Tempest, i. 2.

Millions of spirits for his fault amerced
Of heaven, and from eternal splendours flung
For his revolt. —— *P. L.*, ii. 609

He never shall find out fit mate, but such
As some misfortune brings him, or mistake
Id., ix. 900.

For as, by discipline of Time made wise,
We learn to tolerate the infirmities
And faults of others—gently as he may,
So with our own the mild Instructor deals
Teaching us to forget them or forgive.
WORDSWORTH. '*Eccles. Sonnets.*]

Exercise.

It is a great ——— to suppose that children, because they are young and inexperienced, should not be treated as reasonable beings.

There can be little doubt that many of the ——— which are so prevalent in early youth might be much modified, if not altogether prevented, by a judicious education.

The young, though gifted with great abilities, are more liable than their elders to make ——— in the conduct of life, from want of experience.

Instead of prying into the ——— of others, we should take care to be free from them ourselves.

The ——— of the work are so glaring, that it is impossible for the most inattentive reader not to be struck with them.

When my uncle first saw his friend after so long an absence, he was so altered that he did not recognize him, and took him for some casual frequenter of the same hotel; but on discovering his ———, he immediately apologized for his apparent rudeness.

"To be desirous of a good name, and careful to do every thing that we innocently may to obtain it, is so far from being a ———, even in private persons, that it is their great and indispensable duty."

"It happened that the king himself passed through the gallery during this debate, and smiling at the ——— of the dervise, asked him how he could possibly be so dull as not to distinguish a palace from a caravansary."

An idea—a notion

An idea is an impression made on the mind by something external; a notion is whatever we know about a thing.

These words have been much confounded, and in common language are very frequently used the one for the other. If I mention the word *horse* to one who has seen that animal, the word recalls to his mind the idea of the animal; but, if I make any affirmation about the horse—as, the *horse is swift*—I express a notion, or what I know about the horse.

[*Friar.* The idea of her life shall sweetly creep
Into his study of imagination. *Much Ado, &c.*, iv. 1

Macb. ——— that might,
To half a soul, and a notion crazed,
Say, thus did Banquo. *Macbeth*, iii. 1.

Thence to behold this new-created world,
The addition of his empire, how it showed
In prospect from his throne, how good, how fair
Answering his great idea.—— *P L.*, vii 557.

——— unless we ourselves
Seek them with wandering thoughts, and notions vain
Id., viii. 187.

Unhallowed actions—planted like a crown
Upon the insolent aspiring brow
Of spurious notions—worn as open signs
Of prejudice subdued —— '*The Excursion*,' ii.]

Exercise.

It was not long before we found him of no assistance whatever; he had not a single ——— upon the subject, and consequently, he made so many blunders, that he rather retarded than forwarded the work we were engaged upon.

His work, though it displayed no inconsiderable talent, was so full of strange ——— and odd fancies, that few gave themselves the trouble to read it, and it soon was neglected to a degree which it really did not quite deserve.

Those who are deprived of the sense of hearing or sight, can have but very imperfect ——— of sound or colour.

He was full of the most extravagant ——— of the construction of the world, and the planetary system, and would indulge in the wildest theories upon all sorts of speculative questions.

Those who compose for the first time, generally find themselves at a loss in two ways: firstly they want ———, and secondly, when they have them, they do not know how to arrange them.

A method—a mode.

The *method* is the theory upon which the *mode* is built. Method regards the contrivance; mode, the practice. Bell and Lancaster invented methods of teaching. The method is the arrangement of the plan, which is worked out by the modes of practice which it pursues. The method is in the mind; the mode, in the hand. Methods are ingenious or erroneous. Modes are skilful or clumsy. The Chinese method of building differs greatly from that of the English. Running, jumping, leaping, &c., are various modes of action by which a method of gymnastics is worked out.

[*Pol.* Though this be madness, yet there's method in it.
Hamlet, ii. 2.

K. Hen. For all my reign hath been but as a scene
Acting that argument; and now my death
Changes the mode —— 2 *Henry IV.*, iv. 4

Another method I must now begin *P. R.*, iv. 540.

God's altar to disparage, and displace
For one of Syrian mode —— *P. L.*, i. 474.

——— Powers there are
That touch each other to the quick, in modes
Which the gross world no sense hath to perceive
No soul to dream of. —— WORDSWORTH. '*Tour in Scotland.*']

Exercise.

The whole ——— differs from the old one in being much more simple, effecting a great deal more in a shorter time, and in making it much less likely for the machine to get out of order.

A duty being once resolved upon, there will be little difficulty in determining the ——— of performing it.

"Although a faculty be born with us, there are several ——— for cultivating and improving it, and without which it will be very uncertain."

The ——— of teaching used in schools are at the present day far superior to those in general practice fifty years ago.

There are certain ——— of expression which vary with the times, the fashion of our clothes being not more subject to alteration than that of speech.

To understand the nature of a disease, and the proper ——— of curing it, belongs to a skill, the study of which is full of toil, and the practice beset with difficulties.

"———s of speech, which owe their prevalence to modish folly, die away with their inventors."

"Men are willing to try all ———s of reconciling guilt and quiet."

An observance—an observation.

These words are both derived from the Latin *observare*, to keep, and are used as follows:—An *observance*, is the keeping of a rule or law by the performance of the outward ceremonies which it enjoins. An *observation* is the keeping of a fact in the mind, for the convenience of adverting to it at some future time. The intention of an observance is the fulfilment of a religious or moral duty; the intention of an observation is to increase our own information, or that of others. We speak of astronomical observations, and of the observance of the laws.

[*Ham.* ——— it is a custom
More honoured in the breach than the observance.
Hamlet, i. 4.

[*Ham.* All saws of books, all forms, all pressures past
That youth and observation copied there
Id., i. 5.

And from affectionate observance gain
Help, under every change of adverse fate.
WORDSWORTH. '*Dion.*'

The imaginative faculty was lord
Of observations natural. '*The Excursion*,' i.]

Exercise.

Without a strict ——— of the principles of morality, no man can be considered a good citizen, or a useful member of society.

His ——— are full of good sense, and he has treated the whole subject with the greatest perspicuity.

There is no country in Europe where the ——— of the Sabbath is so strictly attended to as in England.

A habit of ———, and the power of concentrating our attention strongly on whatever may be the object of our inquiry, are necessary qualifications for the acquirement of solid information.

During the middle ages, the numerous and various religious ceremonies enjoined to the faithful, together with the strict ——— of fasts and holidays, interfered considerably with the industry of the people, and were a strong bar to the advancement of this country in commercial enterprise.

Many learn more from ——— than from rules.

"Some represent to themselves the whole of religion as consisting in a few easy ———, and never lay the least restraint on the business or diversions of this life."

"The rules of our practice are taken from the conduct of such persons as fall within our ———."

Pride—Vanity.

The *proud* man is self-satisfied—wrapped up in his own estimation—careless of the opinions of others. The *vain* man has little or no merit, and is greedy of praise at the same time that he is conscious of not deserving it. Those who have more merit than others cannot help being conscious of it; but pride does not signify the consciousness of our own superiority; it is the feeling which, in over-rating our own merit, causes us to under-rate that of others. Pride is disagreeable and odious; vanity is ridiculous and contemptible.

The qualities *honest* and *honorable*, when applied to pride, deprive it of its odium, and make it a feeling which no one needs be ashamed to own. He who has raised himself in society by his own unaided exertions will naturally feel an honest and proper pride in his success.

[*Chor.* Being free from vainness and self-glorious pride.
Henry V., v. *Chorus.*

Wol. ——— my high-blown pride
At length broke under me —— *Henry VIII.*, iii. 2.

Dan. As matching to his youth and vanity,
I did present him with those Paris balls.
Henry V., ii. 4

——— had not thy pride
And wandering vanity, when least was safe
Rejected my forewarning —— *P. L.*, x. 874

Till pride and worse ambition threw me down
Id., iv. 40.

If thou be one whose heart the holy forms
Of young imagination have kept pure,
Stranger! henceforth be warned; and know that pride,
Howe'er disguised in its own majesty
Is littleness. —— WORDSWORTH. '*Poems of Youth*'

One lesson, Shepherd, let us two divide,
Taught both by what she shows, and what conceals;
Never to blend our pleasure or our pride
With sorrow of the meanest thing that feels.
'*Hart-Leap Well.*'

——— he was sincere
As vanity and fondness for applause,
And new and shapeless wishes, would allow.
'*The Excursion*,' ii.]

Exercise.

He was a man of low intellect, and had very little general information; and so absurdly ———, that he was the laughing-stock of the whole village.

Nothing can be more intolerable than the ——— of this new-comer; he visits no one, goes nowhere, and keeps himself in every respect aloof from all the visiters of the place.

There is no feeling more satisfactory than that ——— which we experi-

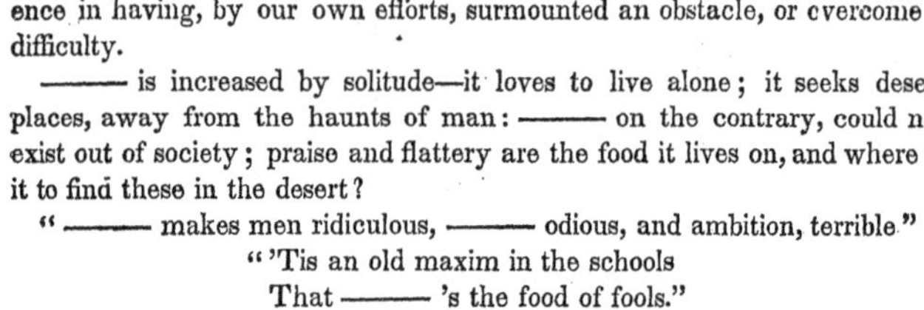

ence in having, by our own efforts, surmounted an obstacle, or overcome a difficulty.

——— is increased by solitude—it loves to live alone; it seeks desert places, away from the haunts of man: ——— on the contrary, could not exist out of society; praise and flattery are the food it lives on, and where is it to find these in the desert?

"——— makes men ridiculous, ——— odious, and ambition, terrible."

"'Tis an old maxim in the schools
That ——— 's the food of fools."

Subsidy—Tribute.

Both these words signify a sum agreed to be paid by one nation to another; but they differ in the following circumstances. A subsidy is voluntary; a tribute is exacted. A subsidy is paid to meet an exigency; a tribute is paid in acknowledgment of subjection. A subsidy is paid to an ally; a tribute is paid to a conqueror.

[*K. Hen.* Nor much oppressed them with great subsidies
3 *Henry VI.*, iv. 8.

Clo. Why tribute? why should we pay tribute? If Cæsar can hide the sun from us with a blanket, or put the moon in his pocket, we will pay him tribute for light; else, sir, no more tribute. *Cymbeline*, iii. 1.

Then meeting, joined their tribute to the sea
P. R., iii. 258.

——— bringing each in turn
The tribute of enjoyment, knowledge, health
Beauty or strength. — '*The Excursion*,' ix.]

Exercise.

"They advised the king to send speedy aids, and with much alacrity granted a great rate of ———."

"They that received ——— money, said: Doth not your master pay ———?"

"The ——— paid by foreign nations was by far the most important branch of the public revenue during the period of Rome's greatness."

"It is a celebrated notion of a patriot, that a House of Commons should never grant such ——— as give no pain to the people, lest the nation should acquiesce under a burden they did not feel."

"The Irish lords did only promise to become ———aries to King Henry the Second; and such as only pay ——— are not properly subjects, but sovereigns."

A quarrel ensued between the king and the Commons. They drew up a petition praying him to send some ———ary troops to defend the Palatinate, to declare war against Spain, and to marry his son to a Protestant princess.

Cæsar landing the next spring, forced the passage of the Thames above Kingston, took Verulamium, received the submission and hostages of several states, and having imposed ———, quitted Britain for ever.

"To acknowledge this was all he did exact,
Small ———, where the will to pay was act."

To abbreviate—to abridge.

To abbreviate and to abridge both signify to shorten: but to *abridge* is to shorten by condensing or compressing; whilst to *abbreviate* is to shorten by contracting or cutting off. In abridgments, we have as much substance, only in a smaller space. In abbreviations, the same meaning, but in fewer characters. Single words are abbreviated; whole works are abridged. Lieut., Dr., Esq., are abbreviations for lieutenant, doctor, esquire. Large histories are abridged for the use of young students. A work in three volumes has been frequently abridged into one.

[*Hol.* —— 'neigh' abbreviated 'ne.'
Love's Lab. Lost, v. 1

Bru. So are we Cæsar's friends that have abridged
His time of fearing death. *Jul. Cæs.*, iii. 1.]

Exercise.

The paper was so full of contractions and ———, that it was with the greatest difficulty I could decipher its contents.

——— are necessary for those who either do not wish, or have not the power to study subjects in detail.

The work was in itself so concise, and every remark it contained was so necessary to the proper understanding of the subject, that it was found impossible to ——— it.

"The only invention of late years which has contributed towards politeness in discourse, is that of ———, or reducing words of many syllables into one, by lopping off the rest."

If we trace the history of the spoken language of any particular country, we shall find ——— and harmony to have been the two leading principles which have influenced its various changes.

"It is one thing to ——— by contracting, another by cutting off."

"I shall lay before my readers an ——— of some few of their extravagancies, in hopes that they will in time accustom themselves to dream a little more to the purpose."

To advance—to proceed.

To *advance* regards the end, to *proceed* respects the beginning of our journey. We cannot advance without proceeding, nor proceed without advancing. In advancing, we approach nearer the end; in proceeding, we leave the beginning farther behind us. The army advanced three leagues into the enemy's country. They proceeded on their journey. We advance further. We proceed farther. (See farther and further.) In fine, to advance refers to the point we are striving to attain, whether in a primary or secondary sense, whilst to proceed refers to the point we start from. The difference then between "to advance in our studies" and "to proceed with our studies" will be obvious.

[*Siw.* Towards which advance the war.
Macbeth, v 4

Wol. —— how far I have proceeded,
Or how far further shall —— *Hen. VIII.*, ii. 4.

Now Morn, her rosy steps in the eastern clime
Advancing, sowed the earth with orient pearl
P. L., v. 2.

Man lives not by bread alone, but each word
Proceeding from the mouth of God ——
P. R., i. 350.

It was the season of unfolding leaves,
Of days advancing toward their utmost length,
And small birds singing happily to mates
Happy as they. —— '*The Excursion*,' vi.

So, from the body of one guilty deed,
A thousand guilty fears, and haunting thoughts proceed!
'*Tour on the Continent*.']

Exercise.

In order to insure our ——— in any particular study, we must ——— diligently and regularly.

We had not ——— far before we found ourselves in a defile, surrounded on all sides by the enemy's horse; in this predicament, the colonel ordered a chosen body of men to ——— and engage the enemy, while he ——— with another band to explore a path by which he might extricate his men from their dangerous position.

As soon as the confusion caused by this interruption had in some degree subsided, the lecturer ——— with his remarks upon the internal condition of the Roman empire, and the state of its literature during this period.

Upon reconnoitring his position, he found he had committed a great error in ——— so far into the country without securing a retreat: but it was now too late to remedy the evil; he therefore ——— to take every means of strengthening his position till reinforcements should come to his assistance.

"It is wonderful to observe by what a gradual progress the world of life ——— through a prodigious variety of species, before a creature is formed that is complete in all its senses"

"If the scale of being rises by such a regular progress so high as man, we may, by a parity of reasoning, suppose that it still ——— gradually through those beings which are of a superior nature to him."

To appear—to seem.

What *seems* is in the mind; what *appears* is external. Things appear as they present themselves to the eye; they seem as they are represented to the mind. Things appear good or bad, as far as we can judge by our senses. Things seem right or wrong as we determine by reflection. Perception and sensation have to do with appearing; reflection and comparison, with seeming. When things are not what they appear, our senses are deceived; when things are not what they seem, our judgment is at fault.

[*Edg.* The fishermen, that walk upon the beach
Appear like mice ——— *King Lear*, iv. 6

Ham. How weary, stale, flat, and unprofitable
Seem to me all the uses of this world!
Hamlet, i. 2.

——— so seemed
Far off the flying fiend. At last appear
Hell-bounds ——— *P. L.*, ii 643

And oft though wisdom wake, suspicion sleeps
At wisdom's gate, and to simplicity
Resigns her charge, while goodness thinks no ill
Where no ill seems.——— *Id.*, iii. 689.

——— to whom, in vision clear
The aspiring heads of future things appear,
Like mountain-tops whose mists have rolled away.
WORDSWORTH. '*Poems to Liberty.*'

No fountain from its rocky cave
E'er tripped with foot so free;
She seemed as happy as a wave
That dances on the sea. '*The Two April Mornings.*']

Exercise.

It ——— that he not only detained the property from the rightful owner, but even appropriated a large portion of it.

As far as I can judge of the question, it ——— impossible to explain it in any thing like a satisfactory manner.

Those who are not accustomed to judge of distances are very often deceived; for many objects which ——— far off, are in reality much nearer to us than we suppose.

I have been informed by persons who have made frequent ascents in a balloon, that, upon those occasions, the earth ——— like a small speck when the balloon has attained its greatest height, and the men and women upon it no bigger than mites in cheese.

In fine weather, at sea, we may often observe a long dark line upon the horizon, which rises up from the water, and ——— like land. This is said to be the effect of the heat, and sailors consider it a sure sign of length of fine weather.

In my dream, I ——— to have taken the shape and size of a bat, and to be flying through the dark air at a rapid pace.

" Lashed into foam, the fierce conflicting brine
——— o'er a thousand raging waves to burn."

" My noble master will ———
Such as he is, full of regard and honor."

To articulate—to pronounce.

To *articulate* is to utter distinctly every syllable of which a word is composed. To *pronounce* is to utter a word in that accent and tone which are assigned to it by custom. Articulation has to do with the distinctness of the syllable; pronunciation, with propriety of the vocalizing. A child who says *possble* for possible, articulates indistinctly; a child who says *passable* for possible, pronounces improperly. Careless readers and speakers articulate badly; foreigners and countrymen pronounce improperly.

[*Macb.* But wherefore could not I pronounce, amen?
Macbeth, ii. 2.

Ham. Speak the speech, I pray you, as I pronounced it to you
Hamlet, iii. 2.

——— language of man pronounced
By tongue of brute, and human sense expressed?
The first, at least of these I thought denied
To beasts; whom God, on their creation-day
Created mute to all articulate sound.
P. L., ix. 553.

——— adjudged to death
For want of well pronouncing Shibboleth.
S. A., 289.

He heard, borne on the wind, the articulate voice
Of God —— 'The Excursion,' iv.

He only judges right who weighs, compares
And, in the sternest sentence which his voice
Pronounces, ne'er abandons Charity.
'Eccles. Sonnets.'

——— the beauty of the sabbath kept
With conscientious reverence, as a day
By the almighty Lawgiver pronounced
Holy and blest. ——— 'The Excursion,' viii.]

Exercise.

Demosthenes is said to have ——— so badly, that in order to cure himself of this defect, he used to recite speeches with small pebbles in his mouth.

Though, in point of information and style, he was an excellent lecturer, he ——— English with so strong a provincial dialect, that it occasionally gave many of his hearers some difficulty to understand him.

In order to ——— properly, we should be accustomed to hear and converse with those who mix in the best society.

Those who have a defect of ——— should be put under the care of an elocution master.

The first requisite for a good reader is a distinct ———. This may be said to resemble perspicuity in style; for whatever beauties our writing may possess, they are without value when unaccompanied by this essential quality.

A bad ——— often arises from carelessness; vicious ——— is the natural consequence of having bad examples for imitation.

"Speak the speech, I pray you, as I ——— it to you."

To attribute—to impute.

Both these words relate to causation. To *attribute* is to refer to as a known, or a natural cause; to *impute* is to refer to as a supposed, or an evil cause. Bad health is sometimes attributed to intemperance. Riots and discontent among a people may be attributed to a bad harvest, or may be imputed to the unpopularity of the government. In attributing, we assign things as causes; in imputing, we assign the feelings or acts of persons as causes. To impute is generally used in a bad sense; to attribute, in either a good or bad sense.

[*Par* — the merit of service is seldom attributed to the true and exact performer.
All's Well, &c, iii. 6.

Jul. And not impute this yielding to light love
Romeo and Juliet, ii. 2.

Where glory is false glory, attributed
To things not glorious, men not worthy fame.
P. R., iii. 69.

Imputest thou that to my default, or will
Of wandering —— *P. L.* ix. 1145.]

Exercise.

"Perhaps it may appear upon examination that the most polite ages are the least virtuous. This may be ——— to the folly of admitting wit and learning as merits in themselves, without considering the application of them."

"This obscurity cannot be ——— to want of language in so great a master of style."

"The imperfection of telescopes is ——— to spherical glasses; and mathematicians have propounded to figure them by the conical sections."

"I have formerly said that I could distinguish your writings from those of any others; 'tis now time to clear myself from any ——— of self-conceit on that subject."

"We, who are adepts in astrology, can ——— it to several causes in the planets, that this quarter of our great city is the region of such as either never had, or have lost, the use of reason."

Whenever a great undertaking fails, the blame is always ——— to those who advised it.

To avenge—to revenge.

We *avenge* others; we *revenge* ourselves. When we revenge, we return evil for evil (real or supposed) done to ourselves. When we avenge, we punish an injury done to another. In both cases, vengeance is exercised; in the former for ourselves, in the latter for another. To avenge is an act of retributive justice; to revenge is an act of passion

[*Clar.* O God, if my deep prayers cannot appease thee,
But thou wilt be avenged on my misdeeds,
Yet execute thy wrath on me alone. *Rich. III.*, i. 3.

Ant. For when I am revenged upon my charm
I have done all —— *Ant. and Cleop.*, iv. 10.

Avenge, O Lord, thy slaughtered saints, whose bones
Lie scattered on the Alpine mountains cold.
MILTON '*Sonnets.*'

——— but his face
Deep scars of thunder had intrenched, and care
Sat on his faded cheek; but under brows
Of dauntless courage and considerate pride
Waiting revenge; —— *P. L.*, i. 604.

He, who by wilful disesteem of life
And proud insensibility to hope
Affronts the eye of Solitude, shall learn
That her mild nature can be terrible:
That neither she nor silence lack the power
To avenge their own insulted majesty.
'*The Excursion*,' iv.

And, guilt escaping, passion then might plead
In angry spirits for her old free range
And the 'wild justice of revenge' prevail.
'*Sonnets on Punishment of Death*.']

Exercise.

"The day shall come, the great ———ing day,
When Troy's proud glories in the dust shall *lay*."*

"'Your health, my Glaucus,' said he, quaffing a cup to each letter of the Greek's name with the ease of the practised drinker; 'will you not be ——— on your ill-fortune of yesterday? See, the dice court us.'"

"Come, Antony, and young Octavius, come,
——— yourselves alone on Cassius."

"It is a quarrel most unnatural,
To be ——— on him that loveth thee."

"With heart of fire, and foot of wind,
The fierce ———er is behind."

"By a continued series of loose, though apparently trivial gratifications, the heart is often as thoroughly corrupted as by the commission of any one of those enormous crimes which spring from great ambition, or great ———."

"May we, with the witness of a good conscience, pursue him with further ———?"

With tears in her eyes, she related the insult she had just received, and entreated me to ——— her.

"The just ———er of his injured ancestors, the victorious Louis, was darting his thunder."

To compare to—to compare with.

One thing is compared *to* another when a resemblance is found between them: Anger is compared *to* a tempest. One thing is compared *with* another when our object in bringing them together is to discover the relative worth of each. Art when compared *with* nature is found wanting. Great things may be compared *with* small.

[*K. Rich.* I have been studying how I may compare
This prison, where I live, unto the world.
Rich. II., v. 5.

* It is needless to remark, that Pope is here guilty of a gross grammatical error.

Ham. I dare not confess that, lest I should compare with him in excellence ——
Hamlet, v. 2.

So, if great things to small may be compared
Xerxes, the liberty of Greece to yoke
From Susa, his Memnonian palace high
Came to the sea —— *P. L.*, x. 306.

Alas, how simple, to those cates compared,
Was that crude apple that diverted Eve!
P. R., ii. 348.

As when Earth's son, Antæus, (to compare
Small things with greatest,) in Irassa strove
With Jove's Alcides —— *Id.*, iv. 564.

—— this earth, a spot, a grain,
An atom, with the firmament compared
And all her numbered stars —— *P. L.*, viii. 18.

And Fancy, not less aptly pleased, compares
Your squadrons to an endless flight of birds
WORDSWORTH. '*To the Clouds.*

—— compared
With him who grovels, self-debarred
From all that lies within the scope
Of holy faith and christian hope. '*Rydal Chapel.*']

Exercise.

In point of learning, he is not to be compared —— his rival candidate, though he is far superior to him in natural abilities.

Human life has been compared —— a lamp, which, for want of fresh oil to feed its flame, burns but for a little while, becomes gradually fainter, and is at length extinguished.

We have but to compare the paintings of these two masters —— each other, to perceive how far superior, in every respect, the original is to the copy.

My brother and I had both travelled, at different times, over the same country; and I found, on comparing my notes —— his, that our opinions on the scenery, manners, and habits of the people, agreed in almost every particular.

Burke, in one of his writings, speaking of the necessity of large open spaces for the recreation and exercise of the poor, compares the parks of the metropolis —— the lungs of the human body.

What a difference do we find when we compare the gaiety and light-heartedness of boyhood —— the cares and anxiety of more advanced life! how imperceptibly does the step lose its light, firm, and elastic tread, and the voice its full and commanding tone!

"Solon compared the people —— the sea, and orators and counsellors —— the winds; for that the sea would be calm and quiet if the winds did not trouble it."

To compare—to contrast.

Things which bear some resemblance to each other may be *compared*. Things which are strikingly unlike each other are *contrasted*. When we compare, it is with a view to shew a likeness; when we contrast, it is in order to dissimilitude. The dreadful ravages of war cannot be compared to, but may be contrasted with, the quiet blessings of peace. A man may be compared to a tree, because we can discover many points in which they resemble each other. White is contrasted with black.

[Not from his fellows only man may learn
Rights to compare and duties to discern.
WORDSWORTH. '*Humanity.*'

But stoop, and place the prospect of the soul
In sober contrast with reality
And man's substantial life. —— '*The Excursion*,' v.]

Exercise.

When we —— the squalid poverty of the artisan or labourer with the comforts and refinement of the middle and higher classes, how striking is the difference!

These two men differed so widely in character and habits, that it would be absurd to attempt to institute a —— between them.

On entering this abode of desolation, what a —— presented itself! I had just left a company of light-hearted, joyous companions, full of mirth and jollity:—here I found the silence of sadness, interrupted only by the sobs of despair, or the fitful shrieks of painful disease.

On —— the two books, I found that both writers had treated the subject in nearly a similar manner, and that they differed only in detail.

He who is in the habit of —— his own condition with that of others, will be obliged to confess that, whatever disappointments or reverses it has been his lot to suffer, he has many reasons to consider himself fortunate.

"I will hear Brutus speak:—
I will hear Cassius, and —— their reasons."

"In lovely —— to this glorious view,
Calmly magnificent, then we will turn
To where the silver Thames first rural grows."

To conciliate—to reconcile.

To *conciliate* is to gain the good-will of others for ourselves; to *reconcile* is to bring together those who have been at variance. One man conciliates the esteem of another. A common friend reconciles two persons who have quarrelled. In conciliating, we attract others to ourselves; in reconciling, we bring two others together. Our manners conciliate; our influence reconciles.

When we reconcile *ourselves* to things or persons, we make the first advances to them. When we conciliate others, we behave in such a way that they make the first advances to us.

[*Macd.* Such welcome and unwelcome things at once
'Tis hard to reconcile. —— *Macbeth*, iv. 3.

——— yet winds to seas
Are reconciled at length, and sea to shore.
S. A., 962.

Am pleased by fits to have thee for my foe
Yet ever willing to be reconciled.
WORDSWORTH. '*Miscel. Sonnets.*']

Exercise.

The kindness and clemency of Julius Cæsar soon ——— the minds even of those who had been his most implacable enemies

The two parties entertained such a violent hatred towards each other, that it required all the experience and tact of the minister to ——— them.

It was no easy matter o ——— such fierce and savage tribes, and induce them to submit to the absolute dominion of foreign power.

I shall never be able to ——— myself to a life so full of difficulties and dangers.

By the mediation of a third party, the quarrel was at length made up, and both parties declared that they were wholly ——— to each other.

The most difficult task for a minister is to ——— all the parties which exist in the state to his own interests, and to ——— conflicting factions to each other.

"The preacher may enforce his doctrines in the style of authority, for it is his profession to summon mankind to their duty; but an uncommissioned instructor will study to ———, whilst he attempts to correct."

"It must be confessed a happy attachment, which can ——— the Laplander to his freezing snows, and the African to his scorching sun."

To confess—to acknowledge.

To *acknowledge* is to make known by any means of communication; to *confess* is to make known by speaking. An acknowledgment is public; a confession is private. The former is said of a fault, or a mistake, and is used in reference to venial errors; the latter applies particularly to graver charges. We acknowledge an omission of duty; we confess a commission of sin. A debt is acknowledged; a crime is confessed.

[*Oth.* ——— as truly as to heaven
I do confess the vices of my blood. *Othello*, i. 3.

K. Hen. Through all the kingdoms that acknowledge Christ
1 *Henry IV.*, iii. 2.

Father, I do acknowledge and confess
That I this honour, I this pomp have brought
To Dagon —— *S. A.*, 448

——— till peace obtained from fault
Acknowledged and deplored —— *P. L.*, x. 939.

——— and there confess
Humbly our faults and pardon beg ——
Id., 1088.

Then mark him, him who could so long rebel
The crime confessed, a kneeling Penitent
Before the Altar, where the Sacrament
Softens his heart, till from his eyes outwell
Tears of salvation.
Wordsworth. '*Sonnets on Punishment of Death.*'

——— Doth the will
Acknowledge reason's law? —— '*The Excursion*,' v.]

Exercise.

It is not sufficient that we ——— our faults; we ought also to endeavour to compensate for the injury which our errors may have caused to others.

The police officer ——— that he had done wrong, in allowing the man to quit his presence even for a moment; but he strongly denied that the prisoner's escape had been effected by his connivance.

It was not till after he was tried and convicted on the clearest evidence that the prisoner ——— his guilt, and made a long statement of all the circumstances connected with the robbery.

Fourteen of the conspirators were condemned and executed; seven of whom died ——— their crime.

Dangerfield, being committed to Newgate, ——— the forgery, which, though probably of his own contrivance, he ascribed to the Earl of Castlemain, the Countess of Powis, and the five lords in the Tower.

They died penitent, ——— the justness of the sentence by which they were executed.

To confute—to refute.

When one argument is neutralized by another, it is confuted; when an assertion is proved to be false, it is refuted. A confuted proposition is reduced to an absurdity. When a charge is refuted, the refutation remains triumphant, but does not alter the character of the charge. In confuting, we prove the absurdity—in refuting, we prove the falsehood of an assertion. Opinions, arguments, paradoxes, &c. are confuted; slander, insinuations, accusations, &c. are refuted.

[*Isab.* ——— after much debatement
My sisterly remorse confutes mine honour.
Meas. for Meas., v 1.

——— Satan stood
Awhile, as mute, confounded what to say,
What to reply, confuted, and convinced
Of his weak arguing and fallacious drift:
P. R., iii. 3

How wilt thou reason with them, how refute
Their idolisms, traditions, paradoxes?
Id., iv. 233.]

Exercise.

"'Tis such absurd, miserable stuff, that we will not honor it with especial ———ation."

"The learned do, by turns, the learn'd ———,
Yet all depart unaltered by dispute."

"Philip of Macedon ——— by the force of gold all the wisdom of Athens."

"He could on either side dispute,
———, change hands, and still ———."

"He knew that there were so many witnesses in these two miracles, that it was impossible to ——— such multitudes."

"The arguments employed on the opposite side, in favor of this view of the question, were so weak and inconclusive, that we had no difficulty in ——— them."

He made some slight effort to ——— the charge brought against him, but without success; and his reputation thus received a blow from which it never afterwards wholly recovered.

"Self-destruction sought, ———es
That excellence thought in thee."

To conjecture—to guess.

We guess about the fact; we conjecture on the possibility of the fact. A conjecture is more vague than a guess. We may have a reason for guessing, but conjecture is pure hazard. We guess a person's age from his appearance. When we are utterly at a loss to comprehend a sentence, all we can do is to conjecture its meaning. A guess is an approach to the truth. A conjecture may, or may not, be near the truth. In guessing, we arrive at a probable conclusion from imperfect premises; in conjecturing, we arrive at a possible conclusion from uncertain premises.

[*Gent.* 'Tis likely
By all conjectures. —— *Henry VIII.*, ii. 1.

Cleo. Guess at her years, I pr'ythee.
Ant. and Cleop., iii. 3.

——— for this day will pour down
If I conjecture aught, no drizzling shower
But rattling storm of arrows barbed with fire.
P. L., vi. 545.

Already by thy reasoning this I guess,
Who art to lead thy offspring —— *Id.*, viii. 85

Who comes not hither ne'er shall know
How beautiful the world below;
Nor can he guess how lightly leaps
The brook adown the rocky steeps.
WORDSWORTH. '*The Pass of Kirkstone.*']

Exercise.

The settled gloom of his countenance, his restless eye, and anxious expression, made it easy to ——— the unhappy state of his mind.

Not having seen his friend for a long time, he ——— that illness was the cause of his absence.

The blind man, after carefully passing his hand over the stranger's countenance, ——— immediately that it was the same person who had taken shelter in his cottage a few weeks before.

Some children ——— riddles much more readily than others.

Having no suspicion of poison, the physician was at a loss to ——— the cause of such violent symptoms.

The landlady, ———ing by my exterior that I was not likely to be a profitable customer, replied that she had no accommodation for gentlemen of my appearance.

The mariners ——— by the clouded state of the horizon, and the sudden gusts of wind, that a storm was rapidly approaching.

"Persons of studious and contemplative natures often entertain themselves with the history of past ages, or raise schemes and ——— upon futurity."

"And these discoveries make us all confess
That sublunary science is but ———."

To contemplate—to meditate.

We *contemplate* sensible objects; we *meditate* on actions or abstract qualities. The starry heavens and the rising sun are fit objects for contemplation. Ingratitude, friendship, benevolence, &c., are proper subjects for meditation.

When these words are used in the sense of *to intend*, there is this difference between them, that *contemplate* is more immediately followed by the intended action than *meditate*. In this sense, what we contemplate, we look upon as likely; what we meditate, we consider as probable, but more remote. We contemplate a journey into the country; we meditate an excursion abroad.

[*K. Hen.* So many hours must I contemplate
3 *Henry VI.*, ii. 5.

Jaq. — indeed the sundry contemplation of my travels, in which my often rumination wraps me, is a most humourous sadness. *As You Like It*, iv. 1.

Kath. ——— whilst I sit meditating
On that celestial harmony I go to. *Henry VIII.*, iv. 2.

Grif. ——— full of repentance
Continual meditations, tears and sorrows,
He gave his honours to the world again,
His blessed part to heaven, and slept in peace.
Henry VIII., iv. 2

——— I have not lost
To love, at least contemplate and admire
What I see excellent in good, or fair,
Or virtuous —— *P. R.*, i. 380.

Wrapped in a pleasing fit of melancholy
To meditate my rural minstrelsy *Comus*, i. 547

——— with the thing
Contemplated, describe the Mind and Man
Contemplating; and who and what he was,—
The transitory Being that beheld
This Vision —— '*The Excursion*,' (*Preface.*)

——— The food of hope
Is meditated action; robbed of this
Her sole support, she languishes and dies.
Id., ix.]

Exercise.

The ——— of nature fills the mind with the sublimest thoughts.

During the long period of his confinement, he had full leisure to ———

on his past follies; and he left the prison with a strong determination to reform his life, and become a respectable and useful member of society.

He was aroused from his ——— by the loud report of a gun, and turning his head to the right, he perceived two men, in the dress of hunters, approaching the spot where he stood.

As they had not ——— any danger, they were unprovided with weapons of defence.

In ——— the nature of the Divine Being, the soul is lost in her own insignificance, and is utterly confounded by the immensity and infinity of the object.

I have been for some months ——— a journey to Italy, but I am now so overwhelmed with business, that I see no likelihood of its taking place this year.

The poet stood on a lofty eminence, formed by the peak of a craggy rock, and ——— the scene below him with unmixed delight.

"I sincerely wish myself with you to ——— the wonders of God in the firmament, rather than the madness of man on the earth."

"But a very small part of the moments spent in ——— on the past produce any reasonable caution or salutary sorrow."

To copy—to imitate.

To *copy* has to do with the outward appearance; to *imitate*, with internal signification. We copy words; we imitate meaning. The result of a copy is a likeness to the eye; the result of an imitation is likeness to the mind. In copying, we multiply the original; in imitating, we present a variety of the original. In copying a sentence, we transcribe the words which it contains; in imitating a sentence, we construct one in a similar manner to the one placed before us. The hand copies; the mind imitates. A painting may be copied; the style of a painter may be imitated.

[*Ham.* ——— from the table of my memory
I'll wipe away all trivial fond records,
All saws of books, all forms, all pressures past
That youth and observation copied there.
Hamlet, i. 5

P. Hen. Yet herein will I imitate the sun
1 *Henry IV.*, i. 2

We, that are of purer fire,
Imitate the starry quire,
Who in their nightly watchful spheres
Lead in swift round the months and years.
Comus, 112

Stoop from your height, ye proud, and copy these!
Who in their noiseless dwelling-place, can hear

The voice of wisdom whispering scripture texts
For the mind's government, or temper's peace.
'*The Excursion*,' v.

Where the bare columns of those lofty firs,
Supporting gracefully a massy dome
Of sombre foliage, seem to imitate
A Grecian temple rising from the Deep
Id., IX.]

Exercise.

"Poetry and music have the power of ———ing the manners of men"

"Since a true knowledge of nature gives us pleasure, a lively ——— of it, either in poetry or painting, must produce a much greater; for both these arts are not only true ——— of nature, but of the best nature."

"The Romans having sent to Athens and the Greek cities of Italy for the ——— of the best laws, chose ten legislators to put them into form."

"I have not the vanity to think my ——— equal to the original."

"We should remember that although it be allowable to form our general style upon that of some eminent writer, yet that a close and servile ——— of the style of *any* author will lead us to adopt its faults as well as its beauties."

The two paintings so closely resembled each other, that it was extremely difficult to determine which was the ——— and which the original.

——— the six first stanzas of this poem.

"Some imagine that whatsoever they find in the picture of a master who has acquired reputation, must, of necessity, be excellent; and never fail, when they ———, to follow the bad as well as the good things."

To decrease—to diminish.

To *decrease* is to grow less; to *diminish* is to make or become less. To decrease is relative and gradual; to diminish is positive. To decrease is an internal, and to diminish an external action. In addition to which distinction it may be proper to remark, that to decrease is more frequently applied to quantity or size, and to diminish, to number. Things decrease when they grow less from within, or when the cause of their growing less is imperceptible. They are diminished when something is taken from them from without, or when the cause of their becoming less is more evident. Water exposed to the sun decreases in quantity. A snowball during a thaw will decrease in size. An army is diminished in numbers by disease or famine. Many substances decrease in size by shrinking, such as flannel, cloth, &c.

[*Ch. Just.* Have you not a moist eye? a dry hand? a yellow cheek? a white beard? a decreasing leg? 2 *Henry IV.*, i. 2.

Edg. ——— yon tall anchoring bark
Diminished to her cock; her cock, a buoy
Almost too small for sight. —— *King Lear*, iv. 6.

——— at whose sight all the stars
Hide their diminished heads —— *P. L.*, iv. 35.]

Exercise.

As we approach winter, the days gradually ——— in length.

That which we call good is apt to cause or increase pleasure, or ——— pain in us.

Upon instituting an examination of his affairs, it was discovered that, from a long course of reckless extravagance, his income was ——— by at least one-half.

By some untoward accident, the gas was allowed to escape much more quickly than was intended; in consequence of which, the balloon ——— in size so rapidly, that the aëronauts were in imminent danger of being precipitated to the earth.

"When the sun comes to his tropics, days increase and ——— but a very little for a great while together."

"Crete's ample fields ——— to our eye,
Before the Boreal blasts the vessels fly."

To dissert—to discuss.

In a dissertation, we expatiate upon a subject, and engraft upon it our own ideas in order to explain it more fully. A dissertation is then an amplified discourse. In discussing, we examine the real meaning of what is before us, by shaking out, as it were, its points singly and separately. The object both of a dissertation and a discussion is to arrive at a more perfect knowledge of a subject. In disserting, we add our own ideas by way of illustration; in discussing, we examine, to come at the real meaning.

Exercise.

"A country fellow distinguishes himself as much in the church-yard as a citizen does upon 'Change; the whole parish politics being generally ——— in that place either after the sermon or before the bell rings."

"Plutarch in his ———ion on the poets, quotes an instance of Homer's judgment in closing a ludicrous scene with decency and instruction."

"This knotty point should you and I ——,
Or tell a tale?"

"Could I, however, repeat to you the words of a venerable sage, (for I can call him no other,) whom I once heard ——ing on the topic of religion, and whom still I hear, whenever I think on him; you might accept perhaps my religious theories as candidly as you have my moral."

"We are here to —— only those general exceptions which have been taken."

——ions are frequently written on disputed points in literature, such as Bentley's —— on the Epistles of Phalaris, De Pauw's —— on the Egyptians and Chinese, &c., &c.

To equivocate—to prevaricate.

To *prevaricate* is to evade a question so as to escape detection; to *equivocate* is to answer a question in such a way that two senses are involved. The object of the prevaricator is to escape detection; that of the equivocator is to deceive his questioner. The prevaricator shuffles; the equivocator deceives. An equivocator conceals the real meaning under the one put forth; a prevaricator gives us no information on the subject of our question.

[*Port.* —who committed treason enough for God's sake, yet could not equivocate to heaven. *Macbeth*, ii. 3.]

Exercise.

The evidence of this witness was so full of ——, that the judge ordered that he should be immediately taken into custody, and there held during the pleasure of the court.

A sentence is —— when it is equally intelligible in two distinct senses; as, for example, in the following French expression: "Je voudrais bien l'avoir." This, when pronounced, would leave the meaning ——, for it might signify equally: "I should like to have it," and "I should like to see her."

"Several Romans, taken prisoners by Hannibal, were released upon obliging themselves by an oath to return again to his camp: among these was one who, thinking to elude the oath, went the same day back to the camp, on pretence of having forgotten something; but this —— was so shocking to the Roman senate, that they ordered him to be delivered up to Hannibal."

Irish witnesses are remarkable both for their —— and ——; they either endeavour to avoid the question altogether, or else they answer it in such a way as to give no satisfactory information.

"There is no ——ing with God when we are on the very threshold of his presence."

"A secret liar or ——or is such a one as by mental reservations and other tricks deceives him to whom he speaks, being lawfully called to deliver all the truth."

To foretel—to predict.

We *foretel* by calculation, and with some degree of certainty; we *predict* from pure conjecture. Strictly, no one can predict, though wisdom and experience will frequently enable men to foretel what will happen. Astronomers foretel eclipses; astrologers predict good or bad fortune.

The noun *prediction* expresses what is foretold, as well as what is predicted, but we should not for that reason place the same faith in the predictions of a gipsy or an almanac-maker, as in those of a philosopher or an astronomer.

[*Gaunt.* Methinks, I am a prophet new inspired
And thus expiring, do foretell of him.
Rich. II., ii. 1

Cæs. —— for these predictions
Are to the world in general, as to Cæsar.
Jul. Cæs., ii. 2.

—— whose high office now
Moses in figure bears, to introduce
One greater, of whose day he shall foretell
P. L., xii. 242.

—— prediction still
In all things, and all men, supposes means:
Without means used, what it predicts revokes.
P. R., iii. 356.

And, with this change, sharp air and falling leaves
Foretelling aged Winter's desolate sway.
'*The Excursion*,' v.]

Exercise.

It has been ——, that when London shall join Hampstead, extraordinary changes will take place in England; what these changes are, the prophet did not mention, but there seems every likelihood that the truth of his —— will be soon put to the test.

Astronomers can calculate eclipses with such precision, that they —— the very moment in which they will take place.

Mr. Murphy, whose weather-almanac gained him so high a reputation some years past, goes on —— every year, but no one any longer places faith in his ——.

The Roman augurs, whose office it was to ——— the good fortune or ill success of an undertaking, were themselves so alive to the absurdity of their assumption, that, according to Cicero, they could not look each other in the face without bursting into laughter.

Though their father perceived and ——— all the difficulties and dangers they would have to undergo, the sons turned a deaf ear to his representations, and, being obstinately bent upon the undertaking, lost no time in preparing for its execution.

"Above the rest, the sun, who never lies,
——— the change of weather in the skies"

To go back—to return.

Those who are in a place we have left, speak of us as having *gone back;* those who are in a place at which we are arrived, speak of us as having *returned.* We go back *from,* we return *to.* In the former, the idea of the place we have just left is prominent; in the latter, the idea of the place we are arrived at predominates. A man sets out from London to Liverpool; on his arrival at Birmingham, he finds himself obliged to go back from Birmingham, and return to London.

Though the preposition *to* is not always expressed after the verb return, it is always understood. In such phrases as "The boy returned from school," there is always understood, *to* his father's house, or some such equivalent. The same remark (of the preposition *from*) may be made of the verb "go back."

[*King.* ——— For your intent
In going back to school in Wittenberg
It is most retrograde to our desire. *Haml.* i. 2.

Ham. The undiscovered country, from whose bourn
No traveller returns —— *Id.*, iii. 1.

Return Alpheus; the dread voice is past
That shrunk thy streams; return Sicilian Muse
'*Lycidas.*' 132

Go back to antiqué ages, if thine eyes
The genuine mien and character would trace
Of the rash Spirit that still holds her place
Prompting the world's audacious vanities!
WORDSWORTH. '*Sonnets to Liberty*

——— even if the joys
Of sense were able to return as fast
And surely as they vanish. —— '*Laodamia.*']

Exercise.

"To ——— the business in hand, the use of a little insight in those parts of knowledge is to accustom our minds to all sorts of knowledge."

After remaining with us for two months, during which he had leisure to examine all the curiosities in the neighborhood, he ——— home to his friends in the country, where he is now engaged in writing a work on the natural history of this place.

Having discovered that my trunk had been left behind at Wisbaden, I was obliged to ——— from Biberich to Wisbaden to fetch it, which detained me a night longer than I had intended.

When he had gone through the usual course of study in the medical schools, he ——— from Paris with the intention of establishing himself as a physician in London.

I knocked at my friend's door and asked if he had ——— London; the servant answered that he had been in town, but that he was ———

To prevail with—to prevail upon.

We *prevail with* another, when our influence is sufficiently strong with him to persuade him to do that to which he was not inclined; we *prevail upon* another, when our arguments are sufficiently strong to cause him to do that to which he was violently disinclined. An address to the feelings prevails *with* another; an address to the reason prevails *upon* another. Milton makes Eve say: "The serpent prevailed *with* me." Charles the First could not be prevailed *upon* to give up the command of the army.

[*Men.* —— there is some hope the ladies of Rome, especially his mother, may prevail with him. *Coriolanus*, v. 4.

Pisa. ——— What false Italian
(As poisonous tongued, as handed) hath prevailed
On thy too ready hearing? *Cymbeline*, iii. 2.

But with the afflicted in his pangs their sound
Little prevail —— *S. A.*, 661.]

Exercise.

"There are four sorts of arguments that men, in their reasoning, make use of to ——— them."

"Herod, hearing of Agrippa's arrival in Upper Asia, went thither to him and ——— him to accept an invitation."

Upon assurances of revolt, the queen was ——— to send her forces upon that expedition."

"He was ——— to restrain the Earl of Bristol upon his first arrival"

"——— some judicious friend to be your constant hearer, and allow him the utmost freedom."

"They are more in danger to go out of the way, who are marching under the conduct of a guide, that it is a hundred to one will mislead them, than he that has not yet taken a step, and is likelier to be ——— to inquire after the right way."

"Having reasoned with him for some time on his folly, and seriously entreated him to consider its inevitable consequences, I at last ——— him to revoke the order."

——— obdurate minds nothing ———

To repeal—to revoke.

Both these words mean to call back. Repeal, from the French *rappeler;* and revoke, from the Latin *revocare.*

We *revoke* what has been said, we *repeal* what has been laid down, as law. Hence, edicts are revoked, and statutes are repealed. The proclaimed law is revoked; the written law is repealed. We do not say the repeal—but the revocation of the edict of Nantes: neither do we speak of the revocation—but of the repeal of the Irish Union. Both words are used chiefly in a legal or political sense. It should also be observed that a single individual revokes, and that an assembly repeals. Emperors and kings can revoke a sentence; the Parliament can repeal laws.

[*Cit.* —— repeal daily any wholesome act established against the rich.
Coriolanus, i. 1.

Sic. Let them assemble;
And on a safer judgment, all revoke
Your ignorant election. —— *Id.*, ii. 3.

——— Whence Adam soon repealed
The doubts that in his heart arose —— *P. L.*, vii. 59.

——— and revoke the high decree,
Unchangeable, eternal, which ordained
Their freedom —— *Id.*, iii. 126.]

Exercise.

No arguments could induce the cruel Sultan to ——— the decree he had published against these unoffending people, and in a few weeks, they were all banished from the country.

Such laws as are not found necessary to execute, or which have arisen from circumstances no longer existing, should be immediately ———.

The order was ——— just in time to save the poor prisoner, who, otherwise, would have inevitably suffered death that morning.

The ——— of those taxes which pressed most heavily on the poorer portion of the population was now found absolutely necessary, and a law was passed to that effect, at the beginning of the session.

Seeing the injury they had caused, the king determined ——— these privileges, and to throw open the competition to all ranks of the state.

"When we abrogate a law as being ill-made, the whole cause for which it was made still remaining, do we not herein ——— our own deed, and upbraid ourselves with folly?"

Shall—will.

The following explanations will shew the distinction between these auxiliaries:—

I. When the sentence is affirmative, *shall*, in the first person, expresses purpose or intention; in the second and third, it commands.

Will, in the first person, promises; in the second and third, it expresses purpose.

II. When the sentence is interrogative, *shall*, in the first and third persons, asks the permission or advice of another; in the second, it asks the intention of another.

Will is never used properly (interrogatively) in the first person singular or plural; in the second, it inquires about the will, and in the third, about the purpose of others.

The table below will perhaps more clearly explain the distinction between these words, so puzzling to natives as well as to foreigners.

I. (Affirmatively.)

Singular.

1.	I shall go	=	I intend to go.
	I will go	=	I promise to go.
2.	You shall go	=	I command you to go.
	You will go	=	You intend to go.
3.	He shall go	=	I command him to go.
	He will go	=	He intends to go.

Plural.

1. { We shall go = We intend to go
   { We will go = We promise to go.

2. As the singular.

3. { They shall go = I command them to go.
   { They will go = They intend to go

II. (Interrogatively.)

Singular.

1. { Shall I go? = Do you wish me to go?
   { Will I go? = *incorrect* (never said.)

2. { Shall you go? = Do you intend to go?
   { Will you go? = Do you { choose / wish } to go?

3. { Shall he go? = Do you permit him to go?
   { Will he go? = Does he { choose / intend } to go?

Plural.

1. { Shall we go? = Do you { choose / wish } us to go?
   { Will we go? = *incorrect* (never said.)

2. As the singular.

3. { Shall they go? = Do you choose them to go?
   { Will they go? = Do they intend to go?

[*Com.* ——— we shall hardly in our ages see
Their banners wave again. *Coriolan*-, iii. 1

Sen. —— he shall to the market-place. *Id.*
Cor. Shall remain! ——
Hear you this Triton of the minnows? mark you
His absolute *shall?* *Id.*

Cor. This was my speech, and I will speak 't again
Id.

Sic ——— If you will pass *Id.*

Com. He will shake
Your Rome about your ears. *Id.*, iv. 6.

Ari. What shall I do? say what? what shall I do?
Tempest, i. 2

Ant. Sha.. it not grieve thee? *Julius Cæsar*, iii 1

Men. Wilt thou be lord of the whole world?
Ant. and Cleop., ii. 7

Imo. Will my lord say so? *Cymbeline*, i. 7.

Adam. Master, go on; and I will follow thee
To the last gasp, with truth and loyalty. *As You Like It*, ii. 3

I, too, will have my kings that take
From me the sign of life and death,
Kingdoms shall shift about, like clouds
Obedient to my breath. Wordsworth 'Rob Roy's Grave

This child I to myself will take;
She shall be mine, and I will make
A Lady of my own.
* * * * *
The stars of midnight shall be dear
To her; and she shall lean her ear
In many a secret place
Where rivulets dance their wayward round
And beauty born of murmuring sound
Shall pass into her face. '*Poems of the Imagination.*']

Exercise.

"——— I lift up the veil of my weakness any further, or is this disclosure sufficient?"

"What ——— we say? Which of these is happier?"

"He was a man, take him for all in all,
We ne'er ——— look upon his like again."

"I ——— not urge that private considerations ought always to give way to the necessities of the public."

"The law ——— be known to-morrow to far the greatest number of those who may be tempted to break it."

I ——— go to Brighton to-morrow, and ——— take an early opportunity of calling on your friend there.

"But of the tree of knowledge of good and evil thou ——— not eat; for in the day that thou eatest thereof, thou ——— surely die."

"Thou ——— not leave me in the loathsome grave
His prey, nor suffer my unspotted soul
For ever with corruption there to dwell."

To wake—to waken.

To *wake* is to cease from sleeping; to *waken* is to make to cease from sleeping. The former is an intransitive, the second, a transitive verb. This explanation will be illustrated in the following examples:—"The child *woke* at six o'clock," and, "They *wakened* the child at six o'clock."*

These verbs, when used with the prefix *a*, (awake, awaken,) have a more intensive meaning; thus, one who wakes, no longer sleeps; but one who awakes, rouses himself up from his sleep, and shakes it off. Again, one who wakens another interrupts his sleep; but one who awakens another takes

* By the older authors these two verbs were used indiscriminately in a transitive or intransitive sense; but the difference here explained is observed by all the best modern writers

care that he shall not fall again into his former state of sleep.

[*Pro.* ——— graves, at my command,
Have waked their sleepers —— *Tempest*, v. 1.

Post. ——— Poor wretches, that depend
On greatness' favour, dream as I have done,
Wake, and find nothing. *Cymbeline*, v. 4

Buck. ——— your sleepy thoughts,
Which here we waken to our country's good.
Rich. III., iii 7

Pro. ——— in my false brother
Awaked an evil nature —— *Tempest*, i. 2.

Oli. From miserable slumber I awaked. *As You Like It*, iv 2.

Com. I offered to awaken his regard
For his private friends. —— *Coriolanus*, v. 1

When Adam waked, so customed —— *P. L.*, v. 3.

We may no longer stay: go, waken Eve. *Id.*, xii. 594.

——— now conscience wakes despair
That slumbered; wakes the bitter memory
Of what he was —— *Id.*, iv. 23.

Venus now wakes and wakens Love *Comus*, 124.

——— ere the odorous breath of morn
Awakes the slumbering leaves —— MILTON. '*Arcades*

——— and his next subordinate
Awakening, thus to him in secret spake. *P. L.*, v. 672.

——— I have slept
Weeping, and weeping have I waked —— '*The Excursion*, 1

——— truths that wake
To perish never. '*Intimations of Immortality.*'

Diverting evil purposes, remorse
Awakening, chastening an intemperate grief.
'*The Excursion*,' iv

——— the broad sun
Is sinking down in its tranquillity;
The gentleness of heaven broods o'er the Sea:
Listen! the mighty being is awake,
And doth with his eternal motion make
A sound like thunder—everlastingly. '*Miscel. Sonnets*']

Exercise.

"I cannot think any time, ———ing or sleeping, without being sensible of it."

"When he was ——— with the noise
And saw the beast so small,
What's this, quoth he, that gives so weak a voice
That ——— men withal?"

"The book ends abruptly with his ———ing in a fright."

"Alack, I am afraid they have ———
And 'tis not done!"

"The soul has its curiosity more than ordinarily ——— when it turns its thoughts upon the conduct of such who have behaved themselves with an equal, a resigned, a cheerful, a generous, or heroic temper in the extremity of death."

"Death is a scene calculated to ——— some feeling in the most obdurate breast."

I ——— at five o'clock, and rising immediately, prepared for my departure.

I desired the servant to ——— me at seven the next morning.

All—Every—Each.

All is collective; *every* is distributive; *each* is restrictive. All describes things or persons taken together; every describes them taken singly; and each describes them taken separately. In the three following phrases,—1. All the men. 2. Every man. 3. Each man,—the first designates a body of men taken together; the second may designate the same number and in the same position, but considered singly; the third considers them apart from each other. Besides these distinctions, it is to be remembered, that each relates to two or more individuals; every, always to several.

[*Jaq.* All the world's a stage,
And all the men and women merely players.
As You Like It, ii. 7

Duke. And this our life, exempt from public haunt,
Finds tongues in trees, books in the running brooks,
Sermons in stones, and good in every thing.
Id., ii. 1

Flo. ——— When you do dance, I wish you
A wave of the sea, that you might ever do
Nothing but that; move still, still so, and own
No other function: Each your doing
So singular in each particular,
Crowns what you are doing in the present deeds,
That all your acts are queens. *Winter's Tale*, iv 3

By all the nymphs that nightly dance
Upon thy streams with wily glance. *Comus*, 883.

I know each lane and every alley green,
Dingle, or bushy dell of this wild wood,
And every bosky bourn from side to side.
Id., 311.

——— the brook itself,
Old as the hills that feed it from afar,
Doth rather deepen than disturb the calm
Where all things else are still and motionless.
WORDSWORTH. '*Airey Force Valley.*

——— As Deep to Deep,
Shouting through one valley calls,
All worlds, all natures, mood and measure keep
For praise and ceaseless gratulation, poured
Into the ear of God, their Lord! ' *On the Power of Sound.*

The humblest rivulet will take
Its own wild liberties;
And every day the imprisoned lake
Is flowing in the breeze. ' *Poems on the Affections* '

The Child is father of the Man;
And I could wish my days to be
Bound each to each by natural piety. ' *Poems on Period of Childhood.*

From ancient Rome, downwards through that bright dream
Of commonwealths, each city a starlike seat
Of rival glory. —— ' *Tour in Italy.*']

Exercise.

" ——— man's performances, to be rightly estimated, must be compared to the state of the age in which he lived."

"Taken singly and individually, it might be difficult to conceive how ——— event wrought for good. They must be viewed in their consequences and effects."

"Harold, by his marriage, broke ——— measures with the Duke of Normandy."

"And Brutus is an honorable man,
So are they ———, ——— honorable men"

" ——— one that has any idea of a foot, finds that he can repeat that idea, and joining it to the former, make the idea of two feet."

"Wise Plato said the world with men was stored,
That succour ——— to other might afford."

"Aristotle has long since observed how unreasonable it is to expect the same kind of proof for ——— thing, which we have for some things."

Though it is our duty to live amicably, we cannot live in friendship, with ——— men.

Any—Some.

Some is a certain individual or collective quantity, in other respects indefinite. *Any* is whatever individual or quantity you please; it is applied to all individuals of every species, and is indefinite in every respect.

Some men wish to speak to you.

I do not wish to see *any* men.

Some houses are more convenient than others.

Any houses are more convenient than this.

*Some*thing has happened to vex me.

I never knew *any* thing so provoking.

[*Orl.* If ever you have looked on better days,
If ever been where bells have knolled to church;
If ever sat at any good man's feast. *As You Like It*, ii. 7.

Ulys. ——— O heavens, what some men do,
While some men leave to do!
How some men creep in skittish fortune's lull,
While others play the idiots in her eyes! *Troil. and Cress.* iii 3.

Can any mortal mixture of earth's mould
Breathe such divine enchanting ravishment?
Comus, 244.

Some natural tears they dropt, but wiped them soon.
P. L., xii 644.

Stranger! henceforth be warned; and know that pride
Howe'er disguised in its own majesty
Is littleness; that he who feels contempt
For any living thing, hath faculties
Which he has never used; that thought with him
Is in its infancy. —— WORDSWORTH. '*Early Poems.*'

No—man is dear to man; the poorest poor
Long for some moments in a weary life
When they can know and feel that they have been,
Themselves, the fathers and the dealers out
Of some small blessings —— '*The Cumberland Beggar.*']

Exercise.

I have seen ——— thing to-day which struck me as very remarkable.

I never saw ——— thing equal to that fellow's stupidity.

If you will call on me to-morrow between five and six o'clock, I have ———thing curious to shew you.

Shall I send you ——— fruit? Not ———, I thank you.

We must converse on that subject ——— day when we are alone, and there is no one to interrupt us.

I shall be at home all day to-morrow; and shall be happy to see you at ——— hour you choose to come.

At ——— rate, I shall be sure to see you ——— time before your departure for India.

Never allow your time to pass in total inactivity: ——— occupation, however insignificant, is better than being idle.

——— children have a quicker perception than others; but those who have common sense can generally understand what is clearly explained.

"——— of them did us no great honor by their claims of kindred."

"How fit is this retreat for uninterrupted study! ——— one that sees it will own, I could not have chosen a more likely place to converse with the dead in."

"——— to the shores did fly,
——— to the woods, or whither fear advised,
But running from, all to destruction hie."

Common—Ordinary.

1. The distinction between these words when they signify *of frequent use* is this: What is *common* is done by many persons; what is *ordinary* is repeated many times. Ordinary has to do with the repetition of the act; common, with the persons who perform it. Thus, to dine is a common practice, because it is done by many persons; and it is an ordinary practice, since it is repeated every day. As nouns, the same difference exists between the two words; a common is a piece of ground which many persons have an equal right of enjoying; an ordinary is a meal repeated daily or weekly.

2. In the sense of *low*, ordinary wants distinction; common wants attraction.

[*Sil.* ——— The common executioner,
Whose heart the accustomed sight of death makes hard,
Falls not the axe upon the humbled neck,
But first begs pardon. —— *As You Like It*, iii. 5

Cas. Were I a common laugher, or did use
To stale with ordinary oaths my love
To every new protester. —— *Julius Cæsar*, i. 2.

——— This would surpass
Common revenge —— *P. L.*, ii. 371.

Nor do I name of men the common rout,
That, wandering loose about,
Grow up and perish, as the summer-fly,
Heads without name, no more remembered. *S. A.*, 674.

Whose powers shed round him in the common strife,
Or mild concerns of ordinary life,
A constant influence, a peculiar grace.
WORDSWORTH. '*Character of the Happy Warrior*'

——— 'Tis a common tale,
An ordinary sorrow of man's life. '*The Excursion*,' i.]

Exercise.

"Men may change their climate, but they cannot their nature. A man that goes out a fool, cannot ride or sail himself into ——— sense."

"Though in arbitrary governments there may be a body of laws obscured in the ——— forms of justice, they are not sufficient to secure any rights to the people, because they may be dispensed with."

"Though life and sense be ——— to man and brutes, and their operations in many things alike; yet by this form he lives the life of a man, and not of a brute, and has the sense of a man, and not of a brute."

It is a ———ly received opinion that art cannot flourish without patronage; that is, that unless, in every country, individuals of rank and wealth bestow some of their riches in encouraging the efforts of the artist, those efforts must fail, and their originator must languish in poverty and neglect.

"Neither is it strange that there should be mysteries in divinity, as well as in the ——— operations of nature."

"Every ——— reader, upon the publishing of a new poem, has will and ill-nature enough to turn several passages of it into ridicule, and very often in the right place"

Enormous—Immense.

Enormous is out of rule; *immense*, beyond measure. Enormous is properly applied to magnitude; immense, to extent and distance. A giant is enormous; the ocean is immense. A man of enormous strength is one who is stronger than most men; a man of immense strength is one whose strength is incalculable. Immense expresses a higher degree than enormous. Milo of Crotona was said to possess enormous strength; Samson was endowed with immense strength.

Men In what enormity is Marcius poor, that you two have not in abundance?
Coriolanus, ii. 1.

——— Titan, heaven's first-born,
With his enormous brood, and birthright seized
By younger Saturn. —— *P L.*, i. 511.

——— lifted up so high,
I 'sdained subjection, and thought one step higher
Would set me highest, and in a moment quit
The debt immense of endless gratitude,
So burdensome; still paying, still to owe. *P. L.*, iv. 52

Thither the rainbow comes—the cloud—
And mists that spread the flying shroud;
And sunbeams; and the sounding blast,
That, if it could, would hurry past;
But the enormous barrier holds it fast. WORDSWORTH. '*Fidelity.*

The eminence whereon her spirit stood
Mine was unable to attain. Immense
The space that severed us! But, as the sight
Communicates with heaven's ethereal orbs
Incalculably distant; so, I felt
That consolation may descend from far. '*The Excursion*,' iii.]

Exercise.

The national debt of Great Britain is calculated at between eight and nine hundred millions sterling; an ——— sum, and which would appear sufficient to crush the energies of the most industrious nation on earth.

The hydro-oxygen microscope magnifies to 10,000 times, so that mites in cheese, when seen through its tube, appear of an ——— size.

The greater part of North America, when first colonized, was covered with ——— forests, which have been gradually cleared away, as the settlers increased, and required the ground for cultivation.

"It is related of Maximin, the Roman emperor, that he was a man of such ——— size, that his wife's bracelet usually served him for a thumb-ring; and also that his strength was so ———, that he could break a horse's leg with a kick."

The ——— expanse of ocean which here presents itself to the eye of the astonished beholder, fills him with the sublimest thoughts.

His appetite was so ———, that one of his usual meals would have sufficed to satisfy the desires of four ordinary men.

"The Thracian Acamas his falchion found,
And hew'd the ——— giant to the ground."

"O goodness infinite! goodness ——— !
That all this good of evil shall produce!"

Ferocious—Savage.

The etymology of the word *ferocious* is, partaking of the nature of beasts; the derivation of *savage* points to a particular mode of life; viz., that of the woods. Ferocious is, therefore, like a wild beast; savage, like an inhabitant of the woods. Ferocious is opposed to gentle; savage, to civilized. The cruelty of a savage is the consequence of his mode of life, of his want of intercourse with his fellow-men, &c.; the cruelty of a ferocious man arises from his natural disposition. Savages are not always ferocious; many of them have been remarkable for their gentleness of disposition. The savage man requires culture and civilization; the ferocious man requires taming.

[*Orl.* Speak you so gently? Pardon me, I pray you;
I thought that all things had been savage here.
As You Like It, ii. 7

——— O, might I here
In solitude live savage, in some glade
Obscured ——— *P. L.*, ix. 1085

In him the savage virtue of the Race,
Revenge, and all ferocious thoughts were dead:
Nor did he change; but keep in lofty place
The wisdom which adversity had bred
WORDSWORTH. '*Song of Brougham Castle.*

A savage horde among the civilized,
A servile band among the lordly free! '*The Excursion*,' ix.]

Exercise.

Among civilized men, we have as many examples of ——— brutality, as among the untutored savages of the woods.

The parties of American Indians who lately visited London exhibited all the varieties of a ——— life before their spectators; they pitched their tents, sang, danced, shot at a target, &c.

The Romans were considered a civilized people, and yet, where do we find more frequent examples of a ——— disposition than among the Roman soldiery?

It is an error to suppose that the habits of a ——— life necessarily involve cruelty of disposition, though it must be admitted that they frequently produce that result.

Of all the ——— tribes which contributed to the destruction of the Roman empire, the Huns were the most ——— and the most formidable.

The victory which the rebels had thus gained was followed by the most ——— cruelties.

The ——— nature of the young barbarian was soon softened by his intercourse with the inhabitants of civilized nations.

"The ——— character of Moloch appears both in the battle and the council with exact consistency."

"Thus people lived altogether a ——— life, till Saturn, arriving on these coasts, devised laws to govern them."

Grecian—Greek.

The adjectives Greek and Grecian are often indiscriminately used. The distinction which ought to be observed between them is as follows:—Greek signifies belonging to Greece; and Grecian, relating to Greece. We may speak of a Greek poet, the Greek language; and of Grecian architecture, or Grecian history. An imitation of what is Greek, is Grecian. A Greek helmet is one preserved as a piece of antiquity; a Grecian helmet is one made of the same form and shape. A Greek temple is a temple in Greece; a Grecian temple is one built upon the model of a Greek temple.

[Where the bare columns of those lofty firs,
Supporting gracefully a massy dome
Of sombre foliage, seem to imitate
A Grecian temple rising from the Deep. '*The Excursion*,' ix.

——— characters of Greek or Roman fame.
'*Eccles. Sonnets*.']

Exercise.

"I shall publish, very speedily, the translation of a little ——— manuscript."

"Look upon Greece and its free states, and you would think its inhabitants lived in different climates, and under different heavens from those at present; so different are the geniuses which are formed under Turkish slavery, and ——— liberty."

"In the ——— tongue he hath his name Apollyon."

"The whole school of the ——— rhetoricians of that time, (the reign of Hadrian,) who looked upon themselves as forming a second golden age of oratory, spoke and wrote from the models of the ancients, but, unfortunately, there is no substance in what they spoke and wrote."

"It is not surprising, however culpable, that in opposition to the general taste of mankind, many still admire, and labour to restore, the Gothic architecture; or that, tired of ——— beauty, they endeavour to import into northern climates a style often mixed and modified with their own grotesque or puerile inventions."

Handsome—Pretty.

Handsome qualifies what is at once striking and noble. *Pretty* is said of that which combines the qualities small, regular, graceful, and delicate. We admire what is handsome; we love what is pretty. Trees are handsome. Flowers are pretty. Neither handsome nor pretty is of necessity combined with expression, though they do not exclude it. A man may be handsome, and a woman pretty, without either of them having an intelligent expression. The words imply merely regularity, proportion, and symmetry.

[*Iago.* ——— the knave is handsome, young ——
Othello, ii. 1.

Obe. And that same dew, which sometime on the buds
Was wont to swell, like round and orient pearls,
Stood now within the pretty flowrets' eyes,
Like tears, that did their own disgrace bewail.
Mid. N. Dream, iv. 1.

And in my leaves—now shed and gone
The linnet lodged, and for us two
Chanted his pretty songs, when you
Had little voice or none. WORDSWORTH. '*Poems of the Fancy.*']

Exercise.

At the foot of the hill stood a ——— cottage in the midst of a beautiful garden filled with the choicest plants and flowers.

The town-house is a ——— building of the Doric order, extending three hundred yards along the river, and has a very striking appearance from whatever side you approach it.

Belzoni, the traveller, was a tall, ——— man, of extraordinary muscular strength, and able to support the greatest fatigues.

I had got over the stile, and was walking through the field, when I perceived a group of children amusing themselves in the neighbouring meadows. They were dancing in a ring round one of the ———est little girls I ever beheld, and repeating, as they danced, some lines, which I was not near enough to understand.

The Forget-me-not, one of the ———est flowers I ever saw, grows wild on the hills of Prussia and Nassau.

"Dresden is the neatest town I have seen in Germany; most of the houses are new built, and the Elector's palace is very ———."

"The Saxon ladies resemble the Austrian no more than the Chinese do those of London; they are very genteelly dressed, after the English and French modes, and have generally ——— faces."

Impertinent—Insolent.

Impertinent and insolent are both Latin words. We are impertinent when we do or say any thing which does not belong to us, or which is not our business. We are insolent when we are heedless of the rank or position in society of those whom we address. The impertinent man shews a want of discretion; the insolent man, a want of humility, or self-respect.

> [*Pro.* ——— without the which, this story
> Were most impertinent. ‘*Tempest*,’ i. 2.

> *Bru.* Caius Marcius was
> A worthy officer i' the war; but insolent,
> O'ercome with pride, ambitious past all thinking.
> *Coriolanus*, iv. 6

> ——— but to know
> That which before us lies in daily life,
> Is the prime wisdom; what is more, is fume,
> Or emptiness, or fond impertinence. *P. L.*, viii. 195

> No less the people, on their holy-days,
> Impetuous, insolent, unquenchable. *S. A.*, 1422.

> ——— I should be loth
> To meet the rudeness and swilled insolence
> Of such rude wassailers. — *Comus*, 178.

——— you would I extol
Not for gross good alone which ye produce,
But for the impertinent and ceaseless strife
Of proofs and reasons ye preclude —— *'The Excursion,'*

——— if, need be, defy
Change, with a brow not insolent, though stern.
'Tour in Italy']

Exercise.

It is much more difficult to bear the ——— haughtiness of our superiors, than the ——— behaviour of our equals or inferiors.

His indiscretion was unparalleled; and his curiosity so insatiable, that he was continually asking the most ——— questions.

——— is a quality peculiar to little minds, and results from want of discretion and good sense; ——— may exist in combination with a strong judgment, and is nearly allied to conceit and egotism: the former excites our pity or contempt, the latter is always odious.

A modest and respectful deportment sits well upon all persons, especially upon the young, in whom an ——— forwardness, and prying curiosity, are most reprehensible qualities.

Finding that his deceit was likely to be discovered, and having exhausted all his arts of concealment, he assumed an ——— tone, expecting to frighten his accusers into a belief of what he could not persuade them was true.

On being questioned by the master about what he knew of the matter, the boy replied, with great ———, that he was his own master when the school-hours were over, and that he was not responsible for his actions to any one but his parents.

"The ladies whom you visit think a wise man the most ——— creature living; therefore you cannot be offended that they are displeased with you."

"We have not pillaged those provinces which we rescued; victory itself hath not made us ——— masters."

Ingenious—Ingenuous.

Ingenious respects the intellectual; *ingenuous*, the moral man. Ingenious appears in the work; ingenuous, in the face. Men are ingenious who invent or contrive what raises our admiration. Children are ingenuous in whose character there is no deceit. An ingenious contrivance; an ingenuous answer. Both these words, in their derivation, lead us to the idea of a natural, *inborn* quality; the one moral, the other intellectual.

[*Glo.* ——— O, 'tis a parlous boy;
Bold, quick, ingenious, forward, capable. *Richard III.*, iii i.

Gay, volatile, ingenious, quick to learn
And prompt to exhibit all that he possessed,
Or could perform. —— '*The Excursion*,' vi.

He was among the prime in worth
An object beauteous to behold,
Well-born, well-bred; I sent him forth
Ingenuous, innocent, and bold '*Poems on the Affections*']

Exercise.

He who does not choose to screen himself from punishment by a falsehood, will ———ly confess his fault.

An ——— behaviour is, in some degree, a compensation for faults committed.

He is ——— who is apt at inventing modes of evading difficulties, or who can with facility construct machines which shall answer certain intended purposes.

It is ——— to disclaim a title to that praise which we are conscious of not deserving.

An ——— artisan is ready at contrivances, and is quick at applying them to his handicraft.

The youngest son is a noble boy, with a frank and ——— countenance, and by far the handsomest of the family.

What is there which the ——— of man will not at length accomplish! He skims over the surface of the ocean, dives into the deepest recesses of the earth, and even soars into the regions of the sky in search of knowledge.

On being asked the question, the boy ———ly acknowledged his fault, and told every thing he knew of the transaction.

"Compare the ——— pliableness to virtuous counsels which is in youth, to the confirmed obstinacy in an old sinner."

"——— to their ruin, every age
Improves the arts and instruments of rage."

Irksome—Tedious.

Irksome is from the Saxon *weorcsam*, bringing pain, hurtful; *tedious* is from the Latin *tædium*, weariness caused by time. Irksomeness is the uneasiness of mind caused by the contemplation of what must be done, and is disagreeable to perform. Tediousness is the uneasiness caused by continuing for some time engaged in the same action. The nature of the thing to be done makes it irksome; the time it takes doing makes it tedious. Tedious, then, can never be said of what is to be done, since it is the consequence of action already begun and continued. A work to be done may be irksome, a work nearly completed may be tedious.

[*Phe.* Thy company, which erst was irksome to me,
I will endure. —— *As You Like It*, iii. 5.

Lew. Life is as tedious as a twice-told tale,
Vexing the dull ear of a drowsy man. *King John*, iii. 4

For not to irksome toil, but to delight
He made us, and delight to reason joined. *P L*, ix. 242

More solemn than the tedious pomp that waits
On princes —— *Id.*, v. 355

Ne'er can the way be irksome or forlorn
That winds into itself for sweet return.
WORDSWORTH. '*Tour in Scotland.*

—— I feel
The story linger in my heart; I fear
'Tis long and tedious —— '*The Excursion*,' i.]

Exercise.

"There is nothing so ——— as general discourses, especially when they turn chiefly upon words."

"They unto whom we shall seem ——— are in nowise injured by us, because it is in their own hands to spare that labour which they are not willing to endure."

Many persons find it very ——— to give and receive visits.

Having neither books, nor companions, he was at a loss to know how to employ the ——— hours, when, to his great surprise and satisfaction, he received a letter which informed him that an intimate friend was then residing at a house not three miles from the place.

Such is the perversity of human nature, that we frequently find our occupations ——— simply from the consciousness that we are obliged to be engaged in them.

At last we arrived at the end of our ——— journey, the inconveniences of which I must relate to you in detail the first opportunity.

"For not to ——— toil, but to delight
He made us."

"On minds of dove-like innocence possessed,
On lightened minds that bask in virtue's beams,
Nothing hangs ———."

Liable—Subject.

What we are *subject* to arises from the nature of our moral or physical constitution. We are rendered *liable* by the circumstances of our position. We *are* subject; we *become* liable.

All men are subject to death; whoever sits in a draught is liable to cold. We incur liabilities; we are subject by nature. He who runs into debt is liable to arrest. Many men of irritable temperament are subject to paroxysms of rage. They who calculate badly are liable to sustain loss.

[*K. John.* Apt, liable, to be employed in danger. *King John*, iv. 2

Const A widow, husbandless, subject to fears. *Id.*, iii. 1.

Proudly secure, yet liable to fall
By weakest subtleties — *S. A.*, 55.

And who attains not, ill aspires to rule
Cities of men, or headstrong multitudes,
Subject himself to anarchy within
Or lawless passions in him, which he serves. *P. R.*, ii. 471

Knowledge for us, is difficult to gain—
Is difficult to gain and hard to keep—
As virtue's self; like virtue is beset
With snares; tried, tempted, subject to decay. '*The Excursion*, v.]

Exercise.

We are all —— to the infirmities and weakness of our mortal condition, from which no privilege can exempt any individual.

Those who indulge in excess of any kind render themselves —— to many pains and troubles from which the sober and moderate are exempted.

The unworthy are always the most —— to suspect the motives of others, because they are conscious of their own unworthiness, and judge of others by themselves.

Every man is —— to death, from which no human being has ever escaped, or will ever escape.

He was for many years —— to violent fits of coughing, which attacked him suddenly, and so weakened his constitution, that for a long time it was thought that he would never recover his health.

In many of the offices of this institution, the clerks, by omission or neglect of duty, render themselves —— to certain forfeits.

Ever since they have been in this climate, the men have become much more —— to fever and ague than they were before their arrival here.

"The devout man aspires after some principles of more perfect felicity, which shall not be —— to change or decay."

"This, or any other scheme, coming from a private hand, might be —— to many defects."

Little—Small.

Little wants dimension; *small* wants extension. Little is opposed to big or great; small is opposed to large. Little is derived from the Saxon *lyt dael*, a light portion or part. Small, from *smæl*, slender. Little boys become big by growing. Small children become larger. A little piece does not weigh much; a small piece does not present much surface to the eye. The word little is often used in a secondary sense for mean; as, "a little action." This signification may be accounted for by its root, *light*, that is, without weight, light of estimation.

[*Lady M.* —— all the perfumes of Arabia will not sweeten this little hand.
Macbeth, v. 1

Lor. There's not the smallest orb, which thou behold'st,
But in his motion like an angel sings,
Still quiring to the young-eyed cherubins. *Merch. of Venice*, v. 1.

And gives them leave to wear their sapphire crowns
And wield their little tridents —— *Comus*, 27.

——— slumbering on the Norway foam,
The pilot of some small night-foundered skiff.
P. L., 204

Ye who are longing to be rid
Of fable, though to truth subservient, hear
The little sprinkling of cold earth that fell
Echoed from the coffin-lid;
The convict's summons in the steeple's knell,
'The vain distress-gun' from a leeward shore,
Repeated,—heard, and heard no more!
WORDSWORTH. '*On the Power of Sound.*

As on a sunny bank, a tender lamb
Lurks in safe shelter from the winds of March,
Screened by its parent, so that little mound
Lies guarded by its neighbour; the small heap
Speaks for itself; an Infant there doth rest.
The sheltering hillock is the Mother's grave. '*The Excursion*,' vi.]

Exercise.

I saw a pretty ——— girl standing at the garden-gate with her lap full of roses.

The garden, though very ———, was extremely well kept, and full of the choicest plants and flowers.

This ——— boy is a very ——— and delicate child, and will require great care in rearing.

The ———est heads do not always belong to the most stupid persons; frequently, the very reverse is the fact.

My words, I know, will have but ——— weight with you; nevertheless, I think it my duty to warn you of the consequences of your present course of life.

There are some insects so ——— as not to be discernible with the naked eye; and these have a nervous system, circulation of the blood, pulsation of the heart, &c.!

This piece of lead is too ——— to weigh against every thing that is in the other scale; and it is far too ——— to fill up the space in the wainscot between those two boards.

"The talent of turning men into ridicule, and exposing to laughter those one converses with, is the qualification of ———, ungenerous tempers."

"He whose knowledge is at best but limited, and whose intellect proceeds by a ———, diminutive light, cannot but receive an additional light by the conceptions of another man."

Ludicrous—Ridiculous.

Ludicrous conveys an idea of sport or game. Ridiculous, that of laughter. Ridiculous includes an idea of contempt, which ludicrous does not convey. Persons make themselves ridiculous when they do or say that which excites our laughter, mixed with contempt. The affected are ridiculous. The ludicrous is found in circumstances which excite laughter, but which are not disparaging to the person laughed at. A monkey's tricks are ludicrous. The ridiculous makes us laugh, and at the same time lowers our estimation of the person or thing laughed at. He who talks confidently of what he does not understand, in the presence of competent judges of the subject of his remarks, makes himself ridiculous.

[*Sal.* ——— or with taper-light
To seek the beauteous eye of heaven to garnish
Is wasteful, and ridiculous excess. *King John*, iv. 2.

——— thus was the building left
Ridiculous, and the work Confusion named. *P. L.*, xii. 62.]

Exercise.

There is no folly more carefully to be avoided than affectation: it annihilates all that charming simplicity which is the great attraction of youth, and renders us ——— in the eyes of all sensible persons.

It has been objected to Shakespere that by introducing ——— scenes into his tragedies, he calls off the attention of the audience from the main plot, and disturbs the action of the drama.

Those who endeavour to make the wise and good appear in a ——— light deserve the strongest reprehension.

If any one, fifty years ago, had predicted that we should be able to travel at the rate of sixty miles an hour the idea would have been treated by his contemporaries as ———.

Nothing can be more ——— than the attempts which a tipsy man makes to endeavour to prove to others that he is perfectly sober.

"Plutarch quotes this instance of Homer's judgment, in closing a ——— scene with decency and instruction"

"Gifford was not content with making the author ———; he desired to heap scorn on his person, and to make him out a fool, a knave, or an atheist."

Mature—Ripe.

Both these words qualify those things which are arrived at the perfection of their development. Between them, however, the following distinctions are to be observed. *Ripe* is used in both a proper and a secondary sense; whereas *mature* is generally used figuratively. We may say equally, a ripe fruit, and a ripe judgment; but we cannot correctly say, mature fruit. Again, ripe signifies brought to perfection by growth; mature, brought to perfection by time. A project becomes ripe for execution from the combination of those circumstances which tend to its development. Judgment arrives at maturity by time only.

[*Rom.* ——— they are in a ripe aptness, to take all power from the people, and to pluck from them their tribunes forever. This lies glowing, I can tell you, and is almost mature for the violent breaking out.

Coriolanus, iv. 4.

Vol. ——— thy stout heart,
That humble, as the ripest mulberry
Now will not hold the handling. ——— *Id.*, iii. 2.

——— till, like ripe fruit, thou drop
Into thy mother's lap; or be with ease
Gathered, not harshly plucked; for death mature:
P. L., xi. 535.

Yet years, and to ripe years judgement mature,
Quench not the thirst of glory, but augment—
P. R., iii. 37.

Of man mature, or matron sage.
WORDSWORTH. '*Poems of the Fancy.*'

Like a ripe date which in the desert falls
Without a hand to gather it. '*The Excursion,*' ii.]

Exercise.

On ——— reflection, he perceived the danger he incurred in associating with these men, and withdrew from their company just in time to save himself from ruin.

The fruit, when ———, is gathered in large baskets, and after being carefully picked from the stalk by children employed for the purpose, is thrown into shallow wooden tubs, in which it is mashed and left to ferment.

Though the greatest precaution was used in conducting the plot, and the conspirators had the most unbounded confidence that they should be able to carry out their design, scarcely were their plans ———, for execution, when they were all arrested, and thrown into prison.

The young, whatever natural abilities or quickness of perception they may possess, cannot have that experience and knowledge of the world which ——— years alone can give.

"Th' Athenian sage, revolving in his mind
This weakness, blindness, madness of mankind,
Foretold that in ———er days, though late,
When time should ripen the decrees of fate,
Some god would light us"

Modest—Bashful.

Modest, as synonymous with *bashful* signifies that retiring manner of behaviour which is opposed to self-sufficiency and conceit. *Bashful* implies an awkwardness of manner arising from want of self-confidence. The modest have not too high an opinion of themselves. The bashful blush, hang down their heads, and stammer when spoken to. It is as charming to converse with the modest, as it is painful to converse with the bashful. The modest are confident, though not conceited; the bashful have no self-possession.

[*K. Hen.* In peace, there's nothing so becomes a man,
As modest stillness, and humility *Henry V.*, iii. 1.

K. Rich. Make bold her bashful years with your experience.
Richard III., iv. 4

——— to wisest men and best,
Seeming at first all heavenly under virgin veil,
Soft, modest, meek, demure. *S. A.*. 1036.

By playful smiles, (alas, too oft
A sad heart's sunshine) by a soft
And gentle nature, and a free
Yet modest hand of charity, &c. WORDSWORTH. '*Epitaph.*'

——— the bashful maid
Smitten while all the promises of life
Are opening round her —— '*The Excursion*,' v.]

Exercise.

His kindness, affability, and ——— deportment, together with his well-known courage and great talent, gained him the universal love and respect of his countrymen.

"He looked with an almost ——— kind of modesty, as if he feared the eyes of man."

"Antiochus wept, because of the sober and ——— behaviour of him that was dead."

——— authors, in their first attempts at writing, either conceal their names, or appear before the public with an assumed title.

Conquerors should be ———, for in prosperous fortune, it is difficult to refrain from pride and conceit; indeed some good and great captains have, in like cases, forgotten what best became them.

His downcast look and timid air immediately betrayed his ——— to the whole company; and when he was addressed, he was so agitated that he could not utter a word in reply.

"Our author, anxious for his fame to-night,
And ——— in his first attempt to write,
Lies cautiously obscure."
"Your temper is too ———,
Too much inclined to contemplation."

Alone—Only.

These two words, when used as adverbs, are to be distinguished as follows:

Only excludes other things or persons from our consideration. *Alone* signifies, of itself, of its own power. Thus: "He only could do it," means that no other but himself could do it. "He alone could do it," signifies that he, without the assistance of others, could do it.

[*Const.* —— leave those woes alone, which I alone
Am bound to under-bear. *King John*, iii. 1

Buck. His noble friends, and fellows, whom to leave
Is only bitter to him, only dying. *Henry VIII.*, ii. 1.

Mortals, that would follow me,
Love Virtue; she alone is free:
She can teach ye how to climb
Higher than the sphery chime;
Or, if Virtue feeble were,
Heaven itself would stoop to her. *Comus*, 1019.

His mighty champion, strong above compare,
Whose drink was only from the liquid brook.
S. A, 557

——— O be wiser, Thou!
Instructed that true knowledge leads to love;
True dignity abides with him alone
Who in the silent hour of inward thought
Can still suspect, and still revere himself
In lowliness of heart. WORDSWORTH. '*Early Poems*

A violet by a mossy stone
  Half hidden from the eye!
Fair as a star, when only one
  Is shining in the sky. '*Poems on the Affections.*']

Exercise.

He ——, of all their number, had sufficient resolution to declare himself ready to proceed immediately upon this expedition.

When we heard what was proposed by the opposite party, all our friends exclaimed loudly against the proposition, and declared that the last argument —— was sufficient to shew the weakness of their cause.

—— one more circumstance remains to be mentioned, which will shew most clearly what were the intentions of this designing man, and how much we may congratulate ourselves upon having escaped from his clutches.

This circumstance —— is sufficient to prove the utter worthlessness of the criticism; and shews us how careful we should be not to admit the theories of enthusiasts as sound evidence.

I shall speak —— of facts, without making any comment upon them; and shall leave you to draw your own conclusions on this extraordinary affair.

On mentioning the fact, and questioning them as to their knowledge of it, they all denied it excepting one ——, on whose countenance I could trace evident signs of conscious guilt.

  "Homely but wholesome roots
My daily food, and water from the nearest spring
My —— drink."
  "Here we stand ——,
As in our form distinct, preëminent."

Almost—Nearly.

That which is begun and approaches its completion is *almost* done; that which is on the point of being begun is *nearly* begun. A man is almost killed who receives so severe an injury that his life is despaired of; a man is nearly killed who narrowly escapes an injury which is sure to cause his death. It is almost twelve o'clock when the greater part of the twelfth hour has elapsed; it is nearly twelve o'clock when it is just on the point of striking twelve. The idea contained in almost is incompleteness; the idea contained in nearly is imminent action. *Nearly* regards the beginning, and *almost*, the end of an act.

[*Chor.* ——— the fixed sentinels almost receive
The secret whispers of each other's watch. *Henry V.*, iv. *Chorus.*

Since light so necessary is to life
And almost life itself, if it be true
That light is in the soul,
She all in every part —— *S. A.*, 91.

How beautiful is holiness!—what wonder if the thought
Almost as vivid as a dream, produced a dream at night.
WORDSWORTH. '*The Poet's Dream.*']

Exercise.

I have ——— finished writing my letters; as soon as I have finished them, I shall be happy to accompany you to your friend's house.

On their return from India, the vessel in which they had embarked encountered several severe storms, and on one occasion she ——— foundered.

I had ——— reached the end of my journey, when, driving through a dark lane, I heard voices as of men conversing together, and who seemed to be walking in a direction towards me.

The night was so dark, that I could not see a yard before me, and I had ——— driven over him before I even caught a glimpse of his figure.

The two rivals had ——— met each other; for the one had not left my lodgings five minutes before the other arrived.

He was so excited on the receipt of this news, that he was ——— out of his wits with joy.

The sailor was so weak when taken out of the water, that he ——— fainted from exhaustion.

Also—Likewise—Too

Also means *as-well-as*; *likewise* means *in a similar manner*, *too* means *in addition*. Likewise is one of those words which are fast disappearing from our language. It is seldom used in written language, and still seldomer heard in conversation. The strict distinction between also and likewise is, that *also* classes together things or qualities, whilst *likewise* couples actions or states of being. Thus Milton—"In Sion *also* not unsung," *i. e.* as well as in other places. He did it *likewise*, *i. e.* in the same manner as others. He did it *too*, would mean, "he did it in addition to others;" also is now generally used for likewise, but not always correctly.

[*Fals.* ——— not in words only, but in words also.
1 *Henry IV.*, ii. 4.

Rom. I bear no hatred, blessed man; for, lo,
My intercession likewise steads my foe. *Rom. and Jul.*, ii

Jul. Some say, the lark and loathed toad change eyes,
O, now I would they had changed voices too!
Id., iii. 5.

For God is also in sleep; and dreams advise
Which he hath sent propitious, some great good
Presaging —— *P. L.*, xii. 611.

That Cross belike he also raised as a standard for the true
And faithful service of his heart in the worst that might ensue
Of hardships and distressful fear, amid the houseless waste
Where he, in his poor self so weak, by Providence was placed.
WORDSWORTH. '*The Norman Boy.*'

Have I not seen—ye likewise may have seen—
Son, husband, brothers—brothers side by side,
And son and father also side by side
Rise from that posture —— '*The Excursion*,' ii

The smoothest seas will sometimes prove
To the confiding Bark, untrue;
And, if she trust the stars above,
They can prove treacherous too '*Inscriptions*

Exercise.

"His chamber ——— bears evidence of his various avocations; there are half-copied sheets of music, designs for needle-work, sketches of landscapes indifferently executed, &c."

"All the duties of a daughter, a sister, a wife, and a mother may be well performed, though a lady should not be the finest woman at an opera They are ——— consistent with a moderate share of wit, a plain dress, and a modest air."

"Let us only think for a little of that reproach of modern times, that gulf of time and fortune, the passion for gaming, which is so often the refuge of the idle sons of pleasure, and often ——— the last resource of the ruined."

"And Jesus answered and said unto them: I ——— will ask you one thing, which if ye tell me, I in like wise will tell you by what authority I do these things."

"In these two, no doubt, are contained the causes of the great Deluge, as according to Moses, so ——— according to necessity; for our world affords no other treasures of water."

On this account ——— his style is highly exceptionable.

"But as some hands applaud, a venal few!
Rather than sleep, why John applauds it ———."

"Your brother ——— must die;
Consent you, Lepidus?"

At last—at length.

What is done *at last* is brought about notwithstanding all the accidents or difficulties which may have retarded its accomplishment; what is done *at length* is done after a long continuance of time. In the former expression, obstacles or obstructions are the causes of delay; in the latter, the nature of the thing to be done, or the quantity of labour expended upon it, causes it to occupy a long space of time. He who has had many difficulties to encounter accomplishes his ends at last; what takes a long time to do is done at length.

[*Grif.* At last, with easy roads, he came to Leicester,
Lodged in the abbey —— *Henry VIII.*, iv. 2.

Wol. ——— my high-blown pride
At length broke under me —— *Id.*, iii. 2.

And may at last my weary age
Find out the peaceful hermitage. MILTON. *Il Pens*'

——— till the moon
Rising in clouded majesty, at length
Apparent queen, unveiled her peerless light
And o'er the dark her silver mantle threw. *P. L.*, iv. 607.]

Exercise.

By means of working day and night for many weeks, the task was ——— completed, and presented in time for the approbation of the judges.

The bridge, which had occupied many years in its construction, was ——— opened with the usual forms and ceremonies.

——— after a long interval of anxious suspense, we received news that the vessel had been seen off the coast, and was expected to arrive in port in a few days.

"———!" exclaimed my friend, "——— I see you once more, and after all your wanderings and dangers shall again enjoy the pleasure of your society and conversation!"

———, after a siege of ten years, the city of Troy was taken and burnt to the ground, and its inhabitants carried away into slavery.

After many fruitless attempts, in which he experienced much vexation and disappointment, he ——— succeeded in bringing his invention to perfection.

"A neighbouring king had made war upon this female republic several years with great success, and ——— overthrew them in a very great battle."

"——— being satisfied that they had nothing to fear, they brought out all their corn every day."

Between—Betwixt.

The word *betwixt* has become almost obsolete in colloquial language, where it has given place to *between*. As long, however, as it is used in writing, the distinction which it is undoubtedly entitled to should be maintained. *Betwixt* connects two things that are at a distance from each other; *between*, joins two objects that would be contiguous but for what separates them. What fills up the whole intervening space, is between two objects; what is placed at an equal distance from each of two objects, and yet does not touch either of them, is betwixt them.

"Hard by, a cottage chimney smokes,
From *betwixt* two aged oaks."
MILTON, *L'Allegro.*

The number seven comes between six and eight; the number four is betwixt one and seven.

[*Bru.* Between the acting of a dreadful thing
And the first motion, all the interim is
Like a phantasma, or a hideous dream. *Jul. Cæsar*, II. 1.

Gent. I cannot, 'twixt the heaven and the main,
Descry a sail. *Othello*, ii. 1

——— the swan, with arched neck
Between her white wings mantling proudly, rows
Her state with oary feet —— *P. L.*, VII. 439

——— when Argo passed
Through Bosporus betwixt the justling rocks.
Id., ii. 1018.

Behold! the mantling spirit of reserve
Fashions his neck into a goodly curve;
An arch thrown back between luxuriant boughs
To which, on some unruffled morning, clings
A flaky weight of winter's purest snows! WORDSWORTH. '*Dion*'

——— Self-stationed here
Upon these savage confines, we have seen you
Stand like an isthmus 'twixt two stormy seas
That oft have checked their fury at your bidding.
'*The Borderers.*']

Exercise.

"Friendship requires that it be ——— two at least; and there can be no friendship where there are not two friends."

"Hovering on wing under the cope of hell,
'——— upper, nether, and surrounding fires."

The animosity which had been long suppressed with difficulty on both sides, now burst forth, and war was solemnly declared ——— the two nations.

"Methinks, like two black storms on either hand,
Our Spanish army and your Indian stand,
This only place ——— the clouds is clear."

About this time the animosity ——— Octavian and Antony became violent, and each suspected the other, perhaps not unjustly, of attempts at assassination.

Children quickly distinguish ——— what is required of them and what is not.

Further—Farther.

The positive degree of the first of these words is *forth*, which is compared thus:—forth; further; furthest. The second word is compared thus: far; farther; farthest. *Further*, then, means more in advance; *farther*, at a greater distance. When we are further on our journey, we are farther from the starting place. In abstract language, the same distinction should be maintained. One boy may be much further (in his studies) than another. After many trials, we may be farther than ever from success.

[*Jul.* 'Tis almost morning, I would have thee gone;
And yet no further than a wanton's bird;
Who lets it hop a little from her hand,
Like a poor prisoner in his twisted gyves,
And with a silk thread plucks it back again,
So loving jealous of its liberty. *Rom. and Jul.*, ii. 2

Wol. I have no farther gone in this, than by
A single voice. – – *Henry VIII.*, i. 2.

A little onward lend thy guiding hand
To these dark steps, a little further on. *S. A.*, 2

They followed from the snowy bank
Those footmarks, one by one,
Into the middle of the plank,
And further there were none.
WORDSWORTH. '*Lucy Gray*

Though to give timely warning, and deter
Is one great aim of penalty, extend
Thy mental vision further and ascend
Far higher, else full surely shalt thou err
'*On Punishment of Death.*'

The Youth, who daily farther from the east
Must travel, still is Nature's Priest,
And by the vision splendid
Is on his way attended;
At length the Man perceives it die away,
And fade into the common light of day
'*Intimations of Immortality.*]

Exercise.

It may be remarked, ———, that all the knowledge we possess on any subject is, in reality, abused, whenever we employ it for any other purpose than to improve ourselves in virtue, or to alleviate the distresses of others.

He had strayed many miles ——— from home than he had ever done before; the night was gathering in, and looked black and stormy, and he began to speculate upon the not very pleasing probability of being obliged to spend the night in one of the forest trees.

The advocate, after speaking with great eloquence in his defence, alleged ———, that the extreme youth and inexperience of his client should certainly be admitted, in this case, as powerfully extenuating circumstances.

I had not proceeded much ———, when a troop of urchins, vociferating with all their might, burst from the door of one of the village cottages, and immediately spreading over a wide green, began, with the greatest activity, to engage in a variety of sports.

"What ——— need have we of witnesses?"

Nevertheless—Notwithstanding.

Nevertheless excludes subtraction; *notwithstanding* excludes opposition. "He did his duty nevertheless," signifies that circumstances did not make him do less of his duty, or did not diminish the activity with which he performed it. "He did his duty notwithstanding," means that opposing circumstances had not the effect of preventing him from doing his duty. Nevertheless is for "not the less," or nathless, as Milton uses it; notwithstanding signifies "nothing opposing." Notwithstanding is often used as a preposition: as in the phrase "notwithstanding my exertions"—nevertheless is never so used. Nevertheless is more frequently used with a verb; notwithstanding, with a noun.

[——— nevertheless
Restored by thee, vile as I am, to place
Of new acceptance ——— *P. L.*, x. 970.

Nathless he so endured, till on the beach
Of that inflamed sea he stood ——— *Id.*, i. 299.

They, notwithstanding, had much love to spare,
And it all went into each other's hearts.
WORDSWORTH. '*The Brothers.*']

Exercise.

——— all the opposition of the nobles, Tiberius Gracchus had sufficient influence to procure the passing of the Agrarian Law.

Though opposed by the whole body of the Roman aristocracy, Gracchus persisted ——— in carrying out his measures to secure an improved condition to the poorer classes of Rome.

"Many of the men were gone ashore, and our ships ready to depart; ——— the admiral, with such ships only as could be put in readiness, set forth towards them."

——— all the losses he has sustained from unfortunate speculations, and from over-confidence in the unworthy, he is still so rich, that if he chose, he could retire from business, and live in the greatest luxury on his property.

This sudden change of fortune had no apparent effect upon his mind; for though he was unexpectedly put in possession of immense wealth, he was ——— as attentive to his duties and as industrious in his habits as before.

Here—hither. Where—whither. There—thither.

The proper distinction between *where* (in what place), and *whither* (to what place), is not always maintained; indeed, a strong tendency exists to banish the latter word from our language altogether. These adverbs, with their cognates here—hither, and there—thither, have become so confounded as to make a distinction between them almost hopeless. It is very common to hear, "*Where* are you going? Come *here*." These sentences strictly mean, "In what place are you going?" "Come in this place;" which are manifest absurdities. *Here*, *there*, and *where*, should be used where rest is implied. *Hither*, *thither*, and *whither*, after verbs of motion. Thus: Stay *here*. Come *hither*. *Where* do you live? *Whither* are you going? I saw him *there;* he proceeded *thither*.

[*Const.* ——— here I and sorrow sit;
Here is my throne, bid kings come bow to it. *King John*, III. 1

Eli Come hither, little kinsman; hark a word.
K. John. Come hither, Hubert. *Id.*, iii. 3.

Cym. ——— Where, how lived you?
And when came you to serve our Roman captive?
How parted with your brothers? how first met them?
Why fled you from the court? and whither? *Cymbeline*, v. 5.

King. Where is Polonius?
Hamlet. In heaven; send thither to see; if your messenger find him not there seek him i' the other place yourself. *Hamlet*, iv. 3.

Peace with you, brethren; my inducement hither
Was not at present here to find my son,
By order of the lords new parted hence
To come and play before them at their feast
I heard all as I came; the city rings
And numbers thither flock.—— *S. A.*, 1445.

——— to descry the distant foe,
Where lodged, or whither fled;—— *P. L.*, vi. 531.

To teach thee that God attributes to place
No sanctity, if none be thither brought
By men who there frequent or therein dwell. *P. L.*, xi. 837

—Come hither in thy hour of strength:
Come, weak as is a breaking wave!
Here stretch thy body at full length;
Or build thy house upon this grave.
WORDSWORTH. *'A Poet's Epitaph*

——— Fluttering,
Here did it enter; there, on hasty wing
Flies out, and passes on from cold to cold;
But whence it came we know not, nor behold
Whither it goes.—— *Eccles. Sonnets.*

There let me see thee sink into a mood
Of gentler thought, protracted till thine eye
Be calm as water when the winds are gone,
And no one can tell whither.—— *'To Lycoris.'*

——— the clouds,
The mist, the shadows, light of golden suns,
Motions of moonlight, all come thither—touch,
And have an answer—thither come, and shape
A language not unwelcome to sick hearts
And idle spirits:—there the sun himself,
At the calm close of summer's longest day,
Rests his substantial orb; between those heights
And on the top of either pinnacle,
More keenly than elsewhere in night's blue vault,
Sparkle the stars, as of their station proud. *'The Excursion,'* ii.

Hence in a season of calm weather,
Though inland far we be,
Our Souls have sight of that immortal sea
Which brought us hither,
Can in a moment travel thither,
And see the children sport upon the shore,
And hear the mighty waters rolling evermore.
'Intimations of Immortality']

Exercise.

"O stream,
Whose source is inaccessibly profound,
——— do thy mysterious waters tend?"
"——— let us tend
From off the tossing of these fiery waves,
——— rest, if any rest can harbour ———."

I shall go to Brighton next week. Shall you be ——— this summer?

"That lord advanced to Winchester, ——— Sir John Berkley brought him two regiments more of foot."

I visited last autumn the place ——— I first had the pleasure of making your acquaintance.

"Who brought me ———
Will bring me hence; no other guide I seek."

Pompey followed Cæsar into Thessaly, ——— the latter had already taken his position in the neighbourhood of Pharsalus, and ——— the hostile armies met each other.

Cleopatra returned to Alexandria, ——— she was accompanied by Antony.

"——— Nature first begins
Her farthest verge."

"Gigantic Pride, pale Terror, gloomy Care,
And mad Ambition shall attend her ———."

"——— Phœnix and Ulysses watch the prey,
And ——— all the wealth of Troy convey."

The following synonymous words, to be classified and explained according to some of the principles before laid down, are offered as a further exercise for the student.

Strife—discord.
Changeable—inconstant
To repeat—to reïterate.
Offensive—offending.
Mercenary—venal.
Will—testament.
To refuse—to deny.
Incessant—unceasing.
Electric—electrical.
Pleasant—pleasing.
Cool—dispassionate.
Confident—confiding.
Aversion—dislike.
Disposal—disposition.
Patient—invalid.
Doubtful—uncertain.
Different—unlike.
Attendant—attending
Politic—political.
Injury—disadvantage.
Fervour—ardour.
Warmth—heat.
Abundant—abounding.
Deceit—fraud.
Heroic—heroical.
Faithless—unfaithful.
Dramatic—dramatical.
Worthless—unworthy
Coincident—coinciding.
To weaken—to invalidate.
Comic—comical
To flow—to gush.
Intent—intense.
Fantastic—fantastical.
Signification—meaning.
Always—ever.

INDEX OF SYNONYMES.

(CLASSIFIED.)

SECTION I.

Generic—Specific.

SECTION II.

Active—Passive.

SECTION III.

Intensity.

SECTION IV.

Positive—Negative.

SECTION V.

Miscellaneous.

GENERAL INDEX.

D

E

PAGE.

L

M

N

PAGE

O

P

THE END.

www.ingramcontent.com/pod-product-compliance
Lightning Source LLC
LaVergne TN
LVHW010146110826
845151LV00002B/437

9781425536848